Private Standards and Global Governance

LEUVEN GLOBAL GOVERNANCE

Series Editor: Jan Wouters, *University of Leuven, Belgium*

The *Leuven Global Governance* series comprises high-quality monographs and edited volumes dedicated to innovative research on global governance. The series focuses particularly on the following themes: European Union and global multilateral governance; trade and sustainable development; peace and security studies; human rights, democracy and the rule of law; space governance and comparative federalism. In full recognition of the complex issues involved, the series favours studies approaching global governance from a multidisciplinary, multi-level and multi-actor perspective.

Titles in the series include:

Private Standards and Global Governance: Economic, Legal and Political Perspectives
Edited by Axel Marx, Miet Maertens, Johan Swinnen and Jan Wouters

China, the European Union and Global Governance
Edited by Jan Wouters, Tanguy de Wilde, Pierre Defraigne and Jean-Christophe Defraigne

Private Standards and Global Governance

Economic, Legal and Political Perspectives

Edited by

Axel Marx, Miet Maertens, Johan Swinnen and Jan Wouters

University of Leuven (KU Leuven), Belgium

LEUVEN GLOBAL GOVERNANCE

Edward Elgar

Cheltenham, UK • Northampton, MA, USA

Published by
Edward Elgar Publishing Limited
The Lypiatts
15 Lansdown Road
Cheltenham
Glos GL50 2JA
UK

Edward Elgar Publishing, Inc.
William Pratt House
9 Dewey Court
Northampton
Massachusetts 01060
USA

A catalogue record for this book
is available from the British Library

Library of Congress Control Number: 2012935284

MIX
Paper from responsible sources
FSC® C018575

ISBN 978 1 84980 874 3

Printed and bound by MPG Books Group, UK

Contents

PART III PRIVATE FOOD STANDARDS AND GLOBAL GOVERNANCE: LEGAL PERSPECTIVES

Figures

Tables

Editors

Axel Marx is Research Manager of the Leuven Centre for Global Governance Studies, University of Leuven. He studied sociology and political science at the University of Leuven, the University of Hull and the University of Cambridge. He holds a Ph.D from the University of Leuven.

Miet Maertens is Assistant Professor in Agricultural, Food and Natural Resource Use Economics at the Department of Earth and Environmental Sciences, University of Leuven, Belgium. She holds a MSc in Economics and a MSc in Agricultural Sciences from the University of Leuven and a Ph.D from the Georg-August University Goettingen, Germany.

Johan Swinnen is Professor of Economics and Director of LICOS, Centre for Institutions and Economic Performance, University of Leuven, Belgium and Senior Research Fellow at the Centre for European Policy Studies (CEPS) in Brussels. From 2003 to 2004 he was Lead Economist at the World Bank and from 1998 to 2001 he was Economic Advisor at the European Commission. He has been advisor to many international institutions and governments, and was a visiting professor at Cornell University, Wageningen University, the University of Namur and the University of Nitra. He holds a Ph.D from Cornell University.

Jan Wouters, Jean Monnet Chair EU and Global Governance, is Professor of International Law and Law of International Organizations and Director of the Leuven Centre for Global Governance Studies and the Institute for International Law at University of Leuven. He is President of the Flemish Foreign Affairs Council. He studied law and philosophy at Antwerp and Yale University (LL.M. 1990), worked as a visiting researcher at Harvard Law School and defended his Ph.D at University of Leuven (1996). He is visiting professor at the College of Europe in Bruges, has held teaching positions at the Universities of Antwerp and Maastricht and previously has worked as référendaire (law clerk) at the European Court of Justice in Luxembourg.

Contributors

Emilie Bécault is Ph.D Researcher and Junior Member, Leuven Centre for Global Governance Studies, University of Leuven, Belgium.

Fabrizio Cafaggi is Professor of Comparative Law, European University Institute, Firenze, Italy.

Liesbeth Colen is Ph.D Researcher, LICOS Centre for Institutions and Economic Performance, and Junior Member, Leuven Centre for Global Governance Studies, University of Leuven, Belgium.

Ludo Cuyvers is Professor in International Economics, Faculty of Applied Economics, University of Antwerp, and North-West University, South Africa.

Tim De Meyer is Specialist on International Labour Standards and Labour Law, International Labour Office – Subregional Office for East Asia, Bangkok, Thailand.

Nicolas Hachez is Ph.D Researcher, Institute for International Law, and Junior Member, Leuven Centre for Global Governance Studies, University of Leuven, Belgium.

Spencer Henson is University Professor in the Economics of Food, Health and Development, University of Guelph, Canada, and Professorial Fellow, Institute of Development Studies, United Kingdom.

John Humphrey is a Professorial Fellow at the Institute of Development Studies, Brighton, United Kingdom.

Gretchen H. Stanton is Senior Counsellor in the Agriculture and Commodities Division of the WTO and Secretary of the WTO Committee on Sanitary and Phytosanitary Measures (the SPS Committee).

Frans van Waarden is Professor of Policy and Organization at Utrecht University and Fellow of University College Utrecht, the Netherlands.

1. Introduction: private standards and global governance[1]

Axel Marx, Miet Maertens, Johan Swinnen and Jan Wouters

During the last three decades many social scientists have discussed the impact of globalization. Some critics have argued that existing multilateral and governmentally driven initiatives are incapable of addressing the global challenges that result from trade liberalization and increased economic globalization. At the same time, one can observe the emergence of new non-state market regulatory initiatives. These private voluntary regulatory initiatives aim to govern production processes and supply chains across the globe according to a set of 'private' standards. These standards may contain rules with regard to a diversity of issues such as food safety, ecological protection, labour conditions, human rights protection and others. Several authors consider private standards, besides other instruments, as an increasingly important global governance tool.

As a result, across disciplines and focusing on different areas of research, several scholars have started to study this phenomenon. Initial studies have focused on the emergence of private standards, their design and diversity and their legitimacy as a global governance tool. Recently, scholars also started to address their effectiveness as a governance tool. Hence, along with the proliferation of private standards, the scientific literature on this theme has increased tremendously in the last decade. What emerges from these studies is a complex picture of private governance raising several unresolved issues with regard to questions of their effectiveness and legitimacy, their relationship with public policy arrangements, as well as to the overall issue of whether private standards constitute a viable global governance instrument. In addition, a thematic divide, also partially reflected in a disciplinary divide, can be observed with economic and legal scholars focusing mostly on private food standards, and political scientists and governance scholars analyzing labour standards and social and environmental standards for the management of natural resources. The result is a fragmented literature along disciplinary and thematic lines with little interaction, notwithstanding the fact that this scholarship focuses on highly related issues. This volume aims to bridge these disciplinary and thematic research lines and address some of the identified key questions with regard to private standards as a global governance tool. In addition, the book makes a specific contribution to the study of private food standards by including legal and economic analysis of these standards.

The book's origins lie in an international experts' workshop that was organized in November 2008 at the University of Leuven. The workshop conveners, LICOS Centre for Institutions and Economic Performance and the Leuven Centre for Global Governance Studies, brought together practitioners and researchers from different disciplines who focus on different aspects of private standards. This book contains a selection of the papers presented at this workshop, subsequently revised, and a number of additional invited contributions. The book contains nine chapters. Chapters 2–5 provide a broad assessment of private standards with regard to legitimacy and effectiveness across different thematic areas: natural resources, food and labour conditions. The subsequent chapters focus specifically on private food standards. Chapters 6 and 7 provide an economic analysis of food standards. Chapters 8–10 offer a legal perspective. The book ends with a concluding chapter on private standards as a global governance tool.

GLOBAL GOVERNANCE THROUGH PRIVATE STANDARDS: THE CASES OF NATURAL RESOURCES, FOOD AND LABOUR CONDITIONS

Chapters 2–5 introduce and critically discuss three broad areas in which governance through private standards is especially prominent, namely the areas of natural resources management, food safety and labour conditions.

Frans van Waarden in Chapter 2 on '***Governing Global Commons: Public–Private Protection of Fish and Forests***' focuses on the emergence and proliferation of private forms of governance as an important tool for global natural resources management. After a historical overview of public and private regulation of common property resources in which he pinpoints the failure and weakness of (inter)governmental solutions with regard to biodiversity, van Waarden discusses several market-based regulatory solutions to the protection of forests and fisheries. Two certification schemes in particular are given in-depth attention, namely those of the Forest Stewardship Council (FSC) and the Marine Stewardship Council (MSC), which aim to fulfill three functions: standard setting, accreditation of independent certification bodies, and trademark assurance. In the course of this analysis, the author discusses the emergence of the two certification schemes, provides a comparative analysis and discusses some problems such as the management of diversity, the problem of enforcement (limited audit resources) and issues concerning the maintenance of certificate credibility and reputation.

These problems point to shortcomings of certification mechanisms and call for solutions. Van Waarden emphasizes that there is a need to certify the certifiers, which can be achieved through different means either private or public. Van Waarden builds on historical evidence to make the case for public recognition of private standards and identifies some initial current trends in which states join or make use of private arrangements with regard to the protection of forests and fisheries. He concludes his discussion with the observation that the result of these trends is the emergence of new economic governance regimes, combining elements of markets, associations, hierarchies and states. As a result, van Waarden recommends that more should be invested in developing a genuine Ecological Public Private Partnership (EPPP), where private initiatives such as the FSC and MSC are publicly supported but also controlled.

Axel Marx, Emilie Bécault and Jan Wouters, in Chapter 3 entitled **'Private standards in forestry: assessing the legitimacy and effectiveness of the Forest Stewardship Council'**, draw on recent findings in the academic and policy-oriented scholarship to evaluate whether, 20 years on, the Forest Stewardship Council (FSC), one of the most prominent examples of transnational private regulation in global environmental politics, still holds great promise as an alternative to multilateral forest governance. They focus, in particular, on two dimensions of the FSC that figure rather prominently in discussions of transnational policy networks, namely legitimacy and effectiveness. After a brief description of forest certification and the FSC, the chapter examines the legitimacy of the organizational procedures of the FSC from both a normative perspective and a sociological/constructivist perspective. It then assesses various aspects of the effectiveness of the FSC as a global governance tool for the promotion of sustainable forest management practices worldwide. This two-step analysis reveals that despite scoring relatively well under democratic criteria of input and output legitimacy and in terms of process effectiveness, i.e. adoption of FSC certificates, the FSC is still confronted with several challenges. The authors identify, in particular, a strong North–South divide both in terms of formal representation/participation as well as in relation to certificate adoption, limiting the potential of the FSC to respond to forest degradation problems in developing countries. In line with these findings and with similarity to van Waarden's closing remarks, the authors conclude that addressing global forest challenges requires strengthening the interaction between multilateral and private forms of governance in ways that complement and reinforce each other's performance and legitimacy. Greater involvement and supervision by multilateral institutions could be beneficial to the operation of the FSC. Multilateral organizations could notably help in addressing the North–South financial gap in private forest governance, and can also play a key role in supporting much-needed empirical research on the actual effectiveness of forest certification. With respect to the legitimacy dimension, the international public sector could assist the FSC in achieving a higher level of representation of developing countries in its governance structure by providing financial support to the development of poorer and smaller forest organizations in the South so they can more easily access private transnational environmental governance networks.

Spencer Henson and John Humphrey, in Chapter 4 on '**Private Standards in Global Agri-Food Chains**', shed light on the nature of private food standards and how they relate to and differ from public regulations and international guidelines on food safety. In recent years, discussions have emerged about the impact of private standards on developing countries' access to foreign markets and their legitimacy. Henson and Humphrey distinguish between two main types of private standards. Premium standards schemes aim to establish a differentiation across products by attributing specific characteristics related to, for example, animal welfare, ecological production or fair trade, and by communicating these to consumers through labels. Baseline schemes, in contrast, are aimed at meeting the required minimum level of performance. Such baseline standards are often established by large companies. They are a tool for business-to-business governance and are generally 'invisible' to consumers.

The main issues the authors address are the diversity of private standards and the relationship between private standards and public food safety regulation. They further discuss the factors contributing to the emergence and spread of corporate standards. One of the main insights here is that private standards create entire standard schemes. This entails a change in the way monitoring and control is exercised along value chains. They further argue that private standard-setters can be seen as translating the public rules of, for example, the Codex Alimentarius, into standards that provide sufficient guidance for implementers to know what to do and for conformity assessors to determine whether compliance has been achieved. Finally they note that the extensive 'prerequisites' linked to the adoption of private standards potentially cause the greatest problems for developing countries because of costs related to demonstrating compliance.

Ludo Cuyvers and Tim De Meyer in Chapter 5 on '**Market-driven promotion of international labour standards in Southeast Asia – the corporatization of social justice**' focus on private labour standards and analyze whether the pursuit of social justice related to the international liberalization of trade may be left entirely to market forces. The authors present a line of reasoning in which they raise two main questions. First, are states applying social clauses, i.e. making their commitments to liberalize trade and investment conditional upon the observance of labour standards? Second, can markets themselves make up for government failure to allocate correctly the social costs of economic production? They observe that traditional governance methods that rely on public international law are increasingly complemented by market-driven or private initiatives. This 'privatization of social justice' raises questions about the legitimacy and effectiveness of measures used to promote compliance with international labour standards. Cuyvers and De Meyer review the evolution of the social clause and analyze the diversification of governance methods to promote international labour standards through market-driven initiatives.

The authors suggest that the failure of state-centered regulation has been the main driver behind private driven initiatives for international labour regulation. Concerning the effectiveness of private initiatives the authors state that, so far, they only affect certain parts of the economy and they have been more successful in tackling tangible workplace rights violations (e.g. child labour and safety and health) than those that deal with wages, overtime restrictions and freedom of association. Moreover, private labour standards generally face the same challenges as traditional command-and-control regulatory systems.

Cuyvers and De Meyer illustrate some of the analytical aspects highlighted in the literature by describing outsourced regulatory systems from two Southeast Asian nations, Thailand and Cambodia. The authors conclude that it is not yet warranted to say that the pursuit of social justice in the framework of international trade liberalization can be left entirely to market forces. While market-driven initiatives play a crucial role in stimulating work floor awareness and action on labour standards, they are no long-term replacement for traditional labour market institutions.

PRIVATE FOOD STANDARDS AND GLOBAL GOVERNANCE: ECONOMIC PERSPECTIVES

The subsequent five chapters focus on private food safety standards. Chapter 6 and 7 take an economic perspective.

Miet Maertens and Johan Swinnen in Chapter 6 on '**Private standards, global food supply chains and the implications for developing countries**' provide an overview of the arguments and empirical evidence for the development implications of increasing food standards. The proliferation of private and public standards causes dramatic changes in the way food production and trade are organized, with important implications for rural households in developing countries. Understanding the link between standards, the governance of food supply chains and rural incomes in developing countries is crucial from a development perspective. Maertens and Swinnen address the concern that stringent standards will lead to exclusive and exploitative supply chains and result in adverse implications for development. They show that this is not necessarily the case.

The authors first describe how increasing food standards influence the structure and governance system of food supply chains. The need for a consistent supply of high-standard produce, the need for monitoring compliance with standards, and the high costs related to compliance and certification, stimulate consolidation and vertical coordination in food supply chains. The authors subsequently analyze the development implications of increasing standards and the structural changes in food supply chains they induce. Through a thorough review of existing empirical evidence and insights from three original case studies on horticulture exports from Sub-Saharan Africa, the authors provide new insights on how supply chains have responded to increasing standards and how this has impacted development. Evidence suggests that varying degrees of vertical coordination occur, which result in differentiated development effects. The channels through which rural households benefit from high-standards trade are diverse. An important distinction can be made between product market effects and labour market effects. The case studies show that smallholder producers benefit from supplying high-standards produce to exporters under contract-farming arrangements through both direct and indirect effects. In the case of complete vertical integration in the chains, rural households, including the poorest households, benefit from employment opportunities created in the chains. Overall, empirical findings point to positive welfare effects of high-standards trade and modernizing supply chains.

Maertens and Swinnen conclude that, although there are important concerns related to the increased use of public and private standards in the food sector, standards can also bring about important positive effects for rural development and poverty reduction. They show that next to direct product market effects, which have received most of the attention in the literature, benefits can come in various ways through indirect labour market effects. A key issue in understanding these effects is the way in which supply chain structures and governance systems respond to increasing standards.

Chapter 7 builds on the previous one by discussing in detail one specific case study. **Liesbeth Colen, Miet Maertens and Johan Swinnen** in their chapter on '**Globalization, private standards and poverty: evidence from Senegal**' start from the observation that there is a wide consensus among economists that the integration of developing countries in global trade and foreign direct investment flows is an important driver for growth but that poverty effects of globalization are less clear. Trade and investment in high-value agri-food supply chains can potentially benefit the poor because of a direct link with the rural economy and the intensive use of unskilled labour. Yet, increasing food standards, public as well as private, cast doubt on these beneficial effects. The poverty effects of increasing standards and the globalization of food supply chains remain highly debated. Surprisingly, little empirical research has focused on the overall poverty effects of globalization in the agri-food sectors of developing countries. This chapter aims at contributing to fill this gap in the empirical literature.

Colen, Maertens and Swinnen analyze the overall level of household income and the poverty effects of tomato exports and FDI inflows in the tomato sector in Senegal. The tomato export chain is dominated by a single multinational company that applies a strategy of vertical integration at different nodes in the supply chains, including primary production. One could therefore *ex ante* consider the tomato export sector in Senegal as a 'worst-case scenario' of globalization. Using data from secondary sources, several company interviews and a large household survey, the authors attain several important findings. First, tomato exports to the EU increased sharply, despite increasing standards in the EU. Second, tomato exports contribute significantly to poor household incomes and poverty reduction through employment effects. Third, no evidence was found that asset-poor households or unskilled individuals are disadvantaged in accessing employment in the tomato export sector. These are important findings as they show that even in this worst-case scenario of export development – with one multinational company dominating the chain and no smallholder producers involved in the chain – there are positive development effects through labour market effects.

The authors' conclusions challenge a few general views in the literature. First, the study shows that gains from high-standards food trade concentrated with foreign investors and large food companies do not necessarily marginalize the poor in developing countries. Second, the results show that important benefits may come through labour market effects rather than through product markets. Many empirical studies assume that there cannot be benefits for the rural poor when households are excluded as primary producers as a result of increasing standards. This study shows the importance of including labour market effects when assessing the overall impact for the rural poor. Third, the case study on Senegalese tomato exports adds to the existing evidence of the possibilities of high-standards export development in Sub-Saharan Africa and thereby contributes to the need for a balanced perspective on standards as barriers or catalysts to trade.

PRIVATE FOOD STANDARDS AND GLOBAL GOVERNANCE: LEGAL PERSPECTIVES

Chapters 8–10 focus on legal aspects related to global private food governance.

Fabrizio Cafaggi, in Chapter 8 on '**Transnational governance by contract: private regulation and contractual networks in food safety**', provides a general regulatory framework for the analysis of private food standards. The analysis starts from the assumption that there is a direct relationship between the development of transnational private regulation (TPR) and the structure of supply chains in the agri-food industry. This link is then assessed in the framework of changing dimensions of food safety as a public and private global regulatory issue. The main 'shifts' in food safety regulation are: from producer driven and sector specific to retail driven; from state level to transnational; from public to private; from product to process standards (which warrants a supply-chain approach) and from on-site inspection to third-party certification. Cafaggi delves into a situation of increasing outsourcing and vertical disintegration in which private food safety regulation is implemented mainly by means of contract instruments and tort law. In the chapter he develops a coordinated approach which integrates the value supply chain perspective with regulatory theory to show how co-evolutionary patterns explain changes of task allocation in the supply chain and the increasing use of TPR.

The central theme of the chapter revolves around the use of contractual governance in the wider framework of transnational contracting, specifically that of network and collaborative contracts, for the regulation and monitoring of safety in supply food chains. Cafaggi shows how TPR affects the form and the function of a supply chain and requires specific contractual arrangements among suppliers, and further, between suppliers and retailers, to implement safety standards and to monitor their compliance. Cafaggi continues by describing different inter-firm coordination mechanisms that are, or can be, used in food chains, and proposes a wider deployment of contractual networks to enhance the effectiveness of food safety regulation. To this end, he establishes a distinction between contractual networks directed at information production and transfer, and contractual networks concerning risk assessment and risk management. In light of this account, Cafaggi closes with some policy recommendations that can improve regulatory effectiveness and participation in food safety.

The two following chapters by Gretchen H. Stanton and Jan Wouters, Axel Marx and Nicolas Hachez focus on the issue of private standards in international trade law. **Gretchen H. Stanton** in Chapter 9 on **'Food-Safety-Related Private Standards: the WTO perspective'** provides an overview of the discussions that are currently taking place in the World Trade Organization's (WTO) Sanitary and Phytosanitary Measures (SPS) Committee on private standards. The key question is how private food standards impact access to foreign markets and the economic development of poorer countries. This issue has become hotly debated over the past decade and seems to involve and divide more countries with respect to international food safety and health concerns than any other issue to date. In order to fully grasp this debate one has to dig deeper into the SPS Agreement, which is extensively examined in the chapter.

Stanton subsequently focuses on discussions taking place in the context of the SPS Committee. Proponents of private standards argue that they help suppliers improve product quality and gain access to high-quality markets. Antagonists submit that private standards can be more restrictive and prescriptive than official import requirements. Another concern is that they increase transaction costs while suppliers have to meet different requirements for each buyer. Finally, the (high) costs of certification could impose an additional barrier to market access for small- and medium-scale producers. This affects developing countries since they have proportionally many more small producers. A final aspect of the discussion focuses on whether there is a legal basis for disciplining private food standards in the WTO. The author puts forward that developing countries fear that the proliferation of private standards will eventually undermine the value and credibility of international standards and even of the official SPS requirements of governments. Other governments defend that the private sector sets voluntary standards in order to allow companies to differentiate their products and respond to the perceived demands of their consumers. They argue that the WTO SPS Agreement does not apply to the normal commercial practices of the private sector and therefore actions in this regard should be limited. Enhancing the knowledge and understanding of all stakeholders – governmental and private – of the real and perceived effects of SPS-related private standards may open the way to ensuring that such requirements result in safer foods and facilitate trade, particularly for developing countries.

Jan Wouters, Axel Marx and Nicolas Hachez, in Chapter 10 on '**Private standards, global governance and international trade – the case of global food safety**', build on the previous chapter and seek to clarify the relationship of private standards with, and their place in, the multilateral trade regime. The authors first discuss the emergence of private food standards and argue that these standards have grown into institutionalized market governance instruments because of several interrelated driving forces. Moreover, the interconnection and interaction between private standards and public policy-making is becoming increasingly complex since many public policy arrangements are starting to make use of private standards.

The authors then focus on the international trade regime of the WTO and put forward that the SPS Agreement, as it stands, is not equipped well enough to deal with today's global food market reality, notably the trade-offs that now exist between food safety issues and free trade objectives. The Agreement itself is not clear on whether it encompasses private standards and it is unclear what leverage the SPS disciplines could have in order to reduce the trade-restrictive effects of private standards. The authors claim that a strictly public approach to food safety based on the SPS Agreement standards is misguided in light of the fact that private standards are flexible and dynamic policy instruments. A sound strategy in addressing private standards would therefore be to make them part of the solution by embedding them into new policy arrangements acceptable to all.

The authors propose a model that ultimately aims to establish a system of pluralistic food safety governance. This model might encourage WTO members to develop strategies that bring private standards in line with the free trade objective, while securing optimal levels of food safety. Together, relevant public and private actors should reflect on enhancing the positive and tackling the negative effects of private standards while rationalizing the mosaic proliferation of private standard schemes and enhancing their legitimacy. The authors put forward several proposals to achieve these objectives. They end by arguing that a more elaborate and systemic public policy towards private standards might address these issues further and enable private standards to play an important role in new policy arrangements to address global challenges.

The concluding chapter by the editors (Chapter 11) assesses the degree to which private standards constitute a global governance instrument, identifies current gaps in knowledge and advances an agenda for future research.

NOTE

1 This edited volume originated out of a workshop which was financially supported by the Flemish Fund for Scientific Research (FWO) through the GRESI research community grant. The editors greatly acknowledge the support of the FWO and want to thank Mr. Matthieu Burnay of the Leuven Centre for Global Governance Studies for his help in preparing the manuscript.

PART I

Global governance through private standards: the cases of natural resources, food and labour conditions

2. Governing global commons: the public-private protection of fish and forests

Frans van Waarden

1. INTRODUCTION

A main task of the state is to protect its citizens against all imaginable kinds of risks and uncertainties; it is its very legitimation. Citizens have entered into an imaginary contract with the state, offering loyalty, obedience and taxes in exchange for security and prosperity. That was already so in the early days of state formation, when state authority was accepted and duties performed in exchange for protection from dangerous nature, animals and humans, foreign armies and criminals. However, in the modern era states, and especially democratic welfare states, are confronted with a double paradox. While advances in scientific knowledge and technologies have led citizens to demand greater levels of state protection from an ever longer list of risks, the state's capacity to satisfy these expectations has been decreasing. With globalization, more and more sources of risk and uncertainty are beyond the direct control of the nation-state and many emanate from outside its territorial jurisdiction. Thus states are getting squeezed between these contradictory tendencies: more demands, yet less capacity to satisfy them.

Re-regulating global forces is understandably not as easy as re-regulating the domestic sphere. The former requires nation-states to extend jurisdiction beyond their own territorial borders. How do countries try to influence regulatory standards elsewhere? Economically or politically powerful nations can and do occasionally (try to) impose their standards on other nations, through trade relations, that is, through what Vogel (1995) has called the 'California effect'. Alternatively, they can and do use political, diplomatic and even military pressures, as we have seen in the 'war against terrorism'. More frequently used however are less asymmetric forms: inter-national regulatory cooperation and negotiation, harmonization initiatives (mediated) by supra-national organizations that have been created by nation-states in the past. But even if countries manage to export their standards to others, or to agree on more or less binding international regulations, they remain dependent on other countries for their actual implementation and enforcement on the street level, shop floor, or harbor there. Mutual trust between countries in their enforcement practices and value of certificates is complicated because the discretionary authority of street-level bureaucrats and their enforcement styles tend to differ significantly between countries (Vogel, 1986; van Waarden 1999a, 1999b). Given these differences in styles, countries that maintain stricter enforcement procedures may be hesitant to trust others that are known for having less strict ones.

It is mainly as a result of these international challenges to state authority and capacity that private forms of global governance have, over the past two decades or so, emerged as important regulatory tools, especially in the re-regulation of global markets. Unlike states, private actors have the advantage that they are not bound by territorial jurisdictions and can cross national borders more easily. Their identity is a functional rather than a national one; moreover they can use other sanctions. Instead of administrative fines or criminal punishment they can spread information, affect reputations by rating them, engage in naming and shaming, or refuse to buy or distribute products. Private actors can also easily discriminate and be protectionist. Public actors are restrained in doing so as they are bound by international treaties and the law. As Vogel (2007, p. 21) wrote: 'An important advantage of civil regulations as a global regulatory vehicle is that their provisions are not currently governed by the WTO, whose rules primarily apply to regulations formally adopted by governments.' Private regulations also have the advantage that they can mix informants and inspectors from different nations with different traditions of regulatory enforcement, potentially enabling them to overcome or correct for national differences in enforcement styles.

While earlier stages in history saw a move from private to public regulation (van Waarden, 1985, 2011a, 2011b), what we now see is an opposite movement, back again from public to private, as I have argued before in the field of food regulation (van Waarden, 2006). On the new international interface between public and private organizations complex mixes of regulation and standard setting by a variety of public and private organizations emerge. This chapter deals with one such sector, namely the regulation of global commons, in this case the protection of the biodiversity of forests and oceans. After a historical overview of public and private regulation of common property resources, which traces the failure and weakness of (inter)governmental solutions with regard to biodiversity (sections 2 to 5), the chapter discusses several market-based regulatory solutions to the protection of forests and fisheries (sections 6 to 12). Two certification schemes in particular are given in-depth attention, namely those of the Forest Stewardship Council (FSC) and the Marine Stewardship Council (MSC). This comparative analysis reveals that these schemes are confronted with common problems such as the management of diversity, the problem of enforcement (limited audit resources) and issues concerning the maintenance of certificate credibility and reputation, and that solutions are needed to enhance their performance as transnational regulatory mechanisms. Building on historical evidence, this chapter makes the case for increased public recognition of private standards and identifies some initial current trends in which states join or make use of private arrangements with regard to the protection of forests and fisheries (section 12). In the last two sections, the chapter discusses these new economic governance regimes, combining elements of markets, associations, hierarchies and states (section 13) and closes by recommending that more should be invested in developing genuine Ecological Public-Private Partnerships (EPPPs), where private initiatives such as the FSC and MSC are publicly supported but also controlled and sanctioned (section 13).

2. RISKS TO THE ENVIRONMENT: LOSS OF BIODIVERSITY

A major source of risk and uncertainty, which for nation-states comes also – if not largely – from beyond their own borders, is the threatening loss of biodiversity around the globe, that is, the loss of diversity of species, habitats and ecosystems, and loss of genetic diversity. These losses are aspects of one specific dimension of globalization, namely biological international interdependence. This threatening loss is caused by another dimension of globalization: economic interdependence.

Biodiversity is, first of all, a value in itself and its loss is an intrinsic and universal problem. With humanity's power to control and intervene in nature comes a responsibility for its maintenance. However, loss of biodiversity is also a direct threat to our interests. It endangers our very survival. The biosphere is our source of food, shelter, medicine and other basic and less basic needs. Depletion of these resources threatens their future supply. Whatever happens to the environment across our borders affects us indirectly and even directly. This holds for generic consequences, such as global warming and loss of genetic diversity, but also for specific consequences, whether they be from close neighbors (the Dutch suffer from the pollution France and Germany dump in the Rhine and the British in the air) or from distant 'neighbours': concrete pollution can get carried over long distances. A 2004 study found that plumes of dirty air containing poisonous chemicals such as mercury were carried by the jet stream from factories in China all the way to New England, USA (Pottinger et al., 2004). Pollution and the weather moves across borders as do animal and plant species (the latter through their seeds). They move easier using our planes, ships and cars, invading other ecosystems and uprooting the equilibria there. Barriers between ecosystems get broken down, ecological niches disappear, new struggles for survival of the fittest species take place, some species lose out, and cross-breeding, for example, between wild and farmed salmon, reduces genetic variety.

Globalization means interdependence (Chanda, 2007), both in suffering the consequences and in being responsible for the causes. In many different ways and roles we contribute to the loss of biodiversity elsewhere: as consumers, producers, traders, tourists or soldiers. We cause it, along the global trade chains, in global markets that are so typical for globalization. Pollution and species may move, but so do goods, services, finance and ourselves. Hence it is in a way a self-induced risk, coming back to us, but because it takes a detour via other countries it is less directly under our control.

In reaction to our demand for goods and services elsewhere a great variety of natural resources are harvested from the Earth: petroleum, copper, chrome, uranium and other minerals, tropical forests, fish, etc. Not only does this entail a depletion of these finite resources, their mining or harvesting is often carried out under conditions destructive of ecosystems: mining waste pollutes if not poisons entire regions; clear-cutting of forests destroys complete forest ecosystems; mass fishing techniques such as trawling destroy deep sea life and net-fishing for yellowfin tuna (who tend to stay near dolphin pods to seek protection against sharks) also kills many dolphins.

The global demand for agricultural products equally endangers biodiversity. Forest ecosystems disappear from the use of radical 'slash-and-burn' practices to make room for growing crops. If forests are replaced by tree plantations this results in monocultures low in biodiversity. Competitive pressures to increase productivity foster large-scale, resource-intensive industrial farming, using fertilizers and pesticides. Our demand for goods has also fuelled industrialization elsewhere. As world trade has grown, millions of factories have joined the global supply chain. Though in itself a positive consequence of globalization, this also has negative implications. Accelerated burning of coal and the use of chemicals to fuel the export machine pollutes the environment elsewhere and, eventually, also here. The production facilities in many parts of the world are frequently more primitive, and in the absence of effectively enforced regulation, these industries dump their untreated waste directly in the environment: acids used in dying jeans flow into local rivers, and carbon and heavy metals disappear through smokestacks into the air. Industrialization in turn induces increasing prosperity, population growth and further urbanization, with ecosystems being bulldozed.

Even after our consumptive needs have been satisfied, we still contribute to further destruction of natural environments elsewhere, as with the export of used electronic products to developing countries, where they are taken apart by cheap labour to harvest precious materials for recycling. Again, while this in itself is positive, it is done under unsafe working conditions and produces poisonous waste without commercial value that is dumped in the environment.

In addition to buying imports, traveling as tourists to foreign countries may inflict assaults on the local environments: roads are built for our transportation into sensitive ecosystems; fields are cleared for building hotels and growing crops; airplanes, cars and air conditioners burn fossil fuels, etc. Economists tend to see this 'economic globalization' as a contribution to our own prosperity and that of others. But it comes at a price – the exhaustion of nature – and this is often not included in the price consumers pay. It is a typical negative externality, passed on to the public at large, here, there and in the future. In this sense, we are all in the same boat. Biodiversity is a classical common pool resource (Ostrom, 1990) and protective measures have all the characteristics of a common good, a global common good. We cause it, but can we also control it? That depends, among other things, on the specific characteristics of the threatened resources. Let us take a closer look at some of these.

3. FISH AND FORESTS

Fish and forests are typical common pool resources. They are, in principle, both renewable resources and their ecosystems are rather large. However, reproduction takes time, especially in the case of trees, and hence overharvesting can deplete these 'commons'. For a long time, land and sea were seen as inexhaustible sources of resources to feed and house people: forests seemed to be endless and oceans teemed with fish. However, modern technology has increased the scale of harvesting, up to the point that common pool resources threaten to be no longer self-sustaining.

Forests and fish are both species that are threatened because they are cut, slaughtered and traded because they have commercial value as building materials or food. See Richards and Tucker (eds), 1988, and Dauvergne 1997, 2001 on the increasing extent of this trade and

Khatchadourian, 2008 on more recent illegal logging in Russia for Chinese and indirect Western markets. Both fish and lumber are essential and major resources for providing humans with food and shelter. For 2.6 billion people (40 per cent of the world population), fish makes up at least 20 per cent of their annual protein intake. Moreover, 200 million people depend on the fishing industry to earn their 'daily bread'. Fish is also the most heavily traded good in the world. Its value is larger than the value of coffee, tea, rice and sugar exports combined (FAO, 2008).

While fish and forests have commonalities, they also have differences. Fish are mobile and can move freely in and out of different waters, and are either not owned by anyone, as in the open ocean, or can easily leave a marine territory owned by someone. By contrast, trees have a fixed location, on land, and can more easily be appropriated and turned into someone's private property, who then has an interest in caring for this resource. Even where forests are originally a 'commons', enclosure is possible and usually relatively easy. For fish in the open ocean that is much more difficult. Hence privatization and markets can be a solution to the tragedy of the forest commons, but hardly for the tragedy of the fish commons. Where privatization of a common pool resource is not possible (assuming that it is desirable), a 'Leviathan' may have to be called upon, that is, regulation by an actor, or a conglomeration of actors, that can effectively enforce protective regulation. That too is easier in the case of forests, again due to their immobility. They stand on land that is usually within the jurisdiction of a nation-state, which could, in principle, regulate it. The mobility of fish, including in and out of the territorial waters of nation-states, makes their harvesting more difficult to regulate by such states.

Another difference is that trees can be seen and counted; fish, being underwater, are less easily seen and very mobile hence making it more difficult to estimate the biomass of specific species of fish and hence the threat of overfishing. For forests there is less scientific uncertainty as to the size of the resource, now and in the future, and that facilitates long-term sustainable management. With fish there is more uncertainty, which makes protective policies more susceptible to controversy. With forests the problem is less a potential lack of wood (except in a few cases of highly desirable wood in limited supply, for instance, due to slow growth – usually hardwoods such as redwood, mahogany and some other tropical wood) and more the destruction of important ecosystems, such as old-growth or tropical forests. Hence, unlike with fish, rationing of scarcity is less often used as a measure of sustainable policy. Instead, the emphasis is more on sound long-term management of the whole forest. With fish the problem is, in the first place, overfishing. Still, sound fishing management is also important, for example, renouncing destructive fishing methods, such as net-fishing for tuna, the use of cyanide and dynamite, and water pollution, which all affect both threatened species and threatened habitats.

4. PUBLIC REGULATION

Obviously, there is something to be protected here, and this has been recognized by a great variety of actors. Who could do that, how and by which means? Sources of regulation could come, as we have become accustomed, from the state. However, in global markets and as regards to global public goods, the tentacles of the state may not be long enough; its powers may not suffice. Other, private, actors have attempted to fill the void – commercial businesses, associations, communities, hierarchies – either alone, or in close cooperation among themselves, or in cooperation with states. Given the nature of the resource to be protected, some have offered advantages over others.

States have made efforts to protect biodiversity by regulation in so far as it lies within their power, that is, their domestic jurisdiction. Most countries have legislation in place to protect endangered species. Thus the US has its Endangered Species Act of 1973 and its Marine Mammal Protection Act of 1972, the Netherlands its Natuurbeschermingswet 1968, elaborated in the Wet bedreigde diersoorten 1977 and eventually the Flora and Faunawet 2002, and even Thailand, for many years known as a centre for illegal trade and the smuggling of threatened wildlife species, eventually enacted a Wild Animals Reservation and Protection Act in 1992. However, such national regulatory measures have severe limitations, if only because biological niche boundaries do not respect national ones. The Dutch may protect their birds, but if these get shot on their migratory travels over Italy, Spain or Malta then that protection is not very effective. The protection of species in the territorial waters of one nation is less effective as the fish swim into the territorial waters of another or even the open, ‘free’ ocean. As indicated earlier, there is a global interdependency both with regard to the consequences suffered from loss of biodiversity as well as its consequences. Hence international cooperation is required to solve the problems effectively. Global governance is required.

Therefore, international treaties to protect biodiversity have been concluded, usually under the umbrella of the UN. In the course of time several such agreements have been agreed upon, for example the Convention on International Trade with Endangered Species of Wild Fauna and Flora (CITES). It was integrated with other treaties in what was to be an ‘umbrella convention’, the Convention on Biological

Diversity (CBD), signed at the UN Conference on the Environment and Development (UNCED) in Rio de Janeiro, 1992. The first draft was drawn up in 1989 by a private NGO, the International Union for the Conservation of Nature (IUCN). This organization has also been active in identifying species threatened with disappearance and has published 'red lists of endangered species', for instance, the *Global Biodiversity Outlook of 2001*, and a second version in 2006. Other NGOs have been involved in this as well, such as the World Resources Institute in Washington DC, which has drafted the *Millennium Ecosystem Assessment: Ecosystems and Human Well-being*. The Convention has attempted to reconcile ecology with economy, embodied in the concept of 'sustainable development'. It resulted from a compromise of ecological, economic and social interests (the latter of indigenous peoples) and hence addressed not only the issue of conservation of biological diversity, but linked it to economic interests – commercialization of nature, (intellectual) property rights, (exchange) value, distribution conflicts over the use of genetic resources, technology transfer, etc. These economic and social aspects were further elaborated in the Bonn Guidelines on Access to Genetic Resources and Fair and Equitable Sharing of the Benefits Arising out of its Utilization, signed in The Hague in 2002 (Brand et al., 2008).

Before general biodiversity protection treaties were concluded, product- or ecosystem-specific conventions were agreed. As regards ocean fisheries the first treaty was concluded in 1958, the UN Convention on Fishing and Conservation of Living Resources of the High Seas. It was followed by treaties further elaborating protection such as the 1982 UN Convention on the Law of the Sea (UNCLOS) and the 1995 UN Fish Stocks Agreement. In addition, international fishery regulatory organizations for specific species or regions were established. For example, for tuna the International Commission for the Conservation of Atlantic Tunas (ICCAT), the Western Central Pacific Ocean Fisheries Commission, the Inter-American Tropical Tuna Commission, the Indian Ocean Tuna Commission, the International Commission for the Conservation of Atlantic Tunas and the Commission for the Conservation of Southern Bluefin Tuna were established. Among others, the Northwest Atlantic Fisheries Organization (NAFO) focused on cod (Carr and Scheiber, 2004).

Notwithstanding the number of protective treaties that have been agreed upon, and the international fisheries organizations created, biodiversity remains seriously threatened. Forests are depleted, ecosystems destroyed and oceans over-fished. Of 23 commercially exploited types of tuna, nine are classified as fully fished, four as over-exploited, three as critically endangered, and three as vulnerable to extinction. State regulation, whether national or supra-national, does apparently have its problems. The CBD and other conventions have no sanctions and as such are difficult to enforce (Carr and Scheiber, 2004; Vogel and Kagan, 2004). Enforcement is only possible by the national law of individual nation-states. Many have already enacted laws of their own, often with sanctions. The Convention gives such national regulations international legitimacy and norms to go by; what is more, it obliges the countries which have ratified the treaties to enact binding legislation to implement the treaties. This makes countries dependent on one another for effective enforcement.

However, not every national government gives biodiversity an equally high political priority. There are also problems of shortage of administrative resources, lax enforcers and outright corruption in the long principal-agent chains, as well as conflicts with cultural traditions. For instance, the Thai Kaithong restaurant in Chiangmai – paradise for exotic gourmets – boasts of serving 'snake steak' with a picture of a giant king cobra, and other 'exotic delicacies' such as pythons, crocodiles, wild boar, soft-shelled turtles, monitor lizards, mountain frogs, hares, eels and partridges. Patrons can select a live king cobra and have it cooked to their taste for 4,499 bahts (approximately $180) – quite an incentive for poaching or corruption.

How can countries force each other to 'obey the law'? The conventions and treaties allow trade sanctions in so far as they ban possession, trade, transport and import of endangered species or products made from them without a license. These have indeed been applied, and worked sometimes, at first sight. Thus Thailand finally enacted its 1992 endangered species act after the Secretariat of CITES urged its members in 1991 to ban trade with Thailand in any species included in the CITES appendices, notably birds.

But a law-in-the-books is not yet a law-in-action. Black letter law can be patient. It is only affective if it is effectively enforced, and that is frequently missing in many countries. Even if there is effective enforcement, this may only work for species on the CITES endangered species list. Regulation and enforcement is more controversial for species not yet on the endangered species list, but whose over-harvesting threatens the sustainability of the common pool resource; or where the *process* of growing or harvesting threatens the survival of specific ecosystems. Illegal products can be blocked at borders if the political will and the administrative capacity exist, but it is less clear-cut with products whose *production* has negative externalities for biodiversity, such as bad forest management or sea bottom trawling. Processes in other countries are more difficult to regulate than products. An interesting exception to the rule is the well-known tuna–dolphin case, where imports of tuna coming from fisheries or regions suspected to use nets that kill dolphins have been blocked.

Enforcement problems are particularly great in the matter of ocean biodiversity, for one, because of the public good nature of fishing reserves. As long as there is the threat of poaching and free riding by fisheries of other states, countries have less of an incentive to enact and enforce strict rules on sustainable management of ocean fishing stock. Their savings would only benefit others and the goal, preserving the common pool resource, would not be reached. Thus most countries continue to subsidize fishing fleets and encourage fishing by their own fishermen.

The unwillingness to enforce harvesting restrictions is related to inability to do so. Responsible management is frustrated by 'difficulties of policing fishing catches by thousands of highly mobile individual fishing boats, a lack of scientific consensus regarding the size of worldwide and regional fishing stocks, and the ability of fishing vessels to shift registration to countries whose conservation standards, as actually enforced, are less demanding' (Vogel and Kagan, 2004, p. 22). If it is already difficult for nation-states to police their own offshore exclusive economic zones (EEZs), even more difficult will it be for country A to monitor country B whether or not it monitors effectively the thousands of ships in its own thousands of territorial square miles of water, not to speak of their control over large expanses of the open seas. Monitoring forests is a bit easier, if only because they can be observed from the air or space. Paradoxically, states may also be hindered in effective enforcement, just because they are bound by the law. Conventions on free trade under the WTO constrain states in using import bans to enforce regulations protecting biodiversity. Just because they have to 'obey the law', the law (their own protective) is less useful to realize this policy goal. The legal road can be illegal.

These 'government failures' have led states to seek the assistance of, or support, other sources of regulation, notably markets, hierarchies, associations and communities: markets for fish and lumber; hierarchies in the form of manufacturing, trading and retailing corporations; public interest and trade associations; and communities of environmental activists or fishermen. Alternatively, these sources have taken initiatives to provide alternatives to government regulation for protecting biodiversity.

5. MARKET-BASED REGULATORY SOLUTIONS

So-called market-based regulation is not really a rule 'created by markets', but it concerns institutions created by political and/or economic actors with the intention to affect market transactions in such a way that these have less or no negative externalities for biodiversity. The aim is to use the allocation mechanism of the market better, to serve not only private but also public interests. Such institutions may regulate access to the market, structure interests of the transaction partners involved, steer the competitive structure of the market, affect the costs and benefits of certain choices, provide information to influence those choices, or provide other incentives 'to do good'. As value chains 'from fishery to fork' or 'from forest to furniture' usually consist of different markets, vertically related to each other, such institutions can affect one or more of these stages in the chains.

5.1. Privatization

A standard economics solution to solve problems of depletion of common pool resources is privatization: turning communal or public (including no one's) property into private (someone's) property. Owners of forests and fishing rights are expected to have an incentive to care for the sustainability of their resources, because they have exclusive rights to the benefits of their responsible behavior. Forests and fish were originally common property. Privatization of forests began over a thousand years go and has gone quite far. In so far as there are still commons of forests, logging rights can be allocated by state authorities under whose jurisdiction the forests are. The enforcement of such rights is also relatively easy, at least easier than for fish.

For fish stocks in the oceans, privatization has taken place more recently, in several steps. The 'enclosure movement' of the seas first entailed the appropriation of parts of the seas by still collective actors, nation-states. These divided a part of the global commons by agreeing on and recognizing each others' exclusive rights to parts of the sea. The first three miles or 'a cannon shot' from the coastline (formulated in the early eighteenth century by Dutch jurists), extended gradually to 12 miles by many countries in the twentieth century, and eventually to an EEZ (Exclusive Economic Zone) of 200 miles from the coastline (by the 1982 UN Convention on the Law of the Sea, which also codified the 12 mile territorial waters rule).

This collective property of nation-states has subsequently been further privatized in the form of fishing rights for quotas of specific fish ('individual transferable rights' or ITQs) given to fishermen, fishing corporations or fishermen's associations. Thus the open access to fish stocks, typical of the 'open seas' legal philosophy, was changed into restricted access. However, a condition for privatization bringing about responsible stewardship is effective enforcement of property rights. That was not easy for fish in the open seas; effective enclosure is difficult there. First, fish swim in and out of the protected zones where rights have been given, notably the larger fish. Second, the threat of poaching is difficult to avert, given the aforementioned problems with controlling the large open seas. That, in turn, reduces the motivation of quota-owners to restrict themselves to their quota, under the adage, 'If we don't catch the rest, the Japanese or Portuguese will do so'. In order to land and sell their overcatch, fishermen have been known to resort to fraud, or land the fish in countries not involved in the regulation of these waters. Thus the effect of such privatization has been limited. Furthermore, it has not directly affected the harm caused by fishing methods on other species or on the ecosystem.

More effective protection of property rights and control of methods has been provided with a stricter enclosure measure as with fish farming. Many commercial species, including salmon, cod, catfish, barramundi, shellfish and crustaceans are nowadays raised in offshore net pens where sea water flows through or, in the case of freshwater fish like trout, catfish or tilapia, in ponds and lakes. Trees are also farmed in plantations. Though this has taken some of the pressure of overharvesting the common seas and forests, it has not solved the threats to biodiversity. For one, fish farms and plantations are monocultures, themselves low on diversity. These monocultures, as in any case of intensive farming, facilitate the rapid spreading of disease, and where they are in contact with natural environments, they threaten the biodiversity of species, ecosystems and genetic make-up there.

Apart from the danger of disease there is also the risk of genetic pollution of wild species with farmed ones, which could reduce genetic diversity. Farmed fish can also destroy local populations by devouring them literally, as has been the case with the aggressive Nile perch in Lake Victoria (see the movie *Darwin's Nightmare* by Hubert Sauper). Furthermore, even if farming is a good solution, not all species lend themselves to it; and, after all, taking fish and lumber from the commons is cheaper.

Even where privatization and farming may offer a solution to the problem of overharvesting certain species, it still leaves the problem of the externalities of more 'efficient' production on natural and diverse ecosystems. The owner of a forest may care for the reproduction of his trees, but he has less or no interest in the survival of a great variety of bugs and butterflies in his forests, especially when these may also reduce the productivity of his forests.

5.2. Certification

Privatization starts at the production end of the value chain, but other regulatory measures have started at the final consumer end. Attempts have been made to influence final consumer choices, thus using the market mechanism to steer demand for fish and forest products towards varieties that do not harm biodiversity, or do so to a lesser degree. The instruments are information and persuasion. Information about the product and its producer is intended to influence the transactions into which consumers enter. This is done by naming, blaming and shaming both biodiversity-unfriendly products and producers/sellers. 'Bad' products are censured if not criminated; 'good' ones are commended. In order to aid consumers in distinguishing the good from the evil, good products are certified and given a seal of approval (Bartley, 2003; Conroy, 2007; Gulbrandsen, 2004, 2005, 2010; Overdevest and Rickenbach, 2006; Pattberg, 2005). Such certificates provide information, possibly legitimizing higher prices for better rated products, and have been developed for countless markets before: medieval woolen cloth, wine and beer, kosher and halal food, financial services. Not only products have been certified, but also producers and customers. Medieval craftsmen were certified by guild standards; employees are certified by diplomas, reference letters or psychological tests; and consumers applying for a mortgage by their credit rating. The experiences of these many other rating systems can teach us something about the prospects of these biodiversity-safe certification systems.

A problem with biodiversity is that the quality of the product is usually not at stake here (unlike in the case of biosafety issues), so appeals to the self-interest of the consumer are difficult. For consumers, lumber from well-managed forests is not necessarily better than from wild non-managed forests. (Actually, in so far as there is a difference in the quality reputation of the products, 'natural' species like wild salmon or old-growth lumber or tropical hardwood are often considered more desirable – either because it tastes or works better, or because it is more exclusive and hence satisfies the demand for ostentatious consumption.) The source of the product or its production method is problematic. In principle it does not directly affect the utility the consumer derives from the product. Therefore, appeals can only be made to altruistic concerns, emotional feelings or moral values. The altruism may even be narrow: will there be food or a livable environment for one's grandchildren?

Experience shows that such appeals are is not impossible. Even mainstream micro-economists have in the meantime discovered that human actors are not always the narrow minded self-interested actors that their models assumed or used to assume. Economic actors are also socially embedded, influenced by the opinions, approval and disapproval of others, by symbols to take seriously, by honors bestowed or ostracism inflicted on them, by what their culture and society considers appropriate behavior. If enough people define specific species as pitiful and in need for protection, than that can become a social norm to be honored. Experience has, however, also shown that compassion develops more easily for species with which we as humans somehow can identify or sympathize. At the very least they have to move like us humans, they have to be large enough that we can see them, and preferably they ought to be cuddly like a teddy bear. Ideally they will have a high 'caressibility factor'. Not for nothing did the World Wildlife Fund (WWF) adopt the panda as its symbol, and not a supposedly aggressive, cold-blooded slimy creature such as a snake or alligator. Trees and fishes do not directly meet the above mentioned requirements, but forests can at least be associated with the panda: as being their 'home'. However, more abstract concerns can become socially defined as a major concern for humanity, which few actors can afford to negate openly; such has been the case with global warming and its causes.

These social, moral and emotional concerns have induced people to form public interest associations and to further mobilize support for their cause as for example, the Rainforest Alliance, the Rainforest Action Network, Greenpeace and the WWF. Such NGOs are self-appointed representatives of 'global public interests', bundling and focusing these as a kind of 'public interest burning glass' on something that can most easily be targeted. Their direct action led to the formation of certifying organizations for biodiversity-friendly forest products and fish: the Forest Stewardship Council and the Marine Stewardship Council are among the more well-known cases of such regulation through certification. In a way, these are combinations of three sources of economic governance: markets, associations and hierarchies. As we shall see, eventually states also got involved in these intricate systems of market governance.

6. CASE I. FORESTS: THE FOREST STEWARDSHIP COUNCIL

The emergence of the Forest Stewardship Council (FSC) started with associations focusing in on hierarchies. Their activities led to the formation of the FSC, itself also an association. Public interest associations like Friends of the Earth, Greenpeace and the Rainforest Action Network did not see much use in addressing the amorphous mass of consumers directly. Instead, they targeted large firm hierarchies in highly visible retail sectors such as furniture and do-it-yourself/home improvement stores frequented by consumers and with well-known brand images: B&Q in the UK, IKEA, Home Depot, Office Depot, Staples and Kinko's. They staged demonstrations, protests and boycotts, in the media, in front of these stores, and even within the stores, sometimes 'using the store's public address systems to sarcastically announce to consumers where they could purchase wood "ripped from the heart of the Amazon basin".'(Vogel, 2005, p. 115). Thus they have tried to 'burn' the public reputations of these retail capitalists (a form of social and economic ostracism) unless they would switch to selling (only) environmentally certified products.

The first initiatives date from 1985 when Friends of the Earth UK organized a boycott of B&Q and some other retailers selling products from clear-cut logging in tropical forests. A little later the WWF started to develop a tropical forest policy. In April 1991 the Rainforest Action Group, Friends of the Earth UK and Earth First! began a sustained campaign against retail chains. 'They organized mock chainsaw massacres outside stores depicting the destruction of the world's forests. Customers and store managers were systematically leafleted. In some cases, smoke bombs were set off inside home improvement stores. In one weekend, there were around 30 demonstrations outside B&Q facilities alone' (Austin and Reficco, 2006, p. 2). The media amplified the effect of these direct actions by giving them extensive coverage. This social movement in the UK blew over to Germany, the Netherlands and the US.

At the end of 1991, ten UK retailers gave in. They promised to change their sourcing policies and buy wood only from well-managed forests. They would either cut suppliers or convince them to change forest management practices. They did not so much react to a consumer demand for responsible wood but they disliked controversy and feared for their reputation in general. It was a kind of risk management. 'As an executive of UK retailer B&Q stated: "We weren't ever going to have customers demanding sustainable timber in our stores. But we knew that if our name, B&Q, was associated with destruction of tropical forests or even temperate forests, our brand name . . . would be damaged."' (Counsell and Loraas, 2002, p. 12, quoted in Taylor, 2005, p. 142). Market competition worked. Once major retailers like B&Q had come round, the environmental issue became a means of differentiation among competing retailers in the competitive do-it-yourself market. Therefore their competitors felt compelled to follow. Thus major hierarchies like B&Q not only regulated their own suppliers, but indirectly they also regulated their competitors.

The WWF monitored and gave feedback to companies. To this end, it mediated between environmentalists and retailers and formed buying groups in which these participated and discussed policy options. These buying groups gained ground quickly. By 2002, around 700 companies had formed 17 such buyer groups, mostly in Europe and North America. They included the biggest retailers: B&Q, Home Depot, Lowe's, Sainsbury's, Homebase, Texas, Do it All and IKEA. Major timber producers also joined, for example, Canadian exporters to Europe, whose exports to these retailers fell (Austin and Reficco, 2006). The groups formed the Global Forest and Trade Network, which included manufacturers, media, local authorities, environmentalists and end users. Their aim was to regulate the supply chains and bring supply and demand for wood from well-managed forests together. That turned out not to be easy, for one because demand quickly exceeded supply, but also because clear standards were lacking. Soon every retailer claimed to buy environmentally friendly, but claims were hard to substantiate. Thus need arose for a credible system of standardization. This led to the formation in 1993 of the FSC. Its goal was to preserve biodiversity, especially in tropical and old-growth forests, and to support responsible and sustainable forest management, and it would do so via certification.

6.1. Functions

The FSC has three main functions: standard setting, accreditation and trademark assurance.

First, it sets standards for responsible forest management, using an open and transparent process of decision making involving all affiliated stakeholders. These standards are codified in ten principles and criteria of forest stewardship. Typical for these basic FSC standards is that they take a broad view of forest stewardship. They concern, of course, environmental impact: biodiversity, water resources, soils, fragile ecosystems and landscapes, hazardous pesticides and chemicals, and integrity of the forest. But they also examine economic concerns (such as economic viability and efficient use), social concerns (such as rights of indigenous peoples and forest workers, transparency of tenure, use rights of the land and community relations), as well as legal and practical concerns (legality – no corruption, management plans, monitoring and assessment). There are separate principles for high-conservation value forests and forest plantations. Special concern is also shown for cultural or sacred sites and the habitats of endangered animals or plants. The principles also prohibit the cultivation of genetically modified trees.

These principles are elaborated into more specific national, regional or local standards by national working groups, which need approval from the FSC's board of directors. Standards are to be based on 'best available science'. They are formulated in a open and transparent discussion process involving all stakeholders (thus providing legitimacy) and aiming for consensus, meaning there are usually political compromises. Arriving at the standards is both a political and technical activity.

There are standards and certificates for two types of products: a) for forests and their management; and b) so-called 'chain-of-custody certification', for products whose sources are traceable to sustainable managed forest. This requires tracking products along the whole value chain, from forest to final product. For every stage (or 'custody') in the chain, a certificate is issued that informs the subsequent stage about the 'purity' of the intermediate product, for example, that it is not mixed with uncertified wood. Wherever that is difficult to ascertain because certified and uncertified wood were indistinguishable when they went into the subsequent product, as with paper, a special certificate is issued, certifying a percentage claim, minimal X per cent, of certified wood. (Later this was further differentiated in subcategories as 'FSC mixed sources'.)

The second function of the FSC is accreditation. It does not certify itself whether producers comply with the standards, but it recognizes and accredits other certification bodies who do so. These have to be independent third-party organizations that are competent in forest evaluation. Certification has to be carried out following clear and pre-defined procedures. To this end, the FSC has created an Accreditation Manual, which formulates the norms that certification bodies have to meet in order to be accredited. In 2005, the FSC created Accreditation Services International GmbH (ASI) to manage the FSC accreditation program. That is, the FSC certifies the certifiers – and it does so at least once a year. If they are found not to comply, the certificate is withdrawn. Getting certified is formally a voluntary choice by the forest producer; de facto it can, of course, be imposed by the customer.

The certifying bodies are of different natures. Among them are local NGOs, international NGOs present in different countries such as the Rainforest Alliance network, and commercial certifiers such as consultants. It is dependent on what organizations are available in a specific country. Some subcontract the actual implementation and enforcement – for example, SGS Forestry, based in Europe, delegated actual control on the ground in Africa to local subcontractors – thus the control chain was occasionally even longer. The greater principal-agent problems resulted occasionally in questionability of the experience, competence and hence effectiveness and reliability of certification, esepcially where distant local certifiers had to be relied upon. After all, many forests are in out-of-the-way places.

Thirdly, the FSC manages its logo, the FSC trademark. Use of the logo means that products satisfy the FSC standards. The FSC licenses firms, including final consumers, to use the logo on wood products.

6.2. Funding

Originally, the FSC International was funded mainly by donations. In 2001, they came from European governments (40 per cent), American foundations such as Rockefeller and Ford (40 per cent) and environmental NGOs such as the WWF (20 per cent) (Austin and Reficco, 2006). Membership fees and accreditation charges were minimal and covered mostly the costs of those activities. However, dependence on donations was risky and therefore the FSC has tried to reduce its dependency on such donations. By 2008, donations accounted for only 60 per cent of it funding. The other 40 per cent was collected from fees (membership, accreditation, logo-use and others) and services rendered.

Auditing and certification could be expensive, especially where it concerned large tracks of forest in remote areas, and lots managed in a complex fashion in order to increase yield yet abide by FSC norms. Costs could vary from $ 500 to $ 50 000 (Austin and Reficco, 2006). In addition to these initial costs, audits and certification had to be repeated annually, and this cost about 50 per cent of the initial fee. Furthermore, there were the costs for carrying out suggested changes in forest management. These auditing and certification costs had to be borne by the forest owner, therefore deterring many lumber producers, particularly smaller private forest owners in Europe. They could however split the bill by engaging in group certification.

6.3. Success

The FSC has been quite a success story, at first sight. It has grown fast since its inception in 1995. By 2002, 25.5 million hectares of forest – the size of the UK – in 66 countries had been FSC-certified. After another nine years, by May 2011, this had increased almost six-fold to more than 143 million hectares of forest in 81 countries (www.fsc.org; accessed 8 May 2011). As is to be expected, the largest single certificates are given to forests in Canada, Russia, the US and Sweden. Though the majority of certified forests are still in the temperate (54 million hectares) and boreal zones (71 million hectares) of the Earth, there is also some growth in certified tropical forests. In the tropics, a region about which the founders of the FSC were most concerned, growth in certification has been slow. By 2011, 17 million hectares in tropical and subtropical areas had been certified. Altogether, 1041 Forest Management certificates had been issued by May 2011. With 20 257 chain-of-custody (COC) certificates to companies in 105 countries, the number of companies along the forest product supply chain committing to FSC certification has increased substantially. The value of

FSC labelled sales rose from $ 1 billion in 2002 to $ 20 billion in 2008 (www.fsc.org, accessed February 2009). The FSC now has offices in 46 countries. The FAO has called the FSC the fastest growing forest certification system in the world (UN FAO, 2007).

However, the forest area certified is still only a small part of the total forest surface area of the Earth, as pointed out by Marx and Cuypers (2010). The 116 million hectares of forest certified in 2009 constituted only 2.9 per cent of the total world forest area of 3 937 million hectares (data FAO, cited in Marx and Cuypers, 2010). The FSC is notably absent in Africa, with only 7 million hectares certified, mainly in South Africa, Congo and Gabon. Hence, the growth in forest area certified has not yet been able to stop global deforestation (a decrease of 3.3 per cent between 1995 and 2007), as Marx and Cuypers note. They blame this on the limited coverage in developing countries, and conclude that the effectiveness of forest certification does not only depend on the certification itself, but also on some institutional characteristics of the countries involved, such as good governance practices, governmental effectiveness, respect for the rule of law and control of corruption.

The FSC is also increasingly marketing its own product: certification. It has developed a licensing program for the FSC logo, and the increased use of it, especially on all kinds of paper, has substantially increased its visibility to the general public. One can find it on kitchen furniture, pencils, magazines, books, sweepstake tickets, food packaging (recently Tetrapak secured a chain-of-custody certificate and in a short time the logo appeared on 100 million cartons), and even cosmetics and gin (Belgian gin called *Dennenknopj*e made from pine cones from a certified forest). President Obama's inaugural invitations bore the FSC logo.

7. CASE II. FISH: THE MARINE STEWARDSHIP COUNCIL

The Marine Stewardship Council (MSC) had a start somewhat different from the FSC. It was not born from protests, demonstrations and boycotts forcing large firms to consider environmental concerns; on the contrary, one such large firm was, voluntarily, among the major initiators. In 1997, Unilever, together with the WWF, took the initiative to form the MSC. Of course, protests may have indirectly played a role in convincing Unilever to do so. Spectacular environmentalist direct action regarding the forest ecosystems was a recent phenomenon and Unilever would have surely noticed it. Its executives may have feared that the wrath of environmentalists would turn upon them after their success with the FSC.

However, Unilever also had a private interest in sound management of the seas. As the world's largest producer of frozen seafood it had a direct, though long-term, interest in securing the health and continued productivity of the oceans. Here the size of its 'hierarchy' favored environmental governance. It was large enough that it could not so easily externalize the costs to others because it was itself 'these others'. Icelandic fishermen could still reason, 'If we don't catch the fish, the Portuguese will'. But both the Icelanders and the Portuguese might supply Unilever. Whereas smaller actors had no incentive to care for the sustainability of the ocean commons, a large actor like Unilever did. The global fish commons was, in large part, its own pseudo-private 'property', at least in so far as it could itself reap the benefits of responsible management of the renewable resources in the ocean commons.

Unilever's size, diversity and resources also allowed it to take a long-term perspective. Whereas individual fishermen had good reason to be concerned about tomorrow's daily bread, Unilever's survival did not depend on tomorrow's supply. It could wait a bit and diversify risks, allowing it to take a long-term perspective. It could think in terms of decades, when the individual fisherman would be long dead. Hence, Unilever saw the depletion of renewable fish resources as a threat to its long-term interests. Given the difficulty of establishing a global regulatory authority for the oceans, it considered market-based certification a means to govern the global fish commons. As we know from the history of trade association formation at the national level, very large firms may have an incentive to sponsor and even fund collective action of the industry on their own (Olson, 1965; van Waarden, 1992). Not only can they not externalize the costs of free riding, they also cannot reason that their contribution to collective action does not count or that others would not note free riding on their part. Given their size, the benefits that they derive from collective action (even if only the more neutral letterhead) are large enough to outweigh the costs. What is more, the resources needed for collective action are peanuts for such large hierarchies.

So history repeats itself, now at the international level, with a large firm taking the initiative to found an association to regulate the resources on which the sector as a whole depends. Unlike in forests, here the initiative did not come from the retail but from the producer side. For one, in forestry there were no producers the size of Unilever. Furthermore, forestry producers did not have important brand names whose standing could be increased by association with sound resource management. Moreover, Unilever was not only a producer but also a buyer. Certification of fisheries could make it easier to control its many suppliers all over the world.

The MSC was formed in 1997, four years after the FSC. That was no coincidence – the FSC clearly formed a model for the MSC (Gulbrandsen, 2010). It was not only the similarity in name that indicates this. In many ways, as regards to the diversity of stakeholders, functions, structure and finance, the MSC was almost a copy of the FSC. Soon the organization included among its members conservation associations, scientists, fisheries, seafood companies and large food retailers. It set itself fundamental standards, also called 'principles and criteria'. There was certification both for harvesting/source management and for chain-of-custody management. The MSC did not itself do the certification, but accredited certifiers who audited fisheries and canners against the standards. It managed its MSC logo, licensing fisheries, seafood companies, retailers or restaurants to use it if they caught, processed, sold or prepared fish according to its criteria for sustainable fishing. Funding came largely from charitable grants.

The MSC had a bad start. It met various setbacks: suspicion and opposition by large parts of the industry who found that the auditing process was too long, too bureaucratic, and hence too costly; national governments such as those in Scandinavia who thought that certification should be conducted by governments and not by an NGO; tensions with environmentalists who wanted stricter standards; bad management; financial crises. Many of these issues could be traced back to a fundamental problem, which distinguished the MSC from the FSC: as it was difficult to 'see underwater', it was more problematic to evaluate whether fisheries had observed the standards and performed well. As a critical Greenpeace campaign director remarked:

> We disagree fundamentally with MSC's claim to certify sustainable fisheries. We believe that it is nearly impossible to claim that a fishery is sustainable. You need so much data to make that claim. And most fisheries do not have that data. They might have some evidence that they manage the fish stock in a way that it hasn't gone down. But that is not sustainability as we see it, namely managing a stock within a whole ecosystem and wanting the whole ecosystem to restore. (Quoted in Nick, 2006).

The difficulty of demonstrating effective ocean management meant that the credibility of MSC certificates was questioned, and hence also the organization itself. Did 'green stamps for seafood' really mean anything?

Another problem that differentiated it from the FSC was the fact that the MSC was started by firms mid-way along the supply chain – seafood processors like Unilever. Although it had, given its size, quite an influence in global markets, Unilever needed to convince both the original suppliers, the fishermen, and the consumers/retailers to adopt the standard, to live up to it and respectively to demand it. As Nick (2006, p.16) formulated it, the dilemma was 'no supply meant no market and no market meant no supply'. By contrast, the FSC was started at the end of the chain, by the retailers. There, there was an initial market, which looked for suppliers.

After a reorganization, change in leadership, further elaboration of standards and performance indicators, new certification methodology, further research into the benefits of certification, increasing transparency, and new internal checks and balances (such as an accreditation committee that double-checked accreditation decisions), the MSC recovered. In 2008 the MSC eco-labeled the 2000th product, a box of scallops from a Patagonian scallop fishery certified in 2006. Growth has been increasing. It took the MSC seven years to get from the first MSC-labelled product to the 500th, only nine months to get to the 1,000th and another 12 months to the 2000th. By 2008, 28 fisheries had been certified, including the first tuna and shrimp fisheries, and 77 were in the process of being certified. There were 580 companies that had received a chain-of-custody certification. MSC-certified products are available in 36 countries and sales total 250 million items at a net worth of US $ 1 billion (up 100 per cent from 2007). Many major food retailers have committed themselves to selling MSC-certified seafood, such as Loblaws, Tesco, Target, Sainsbury's, Wal-mart, Whole Foods, Carrefour, Metro, Lidl, Casino and Spar. Some of them, like Tesco and Wal-mart, committed themselves for a number of years to sell only MSC-certified fish. In addition to large hierarchies, associations of retailers have joined the program, for example, the association of Dutch retailers agreed that by 2011 all wild caught seafood at every food retailer in the Netherlands would be MSC-certified. In order to organize all this, the MSC set up regional offices in Edinburgh, Seattle, Berlin, Tokyo, Cape Town, The Hague and Australia.

In the meantime, the founder Unilever backed out of the frozen fish market and sold its division, due mainly to fierce competition from retailers creating their own brands. Not only were they cheaper than Unilever's brand products, like Findus and Bird's Eye, they also got preferential access to their shelves.

8. FSC AND MSC AS ASSOCIATIONS: THE PROBLEM OF MANAGEMENT OF DIVERSITY

What distinguishes the FSC and MSC from others certifiers, for example corporations, is that as associations they have members. Together, these members make the policies. The membership base of these international associations is very broad and diverse. It includes representatives from different stages in the value chain who have diverging interests: small and large fishing and forestry businesses, associations and cooperatives of them, the forestry profession, suppliers, processors, distributors and retailers, the scientific community, indigenous peoples' organizations, fishing and forestry communities and conservation groups. Furthermore, the councils also have to deal with other stakeholders outside the organization but in its domain, and that in many different countries where the circumstances and interests in forestry and fishing are very diverse. Both the FSC and MSC are kinds of peak associations: international associations of other national and international associations and organizations, differing by function, sector, region and nationality.

For such diverse interests to cooperate is not easy. Each has been confronted with the choice of being pragmatic or principled. Pragmatic means to cooperate with the others in joining the councils. The benefit is broader representation and legitimation, but at the cost of having to make concessions, diluting one's own pure interests and ideals, and losing legitimacy among the more radical wing of their rank and file. Principled means remaining true to one's own immutable convictions, and not, or only hesitantly, cooperating. The benefit is there is less risk of alienating the rank and file, but at the costs of remaining an outsider and lacking representativeness. It is the typical dilemma in any political arena: from national parliaments to the Israeli–Palestine conflict. In this case, the radical principled were organizations such as Greenpeace, local fisheries and the American forest and paper association. In between were pragmatists such as the WWF and some state foresters.

One reason for cooperation is that the different parties depend on each other. Environmentalists can exert pressure, lobby, publish, criticize, demonstrate and boycott as much as they want, but in the end the responsible management of forests and seas has to be carried out by foresters and fishermen. Retailers are needed to impose standards on producers. Conversely, retailers and producers depend on critical environmentalists to give their sustainability efforts recognition in the public eye, and to legitimize the certification. They may need each other, yet they also can get in each other's way. Standards demanded by environmentalists may be considered unrealistic, too strict or too costly by the industries. Conversely, involvement of industrial interests in the certification process tends to threaten the legitimacy of the certification and could even damage the reputation of the cooperating environmental organizations in the eyes of more critical environmentalists. Critical conservationists quickly call such 'self-regulation' 'greenwashing'. They believe that one should not involve the turkey in decisions about the Christmas dinner.

The management of such diversity poses quite a challenge to these organizations. The governance problems are akin to that of a state, which has citizens as its 'members'. Building broad coalitions requires a careful balancing of interests and the maintenance of some neutrality by the leadership in order to keep the organization together, given the conflicting interests involved. To this end the MSC, and especially the FSC, developed a governance structure that, on the one hand, was intended to engage interested stakeholders and, on the other hand, to balance their interests. There was a general assembly with individuals and representatives from all member organizations. It was divided into three chambers: environmental, social and economic. This allowed the maintenance of a balance between all three types of interest, without having to limit the number of members. Each chamber was, in turn, divided in a North and a South sub-chamber; Northerners were from high income developed countries, Southerners from developing countries. Altogether, there were six sub-chambers each with one-sixth of the vote, a kind of corporatist democracy. Decisions required a 66.6 per cent majority of the votes in the general assembly. The same careful composition was used in the board of directors. Furthermore, the international FSC was decentralized into 'national initiatives', in order to give the organization a grassroots base. These were organized on the same tripartite basis.

A balancing act was required from the leadership; on the one hand to engage members and on the other to keep some distance from individual members/associations in order not to alienate others. Though large member organizations such as Greenpeace and WWF gave the association legitimation and strengthened its reputation with the general public, too much intimacy with them might be counterproductive. Industry could fear a domination of such environmental NGOs and could come to perceive the council as an extension of Greenpeace.

Therefore it remained, certainly in the beginning, a rather unstable coalition. The councils are and remain political organizations. The membership base was a complicated Baptist-bootlegger coalition. It shared an interest in the credibility of fish and lumber, but for very different reasons. The costs of protecting relatively rare species are privately born and concentrated on a few specific industries, for instance, fishermen, foresters, or expanding and polluting industries. The benefits are public, and thinly spread over all of humanity. Public choice theory teaches us that in such a case those for whom costs are concentrated will have a stronger incentive to organize against protective regulation whereas when benefits are diffused among many, the latter will have less of an incentive to organize. Yet this theory is not confirmed in these cases because people are not only motivated by interests but also by ideals. The public interest has been represented by idealistic self-appointed activist NGOs and the scientific community.

Mutual distrust and adversarialism have plagued the councils. Repeatedly, there have been conflicts and walk-outs. At the first meeting of the FSC in Toronto, the more radical environmentalists such as Greenpeace, Friends of the Earth, the Rainforest Action network, and Rettet den Regenwald left the assembly temporarily when the industry was granted representation. The US and Canadian foresters' associations chose to remain outside the FSC and created their own competing certification systems.

The diversity of interests complicated agreement and hence affected the nature and acceptance of private associational standards. Some environmentalists found the councils too soft and wanted stricter standards, whereas others believed that a private market-based regulation could never solve the problem and that governments should be involved more. In their eyes such certification councils might be excuses for inaction. Fisheries, foresters and industries wanted less strict standards. They found certification too bureaucratic and expensive. Territorial diversity required the adjustment of standards and rules to local circumstances, but too much variety in standards could blur their identity, undercut them and threaten their credibility. Different elaborations of standards could even compete with each other.

9. THE PROBLEM OF ENFORCEMENT: USING HIERARCHIES

Typically, associations are voluntary hence they tend to have problems with enforcement of their regulations and standards. They may be able to bind their members through membership contracts, but since these members are free to leave that power is limited. It is even more difficult for such associations to impose standards on outsiders because they do not have the legal sanctions that public authorities have.

Historically, economic associations have been able to impose regulations on outsiders through 'exclusive trade agreements' with other associations. Thus for example members of an association of book printers were only allowed to buy paper from suppliers organized in one paper trade association. Conversely, its members, paper suppliers, were only allowed to supply printers organized in the book printing association. Similar 'closed shop' arrangements existed between employers' associations and trade unions. They forced economic actors to be organized in their respective association and made for 100 per cent density ratios. This compulsion allowed associations to regulate their industries, in the first place their own members, as these did not have an exit option short of leaving the industry. However, it also allowed for one association to regulate the members of another association, usually in exchange for a similar favour. However, the legality of such arrangements is questionable in many countries as they come close to cartels. Furthermore, due to concentration in certain markets, associations have become de facto replaced by large firm hierarchies with dominant market shares.

What associations may not be able to do, firm hierarchies can: they can impose their standards legally on their suppliers, and they also have the resources to control and audit them. The opposite is, of course, also possible: major suppliers can refuse to sell to customers if the latter do not abide by their standards for handling their products, for example, major car producers sell exclusively to car dealers under their control. Yet, rule imposition by those at the end of the commodity chain happens more frequently.

The concentration of the retail sector into a few very large retail hierarchies has given the latter so much market power that they can regulate the markets back up the commodity chain by imposing their own standards. The global furniture retailer IKEA serves as an example. In 2008, the corporation had 631 780 000 visitors (equal to the combined population of Europe and the US) in its 285 stores in 37 countries. Its total turnover was 33.5 billion Euros. Its products are manufactured by 1600 suppliers spread across Europe, North America and Asia. It obtained timber from 44 countries. Products are made according to IKEA's specifications. Its main business, furniture retailing, requires huge quantities of wood. The suppliers of these could damage the reputation of IKEA if they did something illegal or illegitimate. Thus, in addition to its many product quality standards, IKEA developed a code of conduct for its suppliers. In 2000, it introduced the 'IKEA Way of Purchasing Home Furnishing Products' – in short, the IWAY standards. These specified working conditions, labour, environment, chemicals, waste, procurement and forestry management practices that were expected from suppliers. IWAY contained 17 different standards regarding 90 specific issues. In this way, IKEA oriented itself to international treaties like the 1948 UN Declaration of Human Rights, the 1988 ILO Declaration on Fundamental Principles and Rights at Work, and the 1992 Rio Declaration on Environment and Development. From its standards it derived directives for its suppliers, who all had to sign an agreement with IKEA agreeing to comply with the directives. It helped and trained smaller suppliers to adopt environmentally-friendly operations. Among other stipulations, it forbade the use of wood that originates from intact natural forests in their area, using information from Global Forest Watch, an NGO which maps the locations of intact natural forests. Before a first delivery, IKEA would conduct a first IWAY audit of the supplier (ICMR, 2006).

Given such buying power, and their practice of already imposing standards on suppliers, NGOs focused from the very start on such large, highly visible retail firm hierarchies to try to get their biodiversity concerns included in chain regulation. They realized that it would be much more difficult to influence the decisions of millions of individual consumers than those of a few very large retailers. For one, the Olsonian problem of collective action is much more serious in a very large group than in a smaller one (Olson, 1965). Individual consumers, being one among millions, can be tempted to free ride. Even if they support the goal of maintaining biodiversity, they can reason that their individual contribution is so small that the collective goal can be realized without their participation. A small number of very large retailers with dominant market position cannot reason like that. Furthermore, large retailers are much more visible than most individual consumers. As such, they are likely to care more for their reputation as any blemish on it will be known immediately to masses of people, who they have to induce back into their stores as customers.

The NGOs knew that retailers had invested a lot in their brand names, and could be quite sensitive to any damage to their reputation. Thus they tried to instrumentalize the retailers' market power to use it to demand not only low prices or good quality products, but also biodiversity-friendly production. Once they succeeded in convincing retailers, the latter have become the means for the MSC/FSC to impose their certification on fisheries and foresters.

> As consumer demand for certified wood was nonexistent, WWF-buying groups were the motor, the driving force behind the emergence of the certification movement. Indeed, the power of these buying groups appeared considerable: they encompassed about 700 companies, including the biggest retailers – like Home Depot, Lowe's, B&Q, Sainsbury – and controlled about 7 per cent of the industrial roundwood global trade. (Austin and Reficco, 2006, p. 3).

Their domestic market shares in prosperous western countries were even higher.

In food retailing, market shares of supermarket chains are even higher and many food retailers are active internationally. Thus the French Carrefour is, with 15 000 stores in 32 countries and 490 000 employees, the second largest food retailer in the world. It used to have its own 'responsible fishing cod' certificate for its product line Eco-Planète. However, in 2008, it adopted the MSC certificate. Lately, even fast-food restaurant chains have reacted to the pressure. In 2005, McDonald's replaced its much criticized Styrofoam hamburger boxes with cardboard ones made from 75 per cent recycled fibers from FSC-certified wood (for which it even received a prize) and the fish for its fishburgers is also MSC certified.

Not only are such large retailers more responsive than individual consumers, the hierarchies can also aid in informing consumers and propagating environmentally responsible consumption. It is often heard that consumers do not care. While they may be environmentally concerned in their political choices as voters, apparently they are unconcerned or less concerned in their economic transaction choices. Economic leaders, like retailers, can inform and educate them, bring environmental concerns to their attention, and promote environmentally-certified products. Thus they would be like good political and association leaders, who should not only passively aggregate and pass on interests and opinions they receive from their grassroots, but also define and redefine the interests in the context of what is possible, confronting their voters and members with them. Such leadership is not always easy. McDonald's has been trying to promote vegetarian food (as healthier and more environmentally friendly), but salads, french fries, onion rings and veggie burgers make up only 1 per cent of sales (Olthuis, 2009).

What makes wood different from fish (and coffee or sugar) is that the supply chains in wood are longer and involve many stages of processing and transportation: at the simplest they involve foresters, primary manufacturers (for example, of sawn wood), secondary manufacturers (of paper, furniture), wholesalers/exporters and retailers altogether hundreds of companies. Therefore there are frequent changes in product ownership. Along the chain are a large number of different wood products, often produced by different companies. This detracts from the degree of concentration. Yet, at the very beginning of the chain the degree of concentration is increasing. 'Almost half the annual global wood harvest is now processed by 50 forest products companies' (Taylor, 2005, p. 135, quoting WWF). Similarly, the production of frozen fish is also rather concentrated, with Unilever in the past being a major player.

The long supply chains, especially in wood, complicate enforcement and control. Wood and seafood from responsibly managed forests and oceans have to be traceable along the supply chains in order to guarantee the value of the certificates. The FSC and MSC do their best to build in more checks and balances along the chain: DNA testing, unannounced audits, random checks. In addition, they employ commercial auditors and certifiers to do so. If not cumbersome, it is at the very least costly. In principle, retailers could aid in this endeavor. They have inspectors in the field to audit the quality of lumber and fish anyway, and could just as well check whether the FSC/MSC standards are being observed. However, that would require quite some trust between the councils and retailers as well as trust in such arrangements by environmentalists and customers, which is unlikely. Therefore, third-party certification is necessary to double-check.

The certification councils use retail hierarchies and their market power, yet this makes them dependent on such retailers, which entails risks. For one, retailers' association with the certificate could harm the certificate's reputation. Furthermore, such retailers could after a while decide to go at it alone and try to link environmental stewardship directly with their own brand's reputation, setting themselves up in direct competition with the councils. Initial participation in the collective certification can help retailers to begin establishing an environmentally friendly image. This has happened before with, for example, collective certification of French Bordeaux wine growers (Colman, 2003) and the Dutch dairy industry and optician branch (van Waarden, 1992).

Finally, it should be noted that there is something paradoxical in the role of large firm hierarchies as regards the regulatory protection of biodiversity. Their growth and internationalization have at first frustrated this. Multinational organizations (MNOs) have contributed to the increase in international trade, moved capital around the globe, moved resources and their 'vehicles' to different jurisdictions, for instance, reflagging fishing fleets (Carr and Scheiber, 2004), thus undercutting the effectiveness of national state regulation. In general, they have furthered trade and regulatory liberalization. Yet, because they have become such huge private hierarchies, they have also made it easier to control trade flows and regulatory standards if outside parties promoting the public interest can get a grip on these MNOs. Increasingly, the latter have been open to this as their size and broad presence around the globe have made them more visible and concerned about their public reputation.

10. THE PROBLEM OF MAINTAINING CERTIFICATE CREDIBILITY AND REPUTATION

The effectiveness of private certification as a way of protecting biodiversity depends, in the end, on the credibility and reputation of the certificate. Inflation can set in due to pressure from various sides and sources.

10.1. Success Breeds Problems: Shortage of Supply

Problems can come from success. As more and more retailers join the certification scheme, the demand for certified wood and fish increases. The supply may not be able to keep up with the demand. This may induce the certifiers to lower the standards or 'reduce the bureaucratic burdens' for foresters and fisheries in order to increase supply, out of fear of losing retail participants.

The large retailers have an interest in a large, stable, continuous and consistent supply, which is not easy for the FSC and MSC to meet. 'The global corporate demand for certified timber exceeded already in 2001 the levels of supply by more than 10 times' (Austin and Reficco, 2006, p. 6). The process of certification was fastest in the northern boreal and temperate forests of North America and Europe, and not in the tropics, for which the FSC was created in the first place. There were several reasons for this: more difficult access due to remoteness, lack of roads, unclear land ownership, lack of political stability, understaffed forest administration agencies, demographic pressure on the forests, hidden slash-and burn practices, corruption, and so on. Yet the demand for certified wood concerned relatively rare timbers such as teak, mahogany and plywood, and for some of those, supply might never meet demand, as sustainable forest management might require a decrease in cutting.

In order to meet the demand, the certifying council could and did take several measures. First, it focused on those foresters and manufacturers that could more quickly satisfy the need for greater supply, either because they controlled large tracts of land or produced much wood, or because they already had sound management systems in place. This measure threatened to be detrimental to small community-based forestries, especially in developing countries. It affected the competitive position of these smaller and less 'modern' producers negatively (Taylor, 2005)

A second possible measure would be to lower standards, either for the product or for the certification process. Lower standards tend to be cheaper for the forest industry to live up to, and they are likely to be able to supply larger quantities of lumber that satisfy them. This measure might have been popular with the industries participating in the council but it was anathema to the environmentalists (Counsel and Loraas, 2002). Retailers were also cautious because inflation might reduce the usefulness of the certificates. A solution was found in differentiating standards. First, percentage-based certification was introduced, listing on the label the percentage of certified lumber used, with a minimum percentage threshold. Later, the minimum threshold was abandoned, and under the 'truth-in-labeling' regime, the only requirement was that the percentage of certified lumber was clearly indicated. As a result, three separate logos were introduced: FSC 100%, FSC Mixed Sources, and FSC 100% Recycled. The latter two are frequently used for paper. In order to correct for the disadvantages of small and medium-sized foresters vis-a-vis larger ones, the FSC created special certification procedures for SLIME (Small and Low-Intensity Managed Forests), including stepwise certification and aid in getting there.

10.2. Competition

Pressure to lower standards also came from competition. The FSC initiative led to the formation of competing certificates by the forest industry, which resented the FSC standards for their cooperation with environmental and social groups and inclusion of social issues and indigenous peoples' rights. By setting up their own certification schemes they tried to take the wind out of the FSC's sails. Among them were the 1995 Sustainable Forest Initiative (SFI), created by the American Forest and Paper Association (AF&PA), and made compulsory for its members; the 1996 Canadian National Standard on Sustainable Forest Management (CAN/CSA Z809), created by the Canadian Standards Association following industry-directed guidelines; the 1999 Pan European Forest Certification (PEFC), from small and large foresters and industries in Finland, Norway, Sweden, Germany, Austria and France, a decentralized system based on national certification schemes that mutually recognized each other, provided that some basic standards were adhered to, such as independent certification; and the American Tree Farm System for non-industrial forests in the US, sponsored by the American Forest Foundation. In addition, several retailers established their own certification schemes in a desire for their own brand name to stand for responsible forest management. Altogether quite a few schemes emerged. Vogel (2005, p. 118) speaks of 'approximately fifty'. (Such proliferation is, by the way, not uncommon in capitalism, especially in the US where almost all businesses, notably restaurants, claim to be 'award winning', omitting to mention the awarder, who could have been their grandmother.)

Thus a market for ethical certificates developed, and a competition for credibility in the eyes of the different stakeholders: the forest industry, lumber processors, the construction industry, retailers, consumers and environmental NGOs. The latter were suspicious of the independence of the industry schemes and feared particularism and self-servingness. Conversely, many forest industries were resentful of the FSC. By 2006, the majority of US leading forest firms still bet on SFI/CSA. In order to increase the credibility of their industry standard, many forest firms let their operations be audited by PriceWaterhouseCoopers (PWC) on the basis of SFI standards. In addition, in 2000 the SFI created an outside independent board to oversee the certification scheme, involving a variety of interests: environmental NGOs, state and federal officials, and academics. The PEFC tried to export its decentralized system based on mutual recognition across the globe. With the SFI and CSA it formed the International Forest Industry Roundtable Initiative. However, NGOs objected to this 'decentralized mutual recognition arrangement' as they feared a race to the bottom, with the lowest common denominator becoming the de facto global standard.

Such competition could either lead to a 'race to the top', or a 'race to the bottom'. Which one of the two depends first of all on whose favors are most wanted and what is most scarce. If concerned customers are scarce, then quality may have to be raised; however, if suppliers are scarce, costs of certification may be successively lowered and with them the standards. Secondly, it would depend on the transparency of the market, and whether prices or quality are easier to compare. Price comparison tends to be more straightforward and hence easier. Quality comparison is more difficult, in particular when quality cannot be seen directly from the product but, as in the case of such certificates, relies on largely inaccessible detailed lists of standards, endorsements by authorities respected by consumers, and trust and reputation. The proliferation of labels does not make comparison easier. Consumers can no longer see the forest for the trees. After all, who would take the effort to read in detail the standards that were guaranteed by the label? A catchy label, or a familiar one, might be enough to appease one's conscience about buying lumber or fish, which might tempt the retailer to go for the cheapest label. As industry certification schemes had lower standards that were easier and cheaper for foresters to satisfy, retailers might be tempted to be satisfied with using them. That held in particular for buyers who were less visible in the market, such as construction companies. They usually cared less about ethical issues than about price and supply.

So far, the FSC and MSC have managed to keep a competitive edge. Their credibility tends to be higher because of their relative independence from the industries. In the case of the FSC it was also important to certify paper users, like publishers or packaging manufacturers, because they could be licensed to print the FSC logo on their products, thus increasing its visibility and familiarity among consumers. Gradually, their logos have developed as a 'gold standard', a global benchmark for responsible forest and fisheries management. Indeed, industry codes have come closer to these gold standards over time.

Whoever would appear to be winning the competition for a global standard would have a 'first mover advantage', as the WTO Technical Barrier to Trade Agreement (TBT) required national standardization bodies to adopt international standards wherever these existed in order to reduce the diversity of standards, which could become technical barriers to trade. The first system to acquire some 'international' character would have a headstart in becoming enforced by the WTO as the one international standard. Therefore, the FSC applied for membership of the International Accreditation Forum, an international club of accreditation organizations with an increasing reputation. The FSC thus tried to cloak itself in the reputation of that organization.

10.3. 'Lumber Laundering', Adulteration and other forms of Fraud

The reputation of certificates can also be blemished if they are repeatedly falsely used. Just as products can be adulterated, so can quality certificates as has happened already so often in history at the national level. Higher prices or easier access to markets can provide incentives for laundering illegal and non-certified fish and lumber. Fraud is especially easy in these markets, as it often cannot be seen from the products themselves where they come from and whether they deserve a label for coming from responsibly managed sources. 'Stamping' fish or lumber at the beginning of the commodity chain is difficult if not impossible. Such 'stamps' have to be on the accompanying documentation, and that is easy to falsify.

In the lumber market the long commodity chain offers additional opportunities for fraud, especially since on the way, wood from various sources is mixed (for instance, in the production of chipboard, wood-based panels, plywood, construction lumber, paper and packaging) and it is difficult or at least expensive to distinguish and trace wood coming from different sources. Willing processors had often to make an extra effort and incur extra costs to exclusively use certified wood as its supply was highly dispersed geographically and involved additional transportation costs (Austin and Reficco, 2006). This meant that the temptation to shortcut and avoid these extra costs was high, all the more so when customers also did not have an incentive to be fussy and there was usually a shortage of sufficient certified forest products (Counsell and Loraas, 2002; Cashore, 2002; Cashore, Auld and Newsom, 2004). Laundering was furthermore facilitated by the aforementioned problems – the proliferation of certificates and the resulting market intransparency, and the global character of the market with corruption being rampant in many parts of the world, especially in remote locations at sea or in distant forests.

Effective controls and audits required along the long global supply chains to uncover and discourage such fraud are also not easy, even with modern-day satellite, bio and ICT technology. What is often mentioned as a cause of state failure is also a problem for private certification: how to enforce, control and monitor whether lumber in distant places is really coming from well-managed forests and how it travels along the long commodity chains; or whether fish are caught according to the rules set out by the MSC, in distant places and huge expanses of water by fishermen (rugged individuals who have developed a culture of autonomy, individualism and being alone) in expanses of open sea, distant both physically, culturally and emotionally from the 'bureaucrats' drawing up quotas, standards and conditions, whether they are from government or a private certification body.

11. NEED FOR SUPPORTS

All these problems – competition, fraud, certificate inflation, limited audit resources – call for solutions. There is a need for support along the commodity chains, and there is a need to certify the certifiers in order to control for whether they do succumb to the temptations to inflate their certificates. These aids and controls are to help separate the wheat from the fraudulent chaff, to lend authority and trustworthiness to the most effective and independent certifier, and to help exercise caution about the development of perverse incentives, for example, following professionalization of the certifying councils.

Who could control the controllers or certify the certifiers? Just as regulatory standards can come from a variety of sources – the market, commercial businesses, the media, associations, communities, courts, states and international organizations – so can backing or further accreditation. One might yet add respected individuals, such as famous people, charismatic leaders to this list.

Commercial accountancy firms such as PWC can and do get chartered to double-check the audits of the fisheries and forests certifiers.

Public interest *associations* such as Greenpeace and the Rainforest Alliance act as self-appointed watchdogs to critically monitor the work of the FSC and MSC as well that of the organizations that participate in them directly – the foresters, fisheries, processors, wholesalers and retailers. Greenpeace regularly checks retailers' shelves for their use of certified fish and absence of threatened species. Depending on their scores on these criteria retailers get a red, orange or green flag. They also monitor distant fisheries, and the Rainforest Alliance does so for the Brazilian jungles. The media aid in this process by publishing the critical findings of the NGOs and engaging in their own investigative reporting. NGOs help them in this by organizing spectacular, newsworthy events. The WWF has not only stood at the cradle of the FSC and MSC but also aided them in their work. It created regional Forest and Trade Networks, made up of companies from the beginning to the end of the product chain (forest owners, timber producers, wholesalers and retailers of wood products) and large users such as construction companies. Belonging to these networks gave participants access to other firms in the supply chain also in these networks. Through these networks retailers could find their scarce suppliers, vice versa suppliers could find outlets. Thus these networks worked as a go-between for those having and those searching for certified wood.

Other fellow certifying associations, like the Fair Trade Labeling Organizations International, the International Federation of Organic Agriculture Movements, the Marine Aquarium Council and Social Accountability International, organized in the International Social and Environmental Accreditation and Labeling (ISEAL) Alliance, have jointly formulated a Code of Good Practice, and have recognized the MSC and FSC as satisfying that code. Other associations have used FSC or MSC standards and have thus recognized them de facto. Thus the LEED Green Building Rating System of the US Green Building Council is based on FSC standards.

Informal *communities* can also help. Communities of fishermen or of indigenous peoples can aid in enforcement 'on the ground', providing their practical knowledge of sea or the forests. After all, they have an interest in the sustainability of the resource from which they live. However, this requires that collective action problems can be solved, for example, by keeping foreign poachers out. It might also require special, less cumbersome bureaucratic procedures or less formal quantitative data demands. The trade-off is easier enforcement, because it is done largely voluntarily by the fishermen and foresters themselves, but it requires quite a leap of trust, which could be risky.

Such private supports have their limits. They cost money, depend often on highly motivated individuals, have no effective sanctions, and sooner or later their objectivity and neutrality can become controversial. Recent history has again shown that controlling agents such as accountants and commercial rating agencies can, even after long periods of public trust in their objectivity, lose that, following a scandal or crisis. This is all the more likely if the controllers and certifiers get paid by those whom they audit and control.

Furthermore, private market-based regulation is, in the end, dependent on the voluntary cooperation of producers and/or retailers. The emergence of competing private standards indicates that quite a few firms resist joining schemes like those of the FSC and MSC. Voluntariness has its limits, especially when the credibility of the certificates is prone to fraud and inflation. Therefore, sooner or later such arrangements may need public support. After all, they concern a public good – the protection of biodiversity. Public support might be needed for recognition, devolving authority, codifying standards for certification, help in monitoring in distant places, funding auditing, control and development of new technological means to do so, and more generally, backing the standards' reputation, and convincing less active nation-states through international pressure to enforce the standards in their territory.

12. STATE SUPPORT, PUBLIC-PRIVATE PARTNERSHIPS: WILL THE 'GOLD STANDARD' BECOME THE GLOBAL STANDARD?

Such public recognition of private standards is nothing new. It has often happened in history at the national level, even in étatist countries like France. Thus the private Appellation d'Origine Contrôlée Syndicats for French wines are recognized and sanctioned by the state as long as they live up to the standards given by the state for such Syndicats by the INAO (National Institute on Appellation d'Origine), which guards the domains of the 'Produits du Terroir' (Colman, 2003). It has also happened at the international level. Vogel (2005) gives examples of how governments have initiated, stimulated, funded, endorsed and/or recognized private standards. For example, the international Corporate Social Responsibility (CSR) codes on good working conditions in Third World countries were supported and even initiated by the American Clinton government and the British government.

States can and do set minimum standards for access to their markets. They have done so, for instance, for pharmaceuticals. Why are they willing to do so for pharmaceuticals and would they be more reluctant as regards biodiversity? Is the death of a single human being a more accepted legitimation of regulatory intervention that annihilation of complete animal or plant species?

It must be said that the beginnings are there. Interstate treaties ban whaling and trading in endangered species, including trading in goods from those species, such as ivory, coral or turtle shells. In 1990, the US Congress codified a private 'dolphin-safe' tuna certificate, gave it monopoly recognition, and required it for imports. Though this trade ban was subsequently ruled impermissible by a GATT panel in 1991, tuna processors kept requiring 'dolphin-safe' tuna from their suppliers, thus effectively closing the US market to tuna caught in ways endangering dolphins (Carr and Scheiber, 2004). This former public measure gave their policy choice legitimacy in the eyes of the general public. Here public-private cooperation makes possible what either cannot: private actors lack sanctions, public ones lack formal legality. Together, they can impose the standard on the industry.

Should not FSC and MSC standards be elevated to that level? It seems to have come to this position. First, the MSC has been recognized, encouraged, supported and even formally accredited as a credible certifier and eco-labeler by both international public organizations (the UN Food and Agriculture Organization), semi-public ones such as the International Council for the Exploration of the Sea (ICES) and private ones like ISEAL, following its Code of Good Practice. Incidentally, but increasingly, public national and international organizations refer in their informal codes or formal legislation to such private standards and so do national and international courts, thus recognizing and helping to enforce them. In 2005, the UN FAO tried to regulate the certification market by setting minimum requirements for marine eco-labelling and certification, including autonomy, transparency and stakeholder involvement. These principles were pretty similar to the ones the MSC already employed, thus de facto raising its reputation.

More importantly, both the US and the EU have in the meantime banned the import of illegal wood. In the fall of 2008, the US banned the import, sale or trade of all illegally harvested wood and forest products. It was an extension of the US Lacey Act, which has long banned the import of tropical birds, elephant ivory and tiger skins, to illegally harvested wood of any species. All importers henceforth had to declare each type of wood being imported and provide evidence about its origin. The EU followed eventually, though originally it intended not to go as far as the US. The European Commission had proposed to require lumber traders only to search for certificates for their wood. It was the European Parliament, which, inspired by the US example, sharpened the regulation by sanctioning it with an import ban, which has taken effect in 2012. Since then, timber traders need to provide evidence that it is 'no fault wood' (Dutch Volkskrant, Feb. 18, 2009: 'Fout hout in de ban'), that is, evidence about the origin of their wood and, in cases where it comes from suspect regions, evidence that it has been legally felled. However, paper remains as yet exempt from the ban.

These acts have the potential of bringing environmentalists and the lumber industry closer together, as they seal a typical Baptist-bootlegger coalition between environmentalists and domestic foresters. Both share an interest in protectionism against 'unfair' competition from illegally-cut wood. That might come in useful in deciding what 'illegal' means and according to which jurisdiction. In order to determine that, the US and EU may have to rely on private certifications with sufficient credibility as they do not themselves give such certificates. Both may not have enough trust in certificates given by Third World countries. It is conceivable that they may provide monopoly recognition of FSC certificates or else force mergers of the various private certifying programs – there are enough precedents for that. Thus ILO conventions have been implemented by private associations and labels. 'FSC certification of wood products promises to be a pivotal tool in providing independent and credible verification of legality and social and environmental responsibility for companies importing wood', stated Corey Brinkema, President of FSC-US.[1] The FSC immediately marketed its certificate to industry in the same article:

> The Forest Stewardship Council certification offers US companies an important tool for demonstrating that they take legality seriously. The Lacey Act requires companies to know the origin of their wood supplies in order to avoid timber from illegal logging. As a global certification system that includes robust standards for both forest management and supply chain of custody, FSC clearly mandates that all FSC forests comply with national laws and regulations. Besides addressing international concerns on illegal logging, FSC also includes a balanced consideration of key social and environmental issues. 'As the gold standard of forest certification programs, FSC certification is the best way to demonstrate legality and reduce the risk of having products seized and paying fines,' says Phil Guillery from the Tropical Forest Trust (FSC newsletter, Sept. 2008; www.fsc.be).

The US and European measures are classic cases of a California effect: live up to our standards or you do not get access to our markets. FSC certification may be a guarantee for that, however it remains to be seen whether the 'gold standard' can really be enforced by these new laws. Technical standards can, according to the WTO, be a legitimation for protectionism, but they should be internationally recognized standards. Therefore, the gold standard would have to become a global standard.

In reality this comes down to Northern countries putting pressure on Southern ones. The link of forests with the highly salient political issue of CO_2 absorption may strengthen them in doing so. Not only could Northern countries buy CO_2 rights by 'buying' forest rights in the south, they could also use trade bans and certification as means to ensure their continued existence through sound management. Northern states could facilitate that by aiding in the costs of certification. As yet, these costs are borne by the foresters, and these may be too high for small-scale wood-producing communities in developing countries. Such development aid would not only favour Southern countries, but also contribute to the maintenance of a global public good. It would be a form of horizontal financial compensation, much like the horizontal redistribution between regions in federal countries like Germany.

If need be, the costs of certification could be paid out of a global tax on lumber products. Currently, part of the domestic costs of certifying pharmaceuticals are borne by states and financed out of tax income. The same holds for food inspections and many others. Why could what is usual for domestic certifications and inspections not also be used for global inspections of sustainable forest management in our global collective interest?

13. STRENGTHS OF EMERGING MIXED ECONOMIC GOVERNANCE REGIMES

The result of these trends is the emergence of new economic governance regimes, combining elements of markets, associations, hierarchies and states. To these, other more informal ones may be added: communities, networks, circles and round tables.

How effective these emerging networks of organizations actually are in formulating and enforcing standards we do not really know yet. Perhaps it is too early to judge. However, what we can see is that the combination and cooperation of different public and private organizations mutually compensates for each other's weaknesses, liabilities, disadvantages and problems. NGOs and fishing cooperatives lack enforcement capacity at the 'fork side' of the chain but here supermarket chains can provide the required enforcement sanctions. However, the latter often lack credibility as they are easily suspected of narrow rent seeking. Such an image can be corrected by public-interest NGOs willing to cooperate with them, the certificates provided by the Council itself, and its supposedly independent status and reputation, and back-up by public agencies such as the UN FAO. The various participating organizations also complement each other's knowledge and information needed for detailing standards and certificates to make them effective, pragmatic and workable. Different organizations can also help overcome each other's collective action problems. NGOs could monitor and report on the compliance with agreed standards by firm-members of trade associations, including fishing cooperatives, and thus aid the latter in disciplining their members and avoiding free ridership: namely profiting both from a product's positive collective reputation yet making extra profits by individually dodging the standards. This would work in the same way as unions have been used by employer associations to help the latter in enforcing collective agreements among their members, with unions reporting free riding employers. Monitoring is more effective if it is complemented by naming and shaming. This promises to work better in a time of easy global communications, as multinational firms become more sensitive to stains on the reputation of their brand names, in which they may have invested a lot.

More generally, private organizations do not suffer from legal jurisdictional constraints as nation-states do. However, they do have other constraints: different and possibly less powerful sanctions; limited resources to organize thorough and trustworthy inspections; commercial bias reputation; the danger of 'public interests' getting lost behind particularistic ones; lack of authority, neutrality, accountability and hence legitimacy; the danger of piling hallmarks and controls upon controls, leading to confusion and less transparency on the 'markets for certificates'.

Eventually such an organization can only be really effective if its regulations and certificates are recognized and enforced at both ends of the chain 'from fishing to fork', that is, by local fishermen on the sending end and by local distributors and consumers at the receiving end. Thus inclusion of private organizations of producers and consumers at these ends of the chain in such stewardship coalitions would be essential. These are likely to include private organizations, be they informal communities (of fishermen), formal associations (cooperatives of fishermen, fish store trade associations, conscious consumers), firm hierarchies (seafood packers like Unilever, supermarket chains), the media, consultants, advertisers and their associations. Large supermarket chains first of all have to abide by food quality standards in the consuming countries. However, as they care for their reputations among consumers, they tend to adopt standards, such as from these councils, that are not statutory requirements yet, provided that consumers know these standards and consider them important. By advertising these standards, supermarket chains help in making them better known.

Such cooperative networks of organizations increase in stability and effectiveness once their organizations goals, and certificates are recognized and supported by local, national or international public authorities and perhaps even backed up with some statutory privileges and powers, such as the Fairtrade Cities and Towns, or the FAO of the UN. In this way, a private organization like the MSC can become the nucleus of a network of private and public organizations, all contributing to enforcing the agreed standards.

14. CONCLUSION: TOWARD A JOINT ECOLOGICAL PRIVATE-PUBLIC PARTNERSHIP (EPPP)

Around 1900, in the early days of bicycles and cars, a privately initiated association, the Dutch Automobile Association, placed the first direction signs along the rudimentary roads. They were ideal-typical public goods. Eventually, their financing was taken over by a public organization, the state, who funded it out of general tax income, but the association still planned and ordered the placing of the signs. The actual placement was done by a commercial organization. Thus this public good became a collective endeavor of state, association and hierarchy.

Around 2000, in the early days of globalization, privately initiated associations like the FSC and MSC placed biodiversity-friendly signs on products, again typically public goods. Will states eventually also publicly finance and sanction such initiatives? It is already a collective endeavor of associations and hierarchies. Will states join? As indicated earlier, a start has been made. A potential solution, however, could be a joint Ecological Public-Private Partnership (EPPP), where private initiatives, such as the FSC and the MSC, are publicly supported but also chastised and controlled. California and North-Western Europe could, as the most environmentally-concerned states in the US and the EU, take the lead in this.

Support might be needed in providing 'sticks', such as recently enacted trade legislation. This legislation could occasion formal recognition of private certificates in national legislation and perhaps also in international treaties. After all, corporate governance regulation and shareholder protection have also led to formal recognition and regulation of accountants also private certifiers of reliability and quality. Monopoly recognition would go even further, and also reduce the confusion on the market due to the proliferation of certificates. After all, there is a public interest in transparency of the market for certificates. For similar reasons, societies have in the past eventually formally recognized and sanctioned a single weights and measures system. States could also provide recognition through their private role as a buyer on markets. They could, for a start, require FSC certificates for lumber used. Some local governments have already been doing this.

The stick could be made heavier yet by mandating biodiversity-safety certification for all marketed goods domestically. Governments do already set minimum standards for the marketing of pharmaceuticals and food, but why should we protect only the health of the consumer, and not that of the biosphere on which the survival of mankind rests? Maybe a crisis or a scandal is needed. The FDA and the regulations it has to enforce were only initiated after a food poisoning scandal. The link between forest/ocean management and global warming could provide such an occasion, in particular, if it finds expression in more spectacular storms and floodings.

Support could also be given in the form of 'carrots', for instance, financial support. At the moment, FSC and MSC certification is paid for by the recipients of the certificates, which harbors a danger of bias. When word gets out that one can 'buy' a good rating, the reputation of the certificate is shattered. As the saying goes, trust comes on foot, but leaves on horseback. That is not unimaginable, as the Enron-Andersen case has taught us. Certifiers like accountants can be bought: he who pays the piper calls the tune. This is good reason to reduce this dependency by having certification paid for from public funds, filled by a compulsory levy – a tax – on all industry or even all citizens. Industry would still pay, but it would no longer be linked to specific performance, just as is done with the application and implementation of other forms of public regulation.

It might be worth considering something akin to a Tobin tax: a tax on all trade in fish and lumber across the globe. While James Tobin saw this as a means to stabilize global financial markets by putting a penalty on short-term speculation, such a fish/lumber tax might help stabilize biodiversity. Ramonet, editor of *Le Monde Diplomatique*, further elaborated Tobin's idea in his article 'Disarming the markets' (1997), by suggested using the income for public aid. Following on from this, one could use such tax income to fund buying biodiversity reserves, which could then be placed under the stewardship of organizations like the WWF. In addition to UNESCO World Heritage Sites, we might have WWF World Biodiversity Sites. National governments do already create such parks and reserves and frequently place them in the custody of private associations (the National Trust, Natuurmonumenten), but with such tax income they could also be realized in parts of the world, notably the biodiverse tropics, where local governments either do not have the resources or do not give such a policy enough priority to devote scarce resources to. There would be enough justification for such a global tax: the public good would benefit the global public. The income could form the nucleus of an emerging global governance of global public goods. As this might not be immediately realizable at the global level, again the example of the Tobin tax could be followed: local and national governments could start with it, for example, the more environmentally-concerned states in the US and Europe.

Both supportive and sanctioning approaches could come together in public support for the daunting task of monitoring, enforcing and controlling compliance with the standards all over the 'global ground' in combating illegal harvesting and laundering of lumber and fish. Once the state bans illegally-cut lumber or caught fish, it has an interest in effective monitoring. It could do so by auditing the auditors, but also through more specific public-private collaboration: sharing of expertise, experiences, knowledge, technology (for instance, satellite observation), benchmarking, learning, and so on. This could lead to the curious paradox that public agencies might be enforcing private standards. Are there perhaps legal precedents for this?

Finally, the North-Western European experience with consensual and associational politics might inspire cooperation in global EPPPs. The countries of continental North-Western Europe are characterized by more consensual institutions and cultural values: in the economy, in politics, and in the relation between politics and the economy. Cooperation among business firms has been common and accepted, notably in the Netherlands, which used to be considered a 'cartel paradise', both by its own citizens and outside observers such as the OECD or the European Commission up until 1998 (Unger and van Waarden, 1999; van Waarden and Drahos 2002). These associations of employers and employees, which have been able to work well together in institutionalized 'social partnerships', could offer learning experiences for the cooperation of environmentalists and industrialists, and of private and public actors in ecological partnerships, which are what the FSC and MSC aim to be.

NOTE

1 FSC-US Newsletter September 2008 (http://www.fscus.org/news/?article = 525; accessed 8 May, 2011).

REFERENCES

Austin, J., and Reficco, E. (2006), *Forest Stewardship Council*, Case 9-303-047, Cambridge: Harvard Business School.

Bartley, T. (2003), 'Certifying forests and factories: states, social movements, and the rise of private regulation in the apparel and forest products fields', in *Politics and Society*, 31 (3), pp. 433–464.

Brand, U., Görg, C., Hirsch, J. and Wissen, M. (2008), *Conflicts in Environmental Regulation and the Internationalisation of the State. Contested Terrains*, London and New York: Routledge.

Carr, C.J. and Scheiber, H.N. (2004), 'The globalization of conservation standards in marine fisheries', in D. Vogel and R.A. Kagan (eds), *Dynamics of Regulatory Change. How Globalization Affects National Regulatory Policies*, Berkeley: University of California Press.

Cashore, B. (2002), 'Legitimacy and the privatization of environmental governance: how non-state market-driven (NSMD) governance systems gain rule-making authority', in *Governance: An International Journal of Policy, Administration, and Institutions*, 15 (4), pp. 503–529.

Cashore, B., Auld, G. and Newsom, D. (2004), *Governing through Markets: Forest Certification and the Emergence of Non-State Authority*, New Haven: Yale University Press.

Chanda, N. (2007), *Bound Together: How Traders, Preachers, Adventurers, and Warriors Shaped Globalization*, New Haven: Yale University Press.

Colman, T. (2003), *The Politics of Quality: Institutions and Market Stratification in the Wine Sector*, Ph.D. dissertation, Northwestern University.

Conroy, M.E. (2007), *Branded! How the 'Certification Revolution' is Transforming Global Corporations*, Gabriola Island BC: New Society Publishers.

Counsell, S., and Loraas, K.T. (2002), *Trading in Credibility: The Myth and Reality of the Forest Stewardship Council*, London: The Rainforest Foundation.

Dauvergne, P. (1997), *Shadows in the Forest: Japan and the Politics of Timber in Southeast Asia*, Cambridge, MA: MIT Press.

Dauvergne, P. (2001), *Loggers and the Degradation in the Asia-Pacific. Corporations and Environmental Management*, Cambridge, UK: Cambridge University Press.

FAO (2008), *The State of World Fisheries and Aquaculture*, Rome: FAO.

Gulbrandsen, L.H. (2004), 'Overlapping public and private governance: can forest certification fill the gap in the global forest regime?', in *Global Environmental Politics*, 4 (2), pp.75–99.

Gulbrandsen, L.H. (2005), 'Non-state governance for corporate responsibility and accountability: comparing fishery and forestry eco-labeling', Paper presented at the conference on 'Organizing the World: Rules and Rule-Setting among Organizations', SCORE, Stockholm, 13–15 October.

Gulbrandsen, L.H. (2010), *Transnational Environmental Governance. The Emergence and Effects of the Certification of Forests and Fisheries*, Cheltenham: Edward Elgar.

ICMR (ICFAI Center for Management Research) (2006), *IKEA's Environmental Practices. Making Good Business Sense. Case Study no. 706-055-1.* Chennal: Center for Management Research.

Khatchadourian, R. (2008), 'The stolen forests. Inside the covert war on illegal logging', in *The New Yorker*, 6 October, 2008.

Marx, A., and Cuypers, D. (2010), 'Forest certification as a global environmental governance tool: what is the macro-effectiveness of the Forest Stewardship Council?', in *Regulation and Governance*, 4 (4), pp. 408–434.

Nick, A. (2006), *Transforming the Global Fishing Industry: The Marine Stewardship Council at Full Sail?* IMD Case IMD-2-0083, Lausanne: International Institute for Management Development.

Olson, M. (1965), *The Logic of Collective Action. Public Goods and the Theory of Groups*, Cambridge MA: Harvard University Press.

Olthuis, L. (2009), 'Ze komen toch vooral voor het vlees', in *De Volkskrant*, 28 March, 2009.

Ostrom, E. (1990), *Governing the Commons. The Evolution of Institutions for Collective Action*, Cambridge, UK: Cambridge University Press.

Overdevest, C., and M.G. Rickenbach (2006), 'Forest certification and institutional governance: an empirical study of Forest Stewardship Council Certificate Holders in the US', in *Forest Policy and Economics*, 9 (1), pp. 93–102.

Pattberg, P. (2005), 'What role for private rule-making in global environmental governance? analyzing the Forest Stewardship Council FSC' in *International Environment Agreements*, 5 (2), pp. 175–189.

Pottinger, M., Stecklow, S. and Fialka, J. (2004), 'Invisible export – a hidden cost of china's growth: mercury migration. Turning to coal, nation sends toxic metal around globe; buildup in the Great Lakes conveyor belt of bad air', in *The Wall Street Journal*, 20 December.

Richards, J.F., and Tucker, R.P. (eds) (1988), *World Deforestation in the Twentieth Century*, Durham and London: Duke University Press.

Secretariat of the Convention on Biological Diversity (2001) *Global Biodiversity Outlook 1*, Montreal, available at www.cbd.int/gbo1/

Secretariat of the Convention on Biological Diversity (2006) *Global Biodiversity Outlook 2*, Montreal, available at www.cbd.int/gbo2/
Taylor, P.L. (2005), 'In the market but not of it: fair trade coffee and Forest Stewardship Council Certification as market-based social change', in *World Development*, 33 (1), pp. 129–147.
UN FAO (2007) *Forest Products Annual Market Review 2006–2007*, New York and Geneva: UN.
Unger, B., and van Waarden, F. (1999), 'Interest associations and economic growth', in *Review of International Political Economy*, 6 (4), pp. 425–467.
Vogel, D. (1986), *National Styles of Regulation. Environmental Policy in Great Britain and the United States*, Ithaca and New York: Cornell University Press.
Vogel, D. (1995), *Trading Up. Consumer and Environmental Regulation in a Global Economy*, Cambridge MA: Harvard University Press.
Vogel, D. (2005), *The Market for Virtue. The Potential and Limits of Corporate Social Responsibility*, Washington DC: Brookings.
Vogel, D. (2007), 'The private regulation of global corporate conduct', unpublished paper, Dept of Political Science, Berkeley: University of California.
Vogel, D. and Kagan, R.A. (2004), 'Introduction' in D. Vogel and R.A. Kagan (eds) *Dynamics of Regulatory Change. How Globalization Affects National Regulatory Policies*, Berkeley: University of California Press.
Waarden, F. van (1985), 'Regulering en belangenorganisatie van ondernemers', in F.L. van Holthoon (ed.), *De Nederlandse samenleving sinds 1815*, Assen: Van Gorcum.
Waarden, F. van (1992), 'Emergence and development of business' interest associations. An example from the Netherlands', in *Organization Studies*, 13 (4), pp. 521–561.
Waarden, F. van (1999a), 'European harmonization of national regulatory styles?', in J.A.E. Vervaele et al. (eds), *Compliance and Enforcement of European Community Law*, Deventer: Kluwer Law, pp. 95–124.
Waarden, F. van (1999b), 'Elk land zijn eigen trant', in W. Bakker and F. van Waarden (eds), *Ruimte rond regels. Reguleringsstijlen vergeleken*, Amsterdam and Meppel: Boom.
Waarden, F. van (2006), 'Taste, traditions, transactions, and trust: the public and private regulation of food', in C. Ansell and D. Vogel (eds), *What's the Beef? The Contested Governance of European Food Safety*, Cambridge MA: MIT Press, pp. 35–59.
Waarden, F. van (2011a), 'Varieties of private market regulation: problems and prospects', in D. Levi-Faur (ed.) *Handbook on the Politics of Regulation*, Cheltenham: Edward Elgar.
Waarden, F. van (2011b) 'The governance of markets: on generating trust in transactions', in D. Levi-Faur (ed.) *Oxford Handbook on Governance*, Oxford: Oxford University Press.
Waarden, F. van, and M. Drahos (2002), 'Courts and (epistemic) communities in the convergence of competition policies', in *Journal of European Public Policy*, **9** (6), pp. 1–22.
World Resources Institute (2008) *Millennium Ecosystem Assessment: Ecosystems and Human Well Being – Synthesis*.

3. Private standards in forestry: assessing the legitimacy and effectiveness of the Forest Stewardship Council

Axel Marx, Emilie Bécault and Jan Wouters

1. INTRODUCTION

Forests are receiving increased attention from policy-makers and academics. The United Nations declared 2011 International Year of Forests and the European Union is currently preparing an extensive review of its forests policy and strategy. As a result, global forest governance is becoming a hot topic, as exemplified by a recent global assessment report on global forest governance by a set of leading political scientists and governance experts (Rayner et al., 2011). The report, *Embracing Complexity: Meeting the Challenges of International Forest Governance*, provides an extensive overview of the current forest regime and how it developed. It maps the different actors and initiatives involved and discusses the many objectives related to the governance of forests.

Starting with the failure to agree an international forest convention in Rio in 1992, to the establishment of the Intergovernmental Panel on Forests (IPF) (1995–97) and Intergovernmental Forum on Forests (IFF) (1997–2000), to the formation of the UN Forum on Forests (UNFF), one can observe a failure of current multilateral initiatives with regard to forest governance. Dimitrov et al. state with regard to the UNFF that it is 'explicitly deprived of a policymaking mandate' (2007: 243).

In parallel to the developments on the multilateral level one can also observe a rising contestation over this failure. Several NGOs started to protest heavily against deforestation and the destruction of (mainly old growth) forests. One of the key targets in these protests were multinational firms (Meidinger, 2003). These protests proved to be quite effective. As Gereffi et al. observe, 'Protests against brand-name retailers are only 10 years old, but as one Greenpeace activist expressed, "it was like discovering gunpowder for environmentalists'" (2001: 64). As a response, several new initiatives and actors emerged, of which forest certification is one of the most prominent. As Cashore et al. argue, forest certification is 'one of the most innovative and startling institutional [governance] designs of the past 50 years' (2004: 4).

The first initiative for forest certification, the Forest Stewardship Council (FSC), was launched in 1993 and has since been hailed as an innovative and properly functioning global 'soft' governance tool, casting doubts on the necessity to further develop effective multilateral solutions to the current forest crisis. Moreover, the FSC, by promoting in its core principles and criteria compliance with all applicable existing international rules, is increasingly regarded as some kind of legality verification initiative, susceptible at times to bypassing state sovereignty in the diffusion of international law. Principle 4, for instance, requires forest industries to comply with all major ILO conventions irrespective of whether the country in which they operate has ratified them. The same goes for some other major environmental treaties (CBD, ITTO, CITES) for which the country in question only needs to be a signatory (principle 1).

Taking this observation as a starting point, this chapter draws on recent findings in the academic and policy-oriented scholarship to assess whether, 20 years on, the forest certification scheme of the FSC still holds great promise as a global governance tool. In particular, we will address two dimensions of the FSC that figure rather prominently in discussions of non-state network-governance arrangements: legitimacy and effectiveness. To this end, the chapter proceeds in three steps. It begins with a detailed description of forest certification and the Forest Stewardship Council. It then examines the legitimacy of the organisational procedures of the FSC from both a normative (input-output) perspective and a sociological/constructivist perspective. The third section builds on regime theory to assess the effectiveness of the FSC in the promotion of sustainable forest management worldwide. The paper closes with a discussion of our major finding, that in terms of legitimacy and effectiveness, the FSC does not sufficiently provide for the interests of its Southern members and stakeholders, and that addressing the problem of forest degradation ultimately requires strengthening the role of multilateral institutions and actors in ways that might enhance the legitimacy and effectiveness of private forest certification.

2. FOREST CERTIFICATION AND THE FOREST STEWARDSHIP COUNCIL

2.1. Forest Certification

Forest certification, according to Meidinger, 'is a process through which transnational networks of diverse actors set and enforce standards for the management of forests around the world' (Meidinger, 2003: 265). Cashore (2002) refers to these new institutions as 'non-state market-driven' (NSMD) governance systems because rulemaking comes from private actors. Other authors refer to civil regulation (Vogel, 2008) or private governance (Pattberg, 2005).

Currently several systems of forest certification exist, including the Forest Stewardship Council (FSC), the US Sustainable Forest Initiative (SFI), the Lembaga Ekolabel Indonesia (LEI), the Programme for the Endorsement of Forest Certification Schemes (PEFC), the Malaysian Timber Certification Council (MTCC), the Certificación Florestal (CerFlor Brazil), the Canadian Standard Association (CSA) and the American Tree Farm System (ATFS). Most initiatives are characterised by an organisation that defines social and ecological standards and provides verification procedures to ensure that products or production processes conform to these standards (that is, conformity assessment). When products or production processes comply with the defined standards, a certificate is awarded which may or may not be used for external communication (label). However, these initiatives differ in important respects.

Abbott and Snidal (2009) have recently developed a means of classifying these systems. They subdivide the new initiatives on the basis of the actors involved in defining the standards. They distinguish between three major actors: the state, companies and non-governmental organisations which develop rules and standards, either separately or together, that govern the global production chains. These three actors form the 'governance triangle' (see Figure 3.1). Within this triangle, Abbott and Snidal distinguish seven zones, depending on how many parties are involved in defining standards. They place new regulatory initiatives in each of these zones. Three zones contain initiatives whereby one actor develops the standards, three zones contain initiatives whereby two actors develop standards and one zone contains standard-setting initiatives which are developed by the three parties.

Most forest certification initiatives are located in zone 2, which is characterised by company- or industrial sector-driven initiatives. Only one, the Forest Stewardship Council, is located in zone 6, which results from cooperation between companies and NGOs.

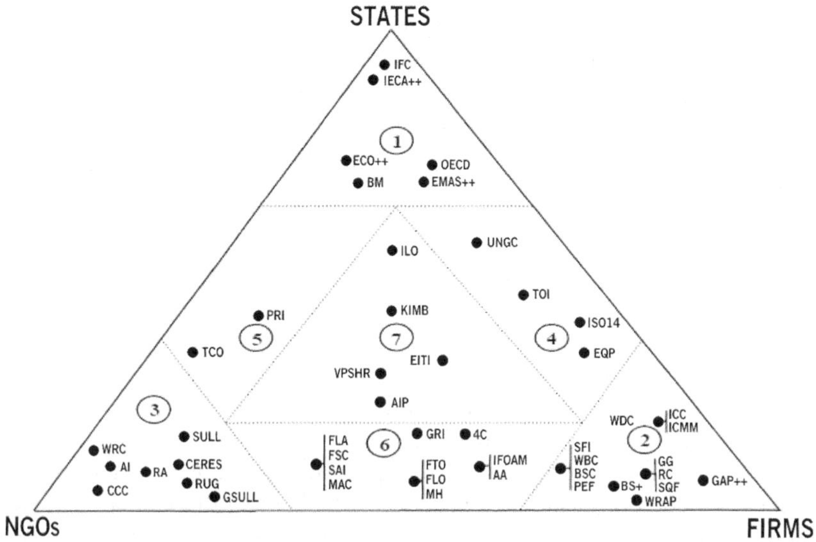

Source: Abbott and Snidal 2009: 513

Figure 3.1: The governance triangle

The Abbott and Snidal classification outlines the diversity of various forms of public-private and private transnational regulation. However, the classification only covers part of the complex tangle of private regulatory initiatives, because it is based mainly on the dimension of who develops standards but pays little if any attention to how the actual implementation or enforcement of the standards is achieved. Defining and developing standards is only one part of the regulatory process. Implementing and monitoring the implementation of standards is another element and this can be done in various ways.

The literature refers in this context to first-party, second-party and third-party certification, in essence referring to the number of parties involved in the standard-setting and standard-enforcement process (Gereffi et al., 2001; van Waarden, 2011). This process, also referred to as the certification process, consists of defining standards, accrediting an organisation that examines conformity with the standards, applying for a certificate, carrying out a conformity assessment (testing whether organisations, systems and products satisfy the proposed standards) and awarding a certificate.

First-party certification is characterised by the fact that a company or an organisation checks compliance with standards, which are defined by the company or organisation itself. In second-party certification the enforcement of standards is done by an entity that is legally separate from the organisation applying for a certificate but not truly independent since they often share similar interests. In this case, the standards are often defined and enforced by an organisation representing the companies who are applying for a certificate such as industrial sector organisations. Most certification initiatives in the wood and paper-processing industry, such as the Standard Forestry Initiative, are second-party certification initiatives. In the context of third-party certification, the standards are developed by an independent organisation, often a multi-stakeholder body, which also accredits organisations to carry out conformity assessments. Accreditation guarantees that the organisation that carries out the conformity assessment is competent to do this and operates independently. These accredited organisations are autonomous bodies that carry out conformity assessments at companies that apply for a certificate. In most cases, a conformity assessment involves an unannounced audit of production sites. In this case, three parties are involved which are independent of each other. These parties are a company applying for a certificate, a body setting the standards and an accredited party enforcing standards. The FSC is a third-party certification initiative. As a result, on both dimensions (setting standards and enforcement) the FSC comes out as the most significant certification initiative.

It should be noted that these systems are not static but operate in a dynamic field and in interaction with one another. Overdevest (2010) showed how the FSC is playing a pivotal role in ratcheting up industry-related forest standards as well as those of rival industry-sponsored certification initiatives. These findings correspond to more general arguments made by Sabel et al. (2000) on the use of technical standards and benchmarking mechanisms in environmental policy.

2.2. The Forest Stewardship Council

The first concept of voluntary forest certification, the Forest Stewardship Council, was established in 1993 following the Rio declaration of the UNCED in 1992 as a response to the slow process of formal discussions on the promotion of sustainable forest management. The FSC is a multi-stakeholder membership-based organisation with a governance structure consisting of a general assembly in which the members are represented, a board of directors and an executive director. The General Assembly of FSC members is the highest decision-making body in the FSC and is made up of the three membership chambers (a tripartite structure) – environmental, social and economic – which are further split into sub-chambers North and South. The purpose of the chamber structure is to maintain the balance of voting power between different interests without having to limit the number of members (FSC, 2010). Standards are developed on the basis of ten principles (see Box 3.1), which are of equal importance. Specific standards, for the purpose of certification, are developed by national standard working groups and reviewed internationally via a two-tier consultation process. Forest management (FM) certification is the cornerstone of the FSC system and refers to the certification of forests. Chain-of-custody certification (CoC), a supply-chain tracking system, refers to the fact that the product with the CoC certificate is made out of products which originate from an FM-certified forest.

***Principle* 1:** Compliance with all applicable laws and international treaties.
***Principle* 2:** Demonstrated and uncontested, clearly defined, long-term land tenure and use rights.
***Principle* 3:** Recognition and respect of indigenous peoples' rights.
***Principle* 4:** Maintenance or enhancement of long-term social and economic well-being of forest workers and local communities and respect of worker's rights in compliance with International Labour Organisation (ILO) conventions.
***Principle* 5:** Equitable use and sharing of benefits derived from the forest.
***Principle* 6:** Reduction of environmental impact of logging activities and maintenance of the ecological functions and integrity of the forest.
***Principle* 7:** Appropriate and continuously updated management plan.
***Principle* 8:** Appropriate monitoring and assessment activities to assess the condition of the forest, management activities and their social and environmental impacts.
***Principle* 9:** Maintenance of High Conservation Value Forests (HCVFs) defined as environmental and social values that are considered to be of outstanding significance or critical importance.
***Principle* 10:** In addition to compliance with all of the above, plantations must contribute to reduce the pressures on and promote the restoration and conservation of natural forests.

Source: Official FSC website: *www.fsc.org*, accessed 20 August, 2009

Box 3.1: Overview of the ten FSC principles

The FSC is the most globally distributed certification system worldwide. The surface area of FSC-certified forests grew steadily during the first decade of its existence to reach 40 million hectares of certified forests in 2003. From 2004 onwards, growth accelerated and almost tripled between 2004 and 2010. By the end of 2010, the surface area of FSC-certified forests almost reached the 140 million hectares (FSC, 2011d).

FSC operates an independent entity called ASI, which is in charge of providing accreditation services to certification bodies, national initiatives and national standards. The FSC has two main tasks. First of all, to ensure that certification organisations have the highest level of credibility and integrity by evaluating, accrediting and monitoring certifiers of forest products based on their adherence to FSC principles and criteria and guidelines for certifiers, which apply to all types of forest. Secondly, FSC promotes forest stewardship by encouraging development of local forest management standards worldwide through an open, consensus-based and participatory process involving consultation with affected stakeholder groups. As noted, FSC standards are developed on the basis of ten principles, which are of equal importance. Specific standards, for the purpose of certification, are developed by national standard working groups. The enforcement of these standards is achieved via a system based on the development of forest management plans by the applicant and the control on the implementation of these plans by independent certifiers.

First of all, the applicant for FSC FM certification invites an inspector who conducts a pre-audit or feasibility study on whether the forests under consideration can be certified. Principle 7 of the FSC requires for a forest management plan. In a second step, a genuine audit is conducted, which assesses the forest management against the standards and criteria. This audit also contains detailed corrective actions requests (CARs), which are necessary in order to gain certification. Step three involves implementing the corrective actions and an assessment of the audit by the applicant. Step four is a new audit, which often contains more corrective actions to be implemented. Step five finalises the process by awarding the certificate, the first two years for one year, then subsequently for five years.

Monitoring and auditing is outsourced to professional accredited organisations and companies such as SGS, the Soil Association, and so on. These monitors work with standardised procedures, which include an analysis of documents and site visits on the basis of surveys and checklists. The FSC uses a mix of information-gathering techniques. It promotes the use of checklists in auditing but goes beyond the checklist approach by including detailed additional information. Checklists are considered to be a useful and efficient way to ensure that an assessor has evaluated all necessary aspects. The checklist provides auditors with a systematic tool for verifying all important aspects of an operation.[1] However, the FSC also stresses that many decisions in forest management are made in the context of local, national and regional conditions. This requires explanation and justification that is not provided by a simple checkmark against a checklist.[2]

> As a result a final certification report is based on a checklist but is supplemented with specific observations, explanations and references that allow the reader to form an independent judgement as to whether the evaluation was rigorous and consistent in implementing the certification system, and whether the forest management observed meets the FSC Principles and Criteria.[3]

The description shows that the FSC has an elaborate institutional framework to develop and enforce standards for sustainable forest management. As the most prominent example of private regulation in global environmental politics (Pattberg, 2005: 76), a large body of literature has – from around the late 1990s onwards – developed around the scheme. Questions of legitimacy and effectiveness have become particularly important. With respect to legitimacy for instance, much has been written on how this innovative multi-stakeholder regulatory system has – in contrast to governments and intergovernmental organisations – succeeded in achieving political legitimacy (Bernstein and Cashore, 2007; Dingwerth, 2007; Pattberg, 2005; Cashore et al., 2004; Cashore, 2002). Considerations about the democratic performance of the FSC's organisational structure have only started to gain some ground, driven in part by the persisting weakness of intergovernmental efforts (Garrelts and Flitner, 2011; Meidinger, 2011; Auld et al., 2008; Chan and Pattberg, 2008; Dingwerth, 2007). With respect to effectiveness, the other key dimension of the global governance literature, a significant body of research now exists on the FSC and forest certification in general. While most studies tend to focus on the micro-level (single country, small number of countries, firm-level dynamics) and seek to evaluate why firms opt for a particular certification scheme, more recent scholarship has turned its attention to evaluating the global impact of the FSC on improving forest management and production practices worldwide (Marx and Cuypers, 2010; Auld et al., 2008). In this chapter, we will draw on these key insights and other relevant work in the literature to take stock of where the FSC currently stands in terms of legitimacy and effectiveness. For each of these two dimensions, we first commence with a brief conceptual discussion and specify the criteria that will be guiding our analysis.

3. DIMENSION 1: LEGITIMACY

As with every concept in the social sciences, legitimacy has been and still is the subject of a broad variety of contending approaches (Hurrelmann et al., 2007). Despite this elusiveness, though, it is generally agreed that legitimacy – by facilitating compliance with norms, rules and political decisions – is a quality crucial to the effective exercise of authority. In the absence of legitimacy, the argument goes, authority rests on fragile foundations. At the same time, what constitutes legitimate authority varies across institutional frameworks, governments and governance systems. In particular, the increasing privatisation or marketisation of authority in global governance requires thinking about legitimacy in non-traditional (that is, non-statist) terms.

To conceptualise and analyse legitimacy in relation to the FSC's institutional framework, the distinction commonly established in the global governance literature between, on the one hand, the normative/prescriptive dimension of legitimacy (input- and output-legitimacy) and, on the other hand, the sociological/constructivist approach to legitimacy, appears particularly useful (Bodansky, 1999). As the following shows, these two perspectives tend to reflect empirically distinct elements of institutional legitimacy and their conceptual flexibility means that they can apply to a variety of institutional contexts.

Normative/prescriptive approaches to legitimacy tend to refer to a set of objective standards about what may constitute appropriate institutional processes and outcomes. Authority in this sense is justified if it conforms to some *a priori*-defined notions of legitimacy, which in almost all cases remain deeply rooted in democratic political theory and practice. In the field of global environmental politics, the deliberative model of democracy has gained prominence as a potential solution to the participatory gap in processes leading to the making of intergovernmental agreements (Dryzek and Stevenson, 2011). With regards to more complex institutional frameworks operating in a post-national and multi-level context, however, Fritz Scharpf's (1997, 1999) concepts of input and output legitimacy constitute more comprehensive normative benchmarks.

Initially developed within the context of the EU multi-level governance system (Scharpf, 1999; Hooghe and Marks, 2003), this two-dimensional conception of legitimacy reflects the basic definition of democracy as a system of 'collective self-determination', a system of 'government by the people, of the people, and for the people', as Lincoln most eloquently described it (Lövbrand et al., 2009; Schmidt, 2011). From an input perspective then, legitimacy is understood as referring to the degree to which political decisions or choices 'reflect the "will of the people" – that is, if they can be derived from the authentic preferences of the members of a community' (Scharpf, 1999: 6). This dimension, in effect, pertains to the participatory and representative quality of the rule-making process and can be assessed by examining whether policy decisions were made according to some set of procedural requirements, such as representation of relevant stakeholders, inclusiveness, transparency and deliberativeness.

On the output side, by contrast, legitimacy relates to the democratic quality of the decisions themselves and asks whether the governance system actually 'governs for the people', that is, succeeds in delivering goods in ways that effectively respond to the collective goals, values and interests of the community to which it is accountable (Scharpf, 1999: 6). In this sense, output-legitimacy echoes in many ways the notion of 'accountability as responsiveness' (Gulbrandsen, 2008, 2004; Koppell, 2003; Romzek and Dubnick, 1987, 1994), which, as Gulbrandsen describes it, focuses on the 'relationship between the standard organisation and various stakeholders' (2008: 566–67). This notion helps to capture the degree to which 'power wielders' meet 'the expectation of relevant constituencies', accept 'answerability on the disposal of their power,' and act upon 'criticisms or demand made of them' (Gulbrandsen, 2008: 567). From an institutional design perspective, and on the output side in particular, this form of accountability is enhanced if stakeholders are given appropriate opportunities to dispute policy decisions they find deeply problematic and if the organisation provides effective, workable and fair procedures for complaints and dispute resolution. A point worth mentioning here is that given its normative underpinnings, the notion of output legitimacy should not be confused with the rationalist concern for 'problem-solving' or 'impact' effectiveness, an aspect of the FSC we will address later on in this chapter. Examining the output-legitimacy of an institution requires evaluating the procedures and mechanisms established to ensure that policy decisions are fairly and efficiently opened to contestation and criticism. The rationalist focus on effectiveness, as we will see, is broader and seeks to evaluate the performance of the governance system in ways that do not necessarily imply an explicit commitment to a normative conception of democracy.

In summary, when considering using this normative framework to evaluate the formal legitimacy of the FSC, our analytical focus on the input side will assess the extent to which the decision-making scheme of the FSC conforms to some procedures and mechanisms that facilitate representation, transparency and deliberation. From an output perspective, we will draw attention to the FSC dispute resolution system so as to assess how the organisation has so far handled complaints and appeals raised by stakeholders about certification decisions or any other issues within the FSC scheme.

A strict focus on the normative approach to legitimacy, however, is not without limitation. While this perspective can help us to make evaluative statements about the democratic quality of specific institutional design features and procedures, it tends to leave out questions related to the broader societal acceptance of an organisation's policies, structures and operations (Bernstein and Cashore, 2004). If these two dimensions may sometime coincide, with popular attitudes reflecting normative ideals of legitimacy, they should remain conceptually and empirically distinct. As Bodansky rightly reminds us: 'the two types of legitimacy need not correspond. People may, in fact, accept authority based on tradition or myth or demagoguery. But this does not mean that such popular attitudes are justified' (1999: 602). Also, while there are times when it may be appropriate to focus on either one or the other dimension, it is justifiable to consider them together when striving for a richer understanding of the various types of legitimacy pressures an institution is likely to face.

Hence, and in contrast to the normative approach to legitimacy which relies on *a-priori* defined notions of procedural fairness, the constructivist/sociological perspective reflects an interpretivist/constructionist ontology, which links the legitimacy of an institution with the perceptions and attitudes of the communities it is expected to affect (Franck, 1990). In this view then, legitimacy is most basically defined as 'the normative belief by an actor that a rule or institution ought to be obeyed' (Hurd, 1999: 381) and assessing the social legitimacy of an institution thus requires evaluating the attitudes and perceptions of the communities in which the institution in question operates. With respect to a multi-stakeholder organisation like the FSC, this form of legitimacy appears particularly crucial. Unlike more traditional forms of international governance, such as international organisations and governments, private transnational governance systems do not possess any form of *de jure* (legal) legitimacy and must in effect more actively seek social support and recognition from a wide variety of members, stakeholders and observers (Beisheim and Dingwerth, 2008; Bernstein and Cashore, 2004, 2007; Cashore, 2002).

In the case of the FSC, the vast array of social, environmental and economic actors that compose the tripartite decision-making structure of the organisation (membership base) have a particularly important legitimacy-granting role. From this angle then, social legitimacy can be assessed by evaluating the degree to which these various actors consider that the standard organisation effectively or actively contributes to the promotion of their respective interests and values. This is not to say that non-members do not matter for the FSC. Achieving greater credibility with governments and intergovernmental organisations, for instance, can help influence public legislation and policies in ways that can further the FSC's own visions and goals. But since the FSC seeks to maintain formal independence from public authorities, our assessment of the social dimension of legitimacy will focus only on the attitudes and evaluations of the various stakeholders (individuals/organisations) that at one point or another have chosen to join the organisation.

What follows is an evaluation of the FSC's legitimacy, which proceeds by first applying the input-output normative framework (that is, legitimacy on the basis of institutional design) and then examining the more social dimension of the FSC's legitimacy (that is, legitimacy on the basis of popular evaluations). Given space constraints, it is clear that our account of the FSC's legitimacy is more illustrative than exhaustive, yet offers a basis for comprehensive conclusions.

3.1. Input Legitimacy in the FSC

There is no doubt that compared to other transnational policy approaches, FSC's institutional framework can be seen as remarkably democratic. As many scholars have suggested, FSC's standard-setting structure encompasses several institutional mechanisms, which from an institutional design perspective tend to score well under democratic criteria of input legitimacy (that is, inclusiveness, participation, transparency, deliberation) (Garrelts and Flitner, 2011; Meidinger, 2011; Gale, 2009; Auld et al., 2008; Chan and Pattberg, 2008; Dingwerth, 2007; Gulbrandsen, 2004; Gale and Haward, 2004). These design features include, most notably, the organisation's membership structure and the decision-making procedures.

One of the primary social goals of the FSC is to provide institutional access and voice to a whole range of forest stakeholders, such as forest owners and managers, stewards of the forest, resident forest-dependent people, local communities, indigenous people and forest workers (FSC, 2003). As noted by several authors, this concern for broad representation and inclusiveness is particularly apparent in the organisation's open and chamber-based membership structure (see Garrelts and Flitner, 2011; Dingwerth, 2007; Gale and Haward, 2004).

Unlike other and more recent private certification schemes, such as the Marine Stewardship Council (MSC), the FSC is indeed an open membership institution: any individual and organisation who shares the scheme's goals and vision can become a member, providing of course that they secure the support of two existing members and the payment of a membership fee (Garrelts and Flitner, 2011; Gale and Haward, 2004). As of December 2010, for instance, FSC's membership reached more than 850 members located in more than 100 countries (FSC, 2010). By June 2011, 69 new organisations and individuals had joined the organisation (FSC, 2011a). By joining the FSC, individuals and organisations can play a significant role in the governance of the institution: they can directly influence the making of important strategic decisions by attending and voting in the FSC General Assembly meetings. They can also elect individuals to the international and national boards, formulate and submit policy motions and participate in FSC activities at the national and regional levels (Dingwerth, 2008; Gale and Haward, 2004; FSC, 2011b).

More importantly and with respect to the democratic criteria of representation and participation, the FSC's governance structure seeks to adequately balance the interests and values of its various stakeholders. As noted earlier in this chapter, the FSC's main decision-making body, the General Assembly (GA) is organised in three membership chambers: environmental, social, and economic, with each possessing equal weight of vote and influence. As Gale and Haward (2004), among others, explain, the purpose of this tripartite-chamber approach is to ensure that no single set of interests dominate the debates within the GA and that policy decisions adequately reflect the three core values associated with sustainable forest management. The GA's tripartite decision-making structure is responsive to the potential dominance of Northern economic interests and is further designed in ways that seek to strengthen Southern interests in the FSC's decision-making process. Article 13 of the FSC by-laws establishes that 'to achieve a balance between Northern and Southern perspectives within each chamber, Northern and Southern organisations and individuals shall have 50% of the voting power. In effect, there shall be Northern and Southern subchambers within each of the three chambers' (FSC, 2009b).[4] With this elaborate membership structure, the FSC's governance system appears to be an inclusive and representative institution, one which provides venues and resources to the poor and the potentially under-represented, and which gives equal importance to the variety of forest stakeholders' interests and values.

A related design feature of the FSC's governance structure that holds great democratic promise, especially in terms of procedural fairness, transparency and deliberativeness, is the FSC's decision-making procedures. The General Assembly, which convenes every three years, is the FSC's supreme decision-making authority (FSC, 2009a, §14). During GA meetings, FSC members can pass resolutions with regard to FSC's Principles and Criteria, its organisational procedures, and act as final arbiters in the case of organisational disputes (Gale and Haward, 2004). The GA's decisions require the affirmative vote of at least two-thirds of the total voting power (FSC, 2009b, § 15) and hence depend on a substantial consensus across all the chambers and sub-chambers (Meidinger, 2011). In sharp contrast to other international initiatives and intergovernmental organisations for which voting shares are generally allocated according to the economic power of their members, the FSC's voting arrangements seek to guarantee an equal distribution of power and influence across all three chambers and six sub-chambers (Gale and Haward, 2004). Each of the three main chambers retain an equal voting share of the GA's total votes (that is, 33.3 per cent). The Northern and Southern sub-chambers, in turn, dispose of 50 per cent of their respective chamber's total votes. Finally, and within each chamber, organisational members dispose of 90 per cent of the votes, with individual members possessing only the remaining 10 per cent (FSC, 2009b, §12–13). As the FSC by-laws stipulate (2009b, §12), '[t]he purpose of the chamber structure is to maintain the balance of voting power between the different interests without having to limit the number of members . . . If additional members join a chamber, the voting power of existing members declines accordingly'.

While the FSC's voting arrangements seek to reflect an equitably-balanced forum at the international level, the decision-making procedure itself within the GA also tends to conform to transparent and deliberative procedures and practices. As Meidinger notes, '[m]ost rules and standards are developed through extensive deliberative proceedings involving stakeholder consultation, "formal public notice and comment processes" and public explanations of decisions' (2011: 419) (see also Meidinger, 2006). The consultation of various stakeholders, in particular, has three objectives. First, it aims to generate comments on the generic standards being used in an assessment. Second, stakeholders can identify controversial and important regional issues in forest management and offer advice on how these issues might be resolved. Third, they might offer or gather information on the performance of a forest company with respect to the standards being used in an evaluation. Of course, the GA is not the FSC's only forum. Other participatory mechanisms exist, providing for additional institutional discursive spaces and close stakeholder consultation (Dingwerth, 2007). Today, the FSC has national initiatives in more than 50 countries and maintains four regional offices – Europe, Africa, Latin America and Asia (FSC, 2011c). These national and regional institutional platforms hold regular meetings that make it easier for stakeholders, especially from developing countries, to share and obtain information, receive coaching and training, and influence the making of national, sub-national and transnational standards (FSC, 2003).

In synthesis, it is clear that from an input-legitimacy perspective, the FSC's membership structure and decision-making procedures seem to adequately reflect the democratic norms of inclusiveness, participation, representation, transparency and deliberation. For some observers, this suggests that forest certification might be part of a process involving the emergence of new forms of democracy at the transnational level (Meidinger, 2011). But despite these positive insights, the democratic potential of the FSC is not without limitation (Dingwerth, 2007; Garrelts and Flitners, 2011). In recent years, many concerns have been raised about the FSC's actual capacity to adequately represent the interests of its different stakeholders (Garrelts and Flitner, 2011; Dingwerth, 2007; Cashore et al., 2004). As Garrelts and Flitner (2011) recently noted, one major problem with the FSC's chamber-base membership structure is that the boundaries between the three main chambers have not been clearly established. Moreover, the three categories (social, environmental and economic) tend to reflect unrealistically homogenous interests. This lack of clarity and flexibility makes it particularly difficult for heterogeneous groups like researchers, labour unions, indigenous groups, to effectively voice their concerns and interests. 'If', as Gale and Haward tell us, the 'system works well for members that are clearly associated with one or another interest . . . there are many individuals and groups that span more than one chamber, and each has to make a judgment as to which group to belong to' (2004: 15–16). While large-scale forest operators clearly seem to belong in the economic chamber, some union representatives might found it strange to be placed in the social chamber. Increasing the number of chambers could be a solution, but as Garrelts and Flitner (2011) rightly conclude, a more fragmented membership structure could in the end further complicate what is already a largely sophisticated decision-making process.

A second widespread criticism concerns the FSC's efforts to achieve an appropriate international balance of interests between its Southern and Northern stakeholders. In his evaluation of the FSC's decision-making processes, Dingwerth (2008) concludes that despite its pioneering efforts to achieve North-South parity, the FSC has so far failed to strengthen the position of Southern interests. Its affirmative procedures, he explains, have not prevented Northern interests from dominating the standard development processes. If over the years, the share of Southern members has continuously increased, particularly in the social and environmental chambers (Dingwerth, 2008), Southern members are still, for the most part, predominantly represented by individuals rather than organisations, which, as noted earlier, only dispose of 10 per cent of their respective chambers' total votes. As of the end of 2010, for instance, the FSC's economic chamber counted around 351 members, including 185 from the North and 166 from the South. On closer examination, however, the distinction between individual and organisational members reveals that while organisations represented 70 per cent of the Northern-sub-economic chamber, in the Southern sub-chamber they accounted for only 35 per cent of the total members (FSC, 2010). Hence despite their growth in membership and the apparently democratic voting structure of the FSC, Southern members have yet to acquire the same representational force as their Northern counterparts.

A final and related argument is that in the absence of a well-defined citizenry or demos, it is clear that forest certification and transnational rule-making institutions more generally, cannot possibly guarantee adequate representation of all relevant stakeholders. With respect to private regulatory schemes, and to use Meidinger's words, 'there is no systematic mechanism whereby everyone who may be affected by the FSC policies can help select its members or nominate individual members to represent them' (2011: 412). On a similar note, it is useful to remember that even the FSC's members themselves – environmental and social NGOs and private companies – generally fall short of the democratic norms of representation, inclusiveness and accountability, and as such cannot be expected to appropriately represent and transmit the concerns and interests of their own constituencies (Glasbergen, 2011).

Upon closer inspection, it is clear that in practice the FSC has yet to more carefully attend to the interests and values of its Southern stakeholders. On paper, however, the organisation's sophisticated governance structure can at least be credited for holding remarkable democratic promise. As Garrelts and Flitner conclude while acknowledging the organisation's limitations, the FSC 'is still one of the most ambitious and far-reaching attempts to build an inclusive and democratic governance structure beyond the classical international regimes' (2011: 398–99). Moreover, by demanding inclusiveness and equitable representation in standard development, encouraging active stakeholder consultation and participation and decision-making transparency, the FSC demonstrates that thinking about procedural normative democracy beyond the nation-state is not an entirely ill-founded task. More importantly, and as many authors tend to suggest, its governance structure can serve as a template, if not inspiration, for the design of other transnational policy initiatives in global environmental governance (Garrelts and Flitner, 2011).

3.2. Output Legitimacy in the FSC

As mentioned earlier, while input-legitimacy reflects evaluative statements about the democratic quality of an institution's decision-making procedures, output-legitimacy, understood here also in normative procedural terms, refers to the democratic quality of the policy decisions themselves. This dimension can be evaluated in particular by studying whether stakeholders are given appropriate opportunities to dispute policy decisions they find deeply problematic and if the organisation provides effective, workable and fair procedures for complaints and dispute resolution. As we can see in regards to the FSC, its system for dispute and complaints resolution has thus far functioned suboptimally, at least until 2009, when the FSC finally launched a set of new guidelines and procedures. It should be noted that no empirical data on the handling of disputes under the old system is publicly available and hence it is difficult to make a full assessment of the functioning of the old procedure. However, on the basis of documents and information available discussing the FSC dispute settlement system, it can be proposed that the system had some significant shortcomings from a legitimacy point of view.

The FSC allows FSC members, certification bodies and stakeholders to resolve any conflicts or complaints they may have with the FSC.[5] A complaint can be about the Board of Directors, the FSC and/or its affiliates, FSC-accredited certification bodies or their FSC certificate holders.[6] All the levels of the FSC's governance structure are involved in the resolution of complaints but to avoid unnecessary expenses, all complaints are first expected to be handled informally, at the level of the affected parties, for example, the forest manager, the certification body and the national initiative.[7] If no informal solution can be found, then the complaint can be elevated to the formal level. For almost a decade (until 2009), the FSC's formal complaint resolution process was conducted under the so-called Interim Dispute Resolution Protocol, which was adopted by the Board on January 1998 and which has been widely criticised for being unworkable and unfairly structured.[8] On closer examination, it is clear that this system was too problematic and inefficient to ensure the FSC's responsiveness vis-à-vis all of its stakeholders' potential concerns and complaints. As several observers have noted, a key problem with the protocol's lengthy and complex procedures is that they were likely to further marginalise smaller and poorer forest stakeholders, especially those located in the South.[9]

The strict membership requirements for initiating a complaint were particularly illustrative in this regard. Under the protocol, only FSC members in good standing were allowed to initiate an informal or formal complaint to the FSC. Non-FSC members, for their part, had to convince a FSC member to lodge their complaint for them.[10] Access restrictions were also reflected in the formal process of the proceedings. At this stage, the protocol required each complainant to opt for either a primary or secondary status and demanded that all complaints be filed by at least one primary complainant and seconded by at least two other FSC members. The difference between these two statuses is a matter of participation: while a primary complainant was entitled to full participation in the proceedings, a secondary complainant had only limited standing and was only allowed to participate in the resolution of a dispute to a limited extent. They were not entitled, for example, to participate in any site visits or evidentiary hearings.[11] While these participation restrictions might have appeared necessary from a financial or logistical perspective, they tended to challenge the democratic notions of inclusiveness and transparency, features that are crucial for the credibility of any kind of checking/judicial mechanism.

Another widespread criticism was that the procedures not only took too long (Gale, 2009), but were too legally complex for certain individuals or small non-governmental organisations to follow. As suggested by a report issued by the Rainforest Foundation in 2002: '[t]he document . . . is written in highly legalistic terms, with many inter-locking and cross-referred clauses. This makes it very difficult for the non-expert use, even where English (the only language in which the Protocol has been produced) is their native tongue' (Counsell and Loraas, 2002: 45). Furthermore, the costs of the proceedings, which required primary complainants to place a deposit of $1000 (US) and each secondary complainant, a deposit of $250 (US), further restricted the capacity of the poorest FSC members to complain through the FSC's internal system (Counsell and Loraas 2002).

Finally, and more importantly, the former FSC dispute resolution mechanisms were vulnerable to criticisms of conflicts of interest. As Gale (2009: 288) justifiably points out in his analysis of the judicial activities of the FSC, a major problem with these arrangements is that they did not rest on a sufficient separation of powers between the FSC's judicial and executive branches. In particular, no truly independent and impartial committee was established to secure the perceived procedural and outcome fairness of the process. The Protocol relied too heavily on the executive branch – the FSC Secretariat, the Board of Directors and ultimately the General Assembly – for the review and resolution of complaints filed against the FSC's certification scheme. As the Protocol suggests:

> All disputes other than challenges to Board decisions or actions are first presented to the Board, along with a recommendation by the Secretariat as to whether the Board should hear the complaint . . . Its decision may ultimately be timely appealed to the Dispute Resolution Committee . . . [which] may only overturn the Board for a clear error of judgment or a clear and substantial abuse of discretion.[12]

When the appellant is not satisfied with the resolutions advanced by the Dispute Resolution Committee, the dispute is ultimately referred to the GA, the FSC's ultimate authority. This insufficient emphasis on impartiality and independence made the system largely ill-equipped to deal with potential conflicts of interest.

These various difficulties and problems have not gone unnoticed. At the FSC GA in 2002, FSC members rightly began to request improvements to the current dispute resolution system.[13] In November 2009, after many debates and consultations with various stakeholders, the FSC finally launched revised guidelines and procedures. While they have yet to prove their value and effectiveness, these new guidelines seem to offer some improvements in terms of accessibility, transparency, timeliness and efficacy. Under the revised system, for instance, FSC membership is not a requirement for potential complainants anymore: now any individual or organisation has the right to lodge a complaint against the FSC certification scheme (including the FSC Accreditation Program).[14] In terms of clarity, the new system also makes a clearer distinction between complaints regarding compliance issues (that is, with the FSC certification or accreditation decisions), complaints arising from administrative decisions (such as policy standards, trademark, membership).[15] In general, the revised procedures appear far less legally complex and cumbersome than the Protocol's, making the complaint and dispute processes more accessible to non-expert use and especially to individuals and small organisations. Most importantly, the revised version seems to be less conducive to potential conflicts of interest. Each formal complaint filed with the FSC and accepted by the Director of FSC A.C. shall now involve the creation of an independent and impartial complaints panel of three members. This stricter requirement for impartiality and independence means that 'Members of the FSC A.C. and FSC/ASI staff, as well as affected stakeholders shall not be eligible to be part of the complaints Panel, unless unanimously accepted by the Parties to the Complaint'.[16] Furthermore, the parties to the complaints also have the right to contest the composition of the panel if they fear potential conflicts of interest.

3.3. Social Legitimacy of the FSC

What is the social legitimacy of the FSC? Despite being repeatedly hailed as the only credible and rigorous label for good forest management (WWF, 2001), the FSC has been facing growing and outspoken criticism over the years. Some environmental and social stakeholders, in particular, have grown increasingly wary of the scheme's capacity to promote environmentally appropriate and socially beneficial forestry management practices.

A detailed report published by the Rainforest Foundation in 2002, which received input from a large number of individuals and organisations around the world, gives us a non-negligible account of the various reasons why the FSC's reputation started to deteriorate by the late 1990s (Counsell and Loraas, 2002). Most notably, the report accused the FSC of violating its own principles and criteria by issuing certificates to non-compliant forest managers. This credibility problem, like many other issues raised by the report, has been linked with the FSC's decision in the late 1990s to pursue a fast-growth organisational strategy so as to rapidly expand the volume and areas of its certified forests throughout the world. This was a quantity-based strategy that promoted certification even in countries where national laws and regulations were clearly incompatible with the FSC's principles and criteria (Counsell and Loraas, 2002). Other areas of concern the report identified were the certifiers' corporate vested interests in granting certificates and the essentially non-functioning disciplinary and control mechanisms of the FSC, two issues that tended to further encourage a flawed certification processes (Counsell and Loraas, 2002). The report, which was presented to the FSC Board and the Secretariat in September 2002, successfully prompted the FSC to write a detailed response, which included – among other things – the promise to remedy a number of these credibility issues.

Today, considerable criticism from environmental groups about the performance of the FSC and the practices of its accredited certifiers still persist. In October 2008, a group of organisational members from the FSC's environmental and economic chambers circulated a Joint Statement in which they asserted that the FSC's severe lack of credibility actually threatened the perceived legitimacy of their own organisation and demanded, as a result, substantial institutional reforms, particularly in regard to the following problems: the poor performance of accredited certifiers, the inefficiency of the complaints and disputes procedures, and the FSC's controlled wood policy.[17] Since then however, a number of long-standing European environmental members of the FSC have decided to withdraw their support from the organisation. In March 2009, the German-based organisation Robin Wood announced that it was ending its membership with FSC International over the organisation's perceived incapacity to prevent the granting of invalid certificates. A year later, in June 2010, the Swedish Society for Nature Conversation (SSNC) decided to resign from FSC Sweden with its President, Mikael Karlsson, issuing the following statement: 'We are disappointed. We initiated FSC in Sweden some 15 years ago but today the number of violations of laws and standards is too high for any environmental organisation to accept. We refuse further greenwashing under the FSC logotype.'[18] Finally in June

2011, FERN, also a long-term European supporter of the FSC announced the resignation of its membership, criticising the FSC over its intention to fully engage in certification of REDD project carbon credits despite the lack of empirical evidence regarding the actual impact of FSC's certified logging on the climate.[19]

If at the time of its creation, back in the early 1990s, the FSC seemed well placed to gain wide recognition, especially from transnational and national environmental groups (Cashore, 2002; Bernstein and Cashore, 2004), today's picture offers a far less enthusiastic assessment of the organisation's long-term capacity to maintain its environmental and social credibility. Without substantial institutional reforms, the FSC might further lose the trust of some of its long-term environmental and social supporters.

When it comes to evaluating how business and economic actors view the FSC, little data has so far been made available. There is no doubt that business use of the FSC in certain parts of the world has been proliferating (Marx, 2011), but this is more an effectiveness issue, the subject of the next part of this chapter. With respect to the sociological dimension of legitimacy, it is clear that in sharp contrast to their environmental and social counterparts, landowners and forest company officials have been far more reluctant to openly criticise or even assess the organisation's credibility and actual performance (Pattberg, 2005). A plausible explanation for this is that, at least initially, corporate actors choose to join and stay with the FSC for pragmatic legitimacy reasons (Bernstein and Cashore, 2004), which mainly include concerns for short-term material incentives, such as the access to new markets or avoiding costs associated with boycott campaigns. This instrumental logic of action also explains why a number of economic and business actors have created more industry-dominated forest certification schemes such as the Programme for the Endorsement of Forest Certification (PEFC) (formerly known as the Pan-European Forest Certification Council) or the Sustainable Forest Initiative (SFI), which now competes with the FSC.

4. DIMENSION 2: EFFECTIVENESS

Forest certification is often regarded as a new global environmental regime (Rayner et al., 2011; Cashore et al., 2004; Gulbrandsen, 2004, 2005). Regimes can be defined, following Krasner, as 'sets of implicit or explicit principles, norms, rules and decision making procedures around which actors' expectations converge in a given area of international relations' (1982: 186) (compare Ruggie (1975) for a state-centric definition of regimes and Young (1980) for a definition from a social institutional perspective). From a regime perspective, effectiveness is often operationalised on six interrelated dimensions, namely problem solving, goal attainment, behavioural effectiveness, process effectiveness, constitutive and evaluative effectiveness (Miles et al., 2002; Tikina and Innes, 2008; Young, 1994). Problem solving refers to the degree to which the problem, which prompted the establishment of the regimes, is solved. Goal attainment refers to the degree to which specific goals, as stated for example in principles and standards, are achieved. Behavioural effectiveness assesses the degree to which the regime generated differences in behaviour and practices, such as differences in forest practices. Process effectiveness evaluates the adoption of a new regime in a region or country. Constitutive effectiveness refers to the acceptance of the regime by a large group of stakeholders. Finally, evaluative effectiveness assesses the regime on a set of criteria such as efficiency equitability and sustainability. Tikina and Innes (2008) translate these dimensions to forest certification and develop a framework for the assessment of the effectiveness of forest certification. They argue it is too early to assess the effectiveness of forest certification in problem solving and goal attainment but that it has been quite successful at process and constitutive effectiveness. In addition, they argue that effectiveness in changing behaviour is less clear and evaluative effectiveness remains to be determined. This chapter builds on this framework to assess problem solving, goal attainment, behavioural effectiveness and process effectiveness for the FSC. Constitutive and evaluative effectiveness are not assessed due to lack of systematic data. For an assessment of constitutive effectiveness, there needs to be more data on general and stakeholder-specific awareness and appreciation of FSC. In addition, one should be able to analyze membership structures and underlying dynamics between different stakeholders.

4.1. Problem Solving, Goal Attainment and Behavioural Effectiveness

Our first assessment concerns problem solving, goal attainment and behavioural effectiveness, which are taken together since they are highly interrelated. A behavioural impact on forest practices will contribute to the attainment of goals which are based on the problems to be solved. Indeed, a change in forest practices, via forest management plans, is the key mechanism by which the FSC attempts to attain its goals.

Tikina and Innes (2008) argue it is too early to assess these dimensions. However, there is already some partial evidence available which assesses the degree to which certification contributes towards sustainable forest management and the three dimensions of sustainability, environmental and social protection and economic viability. Several studies have focused on analysing the ecological, social and economic impact of forest certification (see Karmann and Smith, 2009). These studies provide evidence that FSC certification generates an ecological impact in certified forests in terms of forest management, enhancing biodiversity and other ecological aspects of forest management, social improvements and economic benefits. However, up until now results have been inconclusive for several reasons. First, many studies rely on a few or only one case study (Ebeling and Yasue, 2009; Gulbrandsen, 2005). Such studies are able to explore the impact of certification but do not provide a basis on which to make more general assessments. Moreover, the studies do not provide an in-depth insight in case selection. Hence, it is impossible to assess whether they are typical cases, outlier cases or, more generally, if there is any selection bias. Second, some studies only rely on indirect measurement of effects/impact and do not use longitudinal observational studies or experimental research designs. Hirschberger (2008), for example, analysed the impact of FSC-certification in six countries (Estonia, Germany, Latvia, Russia, Sweden and the United Kingdom) on the basis of audit reports and corrective action reports (CARs). These CARs contain information about which changes in forest management are required in order to obtain a certificate for sustainable forest management. However, they do not investigate the real changes in the ecological profile of a forest. Third, studies often lack a clear framework to assess impacts; this is most obvious in the case of social impacts. Consequently, some studies argue that certification contributes to better working conditions, but does this only on the basis of one or a few dimensions which are relevant in the context of implementing core ILO labour standards as is required by principle 4 of the FSC list of ten principles. Rezende de Azevedo and Giacini de Freitas (2003), for example, analyse the impact of certification on working conditions in the Amazon in Brazil and find that in certified forests the logging camps and safety of forest operations are significantly better than in non-certified forests. However, no assessment is provided with regard to working hours, overtime pay, minimum wages and other key ILO dimensions of working conditions.

Fourth, not all studies point in the same direction. Some raise doubts about the impact of certification. Cerutti et al. conducted a study in Cameroon and concluded that due to the stipulation and application of weak standards forests might not be managed sustainably: 'In only three of the 10 certified forests in Cameroon is the most valuable timber extracted with the application of techniques that are likely to ensure future harvests at the same rate as today' (2011: 188). Schulze et al. (2008) made a similar observation for certification in the Amazon territory. More generally, Holvoet and Muys (2004) found significant variation in sustainable forest standards between countries in their comparison of 164 local and national standards. In addition, their analysis shows that in developing countries sustainable forest management standards focus more on socio-economic aspects. In developed countries, by contrast, they focus more on ecological aspects. These studies point to a potential North-South divide in certification. The same contradictory results emerge in the context of economic benefits. There is evidence that forest certification generates access to mainly European and North American markets (Cashore et al., 2006; Ebeling, 2005; Nebel et al., 2005). Also some studies, mainly by Klooster (2005, 2006), show that forest certification contributes to local community development by developing high-value niche markets in, for instance, furniture. Concerning price premiums – the willingness to pay more for certified products – there is little or no evidence that materialise. Carrera et al. (2006) analysed forest certification in Guatemala and identified one of the negative impacts of certification as disappointment due to false expectations regarding price premiums for certified timber and low returns from forest management once forest owners or concession holders no longer receive subsidies from support organisations.

It is impossible to draw any definite conclusions on the basis of the existing evidence so far. Studies only reveal a very partial and incomplete picture. This lack of clear evidence on impact corresponds to a more general observation with regard to the impact and effectiveness of certification schemes. As Rodrik notes in his recent book. *The Globalization Paradox*: 'we have very little reliable information on how labelling efforts work out in practice' (2011: 226). Moreover, relatively little discussion so far has focused on developing comprehensive frameworks to measure and assess impacts. Such an impact assessment framework coupled to an experimental design could reveal the real impact of forest certification. Such an experiment would identify a number of forest plots and then randomly attribute the intervention – in this case certification – to certain plots and keep the other plots as a control group. Empirical longitudinal observations on several social, economic and ecological indicators would enable researchers to assess the impact of certification.

Assessment with regard to goal attainment and problem solving is confronted with an additional problem, namely the multiplicity of goals and objectives. This becomes obvious in a closer look at principle 1 of the FSC which refers to all applicable laws and international treaties. In practice, this principle brings together a whole range of laws and acts from multiple levels of governance. If one takes the example of the FSC in the US (FSC_US, 2010), principle 1 covers more than 50 laws and acts ranging from the international level, treaties with tribes, federal laws and policies, state law and policies, and local rules and policies. Principle 4 refers to the conventions of the ILO and include conventions on *inter alia* minimum wage (C131), migrant workers (C143), occupational safety and health (C155), indigenous and tribal people (C169), forced labour (C29), freedom of association (C87), right to organise and collective bargaining (C98), equal remuneration (C100), abolition of forced labour (C105), discrimination (C111), minimum age (C138) and the worst forms of child labour (C182) (see Cuyvers and de Meyer, Chapter 4, this volume).

Each of these treaties, conventions, laws, statutes and policies have their own specific objectives which in the case of the FSC are translated into specific standards which have to be reached. Given the multiplicity of goals it is very hard to assess the attainment of specific goals. In addition, very little is known about potential trade-offs between goals. Can all goals be attained at once or does the attainment of one goal work to the detriment of another? The most obvious trade-offs might exist between environmental or economic objectives on the one hand and social objectives on the other hand.

4.2. Process Effectiveness: Adoption of the FSC FM and CoC Certification

The effectiveness of certification is also determined by the adoption of the scheme. Even if we assume that on-the-ground impact is significant, the overall impact remains a function of the adoption of certification. If only a few forests or organisations are certified, the overall impact will remain limited.

In forest certification, two types of certificates are of importance. First of all, there is forest management (FM) certification. In this case, the forests are certified according to a set of principles and standards. They provide the supply of certified wood. Second, other organisations in the supply chain which provides certified wood products to customers can be certified with a chain-of-custody (CoC) certificate. CoC certification can be regarded as an indicator of the demand for certified wood. Figure 3.2 illustrates these two types of forest certification.

Table 3.1 presents an overview of the certification of forests (FM certification) worldwide, broken down by continent. In total, forest certification occurs in 81 countries (FSC Facts and Figures, June 2011). The table shows that mainly forests in Europe and North America are certified. They account for 80 per cent of certified forest surface area. Hence, most certified wood is supplied by European and North American forests.

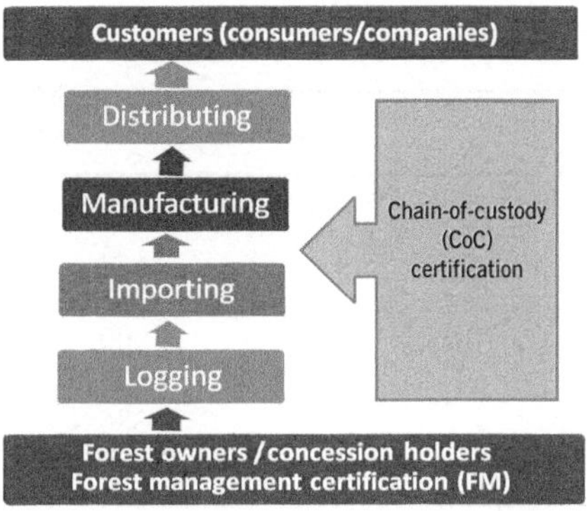

Figure 3.2: FM and CoC certification

Table 3.1: FSC FM certification adoption

Continent	Total area (ha)	Number of certificates	Percentage (ha)
Africa	7 688 716	47	5.37
Asia	3 401 726	111	2.37
Europe	60 094 243	429	41.97
Latin America and the Carribean	13 404 335	222	9.36
North America	56 492 596	205	39.46
Oceania	2 081 365	30	1.45
Total	143 162 981	1 044	100

Source: FSC Facts and Figures, June 2011
Note: 1. 81 countries have certified forests 2. Percentage figures rounded up

Table 3.2 provides an overview of CoC certification worldwide, broken down by continent. It shows again that mainly organisations in Europe and North America demand a CoC certificate. CoC certification occurs in 107 countries, however in many countries (34 in total) only one, two or three organisations are certified (FSC Facts and Figures, June 2011). Europe is even more dominant in CoC certification. Asia has a higher percentage of CoC certification compared to FM certification, which is mainly a result of a significant CoC adoption in Japan (1128 certificates) and China (1563 certificates). The figure for Latin America and the Caribbean is distorted by the fact that Brazil takes the bulk of all CoC certificates (622 in total).

Table 3.2: FSC CoC certification adoption

Continent	Number of CoC certificates	Percentage
Africa	137	0.66
Asia	4 172	20.32
Europe	10 113	49.26
Latin America and the Carribean	900	4.38
North America	4 821	23.48
Oceania	386	1.88
Total	20 529	100

Note: Percentage figures rounded up
Source: FSC Facts and Figures, June 2011

Tables 3.1 and 3.2 show a clear North-South divide with regard to the adoption of FSC FM and CoC certificates. Marx and Cuypers (2010) argue that FSC FM certification occurs most in developed countries in which forests have an important production function. They identify a 'stuck at the bottom' problem for a large number of developing countries with regard to the certification process. This problem is a result of the financial implications of getting certified as certification costs run high.

How adoption will develop in the coming years is difficult to assess. With regard to forest management certification, one can observe some development which might influence the adoption rate of forest certification significantly. First of all, initiatives in the context of the climate change regime, such as REDD+ and CDM provide significant incentives to invest in forest management. Certification is then often regarded as an add-on tool to provide assurance as to the sustainability of these initiatives. Second, and maybe more importantly, forest certification is increasingly considered as a legality verification/due diligence tool in the context of FLEG (Forest Law Enforcement and Governance) initiatives. For example, Article 6 (Due Diligence Tool) of EU Regulation 995/2010 on the prevention of sales of illegal timber and timber products within the EU recognises forest certification as an assurance of compliance with applicable legislation. This compliance with legislation is covered in principle 1 of the FSC.

Increased adoption of FSC CoC in developing countries will be a question of local demand. It is striking that in some countries with significant FSC FM certification, the number of CoC certificates is very limited. Table 3.3 shows the number of CoC certificates (COC #) in the 20 countries with the largest areas of forest which are FSC-FM (FM HA) certified. It shows that in some countries such as Congo, Uruguay, Belarus, Gabon, Bolivia and Cameroon, the number of CoC certificates is very limited notwithstanding significant certified forests. This probably indicates a very limited demand for certified products on the local and/or national market. Forests in these countries are probably certified for export purposes. This might imply that the 'stuck at the bottom' problem will persist for CoC certificates. However, the case of China (see also Table 3.3) might suggest that in fast developing countries CoC certification can gain prominence. In addition, the table shows the number of FSC FM certificate holders (FM #). Concerning the latter, it can be observed that in some countries such as Congo, Croatia, Gabon, Estonia, Cameroon, Indonesia and Belarus, it is only one or a few forest owners/concession holders that have their forests certified.

Table 3.3: Ranking of countries according to FSC-certified surface area (FSC-FM certificate)

Rank	Country	FM HA	FM #	CoC #
1	Canada	42 176 686	61	1 017
2	Russia	28 646 299	65	116
3	United States	13 723 194	114	3 770
4	Sweden	11 321 672	22	244
5	Brazil	6 511 129	79	622
6	Poland	6 427 346	18	602
7	Congo	2 726 996	4	1
8	Uruguay	2 666 441	29	31
9	Croatia	2 018 987	1	147
10	Belarus	1 908 133	8	14
11	Gabon	1 873 505	3	12
12	China	1 791 783	34	1 563
13	South Africa	1 711 419	19	84
14	New Zealand	1 387 148	18	143
15	Bolivia	1 267 547	14	28
16	Estonia	1 086 937	3	103
17	Lithuania	1 046 616	42	106
18	Bosnia and Herzegovina	988 285	2	56
19	Cameroon	763 146	5	13
20	Indonesia	638 455	8	161

Source: FSC Facts and Figures, June 2011

More generally, the future adoption of FSC certification, both FM and CoC, will be a function of state actions. First, with regard to FSC FM certification, an increasing number of governmental bodies are applying for FSC certification for forests which are under their ownership. Marx and Cuypers (2010) showed that most countries with the highest density of FSC (that is, proportion of FSC-certified forest in the total forest area) are countries with significant public control of forests. In order words, states or state-owned forest companies are applying for FSC FM certification. Second, FSC CoC certification is used in public procurement policies in developed countries as a leverage tool (for example, in the EU public procurement constitutes 16 per cent of European GDP). Many countries and local governments are increasingly using sustainability criteria when purchasing goods. Certificates, such as FSC, provide in one label all the information with regard to these criteria and hence are often used when governments have to decide on buying specific goods. Although public procurement laws and rules cannot include references to specific certificates, the result is often that FSC-certified products are bought (Meidinger, 2007; Mechel et al., 2006). Continued state support of FSC adoption will, first, be dependent on how the market for certification evolves, specifically the degree to which competing certification schemes transform themselves from first- or second-party certification schemes to third-party certification schemes. States tend to support more third-party systems than second-party systems. If more competitors move in, adoption rates of FSC certification may slow down or stagnate. To be sure, forest certification is at this point not a zero-sum game and it might very well be the case that in the short term the adoption rates of several certification schemes continue to grow. Second, state support will be dependent on the degree to which certification schemes provide evidence of their impact. As elaborated above, this is still an outstanding issue.

In addition, it should be noted that besides aiming to assess the short-term direct effectiveness of forest certification, one could also consider including positive and negative unintended effects, spillover effects to other certification schemes, and long-term and slower-moving effects, mainly with regard to the impact on national and international rulemaking (see also Auld et al., 2008).

5. CONCLUSION

The FSC is a remarkable governance institution. In 2013, it will celebrate its 20th anniversary and its accomplishments have been impressive on at least five fronts. First, in terms of building an international operational organisation, the FSC has proved it is able to balance many different interests and expand into many different countries by setting up local organisations. The result is an adaptive organisation which is open to change proposed by more than 850 members. Second, from a formal institutional design perspective, there is no doubt that compared to other transnational and intergovernmental regulatory systems, the FSC scores relatively well under democratic criteria of input legitimacy. Its tripartite membership structure and multi-level decision-making procedures constitute a prime example of the so-called multi-stakeholder approach to rule-making in world politics. This, if properly functional, holds great promise for shaping a more pluralistic approach to sustainable forest governance. On the output side, recent institutional reforms in the organisation's complaints and dispute resolution system demonstrate that the FSC can be adaptable and responsive to longstanding criticisms from a variety of forest stakeholders and independent observers. Third, in terms of adoption of the FSC certificates, growth has been spectacular. Both FSC FM and FSC CoC adoption has increased manifold since the start. Fourth, FSC has a distinct impact on the discourse of sustainable forest management (SFM) and seems to win the 'battle' with other forest certification initiatives over what constitutes a legitimate forest certification system which promotes SFM. A recent paper by Overdest (2010) analysed the competition between FSC and PEFC and showed that the presence and discourse of FSC and its recognition in the market has driven up standards and practices in the PEFC. Finally, the FSC is increasingly gaining recognition from public governments.

However, our analysis also shows that from a global governance perspective, the FSC is confronted with several challenges. First, in terms of its social legitimacy, the FSC is now facing a 'confidence' or 'credibility' crisis. This is fuelled mostly by the growing dissatisfaction of environmental and social stakeholders with the performance of some accredited certifiers and the widespread perception that key forest stakeholders, such as local communities and indigenous people, remain marginalised in the FSC decision-making processes and internal dispute resolution system. Second, and most importantly, it is clear that the FSC does not really operate on a global scale. We identified a strong North-South divide both in relation to formal representation/participation as well as in relation to adoption, limiting the potential of the FSC to address forest challenges in developing countries.

On closer examination though, these persisting problems should not be attributed solely to the operations and activities of the FSC. As in other areas of global governance, patterns of inclusion and exclusion are traditionally symptomatic of broader structural inequalities in world politics. The identified North-South divide is partially the result of the costs involved in gaining certification since in the South the gap between current forest management and sustainable forest management as certified by the FSC is enormous (Marx and Cuypers, 2010). Put differently, it is clear that, in sharp contrast to Northern producers, forest companies in developing countries have far less legal, normative and financial incentives to seek certification. The problem of formal representation and participation in the governance structure of the FSC similarly reflects structural gaps in financial, economic and educational capabilities between developed and developing nations (Dingwerth, 2008). Indeed, it is primarily the lack of financial and organisational resources and a more restricted access to transnational networks that explain why the share of Southern membership is so far predominantly composed of individual rather than organisational members.

These remarks suggest that when it comes to enhancing the legitimacy and effectiveness of the certification scheme of the FSC, considering 'bringing multilateralism back in' is not entirely unfounded. In a recent article on the performance of international organisations (IOs), Abbott and Snidal (2010) shed interesting light on the many ways in which IOs can serve as 'global orchestrators' by supporting and shaping the activities and operations of private transnational institutions, and thereby enhancing their own performance. As they indeed describe it:

> orchestration entails mobilizing and working with private actors and institutions to achieve regulatory goals, for example, by catalysing voluntary and collaborative programs; convening and facilitating private collaborations; persuading and inducing firms and industries to self-regulate... Effective orchestration can ameliorate both 'state failure' – the inadequacies of IOG – and 'market failure' – the governance problems that result from the spontaneous creation and decentralized evolution of [regulatory standard setting] RSS. (Abbott and Snidal, 2010: 317)

In a similar vein, we submit that IO orchestration could be beneficial to the FSC's performance both in terms of effectiveness and legitimacy. Multilateral organisations could notably help addressing the North-South financial gap in private forest governance. Some authors (for instance, van Waarden, Chapter 2, this volume) have suggested the establishment of a separate fund (financed by a tax akin to a Tobin tax but on forest-product related trade) to fund certification adoption in the South. In order for such an investment to be legitimate, however, one needs more information on the effectiveness of forest certification. As mentioned earlier, too little empirical evidence is currently available to assess the effectiveness of forest certification and explain possible variation in effectiveness between and within certification systems. Needless to say, multilateral organisations could also play a key role in supporting research on the effectiveness of forest certification. Several multilateral organisations, such as the World Bank, have very strong research departments which could take on this role. A related area for multilateral action is certification of the certifiers. The effectiveness analysis showed that within the FSC there is significant variation between standards and sustainable forest management plans which are implemented. In addition, there is also a significant variation in standards between certification systems. Hence, additional control on forest management plans which are certified constitutes a third challenge which might be addressed by multilateral organisations. A similar proposal in the area of certifying labour standards has been advanced by Sabel et al. (2000). With respect to the legitimacy dimension, multilateral organisations could also assist the FSC in achieving a higher level of representation of developing societies in the governance of the institution. They could also help certifiers better assess and understand questions and issues concerning indigenous peoples' rights in relation to existing land use and tenure patterns and financially assist the development of poorer and smaller forest organisations in the South so that they can more easily access private transnational networks of forest governance.

Ultimately, the question of contemporary global governance is not multilateralism versus private governance, but how the two can interrelate to complement and reinforce each other's performance. As the analysis demonstrates, private forest transnational governance is now playing a key role in the increasing network of organisations addressing forest governance (Rayner et al., 2011), and the current state of global forest governance can be considered as an interesting example of contemporary global network governance with its many challenges (Slaughter, 2004). One of the key questions that needs further enquiry is what contribution forest certification can make and how the impact of this contribution can be optimised by the actors, or otherwise, in multilateral organisations.

NOTES

1 FSC Guidelines for Certification Bodies, Subject 4.1, 2.1
2 FSC Guidelines for Certification Bodies, Subject 4.1, 2.2
3 FSC Guidelines for Certification Bodies, Subject 4.1, 2.3
4 The FSC follows the World Bank definition in its classification of Southern and Northern countries. Organisations that are legally registered in a non-high-income country – that is a country with less than $9,386 gross national income (GNI) per capita – will be placed in a Southern chamber, while those organisations that are based in high-income countries will belong to a Northern chamber. Individual members' placement in turn depends on the country in which they hold citizenship (FSC, 2009b, §14).

5 FSC, 2009. Dispute resolution system, FSC-STD-01-005(V1-0) En.
6 FSC, Disputes Resolution Fact Sheet, p. 1
7 FSC, 2009, Processing Complaints in the FSC Certification Scheme, FSC-PRO-01-008 (V1.0)
8 FSC, Interim Dispute Resolution Protocol (Oaxaca, Forest Stewardship Council, 1998).
9 See, for example, the 2002 report conducted by the Rainforest Foundation (Counsell and Loraas, 2002), the FSC-Watch website at www.fsc-watch.org and Gale, 2009.
10 FSC Interim Dispute Resolution Protocol, p. 2. Exceptions to this membership requirement rule include accreditation bodies or applicant accreditation bodies. They can challenge decisions made on their application status without having to be FSC members.
11 FSC Interim Dispute Resolution Protocol, p. 8.
12 FSC Interim Dispute Resolution Protocol, Summary.
13 FSC, 2002, Final Motions and Results from the FSC General Assembly 2002, Policy 23 'Motion to improve FSC dispute resolution processes,' available at: www.fsc.org/fileadmin/web-data/public/document_center/general_assembly_documents/FSC_General_Assembly_2002_Final_Motions.pdf
14 FSC, 2009, Processing Complaints in the FSC Certification Scheme, FSC-PRO-01-008 (V1.0), p. 6.
15 The new system now relies on five short referenced documents for its application. Compared to the Protocol, which was a unique and lengthy document of 55 pages, this multi-document approach allows stakeholders to more clearly distinguish between the various steps of the FSC's informal, formal and appeal stages of the complaint process.
16 FSC, 2009, Processing Formal Complaints in the FSC Certification Scheme, FSC-PRO-01-009(V1-0)EN, pp.7-8.
17 Position Paper available at: www.fern.org/node/4297 'Regaining Credibility and Rebuilding Support: Changes the FSC needs to make to ensure it regains and maintain its credibility' A Joint Statement by FERN, Greenpeace, Inter-African Forest Industry Association (IFIA), Precious Woods, Swedish Society for Nature Conservation (SSNC) and Tropical Forest Trust, 30 October, 2008.
18 SSNC's press release (16 June 2010) available at: www.naturskyddsforeningen.se/in-english/About-us/latest-news/?news=15246.
19 FERN's statement available at: www.fern.org/leavingFSC. 'FERN Statement to the Forest Stewardship Council: Why Fern is withdrawing its FSC membership', 2 June 2011.

REFERENCES

Abbott, K.W. and Snidal, D. (2009), 'Strengthening international regulation through transnational new governance: overcoming the orchestration deficit', *Vanderbilt Journal of Transnational Law,* 42 (2), pp. 501–578.

Abbott, K.W. and Snidal, D. (2010), 'International regulation without international government: Improving IO performance through orchestration', *The Review of International Organizations*, 5 (3), pp. 315–344.

Auld, G., Gulbrandsen L. and McDermott, C. (2008) 'Certification schemes and the impacts on forests and forestry', *Annual Review of Environment and Resources* 33, pp. 187–211.

Beisheim, M. and Dingwerth, K. (2008), 'Procedural legitimacy and private transnational governance. Are the good ones doing better?', *SFB-Governance Working Paper Series*, No. 14 (June).

Bernstein, S. and Cashore, B. (2004), 'Non-state global governance. Is forest certification a legitimate alternative to a global forest convention?', in J. Kirton and M. Trebilcock (eds), *Hard Choices, Soft Law: Combining Trade, Environment and Social Cohesion in Global Governance.* Aldershot: Ashgate, pp. 33–63.

Bernstein, S. and Cashore, B. (2007), 'Can non-state global governance be legitimate? An analytical framework', *Regulation and Governance* 1 (4), pp. 1–25.
Bodansky, D. (1999), 'The legitimacy of international governance: a coming challenge for international environmental law', *American Journal of Internationall Law*, 93 (3), pp. 596–624.
Carrera, F., Stoian, D., Campos, J.J., Morales, J. and Pinelo, G. (2006), 'Forest certification in Guatemala', in B. Cashore, F. Gale, E. Meidinger and D. Newsom (eds) *Confronting sustainability: forest certification in developing and transitioning countries*, pp. 363–406. New Haven, Connecticut, USA: Yale School of Forestry and Environmental Studies, available at www.yale.edu/forestcertification/symposium/pdfs/guatemala_symposium.pdf (accessed February 2012).
Cashore, B. (2002) 'Legitimacy and the privatization of environmental governance: how non state market-driven (NSMD) governance systems gain rule making authority', *Governance: An International Journal of Policy and Administration*, vol. 15, no. 4 (October), pp. 503–529.
Cashore, B., Auld, G., Bernstein, S. and McDermott, C. (2007), 'Can non state governance 'ratchet up' global environmental standards? Lessons from the Forest Sector', *Review of European Community and International Environmental Law*, 16 (2), pp. 158–72.
Cashore, B., Auld, G., Newsom, D. (2004), *Governing Through Markets. Forest Certification and the Emergence of Non-state Authority*. New Haven, CT: Yale University Press.
Cashore, B., Gale, F., Meidinger, E. and Newsom, D. (2006), 'Confronting sustainability: forest certification in developing and transitioning countries', *Environment*, 48 (9), pp. 6–25.
Cerutti, P. O., Tacconi, L., Nasi, R. and Lescuyer, G. (2011), 'Legal vs. certified timber: preliminary impacts of forest certification in Cameroon', *Forest Policy and Economics*, 13 (3), pp. 184–190.
Chan, S. and Pattberg, P. (2008), 'Private rule-making and the politics of accountability: analyzing global forest governance', *Global Environmental Politics*, 8 (3), pp. 103–121.
Counsell, S., and Loraas, K.J. (2002), *Trading in Credibility: The Myth and Reality of the Forest Stewardship Council*. London, UK: Rainforest Foundation.
Dimitrov, R.S., Sprinz, D.F., DiGuisto, G. and Kelle, A. (2007), 'International non-regimes: a research agenda', *International Studies Review*, 9 (2), pp. 230–258.
Dingwerth, K. (2007), *The New Transnationalism: Transnational Governance and Democratic Legitimacy*. Basingstoke: Palgrave Macmillan.
Dingwerth, K. (2008), 'North-South parity in Global governance: the affirmative procedures of the Forest Stewardship Council', *Global Governance*, 14, 53–71.
Dryzek, J.S. and Stevenson, H. (2011), 'Global democracy and earth system governance', *Ecological Economics*, 70 (11), pp. 1865–1874.
Ebeling, J. (2005), 'The effectiveness of market-based conservation: can forest certification compensate for poor environmental regulation in the tropics?' Paper prepared for the 2005 Berlin Conference on the Human Dimensions of Global Environmental Change 'International Organizations and Global Environmental Governance', Berlin, Germany, 2–3 December 2005.
Ebeling, J. and Yasue, M. (2009), 'The effectiveness of market-based conservation

in the tropics: forest certification in Ecuador and Bolivia', *Journal of Environmental Management*, 90, 1145–1153.

Forest Stewardship Council (1998) Interim Dispute Resolution Protocol, adopted by the board 27 January 1998, Document 1.4.2, Bonn, Germany.

Forest Stewardship Council (2003), FSC Social Strategy: Building and Implementing a Social Agenda, Version 2.1.

Forest Stewardship Council (2009a), FSC Statutes.

Forest Stewardship Council (2009b), FSC By-laws. Bonn: FSC, A.C.

Forest Stewardship Council (2010), FSC members list 2010.12.

Forest Stewardship Council (2011a), FSC New Members 2011, generated 6 June, 2011.

Forest Stewardship Council (2011b), FSC website at www.fsc.org/governance.html (accessed August, 2011).

Forest Stewardship Council (2011c). FSC website at www.fsc.org/fsc-locations.html (accessed August, 2011).

Forest Stewardship Council (2011d), Global FSV Certificates: types and distribution. FSC Forest Area Growth, June 2011 available at www.mx/fsc.org/fileadmin/fsc-mexico/page-content/download/Global_FSC_certificates-EN-pdf

Forest Stewardship Council_US (2010) FSC_US Forest Management Standard (v.1.0) (w/o FF Indicators and Guidance), Recommended by FSC_US Board, May 2010; approved by FSC_IC, July 2010, available at www.fcsus.org/standards-criteria/forest_management.php.

Franck, T.M. (1990), *The Power of Legitimacy among Nations*. New York: Oxford University Press.

Gale, F. (2009), 'An institutional analysis of FSC governance', in Tollefson, C., Gale, F. and Haley, D. (eds) (2009), *Setting the Standard: Certification, Governance, and the Forest Stewardship Council*, Vancouver: UBC Press.

Gale, F. and Haward, M. (2004), 'Public accountability in private regulation: contrasting models of the Forest Stewardship Council (FSC) and Marine Stewardship Council (MSC)', Refereed paper presented to the Australasian Political Studies Association Conference, University of Adelaide, 29 September–1 October, 2004.

Garrelts, H. and Flitner, M. (2011), 'Governance issues in the Ecosystem Approach: what lessons from the Forest Stewardship Council?', *European Journal of Forest Research*, 130 (3), pp. 395–405.

Gereffi G., Garcia-Johnson R. and Sasser E. (2001), 'The NGO–industrial complex', *Foreign Policy*, 125, pp. 56–65.

Glasbergen, P. (2011), 'Mechanisms of private meta-governance: an analysis of global private governance for sustainable development', *International Journal of Strategic Business Alliances*, 2 (3), pp. 189–205.

Gulbrandsen, L.H. (2004), 'Overlapping public and private governance: can forest certification fill the gaps in the global forest regime?', *Global Environmental Politics*, 4 (2), pp.75–99.

Gulbrandsen, L.H. (2005), 'The effectiveness of non-state governance schemes: a comparative study of forest certification in Norway and Sweden', *International Environmental Agreements: Politics, Law and Economics*, 5, pp. 125–149.

Gulbrandsen, L.H. (2008), 'Accountability arrangements in non-state standards organizations: instrumental design and imitation', *Organization*, 15 (4), pp. 563–583.

Hirschberger, P. (2008) 'WWF European Forest Programme (2005): the effects of FSC-certification in Estonia, Germany, Latvia, Russia, Sweden & the United Kingdom: An analysis of corrective action requests (by Peter Hirschberger).' Summary report. Available at: http://assets.panda.org/downloads/fscsummaryanalysisallcountries.pdf (accessed June, 2008).
Holvoet B. and Muys, B. (2004), 'Sustainable forest management worldwide: a comparative assessment of standards', *International Forestry Review* 6 (2), pp. 99–122.
Hooghe, L. and Marks, G. (2003), 'Unravelling the central state, but how? Types of multi-level governance', *American Political Science Review*, 97 (2), pp. 233–243.
Hurd, I. (1999), 'Legitimacy and authority in international politics', *International Organization*, 53 (2), pp. 379–408.
Hurrelmann, A., Schneider, S. and Steffek, J. (2007), 'Conclusion: legitimacy-making sense of an essentially contested concept', in *Legitimacy in an Age of Global Politics*, Houndmills: Palgrave Macmillan, pp. 229–237.
Karmann, M. and Smith, A. (2009), FSC Reflected in Scientific and Professional Literature. Literature Study on the Outcomes and Impacts of FSC Certification. FSC, Bonn. Available at www.fsc.org/fileadmin/web-data/public/document_-center/ publications/FSC_Policy_Series/Impacts_report_-_Karmann_2009.pdf (accessed August, 2010).
Klooster, D. (2005), 'Environmental certification of forests: the evolution of environmental governance in a commodity network', in *Journal of Rural Studies*, 21 (4), pp. 403–417.
Klooster, D. (2006), 'Environmental certification of forests in Mexico: the political ecology of a nongovernmental market intervention', *Annals of the Association of American Geographers*, 96 (3), pp. 541–565.
Koppell, J.G.S. (2003), *The Politics of Quasi Government. Hybrid Organizations and the Dynamics of Bureaucratic Control.* Cambridge: Cambridge University Press.
Krasner, S. (1982), 'Structural causes and regime consequences: regimes as intervening variables', *International Organization*, 36 (2), pp. 185–205.
Lövbrand, E., Rindefjäll, T. and Nordqvist, J. (2009), 'Closing the legitimacy gap in global environmental governance? Lessons from the emerging CDM market', *Global Environmental Politics,* 9 (2), pp. 74–100.
Marx, A. (2011), 'Global governance and the certification revolution: types, trends and challenges', in D. Levi-Faur (2011) *Handbook on the Politics of Regulation.* Cheltenham: Edward Elgar.
Marx, A. and Cuypers, D. (2010), 'Forest certification as a global environmental governance tool: What is the impact of the Forest Stewardship Council?' *Regulation and Governance*, 4 (4), pp. 408–434.
Mechel, F., Meyer-Ohlendorf, N., Sprang, P. and Tarasofsky, R. (2006), *Public Procurement and Forest Certification: Assessing for Policy, Law and International Trade*. Berlin: Eco-Logic in association with Chatham House.
Meidinger, E. (2003), 'Forest certification as a global civil society regulatory institution', in E. Meidinger, C. Elliott and G. Oesten (eds), *Social and Political Dimensions of Forest Certification*. Remagen-Oberwinter, Germany: Forstbuch Verlag, pp. 265–292.
Meidinger, E. (2006), 'The administrative law of global private-public regulation: the case of forestry', *The European Journal of International Law*, 17 (1), pp. 47–87.

Meidinger, E. (2007), Beyond Westphalia: competitive legalization in emerging transnational regulatory systems', in Brutsch, C., Lehmkuhl, D. (eds) *Law and Legalization in Transnational Relations*. Oxford: Routledge, pp. 121–143.
Meidinger, E. (2011), 'Forest certification and democracy', *European Journal of Forest Research*, 130 (3), pp. 407–419.
Miles, E., Underdal, A., Andresen, S., Wettestad, J., Skjaerseth, J.B. and Carlin, E.M. (2002), *Environmental Regime Effectiveness. Confronting Theory with Evidence*. Cambridge, MA: MIT Press.
Nebel, G., Quevedo, L., Jacobsen, J.B. and Helles, F. (2005), 'Development and economics significance of forest certification: the case of FSC in Bolivia', *Forest Policy and Economics*, 7 (2), pp. 175–186.
Overdevest, C. (2010), 'Comparing forest certification schemes: the case of ratcheting standards in the forest sector', *Socio-Economic Review*, 8 (1), pp. 47–76.
Pattberg, P. (2005), 'What role for private rule-making in global environmental governance? Analysing the Forest Stewardship Council (FSC)', *International Environmental Agreements: Politics, Law and Economics*, 5 (2), pp. 175–89.
Rayner, J., Buck, A. and Katila, P. (2011), *Embracing Complexity: Meeting the Challenges of International Forest Governance. A Global Assessment Report by the Global Forest Expert Panel on the International Forest Regime*. Vienna: International Union of Forest Research Organizations.
Rezende de Azevedo, T. and Giacini de Freitas, A. (2003), Annex 1: Forest certification in Brazil: The parallel evolution of community forest management in the Brazilian Amazon and FSC certification', in Molnar, A. (ed.) *Forest Certification and Communities*. Washington DC: Forest Trends.
Rodrik, D. (2011), *The Globalization Paradox. Why Global Markets, States, and Democracy Can't Coexist*. Oxford: Oxford University Press.
Romzek, B.S. and Dubnick, M.J. (1987), 'Accountability in the public sector: lessons from the challenger tragedy', *Public Administration Review*, 47 (3), pp. 227–238.
Romzek, B.S. and Dubnick, M.J. (1994), 'Issues of accountablity in flexible personnel systems', in P.W. Ingraham and B.S. Romzek (eds) *New Paradigms for Government. Issues for the Changing Public Services*. San Francisco: Jossey-Bass, pp. 263–294.
Ruggie, J. (1975) 'International responses to technology: concepts and trends, *International Organization*, 29 (3), pp. 557–583.
Sabel, C., O'Rourke, D. and Fung, A. (2000), 'Ratcheting labor standards: regulation for continuous improvement in the global workplace', Social Protection Discussion Paper No. 0011. Washington DC: World Bank.
Scharpf, F.W. (1997), 'Economic integration, democracy and the welfare state', *Journal of European Public Policy*, 4 (1), pp. 18–36.
Scharpf, F.W. (1999), *Governing in Europe: effective and democratic?* Oxford: Oxford University Press.
Schmidt, V. (2011), 'Democracy and legitimacy in the European Union revisited: input, output and "throughput"'. Paper presented at the 12th EUSA Conference. Boston.
Schulze, M., Grogan, J. and Vidal, E. (2008), 'Forest certification in Amazonia: standards matter', *Oryx*, 42 (2), pp. 229–239.
Tikina, A. and Innes, J. (2008), 'A framework for assessing the effectiveness of forest certification', *Canadian Journal of Forest Resources*, 38 (6), 1357–1365.

Vogel, D. (2008), 'Private global business regulation', *Annual Review of Political Science*, 11, pp. 61–282.
Waarden, F. van (2011), 'Varieties of private market regulation: problems and prospects', in D. Levi-Faur (2011), *Handbook on the Politics of Regulation*. Cheltenham: Edward Elgar.
World Wide Fund for Nature (2001), WWF Position Statement, March 14, 2001.
Young, O.R. (1980) 'International regimes: problems of concept formation', *World Politics*, 32 (3), pp. 331–56.
Young, O.R. (1994), 'The effectiveness of international governance systems', in O.R. Young, *International Governance: Protecting the Enrivonment in a Stateless Society*. Ithaca, NY: Cornell University Press, pp. 140–160.

4. Private standards in global agri-food chains

Spencer Henson and John Humphrey

INTRODUCTION

The evolution of private standards in agri-food chains over the last 10 to 20 years has raised profound questions about the role of public and private institutions in governing food safety and quality and the wider social and environmental impacts of the agri-food system. These standards are applied to production for domestic markets and to food traded across borders. With respect to trade, concerns have been raised about the extent to which private standards can act to exclude producers (and particularly small producers) in developing countries from potentially lucrative international markets (WTO, 2007). Further, the growth of private standards might also challenge the legitimacy of public regulation in spheres such as food safety (see, for example, Fuchs and Kalfagianni, 2010) and established forms of governance of international trade, such as the World Trade Organization (WTO) and the Codex Alimentarius Commission.[1]

The aim of this chapter is to provide clarity regarding the nature of private standards and how they relate to and differ from public regulations and international guidelines on food safety. To do this, the chapter addresses three issues that will be explored in turn. First, it looks at the diversity of private standards, and in particular the distinction between private standards that are oriented to product differentiation and those that are primarily concerned with ensuring compliance with market and regulatory requirements. Second, it examines the reasons why private standards have become important in the global agri-food sector and the interrelationship between private standards and the public sphere, including both regulations on food safety and international guidelines such as the Codex Alimentarius. Third, it discusses the ways in which private standards can be considered to 'go beyond' or be more stringent than public regulations.

PRIVATE STANDARDS: AN OVERVIEW

There are five specific functions involved in operationalising a private standard. These operations define the key characteristics of private standards.

Setting a Standard

Private standard-setting organisations constitute a diverse group. Individual companies may create private standards as part of their strategies to differentiate products. Examples include Tesco's Nature's Choice and Carrefour's *Filières Qualité*. Standards are also created by producer associations, which are often nationally based. These include Swedish Seal, the Label Rouge programme in France and the various sectoral standards united under the Assured British Food label. Retailers and processors may also create standards. These groups have been the driving forces behind international standards such as GLOBALG.A.P.,[2] the British Retail Consortium Global Standard (BRC), the International Food Standard (IFS) and the Aquaculture Certification Council's (ACC) Best Aquaculture Practice (BAP) standard. However, standards can also be created by specialist standard-setting companies, by NGOs or by alliances of different types of organisation, as discussed by Abbott and Snidal (2009). Even governments can create private standards, as was the case with the Safe Quality Food (SQF) standard, first developed by the government of Western Australia.

Standard-setters make decisions about the horizontal and vertical scope of the standards they create. Here horizontal scope refers to the range of issues covered by the private standard. In the case of the food industry, standards that are primarily concerned with food safety also frequently include items relating to environmental impact and labour or social issues. While compliance with food safety standards is a major motive for private standards development, leading companies are also concerned about their brand image and the 'triple bottom line' of profit, planet and people. Vertical scope refers to the extension of the standard along the value chain. Some standards focus on one particular stage in the chain – for example, GLOBALG.A.P. is a pre-farm gate standard, and the BRC Global Standard focuses on processing, while the IFS standard and FSSC 22000 are applicable across the whole value chain.

Adopting a Standard

Standards become tangible when they are adopted. Companies adopt standards when they decide to follow a standard themselves or when they require their suppliers to do so. A private company can adopt a standard by requiring implementation by its suppliers. This could be a standard developed by the company itself, or one it helped to develop, for example, as part of a standards-setting coalition. Companies can also adopt standards created by others. So, for example, a number of seafood companies formed the ACC and developed the BAP standard. Other companies are free to use the standards in their own operations or to require that their suppliers are certified to this standard.

The decision to adopt a standard is an important driver of the spread and influence of private standards. The adoption of private standards for both primary production and food processing by retailers has been an important factor in the spread of private standards, and one of the main factors behind the concerns about private standards raised by developing countries, for example in the WTO. The extent to which private standards are truly voluntary depends on the form and level of power wielded by the entities adopting those standards; that is, the nature of the entities requiring that the standard be implemented by other value chain actors. But, other actors in value chains can adopt standards. Producer organisations develop their own standards as a means of branding their products or in order to gain control over the standardisation process. In some cases, governments adopt private standards. For some products, the EU requires production facilities to be certified to the ISO 9000 standard.

Implementation

Standards are implemented by the organisation that is conforming to the standard. Implementation means following the rules laid down by the standard and creating the systems and processes needed for conformity. In the case of a standard like the BRC Global Standard for Food Safety, the implementer is the company that applies the standard in its own operations.

Conformity Assessment

Standards acquire force when their implementation is verified. Conformity assessment is the process by which compliance with standards is verified. There are various means of assessing conformity, including self-declaration by the implementer of the standard, inspection by the standards adopter (so-called second-party certification) and inspection by a third party (so-called third-party certification). Third-party certification carried out by independent certification bodies has become the norm for many private food safety standards. This practice is in line with the guidelines created by the International Organisation for Standardization (ISO). The ISO has developed guidelines for both the operation of standards schemes and for the conduct of audits by certification bodies.

Enforcement

This refers to the approaches employed in response to non-compliance and sanctions if corrective action is not taken. The standard setter has to have some procedure for responding to the results of the conformity assessment, either by invoking corrective action or withdrawing the right of the organisation to claim certification.

TWO TYPES OF PRIVATE STANDARDS

Not all private standards are the same. Private standards enforced through audit and certification are designed to provide assurances to actors at other points in the value chain that certain hard-to-verify characteristics of products are indeed present. In many cases, these characteristics are extrinsic to the product (for example, products not involving the use of child labour, avoidance of adverse environmental impacts, use of good hygiene practices, safe handling of food, and so on).

Following the line of thought taken by the 2002 Commission on Farming and Food in England (see Kirk-Wilson, 2002), we distinguish between two types of private standards: 'baseline' schemes and 'premium' or 'high-level' schemes. Premium schemes are designed to distinguish food products of particular origins from food products more generally by establishing superior attributes that will appeal to certain categories of consumers. The French Label Rouge scheme for poultry is an example. The scheme certifies farmers that use slow-growing chickens and particular types of feed that are intended to result in a superior-tasting product. Farmers in the scheme also meet certain environmental impact and animal welfare standards through the adoption of practices such as maintaining small flocks, free-range production and limiting the distance travelled to abattoirs (EU/DG Joint Research Centre, 2008). In a quite different way, the Fairtrade certification scheme presents consumers with the opportunity to purchase products that claim to benefit the poor in developing countries to a greater extent than 'mainstream' products. According to the Fairtrade Foundation website, 'Fairtrade is a strategy for poverty alleviation and sustainable development. Its purpose is to create opportunities for producers and workers who have been economically disadvantaged or marginalized by the conventional trading system.'[3] There are many other certification schemes that aim to establish a difference between the products they certify from the general run of products available to consumers. The Marine Stewardship Council (MSC) certifies that fish are sourced from sustainably-managed fisheries. The Kenya Flower Council's (KFC) labelling scheme substantiates claims about environmental impact and working conditions on flower farms. In Germany, the Naturland scheme[4] certifies farmers to organic and Fairtrade standards, while the Neuland scheme focuses on animal welfare and environmentally-friendly production (EU/DG Joint Research Centre, 2006).

Baseline schemes, in contrast, are not designed to establish the uniqueness of particular products. As the name suggests, these are aimed at meeting the required minimum level of performance for access to particular market segments. The specified performance level is 'order qualifying': it is a condition of market access. With respect to private food standards, these performance standards are often established by large companies in retail and processing, and can be either business-to-business or business-to-consumer. The standards developed or adopted by retailer groupings fall into the baseline scheme category. Standards such as SQF 1000 and 2000, FSSC 22000, GLOBALG.A.P., IFS and the BRC Global Standard are all examples of baseline standards. Their primary function is to ensure that internationalised supply chains in the food industry meet certain minimum standards. The primary aim of all of these standards is to ensure that, even though global food value chains are becoming more organisationally complex and more geographically dispersed, food companies have some confidence that the food they are purchasing and selling to consumers is safe. In the case of fruit and vegetable production, this is achieved through providing clear guidelines, backed up by auditing and enforcement, on procedures relating to water and soil quality, pesticide selection and use, and food hygiene practices. In addition to a focus on food safety, such standards may incorporate other issues that are relevant to the brand image of the purchasing companies. These frequently include environmental impact and labour standards, but may also refer to issues such as animal welfare, land rights and impact on communities, according to the particular circumstances surrounding the production and processing of different products. One of the characteristics of these standards, as they are used by retailers and processors, is that they are tools for managing business-to-business relationships and are generally 'invisible' to the consumer.

Retailers and processors are not the only generators of these baseline standards. Producer organisations within particular countries also develop private standards aimed at showing compliance with 'order qualifying' requirements. Examples include the range of product-specific standards grouped under the Red Tractor, or Assured Food Standards, scheme in the UK and the Seal (Svenskt Sigill) scheme in Sweden. For producers, these standards may have the advantage of being more closely tailored to the specific circumstances of national production systems. While such schemes may also make claims about animal welfare, environmental impact, quality and taste, their primary function is to ensure that farming systems are producing food that is safe to eat. Such schemes may pre-empt the international schemes promoted by retailers and processors, or offer an alternative to these.[5] Although these national producer schemes have much in common with the business-to-business standards discussed above, they are usually visible to consumers (for example, the Red Tractor logo). Producers have an interest in implying that their food is superior to that sourced from other countries.

Finally, individual retailers also develop baseline standards. There is, for example, a considerable degree of overlap between Tesco's Nature's Choice standard and the GLOBALG.A.P. standard for fresh fruit and vegetables. Indeed, these standards are sometimes audited simultaneously. However, Tesco's literature on Nature's Choice emphasises quality and environmental impact rather than food safety.

WHY HAVE PRIVATE STANDARDS PROLIFERATED AND WHAT IS THE RELATIONSHIP BETWEEN PUBLIC REGULATIONS AND PRIVATE STANDARDS?

The increasing prevalence of private standards in global agri-food trade, and in particular in the European Union (EU), has led to concerns being expressed about the nature and impact of these standards. The emergence of private standards audited by third parties has been one area of concern raised in recent years at the WTO (WTO, 2007). A recent paper on private standards published by the ISO (ISO, 2010) summarised the concerns felt by a number of international organisations and national governments, particularly in developing countries:[6]

- As they are being developed by the private sector, the standards 'do not necessarily adhere to the same principles as a formal international standardizing organization (i.e., WTO TBT principles of transparency, openness, impartiality and consensus, etc.)' (ISO, 2010, p.6).
- Some concerns have been expressed, especially in developing countries, that certain agri-food private standards (e.g., GLOBAL-

G.A.P. – previously EUREPGAP) may at times exceed requirements (e.g., for certain minimum pesticide residue limits) which are established in regulations or 'international standards'. In this area, these are typically international standards developed by the intergovernmental Codex Alimentarius Commission (CAC) (ISO, 2010, p.7).

- The existence of a growing multitude of private standards in such fields as ICT, agri-food and on social and environmental issues, may ultimately confuse users and consumers, thereby diminishing their important market, safety, social or environmental effect (ISO, 2010, p. 8).

In what sense, therefore, do private standards either 'go beyond' existing public regulations and international guidelines (such as those provided by the Codex) or introduce undesirable elements into standards because of the non-adherents to principles followed by international standardising organisations? Answering this question requires consideration of how private standards were developed in the 1990s, predominantly in response to changing food safety regulations and challenges to consumer confidence. These processes were seen particularly clearly in the UK. In the mid-1990s, three different private standards were developed in the UK. The first was the set of standards that became the UK food assurance schemes grouped under the Red Tractor logo. The Assured Produce Scheme (APS) for horticulture was implemented in 1997, but it was based on a ten-year partnership between retailers and growers (Kirk-Wilson, 2002). Second, at the same time, large European food retailers, grouped together in the European fresh produce retailers working group (Eurep), produced the EUREPGAP standard, which applied similar standards to the APS scheme but also applied them to imported produce.[7] Third, a working group consisting of retailers, inspection bodies, trade bodies and the UK accreditation service began work on the BRC standard for food processing plants. The first edition of this standard was produced in 1998 (Swoffer, 2005).

UK retailers, most notably supermarkets, played an important role in the promulgation of all three of these standards. The first two standards were concerned with the supply chain for fresh fruit and vegetables, while the BRC standard was, according to Swoffer (2005), developed by retailers in order to govern autonomous processing plants that manufactured their own-label products.

The most important factor driving these initiatives was, undoubtedly, the UK Food Safety Act of 1990. This introduced 'strict liability' for food business operators, such that they would be held responsible for the safety of the food that they provided to consumers. The implication was that food businesses could not employ a 'warranty defence' based on assurances from their suppliers that the food or food products they supplied were safe.[8] The Food Safety Act did, however, allow one defence for food business operators. They would not be held responsible if they could show that they had exercised 'due diligence' in ensuring that the supply chain was delivering safe food. The immediate response by retailers to this challenge was to increase monitoring and control of supply chains. However, Swoffer suggests that this led to a 'free for all' in which each company introduced its own approach, creating not only confusion and conflict but also a lack of accreditation and control mechanisms (Swoffer, 2005). The costs for each retailer were also an impediment to competitiveness (Henson and Northen, 1998). The standards introduced in the late 1990s enabled retailers to simplify their control procedures, establish proper procedures for accreditation and certification in line with international standards, outsource some of the monitoring and control processes and pass on much of the attendant costs of compliance to suppliers.

In addition, there was a tightening up of the legislative framework across the EU. In horticulture, more restrictive legislation on pesticide residues reinforced the need for private standards schemes to ensure that on-farm practices and procedures could meet these more stringent requirements. Furthermore, food safety scandals in Europe undermined consumer confidence. In particular, Bovine Spongiform Encephalopathy (BSE) was a key driver of the EU's General Food Law, which placed 'primary legal responsibility for ensuring food safety' firmly onto food business operators (CEC, 2002, preamble to paragraph 30).[9] This devolution of responsibility reflects a more general shift to neo-liberalism, with enhanced fiscal constraints on public regulatory agencies and a belief that regulators should work with the private sector rather than seeing themselves simply as enforcers (Busch et al., 2005). In this context, therefore, baseline private standards should be seen largely as a response to public regulation. In the case of maximum residue levels for antibiotics in farmed fish, for example, the public regulation defines an outcome: EU regulations state that the maximum residue level for chloramphenicol in food of any sort should be zero. In response to this requirement (and similar restrictions in other importing countries), private standards such as GLOBALG.A.P. and the ACC introduced rules that were designed to ensure that the shrimp value chain (including feed producers, hatcheries, ponds and processing facilities) produce shrimp without excessive residues. As feed is one route to antibiotic contamination, the GLOBALG.A.P. aquaculture standard specifies a set of rules to be implemented with respect to record keeping for feed:[10]

- Batches of feed from feed manufacturer must be traceable to batches of fish. System or documentation must be in place.
- Records for fish feed must be in place for purchased feed in the past three years.
- Labels/invoices/statements specifying constituents must be in place kept [sic] for three years. Compound feed used on farms have [sic] to be obtained from a GLOBALG.A.P. (EUREPGAP) approved source.
- Detailed records must be assessed for all additives utilized in feed.
- Feed whose shelf life has expired must not be used. Feed in store must be assessed to assess expiry dates on labels.
- Detailed records of results from tests and analyses must be in place for all relevant contaminants present in feed.

It follows that this part of the GLOBALG.A.P. standard is not 'going beyond' or 'more stringent than' public regulations. Rather, it presents a means of complying with the public regulation. Where private standards do 'go beyond' public standards is when they incorporate additional requirements that are of interest to the adopters of the standard: for example, when the GLOBALG.A.P. aquaculture standard also includes specific control points for shrimp production relating to mangrove swamps and 'social criteria' (GLOBALG.A.P., 2009). Issues relating to environmental impact, preservation of biodiversity, land rights and impacts on local communities are potentially sources of embarrassment and brand damage for retailers, and for this reason are packaged together with food safety.[11]

So, public regulations define product characteristics. Private standards create rules and enforcement procedures so that products meet public regulatory standards. The rules laid down by private standards follow very closely the good practice guidelines produced by the Codex Alimentarius Commission, but complement them with further measures, including prerequisite programmes and specifications of how the guidelines are to be operationalised through managerial practice.

The Codex codes of practice for production, processing, manufacturing, transport and storage are frequently expressed in guidelines that have been drawn from best practice on food safety, codified by Codex and incorporated into numerous standards. These guidelines draw on and influence private standards. So, for example, the HACCP programmes in private standards for food processing (BRC Global Standard, IFS, SQF 2000, and so on) apply the seven HACCP principles defined in the Codex (Swoffer, 2008). Similarly, the Codex principles for food hygiene, first formulated in 1969 and subsequently revised (Codex Alimentarius Commission, 2003b), have been incorporated into many private food safety standards. The general hygiene principles of Codex are complemented by more specific standards for particular products. Comparison between Codex principles for food hygiene in fruit and vegetables (Codex Alimentarius Commission, 2003a) and EUREPGAP shows considerable overlap in the scope of the two documents.[12] In the area of pesticide use, the Codex makes recommendations with respect to only using authorised chemicals, mixing chemicals in a way that avoids contamination of water and land and protecting employees from hazards. It recommends that:

> Growers should keep records of agricultural chemical applications. Records should include information on the date of application, the chemical used, the crop sprayed, the pest or disease against which it was used, the concentration, method and frequency of application, and records on harvesting to verify that the time between application and harvesting is appropriate. (Codex Alimentarius Commission, 2003a, Section 3.2.1.4).

The EUREPGAP standard covers very similar issues, making specific reference to the use of officially-registered or permitted crop protection products, the availability of facilities for the safe and efficient handling of crop protection products and requiring detailed record-keeping about the use of these products, including observation of pre-harvest intervals (EUREPGAP, 2005, section 8).

Given this degree of overlap, why do companies go to the trouble of developing standards at all? Even though a substantial proportion of the costs of standards compliance falls on the supply base, companies still have to work together to develop the standard in the first place. Implementing the standard increases costs along the supply chain, and some of these costs will be reflected in the prices paid to producers. To understand why retailers will go to these lengths to implement standards, further consideration of how standards are constructed is required.

STANDARDS AND STANDARDS SCHEMES

It has already been noted that private standards frequently include additional items beyond those specified in Codex guidelines. This has been the case since the development of the very first private standards schemes. For example, the UK Lion quality scheme for eggs (part of the UK Red Tractor family of standards) includes 'controls on the handling of end-of-lay hens, banning of induced moulting and controls on beak trimming' (Kirk-Wilson, 2002, p.15). Further, EUREPGAP included provisions for environmental impact and worker welfare. But these 'additional' concerns are not the main driver of the standards. Rather, once a standard exists, the designers and promoters of the standard can include additional items of concern to customers at reduced cost. It is important, however, not to distract attention away from the core function of these standards – to assure food safety, with public regulations as the key driver. Similarly, private standards are more agile than international guidelines in responding to new concerns and new hazards.

Companies go to the trouble of creating and promoting private standards directed at securing food safety even though widely-accepted international guidelines exist in this area because they institute standards schemes, not simply standards per se. At the beginning of this chapter, the standardising procedure was divided into five different parts: standard-setting; adoption; implementation; conformity assessment; and enforcement. The Codex guidelines discussed earlier in this chapter identify the objectives to be achieved by food safety systems and particular ways (not necessarily just one) in which these objectives might best be achieved.[13] As a result, they focus almost entirely on the first part of the standardising procedure, which is standard-setting. It is up to others to pursue the other parts. The Codex guidelines are taken up by many agencies and used as the basis for recommended good practice in agriculture, food handling and food processing. The rationale for making these recommendations is that food producers, handlers and processors will have clear guidance on how to improve the safety of the products coming out of their operations. In other words, once the standard exists, it is up to businesses to decide whether or not to adopt and implement it.

The private standards discussed above are very different. When a retailer supports the development of the standard and then decides to make it a condition of access to its supply chain (that is, it adopts the standard) it is demanding that a different firm implements the standard. The standard is a device for changing the way in which monitoring and control are exercised along the value chain, switching from the situation of direct supervision by the purchasing company (or its agents) to third-party certification of suppliers. In these circumstances, the standard has to deliver the same degree of confidence about supplier conformity to the standard as would have been obtained by direct supervision. In other words, the central elements of a standard scheme are implementation (clear guidelines on precisely what is required from the supplier), conformity assessment and enforcement. The first area in which a standard scheme differs from the standard per se is in identifying whether or not the firm intending to implement the standard is in a position to do so, usually through the specification of 'prerequisite programmes'. Swoffer (2009, p.2) defines a prerequisite programme as: 'The basic conditions and activities that are necessary to maintain an hygienic environment suitable for the production of safe food.' These prerequisites are not part of the standard itself, but rather a series of preconditions. Thus, for example, in order for the ISO 22000 standard to be turned into a standard scheme, a prerequisite programme, PAS 220, was formulated by the British Standards Institute (BSI).[14] Once the defined prerequisites are in place, conformity to the control points defined by the standard itself has to be established through third-party audit, following the preparation of documentation and internal audits. To enable the standard to be auditable, it has to be written in a prescriptive fashion. Thus, private standards-setters can be seen as translating the rules of Codex into standards that provide sufficient guidance for implementers to know what they are required to do in order to comply and also for conformity assessors to undertake an objective assessment of when compliance has been achieved. This process of translation is necessary in order that a standard can be audited in a manner that is compatible with ISO guidelines (for example, Guide 65 on General requirements for bodies operating product certification systems). For example, the Codex General Principles of Food Hygiene stipulate that a food safety system should enable traceability, while private standards such as the BRC Global Standard for Food Safety and IFS specify the substantive elements this system should contain, how this system should perform and how the effectiveness of this system should be monitored.

It is probably this central part of the standards scheme that raises most concerns for developing countries. Farm-level standards (such as GLOBALG.A.P. and SQF 1000) require that farmers meet the requirements of prerequisite programmes, and show that they have complied with the control points in the standard that are designed to control hazards. The costs, not only of compliance but also of demonstrating compliance through documentation and the operation of management systems, may substantially affect the competitiveness of small farmers relative to large farmers. A standards scheme relies on maintaining control over producers and processes. Mithöfer et al. (2007) found that Kenyan exporters spent 3.5 hours per acre each week monitoring conditions on smallholder farms organised into outgrower schemes, compared to only 0.1 hours per acre each week on large farms. The biggest challenge, and the greatest expense, of implementing private standards apparently derive not from the extent to which these standards 'go beyond' the principles set down by international guidelines, but rather in the translation of guidelines into standards schemes. These change the fundamental economics of small-scale farms. Thus, GLOBALG.A.P. increases the costs faced by exporters; the costs of operating the certification scheme and maintaining the integrity of its controls is considerably higher in supply chains consisting of appreciable numbers of small farmers than if exporters procure from a limited number of medium- or large-scale producers. Exporters will only procure from smallholders if there are benefits from doing so that offset, in whole or in part, these additional control costs.

Nevertheless, in translating the general rules of the Codex into unambiguous statements about how compliance is to be assessed there is scope for differing degrees of prescription and differing arrangements for establishing equivalence. For example, it is generally accepted that chemicals should be stored safely on a farm, but the arrangements for this can be specified in different ways. EUREPGAP specified that 'crop protection product storage facilities are built in a manner which is structurally sound and robust' (EUREPGAP, 2005, control point 8.8.2). In contrast, the aquaculture compliance criteria of the ACC states specifically that the safe storage of chemicals requires concrete buildings and steel doors of a prescribed thickness. The latter stipulates very specific solutions to the risks identified with chemical storage, while the former states a desired outcome and allows the auditor to judge whether or not the particular means of achieving it are adequate. This is why the development of national equivalent standards (for example, KenyaGAP or ChileGAP, benchmarked to GLOBALG.A.P.) can play an important role in making explicit solutions that are more suited to local circumstances but equivalent in outcome.

CONCLUSIONS

In this chapter we set out to provide greater clarity to debates about the 'rights' and 'wrongs' of private standards relating to food safety. The ongoing discourse about the legitimacy of private standards in global agri-food systems and the potential impacts, for example on vulnerable producers in developing countries, has tended to adopt a rather simplistic view of the forms such standards take, how and why they have evolved, and their relationship to public regulations. Failing to appreciate the complexity of private food safety standards, however, shrouds any real understanding of the implications for food safety governance in global agri-food value chains, and in particular what can be done to address the attendant concerns. As we have seen, private standards *per se* represent just one part of a multi-stage and multi-faceted process by which food safety is governed along agri-food value chains. Thus, private food safety standards are generally implemented as part of standards schemes that aim to provide levels of assurance over food safety, defined predominantly in terms of regulatory compliance, and at the same time act to reduce and/or reallocate the attendant control costs along the value chain. While recognising that private food safety standards do at times 'go beyond' regulatory requirements, it is important to appreciate that the evolution of public regulations has been a major driver of private food safety schemes, most notably in Europe. Seeing public regulations and private standards as distinct entities, therefore, somewhat misrepresents the evolution of food safety governance and confounds attempts to represent one or the other as 'legitimate' versus 'illegitimate'.

NOTES

1 See, for example, the discussion on private standards at the 31st meeting of the Codex Alimentarius Commission in Geneva in 2008 (Codex Alimenatius Commission, 2008). This pointed to the potential for private standards to 'undermine the scientific basis and the democratic adoption of the official standards of the OIE in the field of animal health' (Codex Alimentarius Commission, 2008, p.2) and the need to avoid private standards conflicting with the OIE's own standards.
2 In this chapter, mentions of GLOBALG.A.P. will refer only to the standard for fresh fruit and vegetables, unless explicitly indicated otherwise.
3 See www.fairtrade.org.uk/what_is_fairtrade/fairtrade_certification_and_the_fairtrade_mark/the_fairtrade_mark.aspx
4 See www.naturland.de/organic_fair_one_source.html
5 In the UK, the Assured British Produce standard (one of the Assured British Food standards) is accepted as equivalent to GLOBALG.A.P. although it is not formally benchmarked. GLOBALG.A.P. also benchmarks equivalent national GAP schemes in developing countries such as Chile.
6 The Codex Alimentarius Commission received two papers for discussion on private standards in 2009–10, which also express these arguments, although they do not support them fully (Henson and Humphrey, 2009; Codex Alimentarius Commission, 2010). These issues are also discussed by Busch et al. (2005, p.38).
7 In 2008, EUREPGAP rebranded itself as GLOBALG.A.P. By this time, its membership had extended beyond Europe and included producers, food service firms and standards organisations as well as retailers.
8 A 'warranty' defence is defined as follows:

> A person accused of an offence would escape conviction if they could prove that, when he bought the product, he obtained a written warranty from his supplier that the product could be lawfully sold or dealt with; that there was no reason to believe, when the offence was committed, that the true position was otherwise, and that the product was in the same state as when he bought it. (Humber Authorities Food Liaison Group, n.d.)

The adoption of private standards such as GLOBALG.A.P. and the BRC Global Standard are precisely designed to provide such a due diligence defence. The second paragraph of the BRC Global Standard Food website refers specifically to its role in providing such a defence.
9 For a discussion of how BSE led to changes in EU food safety regulations, see Knowles et al., 2007 and Janning, 2008.
10 The following six bullet points are taken directly, with small edits, from the GLOBALG.A.P. manual control points compliance criteria (GLOBALG.A.P., 2009).
11 The extent to which such additional concerns are packaged with baseline standards varies

considerably between standards developed by different bodies and even between standards developed by GLOBALG.A.P. for different products and at different points in time.

12 For this comparison, EUREPGAP Revision 2, 2005, is used because this is the standard developed at the time the Codex standard was issued (EUREPGAP, 2005).

13 For this distinction, see Codex Alimentarius Commission (2004, p.2).

14 This prerequisite programme (PRP), PAS 220, is part of the FSSC 22000 standard scheme. See www.fssc22000.com/en/

REFERENCES

Abbott, K. and Snidal, D. (2009), 'Strengthening international regulation through transnational new governance: overcoming the orchestration deficit', *Vanderbilt Journal of Transnational Law*, 42 (2), pp. 501–578.

Busch, L., Thiagarajan, D., Hatanaka, M., Bain, C., Flores, L., and Frahm, M. (2005), *The Relationship of Third-Party Certification (TPC) to Sanitary/Phytosanitary (SPS) Measures and the International Agri-Food Trade: Final Report*, RAISE SPS Global Analytical Report 9, Washington: USAID.

CEC (2002) 'Regulation (EC) No 178/2002 laying down the general principles and requirements of food law, establishing the European food safety authority and laying down procedures in matters of food safety', *Official Journal of the European Communities*, 1 February 2002, available http://eur-lex.europa.eu/pri/en/oj/dat/2002/l_031/l_03120020201en00010024.pdf (accessed, February 2011).

Codex Alimentarius Commission (2003a), *Code of Hygienic Practice for Fresh Fruit and Vegetables*, CAC/RCP 53-2003, Rome/Geneva: FAO/WHO.

Codex Alimentarius Commission (2003b), *Recommended International Code of Practices: General Principles of Food Hygiene*, CAC/RCP 1-1969, Rev. 4-2003, Rome/Geneva: FAO/WHO.

Codex Alimentarius Commission (2004), *Code of Hygienic Practice for Milk and Milk Products*, CAC/RCP 57-2004, Rome/Geneva: FAO/WHO.

Codex Alimentarius Commission (2008), *Codex Alimentarius Commission, Thirty-First Session*, CAC/31 INF/4, Rome/Geneva: FAO/WHO.

Codex Alimentarius Commission (2010), *Consideration of the Impact of Private Standards*, CX/CAC 10/33/13, Rome/Geneva: FAO/WHO.

EU/DG Joint Research Centre (2006), *Case Studies 7: Neuland*, Brussels: DG JRC/IPTS.

EU/DG Joint Research Centre (2008), *Case Studies 6: Label Rouge*, Brussels: DG JRC/IPTS.

EUREPGAP (2005), *EUREPGAP Control Points & Compliance Criteria Fruit and Vegetables Version 2.1-Oct04*, EUREPGAP.

Fuchs, D. and A. Kalfagianni (2010), 'The causes and consequences of private food governance', *Business and Politics,* 12 (3), article 5.

GLOBALG.A.P. (2009), *Control Points and Compliance Criteria, Integrated Farm Assurance, Aquaculture Base*, English Version V1.01-1 Apr09, Cologne: GLOBALG.A.P.

Henson, S.J. and J. Humphrey (2009), *The Impacts of Private Food Safety Standards on the Food Chain and on Public Standard-Setting Processes*, Paper prepared for 32nd session of Codex Alimentarius Commission, ALINORM 09/32/9D-Part II, Rome/Geneva: FAO/WHO.

Henson, S.J. and J. Northen (1998), 'Economic determinants of food safety controls in the supply of retailer own-branded products in the UK', *Agribusiness*, 14 (2), 113–126.
Humber Authorities Food Liaison Group (n.d.), *Food Safety Act 1990: Guidelines on the Statutory Defence of Due Diligence*, Kingston on Hull, available www.eastriding.gov.uk/corp-docs/foodservices/Food_Advice_Notes/due_dilligence_guidelines.pdf (accessed March 2008).
ISO (2010), *International Standards and 'Private Standards'*. ISO/TC 34 SC17, Geneva: International Organisation for Standardization.
Janning, F. (2008), 'Risk regulation without political conflicts? risk structures in food safety politics in Germany, Great Britain and the Netherlands', *German Policy Studies*, 4 (1), pp. 67–106.
Kirk-Wilson, R. (2002), *Review of Food Assurance Schemes*, London: Food Standards Agency.
Knowles, T., Moody, R. and Maceachern, M. (2007), 'European food scares and their impact on EU food policy', *British Food Journal*, 109 (1), pp. 43–67.
Mithöfer, D., Asfaw, S., Ehlert, C., Mausch, K. and Waibel, H. (2007), 'Economic impact of EUREPGAP standard on small to large scale producers and farm worker welfare in Kenya', Paper presented at regional workshop on Good Agricultural Practices in Eastern and Southern Africa: Practices and Policies, Nairobi, 6–9 March.
Swoffer, K. (2005), 'EU food safety and the increasing role of private based standards', Paper presented at ERS Conference, Washington DC, 3 November.
Swoffer, K. (2008), 'Global food safety standards', Presentation made at Michigan State University.
Swoffer, K. (2009), 'GFSI and the relationship with Codex', Presentation made at CIES International Food Safety Conference, Paris.
WTO (2007), *Private Standards and the SPS Agreement, Note by the Secretariat*, G/SPS/GEN/746, Geneva: WTO, Committee on Sanitary and Phytosanitary Measures.
http://www.fairtrade.org.uk/what_is_fairtrade/fairtrade_certification_and_the_fairtrade_mark/the_fairtrade_mark.aspx. (accessed, February 2011).
http://www.fssc22000.com/en/ (accessed, February 2011).
http://www.naturland.de/organic_fair_one_source.html (accessed, February 2011).

5. Market-driven promotion of international labour standards in Southeast Asia: the corporatization of social justice

Ludo Cuyvers and Tim De Meyer[1]

INTRODUCTION

Labour must never be made a commodity lest 'working poverty' ultimately undermines the process of wealth creation that serves both as the cause and purpose of political stability. This insight is more than 150 years old, but it took an economic and political cataclysm for the international community to embed it in a global institution, and another one[2] to embed it in the international trade and financial policies deemed necessary to make economies more interdependent and fuel the development of nations gaining full political sovereignty.

Today, the free interplay of supply and demand – better known as 'the market' – is almost universally accepted as the most efficient method for driving the production and distribution of goods and services nationally and internationally. As labour is a production factor, efficiency is served by having it allocated according to market principles, that is, where its productivity and return on investment are the highest, so that both profits and wages can be maximized. To the extent that labour markets 'fail' to subsume costs to society, public authorities may intervene to allocate liabilities or – better still – spread 'the risk of failure' over all those likely to incur them, through social insurance. For example, not all individual employers are likely to assume the cost to society – not to mention the worker and his or her family – of productivity loss and continued medical care resulting from a work-related accident. For this reason, public authorities will legislate to impose employment injury benefit schemes, which force production processes to assume at least part of this cost. The state may even foreclose markets to prevent low-productivity outcomes in the short term, and boost sustainably higher productivity in the longer term. No doubt we can find a ten-year old girl to glue our sneakers at half the wage we would have to pay her father, but if she were given the option of regularly attending school for five more years, she might earn three times her father's current 'labour market value', spend that money on higher-value consumption items, invest more in continued education or better health care, or at the very least acquire the relevant knowledge to discern toxic from non-toxic glue.

This case for labour standards is widely accepted, if not always vigorously pursued, within the confines of national boundaries. Globalization, however, has made it possible to locate or, indeed, relocate production processes. International public authority reaching across national boundaries to allocate liability for the labour and environmental costs to society associated with production is far less well developed. The liberalization of international trade and investment creates at least the potential for stiffer competition to regulate the labour market between different national regimes. Hence, one might expect states to protect their regulatory regimes whenever they undertake commitments to provide greater access to their markets for goods (or services) produced under different regulatory regimes, thereby providing domestic and foreign investors a potential incentive to locate production in countries offering more relaxed rules.

Even if one only considers labour market regulation, the present line of reasoning raises two questions. First, is there evidence to support the assertion that lower labour standards attract foreign investment? Secondly, are states applying social clauses, i.e. making their international commitments to liberalize trade and investment conditional upon the observance of labour standards? Both these questions continue to swell an already impressive body of institutional debate and academic research. In recent years, however, a third question has enriched the debate: can markets themselves make up for government failure to correctly allocate the social costs of economic production? Traditional 'governance' methods that rely on public international law to gradually improve labour standards around the world and establish 'a level (social) playing field' for production are increasingly complemented by 'market-driven' or 'private' initiatives. In essence, these are corporate measures to weed substandard labour practices out of global supply chains, or to determine the stability of emerging portfolio investment destinations. This 'privatization of social justice' raises questions about the sustainability and political and social legitimacy of the measures used to promote compliance with internationally recognized labour standards.

This chapter traces the evolution of the social clause to date, and sets out the gradual diversification of governance methods to promote international labour standards with market-driven initiatives. It briefly analyzes this development by reference to two fairly recent initiatives for corporate social responsibility in export-led, fast-growth economies in Southeast Asia: the Thai Labour Standards mechanism, which promotes the voluntary compliance of Thai exporting companies with a set of labour standards articulated outside the traditional normative frameworks; and the Better Factories Cambodia initiative, which started out as an ILO project to monitor working conditions in Cambodia's nascent garment industry, but has grown into a multi-stakeholder programme rooting Cambodia's competitive edge in compliance with international labour standards and national labour law. The chapter argues that while market-driven initiatives play a crucial role in stimulating shopfloor awareness and action on labour standards, they are not a long-term replacement for traditional labour market institutions such as labour law, collective bargaining, trade unions and labour inspection services.

THE SOCIAL CLAUSE: THE MULTILATERAL DIMENSION

This section examines the extent to which legal or political instruments with a global coverage have made international trading opportunities dependent on the observance of certain labour standards.

The first genuine attempt to improve labour standards on a global scale, and, as part of that effort, protect these standards against predatory competition was made in 1919. As part of the post-World War I reconstruction, the international community decided to establish a multilateral mechanism that would issue international legislation with a view to shielding certain humanitarian requirements (e.g. protecting young children from work in industry; protecting women against night work; protecting all workers against exploitative working hours in industry, and so on) from international competition (Mahaim, 1934). Although the new International Labour Organization did not expressly intend to impact upon international trade and investment flows, the Preamble to its Constitution devoted a full paragraph to considering that 'the failure of any nation to adopt humane conditions of labour is an obstacle in the way of other nations which desire to improve the conditions in their own countries' (ILO Constitution, para.3 of Preamble).

World War II taught a number of hard lessons. The 'conditions of labour . . . involving such injustice, hardship and privation to large numbers of people' (ILO Constitution, para. 2 of Preamble), which the ILO Constitution sought to improve, did not merely result from the exploitative intentions of certain short-sighted employers, but also from fundamental shortcomings in the economic environment (which destroyed job opportunities) and in the political environment (which led to human rights abuses). Mere harmonization of labour standards among competing nations would not fix these shortcomings, and, moreover, would soon prove to present an insurmountable challenge with the rapidly growing number of sovereign nations in the wake of decolonization and, concurrently, the rapidly widening levels of development.

The ILO's Declaration of Philadelphia, adopted in 1944 and annexed to the Constitution of 1919, incorporated these lessons by asserting that social justice cannot be achieved without a fundamental respect for human dignity (Declaration of Philadelphia, II (a), p.4), nor without proactive programmes to create conducive conditions (II (b), p.5), in particular full employment and raised standards of living (III (a), p.5). The Declaration expressly acknowledged that 'national and international policies and measures, in particular those of an economic and financial character' were by no means irrelevant to the pursuit of social justice (II (c)) It noted in particular that a 'high and steady volume of international trade' could contribute to a 'fuller and broader utilization of the world's productive resources necessary for the achievement of the objectives set forth in this Declaration' (IV).

It was hardly surprising, then, when the Havana Charter for an International Trade Organization set about its ambitious plans to expand employment through expanding trade, nor when its Article 7 minced few words in saying that 'unfair labour conditions, particularly in production for export, create difficulties in international trade, and, accordingly, each Member shall take whatever action may be appropriate and feasible to eliminate such conditions within its territory'.[3] The author(s) have explained elsewhere how these plans for an all-encompassing social clause never materialized and how, up until today, efforts to improve labour standards subsequently remained politically divorced from multilateral trade liberalization efforts (De Meyer, 2001).

Political and social forces have not given up all multilateral attempts to make further liberalization of international trade and investment conditional upon the observance of certain international labour standards. The ILO Declaration of 1998 had stressed 'that labour standards should not be used for protectionist trade purposes, and that... the comparative advantage of any country should in no way be called into question by this Declaration and its follow-up' (ILO Declaration on Fundamental Principles and Rights at Work, 1998, para. 5). This provision responded to fears from developing countries that the developed world was not so much keen to promote fundamental labour standards throughout the world for the sake of advancing human dignity, but rather to reduce the developing economies' low-wage advantage, and so protect its own industries (Briefing note for the Doha WTO Ministerial, 2001).

The WTO Doha Ministerial Declaration reaffirmed the status-quo reached in the Singapore Ministerial Declaration of 1996 and the ILO Declaration of 1998, and took note of work under way in the International Labour Organization (ILO) on the social dimension of globalization (WTO Ministerial Conference Fourth Session, 14 November 2001, para. 8). The ILO-backed World Commission on the Social Dimension of Globalization published its conclusions in 2004, formally noting that the Declaration's commitment not to call into question the comparative advantage of low-wage countries implied 'of course, . . . that no country should achieve or maintain comparative advantage based on ignorance of, or deliberate violations of, core labour standards' (World Commission on the Social Dimension of Globalization, 2004, para. 421). This implication, while being presented as a matter 'of course', articulates a significant dimension of the link between international trade and labour standards. The 1998 Declaration's line of reasoning could be read as follows. Developing countries have lower wages because of lower productivity, lower cost of living and a relatively more abundant labour supply. If that gives these countries a comparative advantage producing and exporting labour-intensive goods, then no labour standards – fundamental or other – should alter the equation to the detriment of developing countries. In other words, labour standards present no valid excuse to force up labour costs in developing countries without regard to their productivity or the living conditions of their people. However, the statement in the World Commission's report implies that the reasoning does not simply end there, but that the conclusion depends on a further consideration. The statement does not take issue with a country's comparative advantage of lower wages because of lower productivity. However, if a country suppresses collective bargaining or makes only lukewarm efforts to promote this market-based wage-setting method, and wages fail to keep pace with productivity improvements as a result, then the country is seeking its comparative advantage in a violation of a fundamental principle, so that its comparative advantage may be called into question.

Interestingly, the concept has now been formally enshrined in a new ILO declaration, adopted in June 2008 (International Labour Conference, Declaration on Social Justice for a Fair Globalization, 10 June 2008). The Declaration projects a vision that the main development challenge in our time of globalization is for the world to create decent work for all. Creating decent work is not just about offering men and women hand-to-mouth livelihoods, but also the choice, leverage and platforms to 'market' their work or shape economic decisions affecting their lives, and a degree of protection against loss of income. Much in the Declaration on Social Justice of 2008 is about stressing the indivisibility of 'decent work', and therefore the equal importance of all aspects of 'decent work'.[4] The Declaration appears to reposition international labour standards as authoritative benchmarks of social justice achievement, but no longer as the central means of action.[5] Realizing decent work requires an 'integrated approach', that is, proactive measures at national and international level taken in synchronized fashion across four strategic objectives, but can no longer be expected to result automatically from the effect given to international labour standards. Yet, decent work or the social justice flowing from it will remain a distant dream if the main actors are stifled or if the market dynamics underpinning globalization pull in a fundamentally opposite direction. This explains why the Declaration goes out of its way noting:

> – that freedom of association and the effective recognition of the right to collective bargaining are particularly important to enable the attainment of the four strategic objectives; and
>
> – that the violation of fundamental principles and rights at work cannot be invoked or otherwise used as a legitimate comparative advantage (International Labour Conference, Declaration on Social Justice for a Fair Globalization, 2008, I A (iv)).

Time will tell if this apparent tightening of language will have important consequences for countries in East Asia, where, for example, rights relating to freedom of association and collective bargaining are formally recognized for the most part, but not necessarily widely realized. Most, if not all of the national Constitutions of ASEAN Member States, for example, formally recognize workers' right to organize as a fundamental human right, yet only four out of ten have ratified C. 87, while five out of ten have ratified C. 98.[6] Complaints before the ILO Committee on Freedom of Association point to governments having excessive discretion in authorizing trade unions; interfering with the right of trade unions to independently organize their activities (in particular strike action); or failing to protect trade union leaders or members against harassment, assault or even murder.

The notion that a violation of fundamental labour standards does not constitute legitimate comparative advantage had already found its way into international trade agreements before the Social Justice Declaration. For example, the Memorandum of Understanding on Labour (MOU) Cooperation, concluded in June 2005 in connection with the Trans-Pacific Strategic Economic Partnership Agreement (TPP) provides that:

> 5. The Parties recognise that it is inappropriate to set or use their labour laws, regulations, policies and practices for trade protectionist purposes.
> 6. The Parties recognise that it is inappropriate to encourage trade or investment by weakening or reducing the protections afforded in domestic labour laws. (Article 2(5) and (6) of the MOU, p.2)

This clause is now being copied into other agreements such as the Memorandum of Understanding on Labour Cooperation concluded between New Zealand and China in October 2008 (paras. 3 and 4).

It is worth noting that the TPP commitment reaches beyond violations of fundamental labour standards and effectively encompasses violations of all labour standards covered by domestic labour law. On the other hand, the clause does not appear to offer any protection against violations of fundamental or other standards as such, but only against the lowering of existing standards in domestic labour law, regardless as to whether these standards meet the international benchmark. Some commentators are advocating a 'no standards lowering clause' as a realistic and useful starting point in trade agreements.[8] This is potentially significant, considering the vast discrepancies in Asia between the text of labour laws on the one hand, and the presence of labour market institutions ensuring compliance with such laws on the other hand.[9]

This observation has obviously not been lost on the trade unions in the respective TPP countries. In the Joint Declaration they issued at the start of the negotiations in 2010, they noted upfront:

> Unfortunately, most of the agreements among the proposed TPPTA parties contain either no labor provisions or very weak ones. The TPPTA must at a minimum require that each party adopt and maintain laws and regulations consistent with the International Labor Organization (ILO) core labor rights and effectively enforce those rights, as well as all domestic laws with regard to wages, hours of work and safety and health. Further, parties must commit not to derogate from these laws. A violation of these and other labor obligations should be subject to effective dispute resolution procedures with strong remedies up to and including trade sanctions should more cooperative efforts fail. The monitoring of these provisions should include workers' and employers' representatives, and the agencies responsible for enforcement must be adequately resourced. (Labor Declaration On The Negotiation Of The Trans-Pacific Partnership Trade Agreement, 15 March 2010, p.2)

Whatever the future implications, the political position appears consistent with a steadily growing body of literature that finds no significant correlation between lowering fundamental labour standards and the ability to attract foreign direct investment. Couched in more positive terms, the literature holds that comparative advantage does not need to be sought in violations of fundamental labour standards as respect for these standards embodies good governance and, together with many other factors, creates rather than undermines a favourable investment climate.

THE SOCIAL CLAUSE – THE PLURILATERAL (REGIONAL), BILATERAL AND UNILATERAL DIMENSIONS

In summary, it would probably be fair to state that multilateral attempts at creating a social floor for globalization have not reached far beyond promotional efforts to strengthen national capacity to govern labour markets, declaratory resolve that development is not sustainable without decent work for all, and more recently, warnings that international competitive advantage must not be sought in violations of fundamental international labour standards. New multilateral rounds for the liberalization of international trade – most recently the Doha round – have stalled, but this has not dented the leverage of the world's major export markets. As a result, bilateral trade agreements and unilateral trade preferences are featuring social clauses to exert pressure on labour market governance in developing countries.

The United States has included labour rights provisions in its regional, bilateral and unilateral trade arrangements. These are briefly reviewed as an illustration of the apparent public incapacity to introduce and promote international labour standards in international trade relations. While other countries or trading blocs (such as the European Union, Australia, New Zealand or Canada) have linked and do link trade liberalization measures to respect for labour standards, it is the initiatives of the United States that have received most attention as the boldest in articulation, the commercially most significant and, at times, the politically most controversial.

1. Regional Arrangements

The United States currently maintains two regional trade arrangements, both of which feature commitments to respect labour standards.

1.1. The North American Free Trade Agreement

The North American Free Trade Agreement (NAFTA) has a labour side agreement named the North American Agreement on Labour Cooperation (NAALC). The NAALC does not actually set labour standards for the Free Trade Area but only features a commitment to 'promote compliance with and effectively enforce its domestic labour law through appropriate government action' (NAALC, Art. 3). Unions in all these three countries (US, Canada, Mexico) have not generally been satisfied with the NAALC mechanism (Dicaprio, 2004). One reason is that while the notion of domestic labour law encompasses at least 11 categories of labour standards (including, for example, freedom of association, collective bargaining and forced labour), only three of these categories are able to eventually give rise to a panel ruling that could recommend sanctions: labour protections for children and young persons, minimum employment standards, and prevention of occupational injuries and illnesses.

1.2. The United States-Dominican Republic-Central America Free Trade Agreement (US-DR-CAFTA)

The US-CAFTA, encompassing the US, Costa Rica, El Salvador, Guatemala, Honduras and Nicaragua was signed in May 2004, and the Dominican Republic became an additional party to it in August 2004.

US-DR-CAFTA's labour provisions do not require CAFTA countries to amend their labour laws to meet international labour standards. In fact, the agreement even authorizes CAFTA states to weaken those laws further in order to gain a trade advantage. States must only 'strive to ensure' compliance with their domestic labour laws, and must only 'strive to ensure' that these laws do not fall short of international labour standards. Anti-discrimination is not included among the five categories of standards outlined under CAFTA. NGOs recently observed that CAFTA's sanctions if the country does not uphold its own labour laws are a marked step back from those that governed U.S. trade policy towards Central America in the years preceding CAFTA, primarily under the Generalized System of Preferences (GSP) trade program.[10]

Only one obligation is subject to dispute resolution – the requirement to effectively enforce domestic laws. Fines for labour disputes are capped, and the level of the cap has been criticized for not having any deterrence effect (Labour Advisory Committee for Trade Negotiations and Trade Policy, 19 March 2004).

2. Bilateral Arrangements

Labour standard clauses also consistently feature in trade liberalization agreements that the United States has concluded with individual states. Some focus on specific goods, such as the US-Cambodia Bilateral Textile Agreement and US-Viet Nam Textile Agreement, while others focus on trade across the board, such as the US-Jordan and US-Singapore FTA.

2.1. Bilateral Textile Agreements

2.1.1. US-Cambodia Bilateral Textile Agreement The US-Cambodia Bilateral Textile Agreement, signed on 20 January 1999, was the first US bilateral trade agreement to include labour provisions in it (Kolben, 2004). This labour provision was actually the result of a confluence of several political forces (Dicaprio, 2004). The American trade unions pressed the administration and advocated to include enforceable, main-text labour provisions in the trade initiatives (Dicaprio, 2004). NGOs such as the International Labour Rights Fund and the Lawyers Committee for Human Rights played supportive roles (Kolben, 2004). The agreement requires that:

> The Royal Government of Cambodia shall support the implementation of a program to improve working conditions in the textile and apparel sector, including internationally recognized core labour standards, through the application of Cambodian labour law . . . the Government of the United States will make a determination . . . whether working conditions in the Cambodia textile and apparel sector substantially comply with such labour law and standards (Agreement between the USA and the Royal Government of Cambodia, 20 January 1999, art. 10)

If the United States made a positive determination that the Cambodian garment industry was in substantial compliance with Cambodian labour law and international labour standards, the US could increase Cambodia's export quotas as a reward (Agreement between the USA and the Royal Government of Cambodia, 20 January 1999, art. 4). To satisfy the requirements of this agreement, a programme was set up and run by the ILO.[11] The ILO provides reports of its monitoring, which are taken into account by the US government and have led to the increase of export quotas.

The US-Cambodia Bilateral Textile Agreement is often said to be one of the most successful in outlining labour provisions in trade agreements, but it also has drawbacks. For instance, the ILO plays a major role in monitoring labour conditions while the inspection capability of Cambodia's labour administration has not been improved (Dicaprio, 2004).

2.2 Bilateral Free Trade Agreements

Between 1985 and 2008, the US signed 12 bilateral free trade agreements (FTAs).[12] FTAs with Israel and Jordan were negotiated before the US president was granted Trade Promotion Authority (TPA) in 2002. The Jordan FTA was the first bilateral FTA to include labour provisions in the main text of the agreement. The weakness of an approach based on the 'strive to ensure' type of commitment, also found in the US-DR-CAFTA agreement, combined with a tentative enforcement approach, was rather quickly exposed when reports emerged of human trafficking and forced labour in factories producing for duty-free export to the US (Kernaghan, 2006). TPA is better known as 'fast-track' authority which authorizes the president to negotiate FTAs with only restricted opportunity for Congress to reject or amend them once they are signed. TPA was set to expire on 30 June 2007 (Bolle, 2007).[13] FTA negotiations with Singapore, Chile, Australia, Morocco, Bahrain and Oman were conducted with 'fast-track' authority and US Congress subsequently approved the signed agreements.

FTAs with Peru, Colombia, Panama and South Korea (the so-called KORUS agreement) were also negotiated with 'fast-track' authority, but it became clear in early 2007 that these agreements would not win Congressional approval without modifications involving, in particular, more enforceable labour and environmental provisions. The TPA-negotiated FTAs featured only one labour provision subject to dispute resolution – the requirement to effectively enforce domestic labour laws, not including fundamental labour standards. Enforcement procedures capped the fine or 'monetary assessment' for labour violations (not commercial violations) at 15 million USD, payable into a fund to improve labour law administration in the violating country. Even a maximum fine is infinitesimal compared to the total value of two-way trade between major economies such as the US and South Korea. At the same time, a party in a commercial dispute could suspend the full original amount of trade benefits (equal to the harm caused by the offending measure) if a monetary assessment (capped at half that value) was not paid. Moreover, paying the monetary assessment for labour violations into a fund in the violating country appeared rather like compensating the violator for its failure to effectively enforce its own laws, even more so as the agreements provided no assurance that the assessment would actually support enforcement.

In that context, the Bush administration and Congress struck a Bipartisan Trade Deal (BTD) in May 2010 for the four pending FTAs (Bolle, 2007). In essence, the BTD required the FTAs to feature an enforceable obligation 'to adopt, maintain and enforce in their own laws and in practice the five basic internationally-recognized labour standards, as stated in the 1998 Declaration' (para. 1(A)); an enforceable obligation not to 'derogate from this obligation in a manner affecting trade or investment' (para. 1 (C)); and a provision that 'labour obligations are subject to the same dispute settlement, same enforcement mechanisms (remedies), and same criteria for selection of enforcement mechanisms (remedies) as all other FTA obligations' (para. 1 (D)). Despite the promising language, commentators have been quick to point out various limitations, suggesting that any significant impact on the observance of labour rights is far from a foregone conclusion. First, non-enforcement of labour obligations must have occurred 'through a sustained or recurring course of action or inaction' (para. 12 (B)). In practice, this makes individual violations not-actionable. Secondly, the provisions only apply to federal labour laws. Thirdly, the dispute settlement provisions may only be invoked by the government (and not, for example, trade unions). Finally, dispute panel decisions are neither self-executing nor able to alter US or other national law (Gantz, 2008).

The Peru FTA was modified accordingly and approved by Congress. Despite similar modifications, the KORUS FTA is still awaiting Congressional approval in both South Korea and the US.

'PRIVATE INITIATIVES' TO IMPROVE WORKPLACE RIGHTS AND CONDITIONS

The preceding sections demonstrate the limitations of public authorities relying on fixed rule-making procedures (including multilateral and bilateral treaties) in realizing improved labour standards in economies around the world; the sovereignty which countries insist upon with respect to the organization of their labour markets and the role these markets play in support of other markets and overall economic growth; the weakness or even absence of labour market institutions (such as trade unions, employer organizations and labour inspectorates) in putting these standards into domestic practice; deficiencies in democratic governance; and the reluctance of importing states to retaliate against persistent violations of international labour standards with trade sanctions (such as punitive tariffs).

Some have quite pointedly argued that the failure of state-centred regulation, including international trade agreements that are merely hortatory, has been the main driver behind 'non-state models of international labour regulation' – such as corporate codes of conduct, international framework agreements and fair trade labelling of internationally traded commodities such as cocoa, coffee, and so on (Wells, 2006). One close examination of US trading arrangements concluded that 'social clauses' do not deserve their 'protectionist' label – neither in intent nor design, and least of all in effect. In fact, the leverage potential of these social clauses has been so limited that trade unions and labour activitists have become disillusioned and turned to other channels of influence (Dicaprio, 2004). Some analysts have documented a 'near consistent failure' of the US to suspend tariff preferences, even in the face of violations of international workers' rights (Compa and Vogt, 2001, p. 199).

In the context of globalization, in particular the growing role of transnational firms in the world's GDP and exports, these limitations inevitably lead to a regulatory deficiency, that is, situations in which economic activity is no longer effectively governed from the viewpoint of the objectives normally served by international labour standards. The literature discussing emerging new forms of governance offers a number of reasons for this regulatory deficiency. Some have pointed to the conflict of interest inherent in global governance being run by distinctly non-global players, that is, states with their sovereignty firmly grounded in national or territorial attributes. At the same time, global governance is undergoing a legitimacy shift from territorial and national factors to factors such as expertise or operant values. It is only logical, then, to contemplate the future of global labour market governance resting in the hands of 'non-state governance structures, including global ones, that derive their coherence, effectiveness, and cultural legitimacy from identities based on non-national, non-state attributes' (Brauer and Haywood, 2010, p. 10).

Others assert that new governance is already a fact of life. International old governance (IOG) characterized by intergovernmental organizations issuing fixed rules in a centralized and top-down manner is gradually being replaced by transnational new governance (TNG), which relies more on 'soft law' and orchestration of various configurations of public and private stakeholders as repositories of regulatory expertise. The reasons for this development are the distinct comparative advantages of TNG over IOG: TNG has the capacity to address regulatory issues in more diverse ways, which is important in increasingly complex and ever more rapidly shifting global production systems. It also involves less risk of loss of sovereignty for states; it engages the energy, agency and expertise of private actors (for example, NGOs) much more actively; and it allows those governed (firms) to have a direct voice, putting less pressure on mandatory regulation (Abbott and Snidal, 2009).

To plug the governance gap in the face of the perceived fluidity of contemporary global production, some models propose to substitute soft law with 'rolling rule systems'. The premise is, as always, that transnational supply chains interweave ever more tiers of formal and informal economy producers that can no longer be reached by state-centred regulatory bodies, fixed-rule regimes, and the ever more extensive inspectorates on which these regimes inevitably have to rely. Public pressure, peer pressure and the desire of businesses to demonstrate accomplishments in competitive fashion may, however, be harnessed to gradually 'ratchet labour standards'. Rolling rule regimes, in which accomplishments are continuously monitored and publicized, do not make compliance too costly for (particularly informal) firms. They build on the capacities for reorganization developed in the course of competition, leave intact incentives to improve as conditions of participation and advancement, accommodate a great diversity in political conditions, community capacities and sector circumstances, and are not easily bent for political purposes. These regimes – besides being complex – are, however, difficult to apply to markets without ethically inclined consumers. They do not cope very well with 'distributive and adversarial contests', particularly labour standards that do not present an immediate win-win to both employers and workers (such as health and safety) but instead offer a short-term win to workers and a cost increase to employers, of which the return may only be expected in the medium to long term at best (Sabel et al., 2000).

Whatever theory may suggest, the empirical fact remains that the globalized sourcing of goods and services has raised the visibility of workplace rights violations, and continues to generate proactive attempts by the private sector to address them. The private sector has various motives to support private governance initiatives that aim to improve workplace conditions and rights without being forced to do so by the public authorities (Vogel, 2008). Self-regulation is a common strategy for avoiding additional government regulation. It reduces pressure from NGOs and consumers, even if it remains to be seen whether consumer behaviour has become notably more politicized. Some businesses may regard labour standards as part of their business objectives. Last but not least, the business principle of 'corporate social responsibility' has gained currency: whatever legal obligations any of the corporate links in any global supply chain may have, it is accountable not only to its shareholders but also to the communities in which it is operating, and this responsibility is proportionate to the corporate power it exerts within the supply chain. Whether a company discharges its corporate social responsibility of complying with labour standards, which may derive from international or national 'hard' or 'soft' law, ultimately determines its business opportunities, or even becomes part of the contractual obligations it has within global supply chains.

Corporate codes of conduct (for example, at Nike and Reebok) were among the first private initiatives to address low standards in global supply chains.[14] These company codes represent the purest form of 'privatized regulation' (O'Rourke, 2003), characterized by firm-internal or industry-internal monitoring and certification with only private sector involvement and little or no public transparency. The rationale behind codes of conduct can be attributed to attempts to remedy the failure of public efforts to advance workers' rights, such as facilitating free trade in the face of political opposition to globalization and social clauses in US free-trade agreements, reducing the scope for liability for violating labour standards (in particular, joint liability of contractors within the supply chain, and connecting to socially concerned consumers (Bartley, 2005).

A trend over the last decades is for 'outsourced regulation' to become more diversified and less 'purely privatized'.[15] The term 'private' is still appropriate in the sense that the initiatives continue to rely on market sanctions – either through interfirm purchasing decisions or NGO consumer campaigns. Yet, more collaborative labour governance models involve a wider range of stakeholders (particularly NGOs), internal as well as external monitoring, brand commitment and public disclosure of information. Examples such as the Fair Labour Association (FLA)[16] have been compared to a supply chain policing system. Socialized regulation models, such as the Worker Rights Consortium (WRC),[17] go one step further in wrestling away governance control from the business side of the labour market by inviting complaints, and then targeting worker empowerment and organizing to negotiate improvements.

In this sense, the term democratization describes developments more accurately than corporatization or privatization of social justice. Yet, even democratization raises questions about the nature of the relationship between public authority and private normative activity. Does the latter have the potential to gradually replace public authority and, indeed, the democratic debate by which it is legitimized? Some have argued that the 'plural formulation of standards' in public and private initiatives alike raises the spectre of confusion and ultimately normative dilution. For example, if even some US-sponsored bilateral trade agreements have dropped non-discrimination from the list of fundamental labour standards, what should stop companies from proclaiming full adherence to fundamental labour standards while assuming the right to idiosyncratically determine their content? (Gravel, 2008) Bartley (2005) argues that codes of conducts have not displaced labour law nor ushered in an era of privatization of social justice, but that public law-based efforts to enforce labour standards and private initiatives to advance compliance are complementary – in some cases, private initiatives have helped to define legal liabilities that they were initially designed to shield against, because social activism has resisted the erosion of public accountability

A pressing question, at least from the viewpoint of social justice, is whether these private or semi-private initiatives have the potential to improve workplace rights and conditions. Even the most well-researched scholars admit that much more research is needed to adequately answer that question, and surmise that only a mix of old and new governance techniques will do the trick (Vogel, 2008). One important conclusion so far is that private initiatives only tend to affect various enclaves in the global economy (Vogel, 2005). So, for example, they affect supply chains producing for markets in the European Union and the US, but not for many other increasingly important markets (for example, China); they affect first-tier supplies produced by large-scale manufacturing and other formal sector providers, but not the lower, informal echelons of the supply chain (such as home workers). Some agricultural products (such as coffee, cocoa, bananas) are subject to the influence of private initiatives but many others are not; brand-dependent firms of primary goods are touched, but often not smaller corporations and invisible firms producing secondary goods; supply chains with suppliers owned by the brands or producing for one brand are affected, but not supply chains with multiple tiers all of which produce for multiple sourcing businesses. Private initiatives have seen greater success in remedying the more tangible workplace rights violations (such as child labour and health and safety), but not those that deal with wages, overtime restrictions and freedom of association standards.

Private initiatives encounter many of the same challenges as traditional command-and-control regulatory systems:[18] limited inspection or monitoring capacity resulting in limited coverage of factories and workers; corruption; incentives to evade regulation; businesses hiding behind multiple layers of ownership; and difficulties in reaching the informal economy (in this case because of a lack of ethically inclined consumers). To this may be added unintended consequences articulated in fears that non-governmental regulation will provide public relations cover to brands, may confuse consumers with a proliferation of labels and certifications, and may push workers in developing countries out of a job and into even deeper poverty if market sanctions materialize. There is some merit in the notion that elected governments are actually ceding some of their sovereignty to consumers by outsourcing regulation, and so allowing consumers to 'crowd out' trade unions.

To illustrate some of the analytical aspects highlighted in the literature to date, this chapter will now go on to describe outsourced regulatory systems from two Southeast Asian nations. The countries vary in level of development as well as in experience with market institutions they have accumulated over time: Thailand is a longstanding market economy and an established middle-income country while Cambodia is a least developed country (LDC) recovering from colonialism, the ravages of a genocidal regime and more than a decade of foreign occupation. Being national in scope, these regulatory regimes have not been widely analyzed so far.

THAI LABOUR STANDARDS (TLS 8001-2003)[19]

TLS is a private initiative in the sense that it is the market responding to 'governance failure' to enforce outcome-related labour standards in Thai workplaces to a level at which foreign buyers will feel confident does not entail excessive risk for their brand reputation. The TLS mechanism, however, is not privately owned nor controlled. TLS promotes voluntary compliance among Thai exporting companies[20] to a set of labour standards, which are issued, reviewed and promoted by the Thai Ministry of Labour (MoL) (Suttawet, n.d.).

TLS started out as a five-year Thai Labour Standards Project aimed at increasing 'the quality of life of labor to equal international standards, strengthen export producers' ability to compete, and improve Thailand's image as a country taking responsibility for labor standards' (Serrano, Marasigan and Palafox, 2004, p. 68; Chulalongkorn University, 2004). A Cabinet Resolution of 18 December 2001 approved a project called 'Labour Standard Development Project to support Free Trade Promotion' in response to CSR and labour standards as non-tariff barriers by importing countries. The project was assigned to a new administrative unit within the MoL's Department of Labour Protection and Welfare. The project initially had a budget of over 300 million Thai Baht (Thai Ministry of Labour, 2004).

In 2006, the Thai Ministry of Labour, in collaboration with the private sector, produced the Thai Labour Standards (TLS-8001) under the name 'Thai Corporate Social Responsibility'. The Thai Labour Standard Development Bureau was assigned to 'enhance and support to develop the Thai Labour Standard network', 'audit TLS 8001-2003 certification' and 'study and analyse international labour standards'.[21] TLS 8001-2003 is substantively based on the provisions of Thailand's 1997 Constitution, the law on labour protection (in particular, the Labour Protection Act of 1998), labour welfare, labour relations and occupational safety, health and the environment, as well as international labour conventions and UN human rights treaties. TLS 8001-2003 deliberately emulates other prominent international CSR standards, especially Social Accountability 8000 (SA 8000). It covers a fairly complete range of labour standards including forced labour, remuneration, working hours, discrimination in the workplace, discipline, child labour, female labour, freedom of association and collective bargaining, health and safety in the workplace and worker's welfare.[22]

TLS 8001-2003 incorporates requirements of Thai labour law, for example:

> 5.1.2 The establishment shall provide for and keep a record as evidence demonstrating how the establishment has conformed to the requirements of this standard and for addressing the effectiveness of the management system. The record shall be clearly defined and easily accessible. The record required by law shall be provided in accordance with the form and procedure prescribed by the laws.
> 5.2.1 (1) Top management shall define and formally declare the policy on social and labour accountability. The policy shall express the intention to: (a) conform to the requirements of this standard, to labour laws and to other regulations concerned.
> 5.5.2 For general working conditions, performing overtime work shall be deemed as the right of employee, unless the work is exempted by law.
> 5.11.2 The establishment shall provide the safe working environment to prevent hazards and reduce risks in accordance with the related laws.

Compared to Thai labour law, TLS 8001-2003 occasionally sets higher standards, for example:

> 5.3.2 The establishment shall not require submission or deposit of identity card or any other personal identity paper from an employee either upon commencing employment or after, nor shall the establishment make it a requirement or a condition of employment to do so unless exempted by law. This is not specified by the Labour Protection Act 1998 (LPA 1998).
> 5.4.3 The establishment, at every wage payment, shall provide for employees comprehensive information in writing on the composition of wages and remuneration paid to them. This is not required by the LPA 1998, which only establishes a record-keeping obligation for supervisory purposes (Section 114).
> 5.5.2 The establishment shall specify the hours of overtime work (more than 48 normal working hours per week) as not to exceed 24 hours per week in the first year of standard certification, and not to exceed 18 hours per week in the second year and not to exceed 12 hours per week as condition for certification in the consecutive years. Ministerial Regulation No. 3 issued under the Labour Protection Act (B.E. 2541) only requires 33 hours restriction of overtime work per week (November 1998, p. 347).
> 5.6.1 The establishment shall not engage in or support discrimination in hiring, payment of wage and remuneration, providing welfare and opportunity for training and development, promotion, termination of employment or retirement based on nationality, race, religion, language, age, sex, marital status, sexual orientation, disability, trade union membership, political affiliation or personal opinion. Section 15 of the LPA 1998 establishes a general prohibition of sex discrimination. Section 53 requires equal pay for men and women for equal work (but seemingly not for work of equal value). Discrimination of trade union members is prohibited in the Labour Relations Act 1975, Chapter 9.
> 5.7.3 The establishment shall set up measures to prevent the employees, especially women and young employees, from being sexually harassed by any means – verbal, gesture or physical contact. Section 8 of the LPA 1998 (amended in 2008) prohibits sexual harassment by employers or supervisors,

> but does not require employers to take preventive measures nor to establish a company policy.
> 5.9.1 The establishment shall provide safe working conditions and environment for pregnant employee(s). The protection of pregnant employees is not so comprehensively articulated in the Labour Protection Act 1998 (LPA). The LPA prohibits certain types of work to be performed by pregnant employees (S. 39), and permits a pregnant employee to request a change of duties (S. 42), but does not impose a specific obligation on the employer to provide a safe working environment.
> 5.12 The establishment shall provide, for all employees, the convenience and adequate welfare and facilities as follows: 1. hygienic toilet and bathroom; 2. hygienic drinking water; 3. first-aid equipment as appropriate; 4. sanitary canteen and place for food storage; 5. dormitory, if provided, shall be equipped with clean and safe basic facilities and be ready for use. This is not regulated in much detail in the Labour Protection Law 1998.

In 2004, a total of 304 Thai companies had been certified to comply with the standard, of which 241 were large companies with 200 or more employees.[23] By October 2008, 951 Thai companies had been certified, employing over 940 000 employees. By mid-June 2010, 1 467 companies had been certified, of which 876 were at the completion level and 565 at the basic level. These companies covered 63 provinces and employed 1 302 646 employees.[24]

Exporting companies have been encouraged to implement TLS 8001-2003 and the government offers financial support to companies to improve and meet the standards.[25] The Ministry of Labour provides for two levels of prescription and certification based on companies' compliance with the Thai Labour Standard (TLS 8001-2003):[26]

1. Basic Level. The establishment will be certified with the Thai Labour Standard (TLS 8001-2003), if it complies with requirements no. 5.3 to no. 5.12;[27] and requirements no. 5.1 to no. 5.2 only as regards the documents prescribed by labour law.
2. Completion Level. The establishment will be certified if it complies with all the requirements of TLS 8001-2003 and is prepared to gradually reduce its overtime regime as follows:
   A. Initiative Phase – the establishment complies with all requirements of TLS 8001-2003, and overtime does not exceed 36 hours per week.
   B. Generative Phase – the establishment complies with all requirements of TLS 8001-2003, and overtime does not exceed 24 hours per week.
   C. Progressive Phase – the establishment complies with all requirements of TLS 8001-2003, and overtime does not exceed 18 hours per week.

D. Superlative Phase – the establishment complies with all requirements of TLS 8001-2003, and overtime does not exceed 12 hours per week.

The Ministry of Labour offers financial and logistical support to companies pursuing compliance with TLS 8001-2003 standards: 73,000 Baht[28] for consultancies to help companies internally set up a labour management system mainstreaming compliance in day-to-day management, and the same amount to have the company audited and certified externally.

The Department of Labour Protection and Welfare is the certifying body. The auditors are appointed by the Department, and can be either senior civil servants of the Department, persons recruited by the Department or officers of a legal person that provides auditing services and has qualifications specified by the Department of Labour Protection and Welfare. In practice, civil servants function as auditors for basic level certification or renewal of the certification, while an independent certifying body (a private company), accredited by internationally accepted accreditation bodies such as the National Accreditation System of Thailand (NAC), Social Accountability International (SAI) or the United Kingdom Accreditation Service (UKAS) will audit for completion level certification.

The first step in the certification process is 'self-implementation' by the company. This can be done with the assistance of the Labour Standard Development Bureau ('the Bureau') for which the company may apply to the Bureau. If the Bureau approves the application, it will hire a consultant under its budget to develop the TLS system within the company. The elements of the system are set out in the Manual of the TLS Implementation. This manual provides eight steps to implement the system.[29] For basic level certification, entrepreneurs have to comply with requirements no. 5.3 – 5.12, which concern labour rights and protection. For the completion level, entrepreneurs have to set up a labour management system in accordance with requirements no. 5.1 – 5.2 and meet the limited overtime requirement ranging from 12 to 36 hours.

The second step is that companies may apply for TLS certification at the local or provincial Labour Standard Development Bureau. The Bureau reviews all submitted documents, and decides if the company is ready to be audited. Auditing is the third step, and may be done according to one of two methods: (1) a document assessment or (2) an on-site assessment (Labour Standard Development Bureau, Manual of TLS Implementation, p. 19). If the company's documents and practices are found to comply with TLS, the auditor submits its report to the certifying body. In practice, this determination is made by the sub-committee for TLS certification. The certification is in effect for a year for the basic level and three years for the completion level.

The fourth and last step is surveillance, which is conducted four months after certification (The Labour Standard Development Bureau, p. 18). Surveillance is conceived as a continuous auditing measure to ensure that TLS compliance is sustained and gradually improved. It is also used to renew the certification upon expiry. There are three recognized types of surveillance: (1) surveillance by the company, (2) by customers and (3) by an independent third party. The surveillance report/result is submitted to the sub-committee for TLS certification for consideration. If the company does not comply with the TLS, it may face suspension or revocation of its certification.

The above demonstrates that supervision of compliance with TLS 8001-2003 is, to a large extent, left to companies themselves. This 'fox-guarding-the-henhouse' conundrum raises questions as to its effectiveness from the viewpoint of upholding labour standards.

Every year, the Department organizes a Thai Labour Standards Day presided over by the Minister of Labour. Eligible companies receive their TLS 8001-2003 certificate on this occasion. The agenda of the 10th TLS Day (31 May 2010, unpublished) illustrated the various underpinnings of the system:

1. promoting higher retention and labour productivity by promoting a more satisfied workforce
2. promoting economic growth and sharpening competitive edge in the global marketplace, where countries are 'using issues on labour standards and human rights as trade barriers'
3. preparing for 'ASEAN + 6 FTA' negotiations
4. gaining a competitive edge in the global marketplace, where countries are 'using issues on labour standards and human rights as trade barriers' (in particular child labour, forced labour and migrant workers).

TLS 8001-2003 has not been widely discussed in CSR literature, and nothing suggests that global supply chains give it great credibility. This is hardly surprising given the emphasis on self-monitoring or at least closed-circle monitoring. The scheme, despite a gradual expansion and nationwide aspirations, still only covers less than 3 per cent of the workforce. No domestic stakeholders, such as trade unions or employers, take part in the monitoring system even though they cooperated with the government to create the standard. Disregarding stakeholders is bound to make the TLS less sustainable. While it is designed to improve labour standards, so is labour law. Whether labour standards regarding working conditions are complied with should be monitored on a day-to-day basis by workers and the employer, and verified for consistency by a labour inspection system operating under central authority, as required by the ILO Labour Inspection Convention, 1947 (no. 81).[31] Only then can companies compete with each other on a level social playing field.

One of the few commentators on TLS 8001-2003 notes several reasons for the scheme's relative unpopularity with companies' international buyers:[32]

1. TLS 8001-2003 does not dovetail well with international requirements. Many companies disregard them because the standards and management system vary, if not always much, from the labour standards or codes of conduct in multinational firms' home countries. Local firms still need to follow the labour standards of the client company, so compliance with the Thai standard is a further unnecessary cost. This suggests international buyers have little incentive to recognize and rely on TLS 8001-2003.
2. The government initially offered financial support to help firms improve and qualify for the standards. As firms become responsible for the cost of maintaining compliance, they no longer found it worthwhile.
2. The unpopularity of TLS 8001-2003 is also due to prescriptive and inflexibile standards such as employee welfare and the reduction of overtime hours from 36 to 12 hours per week in three years. When firms need to increase their production suddenly due to the amount of orders they receive, they often have insufficient overtime hours to meet the orders. Excessive overtime has long proven intractable in Thailand, as workers request overtime to top up regular wages that are considered inadequate. This should be seen in the context of low trade union density in the private sector (even by Asian standards) and virtually non-existent collective bargaining, leaving wage policy reliant on occasionally adjusted minimum wages.
4. Other problems in the government sector include a limited budget, limited experts and limited ability to improve the standard due to rules and regulations. In addition, the frequent change of governments in Thailand causes the improvement process to decelerate or come to a halt.

BETTER FACTORIES CAMBODIA (BFC)

In 2001, the ILO initiated a project to improve working conditions in Cambodian garment factories in accordance with Cambodian labour law and international labour standards.[33] The ILO Garment Sector Project was rebranded Better Factories Cambodia (BFC) in 2004.

BFC grew out of the US–Cambodia Textile Agreement (UCTA, 20 January 1999). More precisely, it was inspired in no small measure by US trade unions and labour rights activists disappointed by the ineffectiveness of earlier US trade agreements to further or enforce workers' rights (Wells, 2006). The UCTA provided for annual increases in export quotas for garments from Cambodia to the US, on condition that Cambodia's garment sector 'substantially comply' (UCTA, 20 January 1999, article 10 (D)) with 'internationally recognized core labor standards' and Cambodia's Labour Law adopted in 1997 (UCTA, 20 January 1999, Article 10 (B)). The quota increases could only be tapped if Cambodia demonstrated improvement in labour standards first, to which end the government had to 'support the implementation of a program to improve working conditions in the textile and apparel sector' (UCTA, 20 January 1999, Article 10 (B)). The commercial rewards from the US followed.[34] The ILO was then drawn in at the request of both parties to the UCTA for its expertise and credibility in the area of labour standards, even though it had never engaged in monitoring factories before (Kolben, 2004).

Consonant with the ILO's principle of tripartism, BFC was guided from the very beginning by a tripartite Project Advisory Committee (PAC) with equal representation from the Cambodian government, the Garment Manufacturers Association of Cambodia and the Cambodian trade union movement. The committee evaluates the project's monitoring and reporting system, including registration of participating factories, procedures for monitoring and reporting on visits, and procedures on reporting overall findings.[35] BFC thus represents a convergence of common interests in the industry, international buyers, the desires of western consumers for sweatshop-free products, and the need for more and better jobs in one of the poorest countries of the world. It is funded by the US Department of Labor (USDOL), USAID, the Agence Française de Développement (AFD), the Royal Cambodian Government (RGC), the Garment Manufacturers Association of Cambodia (GMAC) and international buyers.

In order to achieve the basic objective of the project – improving working conditions in Cambodia's textile and apparel sector – BFC operates a system of monitoring factories, which voluntary sign up.[36] Independent monitors visit factories to check working conditions on the basis of a checklist of over 500 questions. The checklist is endorsed by the PAC.[37] Data are collected, stored and analyzed in a computerized information management system (IMS) that permits ready access and immediate comparison among factories or issues. Compliance levels are now further being refined, for example, by computing the number of workers affected by certain issues.[38] The key monitoring steps include registration,[39] unannounced visits,[40] report preparation,[41] publication of the report in the IMS, objections and development of Corrective Action Plans (CAPs),[42] and follow-up visits[43] (ILO, BFC, Monitoring Process Brochure, p.2).

In the six months before 31 October 2009, 172 out of a total of 243 active factories, employing 278 398 workers were monitored (ILO, BFC, 23nd synthesis report, p.2). The project's monitoring covers core international labour standards as well as provisions of the Labour Law (1997) and executive ministerial decrees regarding wages, hours of work, contracts of employment, leave, occupational health and safety, welfare and labour relations. Two kinds of reports are provided after monitoring: confidential factory reports on the findings at each factory, and publicly available 'synthesis reports' with overviews of monitoring results.[44] The confidential reports provide factory managers with the findings and include specific suggestions for improvement touching on issues as diverse as child labour, freedom of association, employee contracts, wages, working hours, workplace facilities, noise control and machine safety.[45] After time for discussion and follow-up action, the monitors visit the factory again to check progress. Factories are named and their progress on implementation is identified in all reports made after the second visit. The synthesis reports were obviously determining the US government's decisions about annual quota increases (Wells, 2006, p. 364). BFC does not only engage in monitoring, but also creates services to help the industry improve working conditions, while at the same time improving quality and productivity. A range of training opportunities and resources, such as the Modular Training Programme and Single Issues Seminars, are being offered progressively to the industry.[46]

Better Factories Cambodia is complemented by an ILO Labour Dispute Resolution Project (LDRP) with funding from the US Department of Labour and USAID. The LDRP helped establish Cambodia's first national labour rights dispute settlement body (called the Arbitration Council) and has developed an agreed National Strategy on Labour Dispute Prevention and Settlement in Cambodia. It is a key element in the promotion of the Cambodian garment industry to international buyers concerned with compliance issues.[47] From its establishment in May 2003 until 31 December 2008, 650 cases have been filed with the Arbitration Council, the vast majority of which were settled successfully with a settlement agreement or arbitral award.[48]

BFC continues to attract considerable attention from researchers who have identified the following achievements:

1. The BFC initiative has grown into a multi-stakeholder programme rooting Cambodia's competitive edge in compliance with international labour standards and national labour law.[49]
2. The IMS provides a world-first information management system for monitoring and reporting. The IMS streamlines and integrates the data collected during factory monitoring visits on working conditions and labour standards. By managing the data in this manner, BFC can help factories improve their business performance. Since the information is managed electronically, BFC can automatically generate reports for individual factories as well as for groups of factories or the entire industry, showing their compliance and progress, while making suggestions for improvement. The IMS also benefits international buyers since the electronic information management system can 'provide better quality, easy-to-read reports; provides convenient, on-line access to factory reports; generates tailored reports comparing compliance levels for selected factories; reduces duplicative monitoring and cuts costs' (IMS Brochure). Other stakeholders, such as the employers' organization (CAMFEBA), trade unions and the public also benefit from the IMS because it can 'contribute to the garment industry's sustainability, provide online access to timely, user-friendly information, increase the transparency of monitoring and reporting and generate analytical data' (IMS Brochure).
3. There is substantial evidence that the programme has benefited garment workers in Cambodia. For instance, employment in the garment industry more than quadrupled from 79 000 in 1998 before the agreement to over 350 000 in April 2008 before the global crisis forced a number of factories to close (ILO, 2005). On the other hand, reports and surveys provide evidence of significant improvement in compliance with several labour standards (ILO, BFC, 30 April 2008). Research in 1999, before the UCTA came into effect, disclosed that labour standards went 'largely unchecked' and that '[l]ack of enforcement, rather than inadequacy of existing legislation, pose[d] the greatest obstacle to guaranteeing basic rights to workers in the garment industry in Cambodia' (Hall, 2000, pp. 119, 126). By contrast, after several years of UCTA quota incentives and ILO monitoring, a World Bank survey of international buyers found that

Cambodia's labour standards compliance ranked ahead of all its regional competitors (Foreign Investment Advisory Service, World Bank, Dec. 2004). In addition, according to the 8th synthesis report of BFC, on the whole, while a few factories made 'little effort to improve', in most factories progress has been made in improving working conditions (ILO BFC, July 2008, p. 89). The growth of the garment sector and the democratic transition in Cambodia has also prompted the emergence of an active trade union movement in the country.[50] A September 2004 survey of trade unions in Cambodia estimated total union membership in the country at 337 000, of whom 83 per cent are women. The largest number of unions and union members are found in the garment industry, where several union federations compete for members (Foreign Direct Investment Advisory Service, World Bank, December 2004). Working conditions, particularly as regards payment of wages and entitlements, have improved considerably as a result of BFC. Areas where further improvements could be made include freedom of association, discrimination and occupational health and safety.[51]

4. According to a 2004 World Bank survey of Cambodia's top fifteen buyers, which account for 45 per cent of the Cambodian garment industry's exports in the textile and garment sector, nine buyers intend to increase sourcing in Cambodia and six intend to continue sourcing at the same level even after the quota period.[52] The strong majority, 78.6 per cent, of respondents felt that voluntary certification/audit schemes would be of major or critical importance when they consider sourcing post quotas in 2005. Good labour standards rated first out of 12 possible country-specific reasons to source from a country.
5. Buyers felt that improved labour standards had positive effects on workplace accidents, workforce productivity, product quality, worker turnover, absenteeism and the quality of applicants for jobs.[53] They also rated Cambodia's compliance with labour standards slightly above Thailand and well ahead of China, Viet Nam and Bangladesh.
6. Perhaps the most significant achievement of BFC to date is that ILO and IFC have embarked on a joint programme to bring the experience in Cambodia to scale with pilot projects in Viet Nam, Jordan and Lesotho.[54]

Commentators, particularly in the US, have hailed the BFC model as the key to effectively linking trade and labour standards in an effort to use trade incentives as a tool to gradually improve labour market governance in developing countries. The failure of state-centred regulation, including international trade agreements, to be more than merely hortatory lies at the basis of experiments with non-state models of international labour regulation such as BFC. The BFC model is particularly successful because it relies on incentives, it depends on ILO as a more legitimate alternative to monitoring by non-descript firms or NGOs, and it focuses on compliance with both domestic labour law and ratified ILO conventions as opposed to eclectic corporate codes of conduct with no firm grounding in the local legal consciousness (Wells, 2006). Factors identified as critical to its success include the alignment of the government's objectives with those of the private sector through positive incentives, and the fact that the ILO's monitoring project made information on compliance findings immediately available to factory managers, interested parties and buyers, who were then in a position to redirect their purchases away from non-complying factories towards complying ones (Polaski, 14 July 2004).

The success of the BFC model should not blind anyone to its conditionality and drawbacks, however. It worked because it was nurtured in a controlled environment: it had a quota system that allowed for tangible incentives, an industry with little or no room to outsource supply operations to sub-standard working environments inside the country, and a nation heavily dependent on exports and employment for the success of the industry. From the beginning, local actors on the employer and worker side were not involved in the negotiations on ILO monitoring. The monitors may find violations but have no power to force compliance, underlining the fact that no monitoring system can substitute for a sovereign labour inspectorate with the power and domestic legitimacy to back up compliance efforts up with sanctions. Moreover, the reward of increased quotas was collective rather than individual, creating a free-rider problem (Wells, 2006).

CONCLUSIONS

This chapter's review of social clauses in trade agreements, the debate on their effectiveness and desirability, and the private social justice initiatives to which they have given rise permits at least five conclusions.

First, the demand for accountability as to how countries govern their labour markets and how companies operating on those markets treat their workforces remains high. No sooner is accountability at one level found wanting than new, mostly complementary, levels are being explored – including through private or market-based initiatives.

Secondly, at the multilateral level of public rule-making, there is a declaratory consensus that certain fundamental labour standards must be promoted, and that countries' violation of these makes any resulting comparative advantage in the international trading order illegitimate. This declaratory consensus appears to legitimize the continued use of trade as a tool to promote good governance, even if the use of trade sanctions remains controversial.

Thirdly, the US has led the way in consistently attempting to make bilateral trade liberalization subject to the observance of labour standards. The level of commitment sought in bilateral agreements as regards respect for fundamental labour standards and enforcement of labour law has strengthened somewhat in the last decade, but sanction-based enforcement of labour provisions is clearly avoided to the extent that any significant positive impact of such provisions on the observance of labour standards has been highly questionable.

Fourthly, a variety of private initiatives have sprung up to induce short-term changes on the shopfloor that more traditional public governance systems have failed to bring about. In many cases, these private initiatives make essential contributions to increased awareness both of legal provisions and of global market expectations, and foster immediate improvements with respect to some outcome-related labour standards (for example, child labour and health and safety, but not regular payment of wages nor overtime restrictions). However, their success in the longer term appears to depend on the same governance institutions that process-related labour standards (most notably freedom of association) aim to improve: participatory decision-making for the labour market (for example, tripartite consultations to ensure a uniform set of informed and viable labour standards) and on the labour market (for example, market-based, negotiated terms and conditions of employment), and respect for the rule of law. The success of private initiatives in improving observance of labour standards has so far been mixed at best. More companies in more sectors (at least export-oriented sectors) are assuming responsibility for improving working conditions, even if that has not delivered a larger market share nor the power to command higher prices. The question remains if that success can be maintained in an environment that is increasingly competitive and in which media attention on sweatshop abuses is fluctuating. It was precisely the need to reduce corporate competition in labour standards that prompted national and international public rule-making on labour standards.

Fifthly, the success of BFC in gradually improving labour standards in garment factories results in no small measure from private buyers' interest in decent labour standards being backed up by a national public authority that makes export opportunities for factories dependent on monitoring by an international public authority as a result of pressure by the public authority of another country. The day when the pursuit of social justice may be left entirely to market forces does not appear to have arrived as yet.

NOTES

1 We are indebted to Ms. Ling Lin for invaluable research assistance. Ms. Lin graduated from the Law School of Tsinghua University, and holds a LL.M. in International Economic and Business Law from Kyushu University.
2 In Western historiography, the cataclysms are referred to respectively as World War I and World War II.
3 For the full text of the Havana Charter, see www.worldtradelaw.net/misc/havana.pdf
4 These aspects are commonly broken down into four strategic objectives, i.e. promoting employment; developing and enhancing social protection measures; promoting social dialogue and tripartism; and respecting, promoting and realizing fundamental principles and rights at work.
5 See Maupain, 2009.
6 This is even without taking account of the persistent and sometimes serious issues of application by countries that have ratified either of these Conventions.
7 The Trans-Pacific Strategic Economic Partnership Agreement (TPP) is a free-trade agreement concluded between Brunei Darussalam, Chile, New Zealand and Singapore in June 2005. In 2008, Australia and the United States expressed interest in joining the Partnership, and in March 2010, negotiations started involving also Peru and Viet Nam as well.
8 See Aaronson and Rioux, n.d.
9 These labour market institutions include strong, representative and independent organizations of employers and workers; properly staffed, trained and resourced labour inspectors; a coherent body of labour law adopted on the basis of prior consultations with trade unions and employers' organizations; a system of collective negotiations enabling terms and conditions of employment to keep pace with productivity increases; and widely recognized employment contracts that define rights and duties of employers and workers; and effective labour dispute settlement mechanisms. For a variety of reasons, each of these institutions remain very weak in Asia.
10 USLEAP, November 2010. The US Labor Education in the Americas Project (USLEAP) describes itself as 'an independent, non-partisan, non-profit organization based in Chicago that engages a wide range of organizations and individuals in the U.S. and abroad to promote full respect for the rights of workers in Latin America'.
11 See www.betterfactories.org/aboutBFC.aspc?z = 2&c = 1&
12 See www.ustr.gov/Trade_Agreements/Bilateral/Section_Index.html (accessed 19 December 2010). The figure of 12 bilateral FTAs does not include the agreements with countries participating in the regional arrangements discussed earlier.
13 The TPA is contained in the Title XXI of the Bipartisan Trade Promotion Authority Act of 2002.
14 In October 2003, the World Bank published an extensive review of company codes of conduct in a range of economic sectors. See World Bank, October 2003, Part I and Part II. Part I concerns apparel, footwear and light manufacturing, agribusiness and tourism and Part II focuses on oil, gas and mining.
15 The following useful typology is from O'Rourke, 2003, pp. 19–20.
16 The FLA characterizes itself as 'a collaborative effort of socially responsible companies, colleges and universities, and civil society organizations to improve working conditions in factories around the world'. It claims to add value by offering 'a system to perform due diligence on companies' internal compliance programs through unannounced independent external monitoring and verification; innovative and sustainable strategies for improving compliance with labor standards; public access to all independent external

monitoring reports via the FLA Web site; and a mechanism to address the most serious labor rights violations through our Third Party Complaint process'. See www.fairlabor.org/about-us

17 The WRC describes its mission in the following terms (www.workersrights.org/about/): 'The Worker Rights Consortium (WRC) is an independent labor rights monitoring organization, conducting investigations of working conditions in factories around the globe... The WRC conducts independent, in-depth investigations; issues public reports on factories producing for major brands; and aids workers at these factories in their efforts to end labor abuses and defend their workplace rights.'

18 O'Rourke, 2003, supra note 55, 21–22.

19 We are indebted to Ms. Chayanich Thamparipattra for reviewing this section and undertaking additional research (*The Thai Labour Standard (TLS 8001-2546)*, unpublished). Ms. Chayanich Thamparipattra obtained a Bachelor of Law from Thammasat University.

20 The TLS covers all types of companies in principle, but its functional focus is on exporting companies.

21 Unpublished (on record with author).

22 Social Accountability International (SAI) describes SAN 8000 as 'a comprehensive and flexible system for managing ethical workplace conditions throughout global supply chains' (www.sa-intl.org/index.cfm?&stopRedirect = 1). SA 8000 is an 'auditable certification standard' containing nine elements: child labour; forced labour; health and safety; freedom of association and right to collective bargaining; discrimination; discipline; working hours; compensation; management systems.

23 *Alternatives to Public Sector Inspections: Public-Private Partnerships and Corporate Social Responsibility (CSR)*, Final Report for the Foreign Investment Advisory Service of the World Bank Group, 30 June 2005. Available at: (www.ifc.org/ifcext/economics.nsf/AttachmentsByTitle/CSR-Alternatives + to + Public + Sector + Insepctions + June + 30/$FILE/Alternatives + to + Public + Sector + Insepctions + June + 30.pdf), para. 71.

24 Unpublished (on record with author). To put this figure into perspective, Thailand currently has a workforce of around 35 million people. Note, moreover, that the figures reflect companies that have been passed certification in a given category at a given point of time in the past, so a company that has gone from basic to completion level is counted twice.

25 Unpublished (on record with author).

26 Unpublished (on record with author).

27 Requirements 5.3. to 5.12 deal with the following issues: forced labour; remuneration; working hours; discrimination; discipline and penalty; child labour; female employees; freedom of association and collective bargaining; occupational safety, health and environment; welfare (for example, sanitary facilities and accommodation).

28 The exchange rate of the Thai Baht is about 39 THB per Euro (rate on 20 December 2010).

29 (1) Establishment of the TLS development team. (2) Development of personnel's understanding. (3) Determination of the status. (4) Documents Management. (5) Impose and declaration of the TLS policy. (6) Implementation. (7) Internal Auditor. (8) Revision by the executive officer. (The Labour Standard Development Bureau, The Manual, p. 101).

30 'ASEAN + 6 FTA' negotiations refer to plans to replicate the ASEAN Free Trade Area (AFTA) on a much larger scale. AFTA members have until 2010 to reduce all tariff rates to 0–5 per cent by 2010, and ultimately eliminate them by 2015. An ASEAN + 3 FTA would do the same for an area including China, the Republic of Korea and Japan, and ASEAN + 6 would further expand the area to include India, Australia and New Zealand. The latter two countries traditionally require 'social clauses' to be included in trade agreements.

31 Thailand has not ratified C. 81. Since 2008, ILO has stepped up the promotion of C. 81 as a convention that is particularly important for labour market governance.

32 Suttawet, 67.

33 Ensuring that Working Conditions in the Textile and Apparel Sector of Cambodia Comply with Internationally Recognized Core Labour Standards and the Cambodian Labour Law, p.26, ILO (May 4, 2000) (on file with author). See also Kolben, 2004, p. 100.
34 Quotas increased by 9 per cent in 2000 and 2001, 12 per cent in 2002, 14 per cent in 2003, and 18 per cent in 2004. See Polaski, October 2004, p. 14.
35 See BFC's website: www.betterfactories.org/ILO/aboutBFC.aspx?z = 2&c = 1
36 Although factory registration is voluntary in principle, only registered factories are eligible for export licences. (Wells, 2006, 364). By 24 August, 309 operating factories were registered with Better Factories Cambodia. Registration means that the ILO and the participating factory sign a Memorandum of Understanding (MOU) outlining their duties and responsibilities. The factory agrees to provide ILO monitors with full access to the factory premises for unannounced visits at all times. The factory also agrees that ILO monitors will interact freely with shop stewards, union representatives and factory workers, both inside and outside the factory premises. See www.betterfactories.org/monitoring.aspx?z = 5&c = 1
37 See www.betterfactories.org/ILO/monitoring.aspx?z = 5&c = 1
38 See ILO BFC, 23rd Synthesis Report, 16 December 2009, p. 1. The new system is called the STAR system (Supply Chain Tracking and Remediation).
39 The manufacturer (employer) registers with the programme and gets basic information about the monitoring process.
40 During the unannounced monitoring visit, meetings are held with management, shop stewards, union leaders and workers documents are reviewed and the workplace is observed.
41 Documentary evidence provided by the manufacturer is reviewed, and the report is prepared.
42 The manufacturer can post objections and Corrective Action Plans (CAPs) and/or request clarification on issues of concern.
43 The next monitoring visit may be expected within six months' time, with a possibility of additional single-issue ad hoc checks at any time.
44 The synthesis reports may be consulted at: www.betterfactories.org/synthesisreport-s.aspx?z = 7&c = 1
45 See www.betterfactories.org/ILO/aboutBFC.aspx?z = 2&c = 1 ('About Better Factories').
46 See www.betterfactories.org/ILO/training.aspx?z = 6&c = 1
47 Cambodia, labour dispute resolution (see Heron and van Noord, 2004 and van Noord et al., 2011.
48 See www.arbitrationcouncil.org/AboutUs/TheArbitrationCouncil/tabid/59/Default.aspx
49 Consider, for example, the following observation about the end of textile quotas: 'Cambodia . . . could be quite adversely affected. Garments contribute 76 percent of exports and all of manufacturing employment, but are closely correlated with those sub-categories where China is presently most quota constrained. Productivity levels are less than in China offsetting lower wage levels. The industry is also hampered by longer lead times and a limited domestic textiles production capacity. One potential comparative advantage however is Cambodia's adherence to ILO monitored Core Labour Standards, which are viewed favorably by some classes of buyers. Cambodia and a number of other Least Developed Countries have also asked for preferential duty-free access to the U.S. market, which otherwise imposes a 15 percent duty on garment imports from WTO members.' (World Bank, 2004, p. 23).
50 The garment and textile sector is the most FDI-penetrated sector in Cambodia, with the largest share of FDI coming from China and the ASEAN countries. See Cuyvers et al., January 2008 and Cuyvers et al., 2009.
51 See www.betterfactories.org/content/documents/1/Newsletter%20No.15%20(Eng).pdf
52 See www.betterfactories.org/content/documents/WB%20survey.pdf.
53 Ibid.
54 See www.betterwork.org/EN/countries/Pages/CountiesSites.aspx

REFERENCES

Books and Articles

Aaronson, S. A. and Rioux, M. *Striking a Proper Match? Strategies to Link Trade Agreements and Real Labor Rights Improvements*. Available at www.er.uqam.ca/novel/ieim/IMG/pdf/finalsummary-4.pdf (accessed 28 May 2012).

Abbott, K. W. and Snidal, D, (2009), 'Strengthening international regulation through transnational new governance: overcoming the orchestration deficit', *Vanderbilt Journal of Transnational Law*, 42 (2), pp. 501–578.

Bartley, T. (2005), 'Corporate accountability and the privatization of labor standards: struggles over codes of conduct in the apparel industry', *Research in Political Sociology*, 14, pp. 211–244.

Bolle, M. J. (2007), 'Trade Promotion Authority (TPA) Renewal: core labour standards issues: a brief overview', Congressional Research Service (CRS) Reports and Issue Briefs. Available at http://digitalcommons.ilr.cornell.edu/crs/27 (accessed 28 May 2012).

Brauer, J. and Haywood, R. (February 2010), 'Non-state sovereign entrepreneurs and non-territorial sovereign organizations', Working Paper no. 2010/09, Helsinki: UNU World Institute for Development Economics Research, 10. Available at www.wider.unu.edu/publications/working-papers/2010/en_GB/wp2010-09/_files/82967192285675604/default/2010-09.pdf (accessed 28 May 2012).

Chulalongkorn University (Chula Uniresearch) (2004), *Executive summary of the appraisal project for the Project of Development of Labour Standard for Free Trade Promotion*.

Compa, L. and Vogt, J. (2001), 'Labor rights in the generalized system of preferences', *Comparative Labor Law and Policy Journal*, 22.

Cuyvers, L., Soeng, R. and Van Den Bulcke, D. (January 2008), 'The contribution of MNEs to economic success in small open economies: the case of Cambodia', Cas Discussion paper no. 58, University of Antwerp, Centre for ASEAN Studies.

Cuyvers, L., Van Den Bulcke, D. and Soeng, R. (2009), 'The competitive position of a developing economy: the role of foreign direct investment in Cambodia', in D. Van Den Bulcke, A. Verbeke and W. Yuan (eds), *Handbook on Small Nations in the Global Economy: The Contribution of Multinational Enterprises to National Economic Success*, Cheltenham UK and Northampton: Edward Elgar, pp.244–272.

De Meyer, T. (2001), 'ILO fundamental principles and rights at work in Asia Pacific: emerging standards for emerging markets?' in L. Cuyvers (ed.), *Globalisation and Social Development: European and Southeast Asian Evidence*, Cheltenham, UK: Edward Elgar, pp. 133–170.

Dicaprio, A. (2004), 'Are labour provisions protectionist?: Evidence from nine labour-augmented U.S. trade arrangements', *Comparative Labour Law and Policy Journal*, 26 (1) (published 28 October, 2005). Available at http://www.law.illinois.edu/publications/cllpj/archive/vol 26/issue 1/dicaprioarticle26-1.pdf (accessed 28 May 2012).

Gantz, D. A. (25 July 2008), 'The bipartisan trade deal: Trade Promotion Authority and the future of U.S. free trade sgreements', *St. Louis University*

Public Law Review, XXVIII (1). Available at http://slu.edu/Documents/law/PLR/Archives/TOC Vol 28 No 1.pdf (accessed 28 May 2012).

Gravel, E. (2008), 'Is the appropriation of international labour standards by new actors replacing or complementing the ILO's traditional standards-related work?', in J. C. Javillier (ed.), *Governance, International Law and Corporate Social Responsibility*, Geneva: ILO.

Hall, J.A. (2000), 'Human rights and the garment industry in contemporary Cambodia', *Stanford Journal of International Law*, 36 (1), pp. 119–174. Available at http://ssrn.com/abstract=926407 (accessed 28 May 2012).

Heron, R. and Van Noord, H. (2004), National Strategy on Labour Dispute Prevention and Settlement in Cambodia, Phnom Penh, International Labour Office. Available at www.better/factories.org/content/documents/1/National%20Strategy%20on%20Labour%20Dispute%20Prevention%20and%20Settlement.pdf (accessed 28 May 2012).

Kernaghan, C. (Director National Labour Committee) (14 June 2006), 'Hearing on modern-day slavery: spotlight on the 2006 trafficking in persons report, forced labour, and sex trafficking at the world cup', House Committee on International Relations, Human Trafficking and Involuntary Servitude, Under the U.S.-Jordan Free Trade Agreement. Available at www.globallabourrights.org/alerts?id=0119 (accessed 28 May 2012).

Kolben, K. (2004), 'Note from the field: trade, monitoring, and the ILO: working to improve conditions in Cambodia's garment factories', *Yale Human Rights and Development Law Journal*, 7, pp. 79–107.

Mahaim, E. (1934), 'The historical and social importance of international labour legislation', in J. Shotwell (ed.), *The Origins of the International Labour Organization*, New York: Columbia University Press.

Maupain, F. (2009), 'Refoundation or lost (and last) opportunity? The new ILO Declaration on Social Justice for a Fair Globalization', unpublished.

O'Rourke, D. (2003), 'Outsourcing regulation: analyzing non-governmental systems of labor standards and monitoring', *Policy Studies Journal*, 31 (1), pp. 1–29.

Polaski, S. (14 July 2004), 'Protecting labor rights through trade agreements: an analytical guide', *Journal of International Law and Policy*. Available at http://www.carnegieendowment.org/files/2004-07-polaski-JILP.pdf (accessed 28 May 2012).

Polaski, S. (October 2004), 'Cambodia blazes a new path to economic growth and job creation', *Carnegie Papers*, 51 (14). Available at www.carnegieendowment.org/files/cp51polaskifinal2.pdf (accessed 28 May 2012).

Sabel, C., Fung, A. and O'Rourke, D. (2000), *Ratcheting Labor Standards: Regulation for Continuous Improvement in the Global Workplace*, Washington DC: World Bank.

Serrano, M.R., Marasigan, M.L.C. and Palafox, J.A.F. (1 May 2004), 'Is a social charter possible in the Asean? – Exploring the chances of an Asean social charter in Six Asean member states', *Friedrich Ebert Stiftung Office for Regional Cooperation in Southeast Asia and U.P. School of Labor and Industrial Relations*, 68. Available at http://library.fes.de/pdf-files/bueros/singapur/02590.pdf (accessed 28 May 2012).

Suttawet, C. (2008), *Current Situation of Labour Standards for Trading in Thailand*. Available at http://www.udel.edu/fiber/issue2/world/LaborStandards-Thailand.html (accessed 28 May 2012).

Van Noord, H., Hwang, H.S. and Bugeja, K. (2011) *Cambodia's Arbitration Council: Institution-building in a developing country*, Working Paper No. 24, International Labour Office, Industrial and Emplyment Relations Department, Geneva. Available at http://www.ilo.org/wcmsp5/groups/public- - -ed_dialogue/- - -dialogue/documents/publication/wcms_166728.pdf (accessed 28 May 2012)

Vogel, D. (2005), *The Market for Virtue: The Potential and Limits of Corporate Social Responsibility*, Washington DC: Brookings Institutions.

Vogel, D. (2008), 'Private global business regulation', *Annual Review of Political Science*, 11, pp. 261–282.

Wells, D. (2006), '"Best practice" in the regulation of international labor standards: lessons of the U.S.-Cambodia textile agreement', *Comparative Labor Law and Policy Journal*, 27 (3), pp. 357–376.

World Bank (October 2003), *Company Codes Of Conduct And International Standards: An Analytical Comparison,* Washington DC: World Bank.

World Commisson on the Social Dimension of Globalization, *A Fair Globalization: Creating Opportunity for All*, Geneva: ILO, avalable at www.ilo.org/public/English/wcsdg/docs/report.pdf (accessssed 8 March 2012).

World Trade Organization, *Ministerial Declaration adopted on 14 November 2001 at the Fourth WTO Ministerial Conference (Doha)*, WT/MIN(01)/DEC/1, available at www.wto.or/english/thewto_e/minist_e/min01_e/mindecl-e.htm (accessed 8 March 2012).

Official Documents

Agreement Relating to Trade in Cotton, Wool, Man-made Fiber, Non-Cotton Vegetable Fiber and Silk Blend Textiles and Textiles Products Between the Government of the United States of America and the Royal Government of Cambodia (20 January 1999). Available at http://cambodia.usembassy.gov/uploads/images/M9rzdrzMKGi6Ajf0SIuJRA/uskh_texttile.pdf (accessed 28 May 2012).

Bipartisan Trade Deal (May 2010). Available at http://bilaterals.org/IMG/pdf/05_14_07.pdf (accessed 28 May 2012).

Briefing Note for the Doha WTO Ministerial (2001), *Trade and Labour Standards – A difficult issue for many WTO member Governments*. Available at www.wto.org/english/theWTO_e/minist_e/min01_e/brief_e/brief16_e.htm (accessed 28 May 2012).

Foreign Investment Advisory Service, World Bank (December 2004), *Cambodia: Corporate Social Responsibility and the Apparel Sector Buyer Survey Results*. Available at http://www.betterfactories.org/content/documents/Cambodia%20Corporate%20Social%20Responsbility/pdf (accessed 28 May 2012).

International Labour Office, Better Factories Cambodia (2005), *Facts and Figures*, Geneva: ILO.

International Labour Office, Better Factories Cambodia, *Information Management System*, available at http://www.betterfactories.org/content/documents/1/IMS%20Brochure%20(en).pdf (accessed 13 March 2012).

International Labour Office, Better Factories Cambodia, *Monitoring Process Brochure*, Geneva: ILO. Available at: www.betterfactories.org/resourcedet.aspx?z = 7&iddoc = 95&c = 1 (accessed 28 May 2012).

International Labour Office, Better Factories Cambodia (2008), *Twentieth Synthesis Report On Working Conditions In Cambodia's Garment Sector*, Geneva: ILO. Available at www.betterfactories.org/content/documents/1/20th%20Synthesis%20Report%20Final%20(EN).pdf (accessed 28 May 2012).

International Labour Office, Better Factories Cambodia (16 December 2009), *Twenty-Third Synthesis Report On Working Conditions In Cambodia's Garment Sector*, Geneva: ILO. Available at www.betterfactories.org/content/documents/1/23rd%20Synthesis%20Report%20(en).pdf (accessed 28 May 2012).

International Labour Office, *Constitution of the International Labour Organization, Part XIII of the Treaty of Versailles (Labour)*, 28 June 1919, available at www.ilo.org/iloindex/english/iloconst.htm (accessed 8 March 2012).

International Labour Office, *Declaration Concerning the Aims and Purposes of the International Labour Organisation adopted by the Conference at its Twenty-Sixth Session*, Philadelphia, 10 May 1944, available at www.ilo.org/public/english/century/information_resources/download/phil-en-fr.pdf (accessed 8 March 2012).

International Labour Office, *Declaration on Fundamental Principles and Rights at Work*, Geneva: ILO. Available at http://www.ilo.org/declaration/thedeclaration/textdeclaration/lang--en/index.htm (accessed 28 May 2012).

International Labour Office (10 June 2008), *Declaration on Social Justice for a Fair Globalization*, adopted by the ILO at its Ninety-Seventh Session, Geneva, 10 June 2008, available at http://www.ilo.org/wcmsp5/groups/public/@dgreports/@cabinet/documents/publication/wcms-0997766.pdf (accessed 28 May 2012).

Labour Advisory Committee for Trade Negotiations and Trade Policy (LAC) (19 March 2004), *Report: The US-DR-CAFTA*. Available at: http://www.ustr.gov/archive/assets/Trade_Agreements/Regional/CAFTA/CAFTA_Reports/asset_upload_file63_5935.pdf (accessed 28 May 2012).

Labor Declaration On The Negotiation Of The Trans-Pacific Partnership Trade Agreement (15 March 2010). Available at www.bilaterals.org/IMG/pdf_TPP_Joint_Declaration_Final.pdf (accessed 28 May 2012).

The Labour Standard Development Bureau, 'The Manual of the TLS Implementation'.

The Labour Standard Development Bureau, Department of Labour Protection and Welfare, the Ministry of Labour (12 February), *Report on Certification of the Thai Labour Standard to Promote Quality of Life and Sustainable Business Workshop*, B.E. 2547.

Memorandum of Understanding on Labour Cooperation concluded between New Zealand and China (October 2008). Available at www.chinafta.govt.nz/1-The-agreement/1-Key-outcomes/0-downloads/MOU-NZ.pdf (accessed 28 May 2012).

Thai Ministry of Labour, Department of Labour Protection and Welfare (12 February 2004), *Report on the Certification of the Thai Labour Standard to Promote Quality of Life and Sustainable Business Workshop*, B.E. 2547.

The Trans-Pacific Strategic Economic Partnership Agreement (TPP) concluded between Brunei Darussalam, Chile, New Zealand and Singapore in June 2005.

USLEAP (November 2010), *Labor Protections and the Dominican Republic-Central America Free Trade Agreement (DR-CAFTA)*. Available at www.usleap.org/CAFTA%20Fact%20Sheet_Nov%202010.pdf (accessed 28 May 2012).

World Bank (2004), *East Asia Update. Ministerial declaration*, by the WTO Ministerial Conference Fourth Session, Doha (9–14 November 2001), WT/MIN(01)/DEC/W/1.

FURTHER INFORMATION

www.arbitrationcouncil.org/AboutUs/TheArbitrationCouncil/tabid/59/Default.aspx
www.betterfactories.org/aboutBFC.aspx?z = 2&c = 1&
www.betterfactories.org/ILO/monitoring.aspx?z = 5&c = 1
www.betterfactories.org/synthesisreports.aspx?z = 7&c = 1
www.betterfactories.org/ILO/aboutBFC.aspx?z = 2&c = 1
www.betterfactories.org/ILO/training.aspx?z = 6&c = 1
www.betterfactories.org/content/documents/1/Newsletter%20No.15%20(Eng).pdf
www.betterfactories.org/content/documents/WB%20survey.pdf
www.betterfactories.org/resourcedet.aspx?z = 7&iddoc = 95&c = 1
www.betterwork.org/public/global/programm-countries
www.fairlabor.org/aboutus.html
www.sa-intl.org/index.cfm?&stopRedirect = 1
http://tls.labour.go.th/en/index.html
www.ustr.gov/Trade_Agreements/Bilateral/Section_Index.html (last accessed 19 December 2010)
www.workersrights.org/about/

PART II

Private food standards and global governance: economic perspectives

6. Private standards, global food supply chains and the implications for developing countries

Miet Maertens and Johan Swinnen

1. INTRODUCTION

Standards are increasingly dominating world trade and production. This is particularly important in sectors such as food and agricultural exports (Jaffee and Henson, 2005; Maertens and Swinnen, 2007). Over the past decades food standards have increased, with new regulations and requirements from national and international governments as well as from private actors, and standards have focused on different issues such as product quality, food safety and increasingly also ethical and environmental concerns. Many large food companies, supermarket chains and NGOs have engaged in establishing private food standards – that are often stricter than public requirements – and have adapted food quality and safety standards in certification protocols. Examples include GLOBALG.A.P. (formerly EUREPGAP), the British Retail Consortium (BRC) Global Standards, Ethical Trading Initiative (ETI), Tesco's Nature's Choice, Save Quality Food (SQV) Program, etc. Although private standards are legally not mandatory, many of them have become de facto mandatory because of commercial pressure by a large share of buyers in international agri-food markets requiring compliance with such private standards (Henson and Humphrey, 2008). Private standards often go beyond food quality and safety specifications and include ethical and environmental considerations as well.

Food standards, public as well as private, have emerged mainly from high-income countries and regions,[1] such as the EU and the US, but affect developing countries through trade with high-income regions and the spread of multinational food companies within their borders. With respect to the impact on developing countries, food standards have most often been discussed as new non-tariff barriers to trade. First, standards can be used by high-income countries as protectionist tools to bar imports from developing countries and protect domestic farmers and agri-food companies. Second, standards can act as barriers to trade because of the high costs of compliance and certification. Such costs may be particularly high for developing countries, which generally lack the infrastructure, institutional, technical and scientific capacity for food quality and safety management and who face a wide divergence between national food quality and safety norms and international standards. Third, the inability of developing countries to comply with stringent standards can be very costly and trade distorting. This can at first lead to border detentions and ultimately result in trade restrictions such as import bans for specific products.

On the other hand, standards can act as catalysts to trade as well. They are most often in the interest of public health and can facilitate trade between countries with diverging norms. As such, standards and certification schemes can help to reduce transaction costs, promote consumer confidence in food product safety and increase developing countries' access to international markets (Henson and Jaffee, 2008). In fact, standards provide a bridge between producers in developing countries and consumer preferences in high-income markets and can be used as catalysts for upgrading and modernizing of developing countries' food supply systems and improving their competitive capacity. Indeed, some developing countries have been successful in complying with increasing food standards and upgrading their export sectors as a basis for long-term export growth.

Understanding the link between standards on the one hand, and export competitiveness and performance of developing countries on the other hand, is crucial in the design of a broader development agenda as integration in global markets is generally believed to benefit economic growth (Bhagwati and Srinivasan, 2002; Dollar and Kraay, 2004). Yet, there is a concern that the poor may not benefit proportionately from high-standards international trade. Hence, another critical policy issue is to understand the link between standards, food supply chains and rural incomes in developing countries. The proliferation of stringent private and public standards has caused dramatic changes in the way food production and trade are organized and governed, with important implications for producers and rural households (McCullough et al., 2008; Swinnen, 2007; Wilson and Abiola, 2003). Hence, the costs and structural changes associated with standards compliance can cause significant redistribution of welfare – not only across countries but also along supply chains and in rural societies (World Bank, 2005). Major concerns are that poor farmers and smallholder suppliers are excluded from high-standards food supply chains because of their inability to comply with high standards. The fear is that these farmers are exploited in the chains because stringent standards decrease the bargaining power of small farmers vis-à-vis large food exporters and multinational food companies, and increase the possibilities for rent extracting in the chain. Standards are therefore often seen as barriers to development as well. However, the arguments are subject to debate; empirical studies have come to diverse conclusions about the effects of increasing and tightening public and private food standards on rural households in developing countries.

In this chapter we give an overview of the arguments and empirical evidence on the development implications of increasing food standards. We argue that a key issue in understanding the local welfare implications of increasing high-standards food trade is the way in which supply chain structures and governance systems respond to increasing standards. Moreover, to empirically assess the development implications of public and private standards, there is a need for firm-, farm-, and household-survey data. In this chapter we discuss issues of supply chain governance and the development implications of increasing standards, and we empirically document our discussion with insights from three original comparative case studies that are based on extensive survey data collection.

2. STANDARDS AND SUPPLY CHAIN GOVERNANCE

Increasing public and private standards induce structural changes in food supply chains. These include: 1) increasing levels of vertical coordination (VC) in global supply chains; and 2) increasing consolidation of the supply base with large food companies – often multinationals – dominating the chains.

First, compliance with increasingly complex and stringent food standards and monitoring of this compliance throughout the supply chains requires tighter VC in the chains. In order to ensure large and consistent volumes of high-quality and safe produce, food traders and processors increasingly procure from preferred suppliers or specialized wholesale markets, often on a contract basis, and thereby push the food distribution system towards more VC. In addition, upstream the supply chain VC is increasing. Traditional spot market trading systems with 'middlemen' are generally not effective in high-standards trade because of high transaction costs related to monitoring compliance with standards. Faced with increased standards, agro-industrial food companies and exporters are increasingly changing their procurement system towards more VC (Swinnen, 2005). This can occur through different forms of contract-farming or, in the most extreme case, through complete ownership vertical integration. The latter implies a shift from smallholder, contract-based production towards large-scale vertically integrated estate production by agro-processing and food trading companies. This large-scale vertically integrated method of production increases the scope for standardized production and for meeting high standards at low transaction costs. However, it also entails additional risks and costs for the agro-industry, including labour supervision costs.

There is a substantial number of empirical studies demonstrating these supply chain developments. Some studies have pointed to the development of comprehensive VC schemes with extensive monitoring and complex contracting between large food companies and developing country producers as a result of increasing food standards. For example, Gulati et al. (2007) have noted a sharp increase in animal contract-production in Southeast Asia in response to increasing standards. For the fresh fruit and vegetable (FFV) export sector in Kenya, Jaffee (2003) reports intensified extension services and closer governance in supplier-contracts, motivated by increased standards. Swinnen (2005) identifies increasing standards as one of the main driving forces of increased vertical coordination in different agricultural sectors in transition countries in Eastern Europe and Central Asia. Other authors have presented case-study evidence of a shift towards vertical integration in high-standards export production. For example, Minot and Ngigi (2004) and Dolan and Humphrey (2000) report increased large-scale agro-industrial farming and vertical integrated production in the fruit and vegetable sectors of Kenya and Cote d'Ivoire. How far-reaching the shift is from small-scale contract-based production to large-scale vertically integrated industrial production strongly varies across sectors and countries (Maertens et al., 2010) and has major implications for the way in which producers and local households benefit (see below).

Second, food standards pose specific challenges – arising from financial, technical and institutional constraints – for small agro-food businesses and exporters in developing countries to stay in business in export markets. Although, in general, the cost of compliance with standards might be low relative to total export value, this cost might be very high relative to the means of small firms, leading to the market exit of small and less capitalized firms (Reardon et al., 1999). In addition, smaller businesses might be disadvantaged in contracting with overseas importers and large retail chains because they cannot guarantee the volumes required by these large buyers. Moreover, multinational holdings increasingly seek vertical integration through establishing subsidiaries in developing countries. Foreign direct investment (FDI) in the food export, processing and retailing sectors in developing countries has increased tremendously in the past decade (Colen et al., 2008), which might push smaller firms with less access to capital, poorer technologies and less access to market information out of high-standards export sectors. Increasing food standards and increased FDI in the food sectors of developing countries may lead to weaker players exiting profitable export markets, and hence to consolidation at the export node of the supply chains.

The empirical literature has presented evidence of ongoing consolidation in agricultural export production in low-income countries (Dolan and Humphrey, 2000; Jaffee, 2003). For example, Maertens et al. (2007) report that in the bean export sector in Senegal the number of exporting companies has dropped from 27 in 2002 to 20 in 2005, with mainly smaller exporters leaving the market. This resulted in an increased market share for the three largest companies, from slightly less than half to two-thirds over the same time period.

As we will document in the next sections of the chapter, these structural changes in the governance system of food supply chains are crucial for understanding the welfare implications of increasing food standards for rural households in developing countries.

3. IMPLICATIONS FOR DEVELOPMENT

Participation in international trade is generally considered to be beneficial for poor countries. Yet, the increased proliferation and tightening of public and private food standards has cast doubt on the beneficial effect of trade for rural households in poor countries. Major concerns are that poor farmers and smallholder suppliers are excluded from high-standards food supply chains because of their inability to comply with high standards; and that these farmers are exploited in the chains because stringent standards decrease the bargaining power of small farmers vis-à-vis large food exporters and multinational food companies, and increase the possibilities for rent extracting in the chain.

Concerning the issue of exclusion of smallholder producers there is mixed evidence in the literature. Some studies argue that small farmers, and especially the poorest ones, are increasingly being squeezed out from high-standards export production because of high compliance costs and increasing levels of VC (Gibbon, 2003; Reardon and Barrett, 2000; Reardon et al., 1999). First, at the farm level the individual cost-of-compliance to strict public and private standards and the cost of certification might be prohibitively high for smallholder producers to (continue to) engage in high-standards production, especially when credit markets are imperfect and credit is rationed. Empirical studies that have actually calculated the cost-of-compliance and certification for individual smallholder producers in high-standards supply chains mostly come to different conclusions. For example, Henson (2009) estimates that the initial non-recurrent investment costs of EUREPGAP certification (type II, group certification) for smallholder contract-farmers in the Ghana pineapple sector represent less than 2 per cent of sales value and the recurrent cost of maintaining certification less than 1 per cent of sales value. In addition to these relatively small compliance costs, the variable costs of production were found to be lower due to EUREPGAP certification, mainly because of better and more efficient use of pesticides and other chemicals and general improvements in agronomic practices.

Second, increasing levels of VC in food supply chains may result in a bias against the smallest and poorest farmers, either because they are excluded from contract-farming schemes with agro-processors and traders who prefer to contract with larger suppliers or because smallholder production is replaced by estate production in vertically integrated agro-industries. Contract-farming schemes may be biased towards relatively larger and better endowed farms because of smaller transaction costs (especially for monitoring conformity with standards), and smaller investment costs in terms of farm extension and financial assistance by the contractor firm (Key and Runsten, 1999). However, standards are themselves instruments for harmonizing product and process attributes over suppliers, and can as such reduce transaction costs in dealing with a large number of small suppliers. Moreover, well-specified contracts include farm extension and assistance programmes that can alleviate the financial and technical constraints small farmers face in meeting stringent standards. In fact, high-standards contract-farming with tight contract-coordination and intensified farm assistance programmes could provide a basis for constrained small farmers to participate in high-value export production. In addition, firms might prefer to contract with smaller farms because they might have a cost advantage – especially if it concerns labour intensive production – or because contract enforcement might be less costly with small suppliers.

The actual evidence on smallholder involvement in high-standards supply chains is very mixed. There are cases of complete vertical integration with hardly any smallholder involvement; for example, in the tomato export sector in Senegal (Maertens et al., 2011) and the fruit and vegetable export sectors in Zambia (Legge et al., 2006). On the other hand, there are also many examples of cases where export production – destined for markets where standards are high and increasing – remains dominated by smallholders; for example, the vegetable export sectors in Madagascar (Minten et al., 2009) and Ghana (Legge et al., 2006). In most cases of high-standards export production there is a mix between smallholder contract production and large-scale agro-industrial production (Maertens et al.,

2011). Some studies have pointed to sharp reductions in the share of smallholder production as standards increase; for example, Jaffee (2003) – recognizing the limitations of the available data – estimates that for export vegetables in Kenya the share of smallholder production decreased from 45 per cent in the mid-1980s to 27 per cent in 2001/2002. More recent studies, however, state that these early estimates exaggerate the problem of smallholder exclusion and that in fact more smallholders are involved in Kenyan high-standards horticulture exports than previously estimated (Asfaw et al., 2007; Mithöfer et al., 2008). In general, the figures on horticulture sectors in Africa seem to point to much more smallholder involvement in high-standards production than would be assumed based on the above arguments. Similar observations have been made for several agricultural sectors in transition countries in Eastern Europe and Central Asia (Swinnen, 2005).

Concerning the issue of *exploitation of smallholder producers*, it has been argued repeatedly that the gains from high-standards agricultural trade are captured by foreign investors, large food companies and developing country elites and that standards lead to a more unequal distribution of the gains from trade (for example, Dolan and Humphrey, 2000; Reardon et al., 1999). On the one hand, consolidation of the export supply base and repeatedly VC in the supply chains are said to amplify the bargaining power of large agro-industrial firms and food multinationals, displace decision-making authority from the farmers to these downstream companies, and strengthen the capacity of these companies to extract rents from the chain to the disadvantage of poor farmers and local households (Warning and Key, 2002). On the other hand, VC schemes provide a basis for farmers to access the credit, inputs and technology they need for upgrading their production in terms of productivity and quality and to increase their incomes.

Recent empirical studies have demonstrated a beneficial effect for smallholders participating in high-standards contract production. Demonstrated benefits include productivity gains, increased household income, reduced volatility of household income, technology spillovers, and so on. For example, Dries and Swinnen (2004) show that small dairy farms in Poland gain in terms of productivity and improved quality from contract production with large foreign milk processors. Gulati et al. (2007) provide similar evidence for smallholder animal production in Southeast Asia. Asfaw et al. (2007) show that EUREPGAP certification among smallholder farmers in the Kenyan horticulture sector leads to substantial additional income gains for certified farmers (as compared to non-certified farmers). In addition, these authors find that EUREPGAP certification among smallholder farmers leads to reduced pesticide use and decreased health risks for farmers (Asfaw et al., 2009).

Moreover, an important and much overlooked argument in the welfare analyses of high-standards trade is that poor households may benefit through employment effects. High-standards trade creates new employment opportunities in processing and handling of produce, and on vertically integrated estate farms and large contracted farms. The case studies discussed below show recent empirical evidence that high-standards trade creates substantial employment that is well-accessible for the poor, leading to increased rural incomes and reduced poverty rates.

4. EMPIRICAL EVIDENCE FROM THE HORTICULTURE EXPORTS SECTOR IN AFRICA

In this section we discuss three comparative case studies on the development effects of increasing standards in horticulture export chains in Sub-Saharan Africa (SSA). Before turning to the case studies, we first document the sharply increased importance of horticulture exports in Africa, analyse the structure of the horticulture export supply chains, and examine how and to what extent rural households in Africa are involved in the chains.

4.1. The Horticulture Export Boom in SSA

Exports of horticulture products from SSA to high-income regions have expanded rapidly over the past decades: from less than 2 million tons in 1990 to 6 million tons in 2005 (FAOstat, 2008). From the early 1990s onwards, the export of fruits and vegetables from SSA grew sharply and continuously while the export growth of other, more traditional agricultural commodities (such as coffee, sugar and cotton) was much smaller and less persistent (see Figure 6.1). Several SSA countries, including very poor countries such as Ethiopia, Burkina Faso, Cameroon, Kenya, Uganda, Senegal and Madagascar have become important suppliers of fresh fruits and vegetables to high-income markets in the EU. It is remarkable that many poor SSA countries experienced accelerated growth in fresh fruit and vegetable exports, mostly to the EU, during a period of sharply increased EU food quality and safety standards. Private standards, in particular, for horticulture products have been increasing sharply since the early 2000s. Some private standard-setting bodies and certification schemes have initially focused on fruits and vegetables, for example, the EUREPGAP standards set by a group of European retailers.

It is recognized that horticulture export production entails an important potential for raising rural incomes and reducing poverty because of this

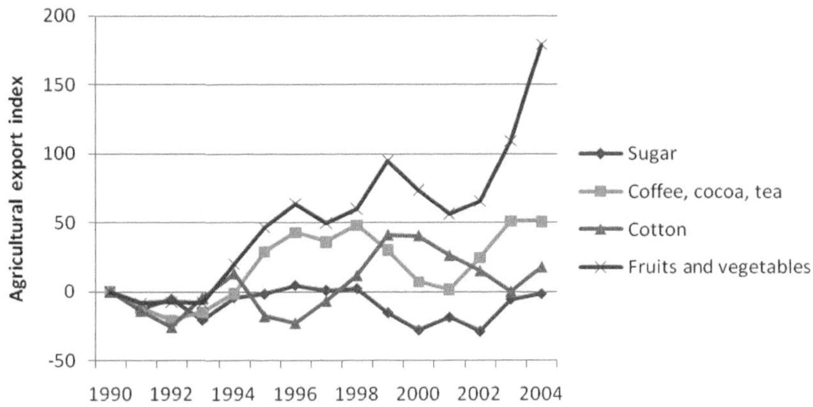

Source: Calculations based on FAO stat statistics

Figure 6.1: Index of agricultural exports from Sub-Saharan Africa, 1990–2005

export's high intrinsic value and labour-intensive production systems (Aksoy and Beghin, 2005; Anderson and Martin, 2005). Many SSA countries therefore pursue the development of horticulture export supply chains as a specific poverty reduction strategy, as documented in many poverty reduction strategy papers of African countries. The World Bank and other international donors have invested heavily in increasing SSA countries' capacity in horticulture exports based on the belief that this will contribute to poverty reduction. Governmental and non-governmental development projects have focused on enhancing the positive welfare effects of rising high-value exports and emerging modern supply chains in SSA. To guarantee the success of such programmes, it is imperative to understand the overall welfare and development implications of increasing horticulture exports and modernizing supply chains, and the channels through which these effects come about.

4.2. Supply Chain Government and Rural Households

As argued before, the structure and governance system of supply chains strongly influences the type of development effects that emerge. High-value export supply chains differ substantially from traditional marketing chains in SSA countries. While traditional chains are based on spot market transactions and often involve a large number of (mainly small) buyers and sellers, the high-value horticulture supply chains are largely based on VC and contract-farming, or on complete ownership integration and agro-industrial farms in the most extreme cases.

As discussed in the previous section, the extent of smallholder inclusion/exclusion in modern and high-value supply chains is still a contentious issue and mainly an empirical question. In horticulture export chains in SSA countries there is a wide variation in the share of produce that is procured from smallholders under contract-farming arrangements. For example, the pineapple and banana sectors in Cote d'Ivoire, the vegetable sectors in Ghana and Madagascar and the fruit sector in Kenya are largely based on smallholder contract-farming while in other sectors export companies rely on procurement from large commercial farms or own integrated estate production (see Table 6.1). Some studies have documented that the share of smallholder contract-farming in export horticulture supply chains in SSA is decreasing as a result of increasing food quality and safety standards (Dolan and Humphrey, 2000; Danielou and Ravry, 2005). Other studies have shown that among the smallholders it is mainly famers with more land and non-land assets that are involved in high-value contract-farming while the poorest are excluded (Legge et al., 2006; McCulloch and Ota, 2002; Minot and Ngigi, 2004).

Table 6.1: Smallholder procurement in Sub-Saharan African export supply chains

Country	Commodity (group)	Year of survey	Share of exports sourced from smallholders (%)	Number of small-holder producers
Ghana	Fruit and vegetables			3 600
	Pineapples	2006	45	300–400
	Papayas	2006	10–15	
	Vegetables	2002	95	
Cote d'Ivoire	Pineapples	1997	70	
	Mangoes	2002	< 30	
	Bananas	2002	100	
Senegal	French beans	2005	52	600–900
	Tomatoes	2006	0	0
Kenya	Fresh fruit and vegetables	2002	±50	12 000–80 000
Madagascar	Fresh vegetables	2004	90–100	9 000
Zambia	Vegetables	2003		300
Zimbabwe	Fruits and vegetables	1998	6	10

Source: Maertens, Minten and Swinnen (2010)

In the previous section we argued that labour markets might also be an important channel by which to involve rural households in modern supply chains, but that evidence for this is still lacking. Involvement through labour markets is indeed important in horticulture export chains in SSA. Table 6.2 shows figures for the number of employees in horticulture export sectors in several countries. These show that in many poor SSA countries, thousands of people are employed in the horticulture export industry. Part of this employment might concern urban jobs in processing units and pack houses but the lion's share is rural employment. Comparing these employment figures with the figures on the number of farm-households involved in horticulture contract-farming in export sectors in Table 6.2, suggests that a much larger number of households is affected through labour markets than through product markets.

Table 6.2: Employment in Sub-Saharan African export horticulture supply chains

Country	Commodity	Year of survey	Number of employees in the FFV agro-industry	Share of female employees (%)
Cameroon	Bananas	2003	10 000	
Cote d'Ivoire	Bananas and pineapples	2002	35 000	
Kenya	Flowers	2002	40 000–70 000	75
	Fruits and vegetables		2 000 000	
Senegal	French beans	2005	12 000	90
	Cherry tomatoes	2006	3 000	60
Uganda	Flowers	1998	3 300	75
Zambia	Vegetables	2002/03	7 500	65
	Flowers	2002/03	2 500	35
South Africa	Deciduous fruit	1994	283 000	53

Source: Maertens, Minten and Swinnen (2010)

4.3. Comparative Case Studies

In the remainder of this section we analyse and compare the insights from three original case studies on high-standards horticulture exports in SSA countries: the vegetable export sector in Madagascar (from Minten et al., 2009); the bean export sector in Senegal (from Maertens and Swinnen, 2009; Maertens, 2009); and the tomato export sector in Senegal (from Maertens et al., 2011). The comparison of these case studies is particularly relevant because the three studies document differences in the way supply chains respond to increasing standards, resulting in varying degrees of VC in the chains and differentiated development effects.

Supply chain structure

First, the vegetable export sector in Madagascar is dominated by one domestic exporting company that relies 100 per cent on smallholder contracting for procurement of primary produce. In response to increasing standards in overseas markets the company has intensified its contract-farming schemes with smallholders. This has led to a VC scheme including almost 10 000 smallholders, often working on very small farms with less than one hectare, in the hillsides of Madagascar. The company relies on an intensive on-farm monitoring system, which includes 300 company agents who regularly visit the contracted farms to provide extension services and technical advice, to monitor adherence to contractual agreements and to avoid side-selling. Moreover, inputs are supplied on credit by the company at the beginning of the growing season.

Second, in the Senegalese bean export sector increasing standards have induced a shift from smallholder contract-farming towards vertically integrated estate production by the exporting companies themselves. It is estimated that smallholder procurement under contract decreased from 95 per cent of export produce in 1999 to 52 per cent in 2005. In particular, the largest companies changed their procurement system and started their own integrated estate farms as part of a strategy to gain EUREPGAP certification. Companies that do rely on smallholder contract-farming usually provide inputs, credit and management assistance to the their contracted suppliers.

Third, the Senegalese tomato export sector is dominated by one multinational company that was established and started exporting tomatoes from Senegal to the EU in 2003. The tomato export supply chain is completely vertically integrated. Smallholder procurement is 0 per cent and production, processing, trade and distribution is completely integrated within the subsidiaries of the multinational companies. This is an extreme case of complete vertical integration.

Welfare effects[2]

Despite the differences in supply chain structure and governance systems across the sectors, the results of the case studies show that in all three cases the growth in modern export chains has had positive welfare effects and a poverty reducing impact. Yet, the channels through which rural households, and specifically the poor, benefit differ: product market effects are important in the vegetable sector in Madagascar where 100 per cent of the produce is supplied by smallholders on a contract basis; labour market effects are important in the tomato sector in Senegal where the chain is completely integrated with no procurement from smallholders; and both effects are important in the bean sector in Senegal where there is a mixed strategy of procurement from contracted smallholders and integrated estate farming. Moreover, households have benefited through direct as well as indirect effects at the household level.

First, in the case of vegetable exports in Madagascar, rural households benefit substantially from contract-farming with the export industry. The vegetables produced under contract and destined for export directly account for 47 per cent of total household income. In addition, technological spillover effects from vegetable contract-farming on rice production are observed. Contract farmers were assisted by the extension agents of the export company to use compost on contracted plots, which resulted in an increase in rice productivity of 64 per cent. The overall impact, through direct and indirect effects, is an increase in rural incomes, an increase in the stability of rural incomes and a reduction in poverty. This is reflected in a substantially reduced 'hungry' season for households engaged in vegetable contract-farming with the export industry (see Figure 6.2).

Second, in the bean export supply chains in Senegal a shift occurred from smallholder contract-farming towards integrated estate farming. This change in supply chain structure has also shifted the way local households benefit: increasingly through agro-industrial employment and labour market effects rather than through contract-farming and product market effects. Both participation in contract-farming and participation in agro-industrial employment has resulted in significantly higher incomes

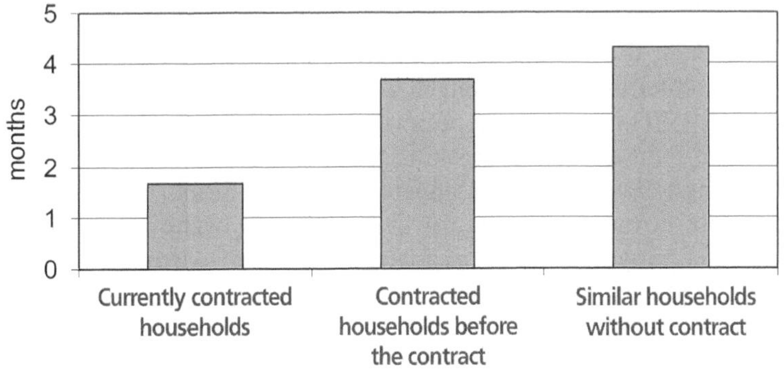

Source: Minten et al. (2009)

Figure 6.2: Impact of vegetable contract farming on the length of the 'hungry' season in Madagascar

(see Figure 6.3). It is estimated that contracting with the export sector has led to incomes that are 110 per cent higher than the average income in the region, while for employment in the export industry incomes are 60 per

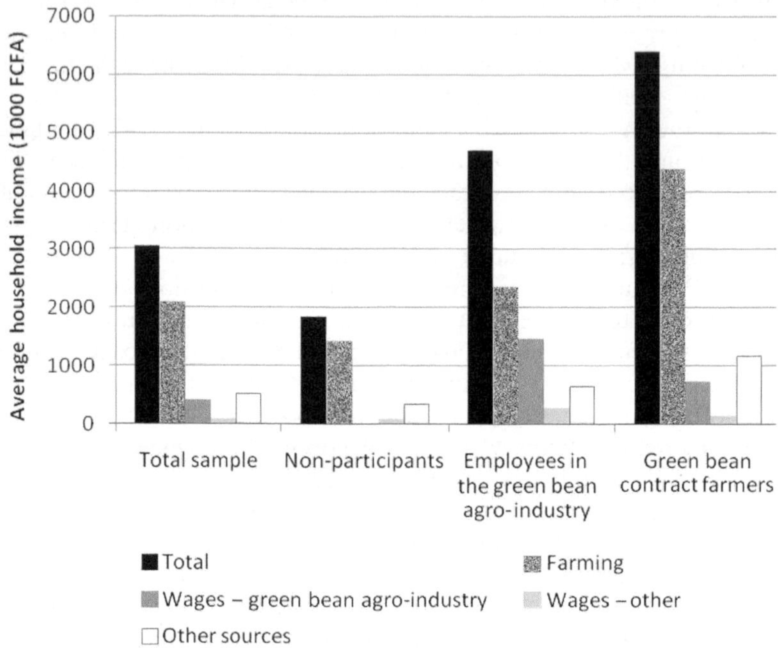

Source: Maertens and Swinnen (2009)

Figure 6.3: Income effects of green bean exports in Senegal

cent higher. Yet, the shift in supply chain structure with increased agro-industrial production has resulted in a stronger poverty-alleviating effect (see Figure 6.4). This is the case because the poorest households, with less land and non-land asset holdings and a lower level of education, mainly benefit through labour market effects and agro-industrial employment while contract-farming is biased towards relatively better-off households. In addition, employment in the export agro-industry is found to not only benefit rural households directly through increased income from wages, but also indirectly through investment linkages. Wages earned in the export industry are partially invested in the households' own farm businesses, mainly in the form of higher input use, leading to higher outputs and farm incomes.

Third, in the tomato export sector in Senegal, rural households only benefit through labour market effects as there is no contract-farming and

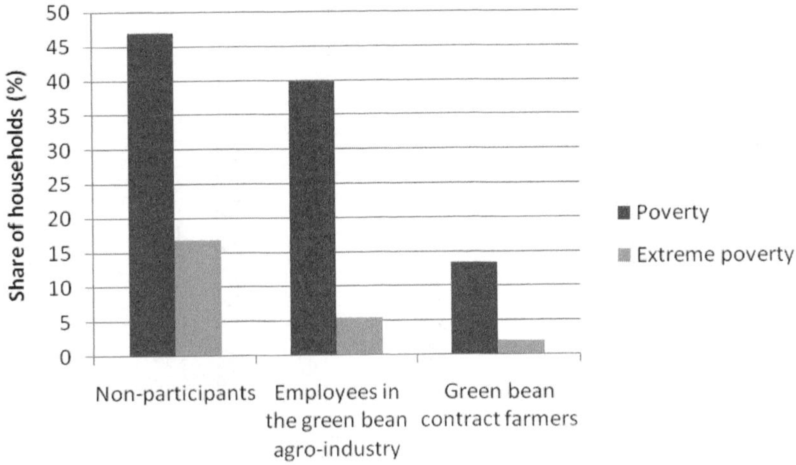

Source: Maertens and Swinnen (2009)

Figure 6.4: Poverty effects of green bean exports in Senegal

procurement from smallholder farms. This case study also shows that it is mainly the poorest households who benefit from the creation of employment in tomato export chains. Households employed in the tomato export industry, either on the fields or in the processing units of the export company, have incomes that are more than double the income of other households in the region (see Figure 6.5) while they initially, before the multinational company was established in 2003, had lower land and non-land asset holdings. Increased tomato exports have resulted in increased employment, increased incomes and ultimately reduced rates of poverty and extreme poverty (see Figure 6.6).

These case studies clearly document that development effects of the growth in modern food supply chains in poor countries can be diverse and emerge in different ways. They show that next to product market effects that have received most of the attention in the literature, labour market effects are important as well, especially for the poorest rural households. The studies from Senegal indicate that even if smallholder farmers are largely excluded as contracted suppliers in modern food chains, there might be important and positive development effects from the growth in modern supply chains that emerge through labour markets. In addition, the studies show that indirect household-level effects are also important in understanding the overall welfare implications of the growth in modern food supply chains in poor countries.

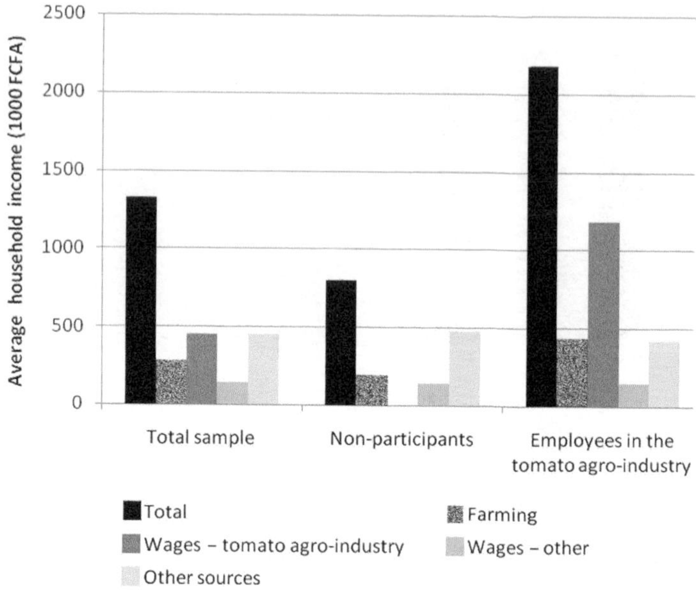

Source: Maertens, Colen and Swinnen (2011)

Figure 6.5: Income effects of tomato exports in Senegal

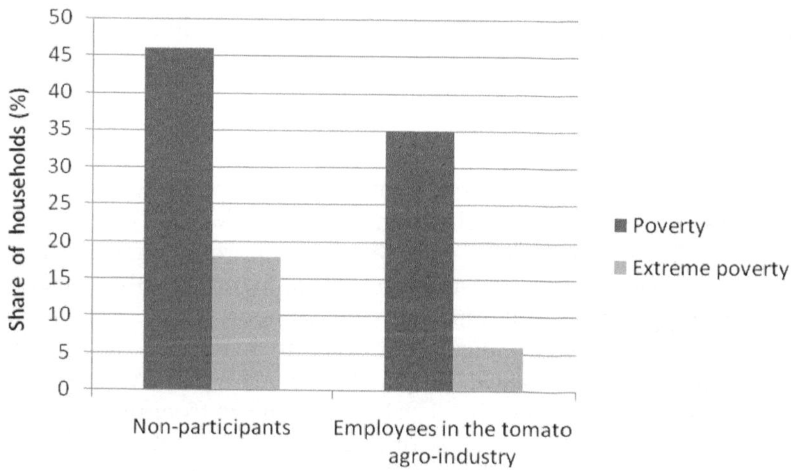

Source: Maertens, Colen and Swinnen (2011)

Figure 6.6: Poverty effects of tomato exports in Senegal

5. CONCLUSION

The main conclusion of this chapter is that, although there are important concerns related to the increased use of public and private standards in the food sector, standards can also bring about important positive effects for rural development and poverty reduction. These effects can come in various ways through product or labour market effects and through direct and indirect effects. A key issue in understanding these effects is the way in which supply chain structures and governance systems respond to increasing standards. We have shown that there is ample evidence that high-standards trade can benefit poor countries and smallholder farmers and rural households in those countries.

NOTES

1. Maertens and Swinnen (2009) discuss the factors that contribute to explaining the increase in public and private food standards.
2. This section discusses and compares the results of three case studies on the welfare and poverty implications of the growth in modern supply chains. The econometric analyses from which these results are derived are described in Minten et al. (2009) for the Madagascar case study, in Maertens and Swinnen (2009) and Maertens (2009) for the Senegal bean case study, and in Maertens et al. (2011) for the Senegal tomato case study.

REFERENCES

Aksoy, A. and Beghin, J.C. (2005), *Global Agricultural Trade and Developing Countries*, Washington DC: The World Bank.

Anderson, K. and Martin, W. (2005), 'Agricultural trade reform and the Doha Development Agenda', *World Economy*, 28 (9), pp. 1301–1327.

Asfaw, S., Mithöfer, D. and Waibel, H. (2007), 'What impact are EU supermarket standards having on developing countries export of high-value horticulture products? Evidence from Kenya', *Paper presented at the 105th EAAE Seminar*, Bologna, Italy, 8–10 March, 2007.

Asfaw, S., Mithöfer, D. and Waibel, H. (2009), 'EU food-safety standards, pesticide use and farm level productivity: the case of high-value crops in Kenya', *Journal of Agricultural Economics*, 60 (3), pp. 645–667.

Bhagwati, J. and Srinivasan, T.N. (2002), 'Trade and poverty in the poor countries', *American Economic Review*, 92 (2), pp. 180–183.

Colen, L., Maertens, M. and Swinnen, J.F.M. (2008), 'FDI as an engine for economic growth and human development: a review of the economic arguments and empirical evidence', *IUAP Working Paper Series*.

Danielou, M. and Ravry, C. (2005), 'The rise of Ghana's pineapple industry', *Africa Region Working Paper Series* 93, Washington DC: The World Bank, Africa Region.

Dolan, C. and Humphrey, J. (2000), 'Governance and trade in fresh vegetables: the impact of UK Supermarkets on the African horticulture industry', *Journal of*

Development Studies, 37 (2), pp. 147–176.
Dollar, D. and Kraay, A. (2004), 'Trade, growth and poverty', *Economic Journal*, 114 (493), pp. 22–49.
Dries, L. and Swinnen, J.F.M. (2004), 'Foreign direct investment, vertical integration, and local suppliers: evidence from the Polish dairy sector', *World Development*, 32 (9), pp. 1525–1544.
FAOstat. Available at http://faostat.fao.org/default.aspx (accessed 2008).
Gibbon, P. (2003), 'Value-chain governance, public regulation and entry barriers in the global fresh fruit and vegetable chain into the EU', *Development Policy Review*, 21 (5), pp. 615—625.
Gulati, A., Minot, N., Delgado, C. and Saswati, B. (2007), 'Growth in high-value agriculture in Asia and the emergence of vertical links with farmers' in J.F.M. Swinnen (ed.), *Global Supply Chains, Standards and the Poor*, Oxford: CABI Publishing.
Henson, S. (2009), 'Standards in agricultural trade: some strategic considerations for Africa', *E-learning Course on Food and Agricultural Trade in Africa*, World Bank Institute, April 2009.
Henson, S. and Jaffee, S. (2008), 'Understanding developing country strategic responses to the enhancement of food safety standards', *World Economy*, 31 (4), pp. 548–568.
Henson, S. and Humphrey, J. (2008), 'Understanding the complexities of private standards in global agri-food chains', Paper presented at the International Workshop on Globalization, Global Governance and Private Standards, November, 2008, Leuven.
Jaffee, S. (2003), 'From challenge to opportunity: Transforming Kenya's fresh vegetable trade in the context of emerging food safety and other standards in Europe', *Agricultural and Rural Development Discussion Paper*, Washington DC: The World Bank.
Jaffee, S. and Henson, S. (2005), 'Agro-food exports from developing countries: the challenges posed by standards', in A. Aksoy and J. C. Beghin (eds), *Global Agricultural Trade and Developing Countries*, Washington DC: The World Bank.
Key, N. and Runsten, D. (1999), 'Contract farming, smallholders, and rural development in Latin America: the organization of agroprocessing firms and the scale of outgrower production', *World Development*, 27 (2), pp. 381–401.
Legge, A., Orchard, J., Graffham, A., Greenhalg, P. and Kleih, U. (2006), 'The production of fresh produce in Africa for export to the United Kingdom: mapping different value chains', Report, Natural Resources Institute, UK.
Maertens, M. (2009), 'Horticulture exports, agro-industrialization, and farm-nonfarm linkages with the smallholder farm sector: evidence from Senegal', *Agricultural Economics*, 40 (2), pp. 219–229.
Maertens, M. and Swinnen, J.F.M. (2007), 'Standards as barriers and catalysts for trade and poverty reduction', *Journal of International Agricultural Trade and* Development, 4 (1), pp. 47–61.
Maertens, M. and Swinnen, J.F.M. (2009), 'Trade, standards and poverty: evidence from Senegal', *World Development*, 37 (1), pp. 161–178.
Maertens, M., L. Colen and Swinnen, J.F.M. (2011), 'Globalization and poverty in Senegal: a worst case scenario?', *European Review of Agricultural Economics*, 38 (1), pp. 31–54.
Maertens, M., Dries, L., Dedehouanou, F.A. and Swinnen, J.F.M. (2007), 'High-

value supply chains, food standards and rural households in developing countries', in J. F. M. Swinnen (ed.), *Global Supply Chains, Standards and the Poor*, Oxford: CABI publishing.

Maertens, M., Minten, B. and Swinnen, J.F.M. (2010), 'Growth in high-value export markets in Sub-Saharan Africa and its development implications', LICOS Discussion Paper No. 245, Leuven: LICOS.

McCullough, E., Pingali, P. and Stamoulis, K. (2008), *The Transformation of Agri-Food Systems: Globalization, Supply Chains and Smallholder Farmers*, London, UK: Earthscan Ltd., p. 416.

McCulloch, N. and Ota, M. (2002), 'Export horticulture and poverty in Kenya', *IDS Working Paper 174*, Sussex: Institute for Development Studies.

Minot, N. and Ngigi, M. (2004), 'Are horticultural exports a replicable success story? Evidence from Kenya and Côte d'Ivoire', *EPTD/MTID Discussion Paper*, Washington DC: IFPRI.

Minten, B., Randrianarison, L. and Swinnen, J.F.M. (2009), 'Global retail chains and poor farmers: Evidence from Madagascar', *World Development*, 37 (11), pp. 1728–1741.

Mithöfer, D., Nang'ole, E. and Asfaw, S. (2008), 'Smallholder access to the export market: the case of vegetables in Kenya', *Outlook on Agriculture*, 37 (3), pp. 203–211.

Reardon, T. and Barrett, C.B. (2000), 'Agroindustrialisation, globalization and international development: an overview of issues, patterns and determinants', *Agricultural Economics*, 23 (3), pp. 195–205.

Reardon, T., Codron, J.M., Busch, L., Bingen, J. and Harris, C. (1999), 'Global change in agrifood grades and standards: agribusiness strategic responses in developing countries', *International Food and Agribusiness Management Review*, 2 (3), pp. 421–435.

Swinnen, J.F.M. (2005), *The Dynamics of Vertical Co-ordination in Agro-Food Chains in Europe and Central Asia*. Washington DC: The World Bank.

Swinnen, J.F.M. (2007), *Global Supply Chains, Standards and the Poor*, Oxford: CABI publishing.

Warning, M. and Key, N. (2002), 'The social performance and distributional impact of contract farming: an equilibrium analysis of the Arachide de Bouche program in Senegal', *World Development*, 30 (2), pp. 255–263.

Wilson, J.S. and Abiola, V. (2003), *Standards and Global Trade: A Voice for AFRICA*, Washington DC: The World Bank.

World Bank (2005), 'Food safety and agricultural health standards: challenges and opportunities for Developing Country Exports, Poverty Reduction and Economic Management Trade Unit and Agricultural and Rural Development Department', *Report No. 31207*, Washington DC: The World Bank.

7. Globalization, private standards and poverty: evidence from Senegal

Liesbeth Colen, Miet Maertens and Johan Swinnen

1. INTRODUCTION

The integration of developing countries in global trade and foreign investments in developing economies have been advocated as important engines for growth and poverty reduction (Dollar and Kraay, 2004; Irwin and Tervio, 2002; Klein et al., 2001). In particular, the enhancement of trade and investment in high-value agri-food supply chains is argued to benefit the poor because of the high surplus created, the direct link the sector has with the rural economy (where poverty rates are often much higher than in urban areas), and because of the intensive use of unskilled labor in the sector (Aksoy and Beghin, 2005; Anderson and Martin, 2005; Carter et al., 1996; World Bank, 2008).

The globalization of high-value supply chains and the integration of developing countries in global trade have been accompanied by the increasing importance of public and private standards concerning food safety and food quality. These have largely shaped the structure of today's global supply chains and have important implications for the different actors in the chain (Swinnen, 2007). The EU imposes a number of requirements regarding food safety and quality and, in addition, a large number of private standards have become important in global agri-food trade (Jaffee and Henson, 2005). Modern retail chains and multinational processing companies play an important role in the development of these standards and in the organization of modern high-value supply chains.

Some papers claim that these changes are detrimental to global poverty reduction (Farina and Reardon, 2000; Reardon et al., 1999). The major concerns are: (a) that raising product and process standards – both public and private – act as new non-tariff barriers, diminishing the export opportunities of the poorest countries for whom compliance is problematic due to financial, technical, and institutional constraints (Unnevehr, 2000);[1] (b) that increasing food standards lead to increased consolidation of the supply base, mostly favouring large foreign-owned companies, which leads to the exploitation of poor farmers because of unequal bargaining power vis-à-vis large multinational food companies; and (c) that poor suppliers are excluded from global food supply chains because of their inability to comply with standards, the preference of food companies to source from larger and more capitalized suppliers, and a shift to large-scale vertically integrated production systems.[2]

Empirical studies on the development implications of these changes in global food supply chains have come to diverse conclusions. Some studies have pointed to cases where increasing food standards are applied to the competitive advantage of developing countries, resulting in successful development of high-standards export sectors, even in poor Sub-Saharan African countries (Minot and Ngigi, 2004; Sautier et al., 2006). Moreover, recent evidence indicates that rather than being exploited, small farmers can make important gain in vertical coordination schemes with the agro-industry through enhanced access to inputs, reduced production and marketing risks, improved technology and productivity, and ultimately higher incomes (Dries and Swinnen, 2004; Gulati et al., 2007; Minten et al., 2009; Swinnen, 2005). The evidence on smallholder exclusion in globalized food supply chains is mixed.[3] Some studies find that the reorganization of global food supply chains has led to a shift from smallholder production to agro-industrial production (Danielou and Ravry, 2005; Farina and Reardon, 2000; Key and Runsten, 1999; Reardon et al., 1999; Maertens and Swinnen, 2009), while other studies find extensive smallholder participation in modern supply chains (Dries and Swinnen, 2004; Jaffee, 2003; Kherralah, 2000; Minot and Ngigi, 2004; Minten et al., 2009). So, while there is consensus that the proliferation of stringent standards is changing the global food supply system with the increased dominance of large multinational food companies, consolidation of the supply base and increased vertical coordination in the chains (Swinnen, 2007; Swinnen and Maertens, 2007; Weatherspoon and Reardon, 2003), the poverty effects of these developments remain highly debated.

Surprisingly little research has focused on the overall poverty effects of globalization in the agri-food sectors of developing countries; most of the abovementioned studies focus only on production. Yet, the poor may benefit through labour markets as well. The intensive use of unskilled labour in agri-food sectors has been identified as an important potential source of poverty reduction (for example, Carter et al., 1996). Only a few studies have pointed to the welfare gains from employment opportunities in the emerging agro-industry (Barron and Rello, 2000; Humphrey et al., 2004; Maertens and Swinnen, 2009; McCulloch and Ota, 2002).

In this chapter, we analyze the overall household-level income and poverty effects of rapidly expanding tomato exports and FDI inflows in the tomato sector in Senegal. Senegalese tomato exports are largely dominated by one single multinational company with a strategy of full vertical coordination. Based on the concerns regarding the globalization of supply chains, many would *ex ante* consider the tomato export sector in Senegal to be a 'worst case scenario' of globalization.

The globalization of the tomato export sector in Senegal has several characteristics, all of which have been argued to be detrimental to the rural poor in developing countries. These characteristics are:

a. Senegal is a very poor country with many institutional problems and market imperfections
b. the fresh fruit and vegetable (FFV) sector has faced rapidly tightening and currently very stringent public and private standards on products and production processes
c. the export tomato chain is characterized by extreme consolidation, as a single company controls all the production, processing, and trade
d. the exporting company is a foreign multinational company
e. the various levels in the supply chain are fully vertically integrated
f. smallholders are completely excluded as all tomatoes for export are produced on large-scale farms owned by the exporting company.

Our study yields some important findings. First, we find that tomato exports from Senegal to the EU have increased sharply over the past decade, despite increasing standards in the EU. Second, despite the extreme consolidation and vertical integration in the supply chain and the exclusion of smallholder farms from export tomato production, tomato exports make an important contribution to poor household incomes and poverty reduction in the tomato-producing regions through employment effects. Third, we do not find evidence that asset-poor households or unskilled individuals are disadvantaged in accessing employment in the tomato export chain.

The chapter is organized as follows. In section 2, we discuss the importance of private standards in the global supply chains of fresh fruits and vegetables. Then in section 3 we describe the tomato export supply chain in Senegal. In section 4, we present details on the survey data and methodology used to analyse the welfare implications of export tomato development. In section 5 we discuss the implications for rural employment, income mobility and poverty. We draw some conclusions in a final section.

2. PRIVATE STANDARDS IN FFV SUPPLY CHAINS

Since the mid-1990s, food standards – both public regulations and private corporate standards – have increased sharply, especially for fresh food products such as fruits and vegetables, and especially in EU markets.

The EU imposes a number of public standards concerning food quality and safety for FFV. In 2001, the marketing standards that specified the quality and different size categories for every type of fruit and vegetable become more specific. Phytosanitary standards, indicating the maximum residue level for pesticides since 1976, became stricter still in 1986 and 1990. In 2002 and 2005, regulations about the treatment of wooden packaging material and contamination by heavy metals for FFV were added. In 2002, the General Food Law was created, including hazard analysis and critical control (HACCP)-based hygiene rules, and in 2005 traceability requirements were added.

Besides these public requirements, private standards have been established by large food companies, supermarkets chains and NGOs and play an increasingly important role in agri-food trade (Jaffee and Henson, 2005). Private standards are often even more stringent than public standards. Ninety per cent of retailers reported that their standards were higher than public ones, and 50 per cent of retailers reported that they were significantly higher (Fulponi, 2007). Besides food quality and safety issues, private standards also increasingly include specifications on ethical and environmental aspects of production.

There exists a large variety of private standards and certification schemes. Some of them apply to one single retailer (for example, Carrefour Filière Qualité, Tesco Nature's Choice) while others are national (for example, the British Retail Consortium Global Standard, or BRC) or international initiatives (e.g. GLOBALG.A.P.). Private standards can be used as a competitive strategy of product differentiation and market segmentation (Henson, 2006; Henson and Humphrey, this volume). However, often private standards are business-to-business standards that are not communicated directly to consumers, so they have no role in product differentiation (Fulponi, 2007). In this case, private companies engage in standard setting to reduce reputational or commercial risks associated with food safety hazards, especially when public food safety capacity is weak. Although private standards are legally not mandatory, they have become de facto mandatory as a large share of buyers in EU markets is requiring compliance with such standards, for example the GLOBALG.A.P. standards (Henson and Humphrey, this volume). In particular, non-traditional, high-value exports such as fruits and vegetables are confronted with high levels of public and private food regulations, since these are often perishable, freshly consumed products that are especially susceptible to food safety risks and quality concerns by consumers. For example, GLOBALG.A.P.[4] has initially focused on fruits and vegetables, which indicates that the demand for increased standards of food quality and safety was especially high for these products (Henson, 2006).

3. THE TOMATO EXPORT SUPPLY CHAIN IN SENEGAL

Horticulture Export Growth

Exports of FFV from Senegal have increased tremendously in the past ten years: from 4800 tons in 1998 to almost 25 000 tons in 2007 (see Figure 7.1). FFV exports also became more diversified. In 1997, more than 75 per cent of FFV exports consisted of one crop (French beans). Since the early 2000s the export of tomatoes and mango has grown importantly. The export volume of tomatoes – mainly cherry tomatoes – has increased from less than 1000 tons in the year 2000 to almost 7000 tons in 2007, accounting for 28 per cent of total FFV exports. The large majority of exported fruits and vegetables are destined for the EU market, mainly France, Belgium, Luxembourg and the Netherlands. Some minor volumes of mangoes and other fruits are exported to neighbouring countries such as Mali, Mauretania and Cape Verde.

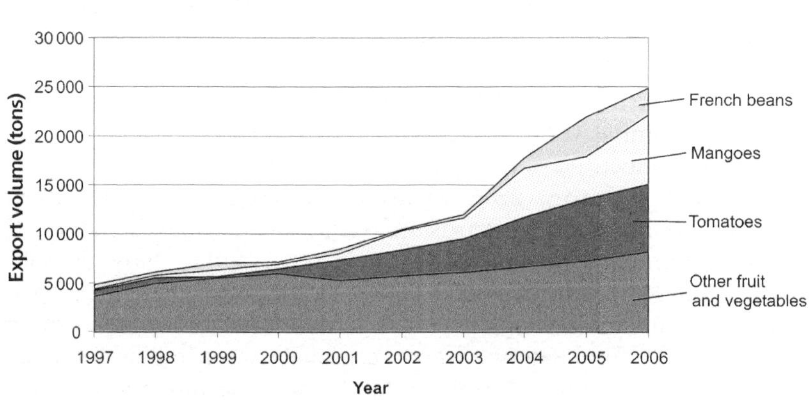

Source: Eurotrans – Senegal

Figure 7.1: Horticulture exports(tons) from Senegal, 1997–2006

Foreign Direct Investment

Foreign direct investment (FDI) has played a major role in the boom of tomato exports. Initially, small volumes of tomatoes were exported by two companies that specialized in bean exports. However, in 2001 a foreign company – Grands Domaines du Senegal (GDS) – a subsidiary of a French holding with food production and distribution affiliates in a number of countries in Europe, Africa and Latin America, entered the market. From 2003 onwards, the company began to export significant volumes of tomatoes from the Senegal River Delta region. The entrance of the FDI company significantly changed the market structure with GDS accounting for more than 90 per cent of exported produce in the 2006/2007 export season.

Public and Private Standards

It is remarkable that Senegal experienced accelerated growth of horticulture exports to the EU during a period when food quality and safety standards increased substantially, especially for fresh food products such as fruits and vegetables, and especially in EU markets. As mentioned above, EU legislation formulates a number of requirements concerning size, pesticide residues, hygiene control, packaging material and so on. The most important private standard for vegetable exports from Senegal to the EU is GLOBALG.A.P.. Other, more stringent, private standards, such as BRC and Tesco Nature's Choice, are only adopted by a few large-scale producers.

In response to increasing food standards, the multinational company GDS has obtained GLOBALG.A.P., HACCP and Tesco Nature's Choice certification for the production and export of tomatoes. In fact, the multinational holding to which the company belongs specifically aims at high-standards production. It therefore seeks compliance with a large variety of private standards focusing on food quality and safety issues as well as on ethical and environmental aspects, and seeks certification by different private schemes such as the British Retail Consortium (BRC) and the Ethical Trading Initiative (ETI).

Consolidation and Vertical Integration

Many studies have documented important structural transformations in the supply chains of fresh produce for export to high-standards markets; these chains have become increasingly consolidated, with fewer and larger firms, while the level of vertical coordination in the chains is increasing

(Dolan and Humphrey, 2004; Swinnen, 2007). In some cases – for example in the Malagasy FFV sector (Minten et al., 2009) – increased standards have led to institutional innovations, such as extensive monitoring and complex contracting, to source from small farmers. In other cases, this is associated with a shift from smallholder contract-based production to large-scale integrated estate production, documented for example by Jaffee (2003) for Kenyan vegetable exports, Minot and Ngigi (2004) for FFV exports from Cote d'Ivoire, Maertens and Swinnen (2009) for green bean exports from Senegal, and Danielou and Ravry (2005) for pineapple exports from Ghana. Increasing quality and safety requirements are usually mentioned as the main driving factor behind the restructuring of the observed supply chains.

The case of tomato exports in Senegal represents an extreme case of these supply chain developments: more than 90 per cent of produce is handled by one multinational company and at several nodes in the chain vertical coordination takes the extreme form of complete ownership integration. Downstream trading, transport and distribution activities are completely integrated within the multinational holding through transport and distribution subsidiaries who own eight specialist vessels, serve four ports in West Africa, including Dakar, and several ports in the EU, and control further distribution within EU countries. Moreover, upstream the tomato supply chain is completely vertically integrated as the company relies solely on their own integrated agro-industrial production for the supply of primary produce. In the Senegal River Delta, GDS has established a conditioning station for handling and processing fresh vegetables and two production sites of 200 hectares in total. The company uses high-technology production techniques, including mechanized and computerized irrigation, fertilization and phytosanitary care in a drip-to-drip system, and improved seeds that are imported from the EU.

The tomato export supply chain excludes smallholder producers completely as production is realized exclusively on the large-scale plantations of the exporting company. It is important to note, however, that this integrated agro-industrial farming was not developed by buying or renting land from small farms, but by investing in previously uncultivated land allocated to the company by the government. During interviews with GDS in September 2005 and March 2006, two main reasons were mentioned for this strategy of complete vertical integration. First, this strategy is in line with the policy of the French holding to which GDS belongs and which owns similar vertically integrated production and exporting facilities in other developing countries (for example, in Mauretania and Côte d'Ivoire). Second, the high EU requirements on quality and food safety, such as traceability, maximum residue levels, and so forth, and especially stringent private standards required by their buyers, combined with the general low capacity and limited access to resources (especially irrigation water) of the local smallholder farmers, induced the company to integrate the production stage of the chain and set up their own agro-industrial farms.

A Worst Case Scenario of Supply Chain Development?

In development literature, consolidation and vertical integration in agri-food supply chains – often produced under pressure of increasing food standards – are usually considered to be particularly detrimental from a development perspective because they lead to the exploitation and exclusion of poor farmers. In this respect, the tomato export sector in Senegal, with its high public and private standards, extreme levels of consolidation and complete vertical integration could be considered a 'worst case scenario'. Moreover, it has been argued that vertical integration limits the possibilities of additional beneficial development effects through spillover effects in down- and upstream activities. In addition, the emergence of monopsonist industries – as is the case in the Senegal tomato industry – would result in rent extraction by these companies and subsequent marginalization of farmers (Gibbon, 2003; Warning and Key, 2002). It is also considered that employment effects might be limited in the case of monopsonist industries as they tend to employ less labour and pay lower wages. So, in many aspects, the sector that we studying represents what could be considered a 'worst case scenario' of supply chain development.

4. DATA AND RESEARCH AREA

To study the welfare implications of the growth of the tomato export chain in Senegal, we conducted interviews with the main tomato-exporting company and with the village representatives, and we organized a household survey for the collection of unique quantitative information on the rural population in the two communities surrounding the company. Both communities are located in the Saint-Louis region, in the north of the country along the Senegal River (see Figure 7.2). Gandon is the community where the company is based, and Ross Bethio is the adjacent community.

We interviewed the main tomato-exporting company GDS (Grands Domaines du Sénégal) in 2005 and 2006, on the developments in the export supply chains, the requirements of the EU market, and on the company's strategy for further growth and recruitment of employees.

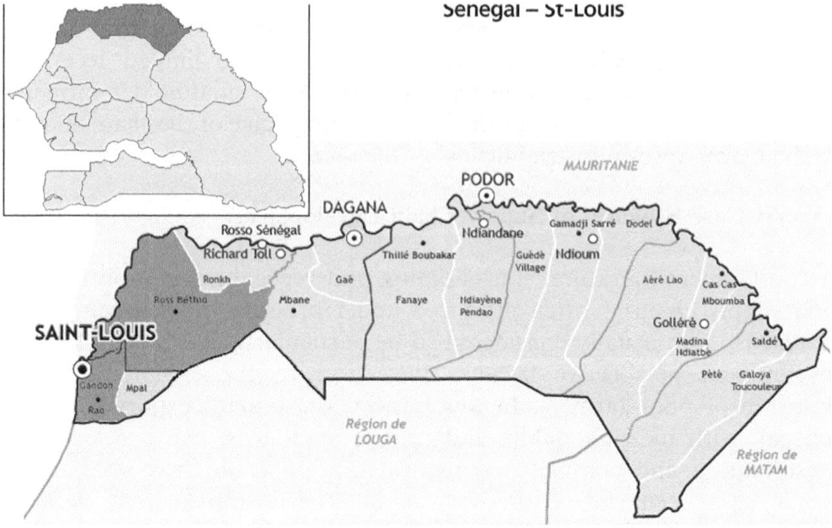

Source: IRD Cartographic

Figure 7.2: Research area: rural communities of Gandon and Ross Béthio selected for household survey

The household survey was organized in the period February–April 2006 and covers 299 households in 18 randomly selected villages in the two rural communities. The household selection resulted in an oversampling of households with members employed in the tomato export industry. To draw correct inferences from descriptive statistics, this oversampling is corrected by using sampling weights that are calculated with information from a village census in all sampled villages.

The survey data – including recall data – provide details on household demographic characteristics, land and non-land asset holdings, agricultural production, off-farm employment, non-labour income, credit, and savings. They allow the calculation of household net income from farm and off-farm sources. For each household we collected detailed and recall information on the employment of household members in the tomato export agro-industry.

5. RURAL EMPLOYMENT, INCOME AND POVERTY

As the chain is completely integrated and smallholder producers are not included in it, the main welfare effects from the growth in tomato exports come from employment creation. In this section, we first describe the participation of local households in this employment and then present some descriptive statistics on how employment is correlated with household income and poverty in the region. We refer briefly to the estimated effects of the net impact of employment on income.

Employment in the Tomato Export Agro-industry

The establishment of GDS and the increase in tomato exports was accompanied by a large increase in employment in this sector. Although part of the production process is mechanized, tomato production and handling remains a labour-intensive business. While irrigation, fertilization and phytosanitary care are completely mechanized and computerized with a drip-to-drip system, the harvesting of tomatoes is done manually and requires substantive amounts of labour. In addition, the processing and handling of tomatoes is labour intensive as packing and labelling is done manually, while sorting is mechanized.

The growth of tomato exports has significantly enhanced employment opportunities in the rural area of the Senegal River Delta. In 2006 GDS employed more than 3000 workers, on the fields as well as in the processing unit. More than 80 per cent of those workers were temporary seasonal workers or day labourers, who were mainly recruited from nearby villages and worked for a daily wage of 1700 FCFA. In our sampled villages more than one-third of households had one or more members working as employee in the tomato export industry. This share increased from 14 per cent in 2003 to 39 per cent in early 2006 (see Figure 7.3). The share was highest – almost 50 per cent of households – in the Gandon community, which includes villages in the immediate surroundings of the GD's production sites and processing unit. However, also in the adjacent community – Ross Béthio – with more distant villages, the share of households employed by GDS is about 30 per cent.

Labour was mostly hired on a day-to-day basis and many households had several members employed in the tomato sector, who sometimes took turns in working for GDS and working on their own farm or household. Not all households participated to the same extent and the total number of man-days worked in the tomato industry – summed over all the participating household members – differed largely across participating households. During the 2005/2006 season, households in Gandon worked on average 816 man-days for the tomato export company compared to 249 man-days on average for households in Ross Béthio.

The impact of tomato export growth and the associated employment on rural income mobility, income equality and poverty reduction depends on which households are selected into this employment and on how much

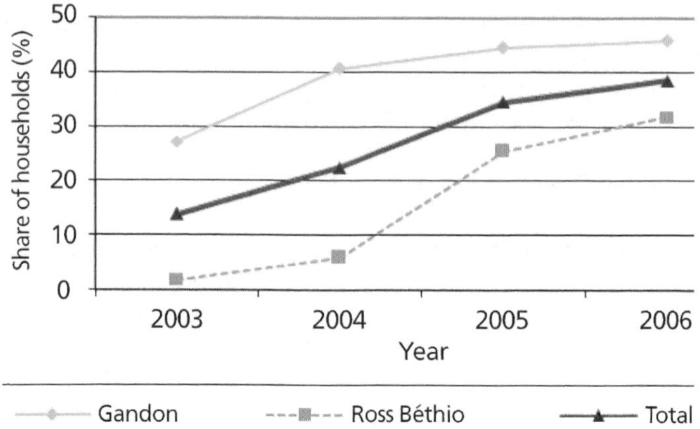

Note: Employed households are household with one or several members working as an employee in the tomato export industry. Based on household survey recall data collected in 2006.

Figure 7.3: Household employment in tomato export industry, 2003–2006

they benefit. Such employment growth could exacerbate rural income inequality if entry-constraints – for example, the need for a minimal level of education or certain assets – exist that limit the off-farm employment opportunities for the poorest households. Such increase of inequality has been observed by Dercon (1998) and Barrett et al. (2001) in studies on rural off-farm employment in Sub-Saharan Africa. However, we find that in the case of employment growth in the tomato export industry in Senegal the poor also benefit.

In Table 7.1 we compare the characteristics of households with one or more members employed in the production and/or handling of tomatoes for export, and households without such employment. The figures show that these two groups of households differ substantially in certain household characteristics. Employees in the tomato export industry come from significantly larger households, with an older household head, significantly larger labour endowments and fewer dependents. There is no disparity between the two groups of households in their level of education or ethnicity. Yet, households with employees in the tomato export industry initially – in 2001, before GDS invested and started to recruit local households – had significantly smaller landholdings. They also have slightly lower initial livestock and non-land asset holdings, but these differences are not significant at the 0.1 level. When we look at how village characteristics influence whether and for which period the households are employed in the tomato export sector,[5] we see that households living in more populated villages and in villages along a paved road are more likely

Table 7.1. Comparison of household characteristics

	Total sample	Household with members employed in the tomato export industry	Households without members employed in the tomato export industry	t – Statistic
Number of households	299	171	128	
Human and social capital				
Household size	13.4	18.1	10.5	7.42***
Age of the household head	56	59	54	3.30***
Labour[a]	6.6	9.3	4.8	7.81***
Dependency ratio[b]	0.511	0.484	0.528	–1.90*
Female-headed households	3.8%	5.5%	2.7%	1.07
Elementary education[c]	26.7%	24.3%	28.3%	–0.66
Ethnicity (non-Wolof)[d]	54.6%	50.4%	57.3%	–1.06
Membership of an organization[e]	49.9%	53.4%	47.6%	0.90
Initial per adult-equivalent assets[e, f]				
Landholdings (ha)	0.18	0.13	0.20	–1.72*
Livestock units[g]	0.79	0.68	0.86	–0.98
Non-land assets[h] (1000 FCFA)	15.5	12.7	17.4	–0.61
Consumer durables[i] (1000 FCFA)	21.9	17.8	24.5	–0.68

Notes: Characteristics of employed households are compared to those of other households using *t*-test. Significant differences are indicated with * : $p < .1$; ** : $p < .05$; *** : $p < .01$

[a] Labour is measured as the number of persons that are older than 17 and able to work.
[b] Dependency ratio is calculated as the number of dependants (children below the age of 17, and those unable to work) over the total household size.
[c] Household head has at least elementary education.
[d] Non-Wolof households refer to ethnic minorities in Senegal.
[e] Organization membership and initial assets are for the year 2001, based on recall data.
[f] Initial assets are expressed in *per adult-equivalent* terms, using the modified OECD adult equivalence scales: a weight of 1 is assigned to the first adult, 0.5 for all other adults and 0.3 for children (under 17 years old).
[g] One livestock unit equals 1 cow/horse/camel, 0.8 donkey, 0.2 sheep/goat/pig.
[h] Non-land productive assets include all equipment and machinery for farming as well as non-farm businesses.
[i] Consumer durables include furniture, vehicles and durable household equipment.

to be employed in the tomato export industry and also spend significantly more time on this activity. The further away the village is situated, the lower the number of days worked in the tomato export sector by the households of that village.

In summary, this comparison indicates that employment in the tomato export industry is not biased towards the better-off or more educated households. In contrast, the employment is biased towards households with smaller landholdings. No major entry constraints in the form of education or wealth seem to exist for entry into employment in the tomato export sector. This is an important finding as many rural off-farm opportunities in developing countries have been found to be inaccessible to poorer households with less assets and lower levels of education because of certain entry constraints (see, for example, Dercon, 1998). We find that households with smaller landholdings and more labour endowments self-select into employment in the tomato export industry. However, the results also indicate that there might be constraints in accessing the labour market that are related to geographic location and access to information. GDS picks up labourers in nearby and easily accessible villages with a large population to assure a sufficient number of daily workers, especially during periods of peak labour demand. Hence, households in more remote and smaller villages where GDS does not directly recruit at the village level face additional constraints in accessing the employment.

Household Income

Total household income is calculated from the survey data for the 12-month period prior to the survey (2005–2006). Comparing incomes for households with member(s) employed in the tomato export industry and households without such employment, we find that employment in the sector is associated with larger total and per adult-equivalent incomes. Households with members employed in the tomato export industry have an average income of 1.95 million FCFA. This is about two times higher than the average income of other households, which is 880 000 million FCFA (see Figure 7.4). Also in per adult-equivalent terms these income differences remain large: 277 000 FCFA for households with GDS employees versus 212 000 FCFA for other households – this is more than 30 per cent higher. Based on statistical analysis of our data we estimated that being employed in the tomato export sector leads to a net increase in household income of 600 000 to 700 000 FCFA.[6]

Hence, the wages received from working on the fields and in the conditioning centre of GDS add substantially to rural incomes. One-third of total household income in the survey region is derived from these wages (see Figure 7.4). For households actually employed at GDS, this is more than half (54 per cent). Hence, the tomato export sector – despite the fact that its activities are very seasonal and associated employment is mostly temporary – has become the main source of income in the region. Nevertheless, most households continue to have diversified income portfolios. Income sources include (apart from wages received from GDS (34 per cent)) farming (21 per cent), self-employment (mostly small trading activities – 18 per cent), other wages (11 per cent) and non-labour income (mostly remittances and public transfers – 16 per cent).

This means that the development of the export tomato sector, largely based on the establishment of GDS in the Senegal River Delta area, has generated employment opportunities for almost 40 per cent of households and has caused a large net increase in rural incomes in this region. These are extremely large and important development effects, emerging through private investment in high-value food supply chains, especially since entry

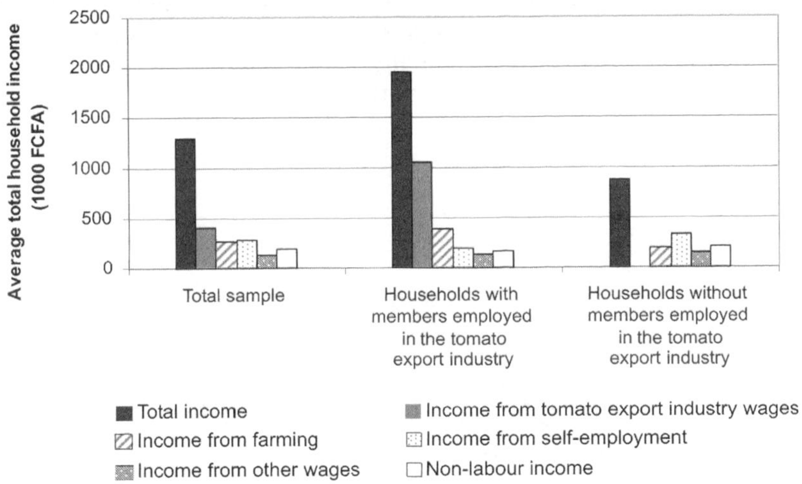

Note: The household total income is yearly income calculated for the 12-month period prior to the survey, February 2005–06. Income from tomato export industry wages is the wage income from employment of household members in the tomato export industry. Farm income is calculated taking into account total production (valued at market prices) in three different seasons ('contre-saison chaude' 2005, 'hivernage' 2005, and 'contre-saison froide' 2005–06), the cost of variable inputs, cost of hired labour, and the depreciation of machinery and equipment. Income from self-employment is income derived from small business or trading activities, taking into account costs of inputs and depreciation of machinery and equipment. Income from other wages are wages resulting from employment in agricultural or non-agricultural activities, different from the tomato export industry. Non-labour income results mainly from remittances and public transfers.

Figure 7.4: Comparison of income from different sources across households

into such employment is biased towards households with smaller land and excess labour endowments.

Poverty Rates

Using a poverty line of 143 080 FCFA for poverty and 31 812 FCFA for extreme poverty,[7] we calculated the share of households living below these national rural poverty lines. The incidence of poverty in the research area is 13 per cent for extreme poverty and 42 per cent for poverty, which is lower than the average national rural poverty rate of 58 per cent (see Figure 7.5). Poverty is much lower among households that are employed in the tomato export industry (35 per cent), compared to those without such employment (46 per cent). The same is valid for extreme poverty: 6 per cent compared to 18 per cent. Poverty is 11 percentage points, and extreme poverty 12 percentage points, lower among households with employment at GDS. These effects are large and appear especially remarkable since our earlier comparison indicated that employment in GDS was not biased towards initially better-off households (see Table 7.1). The figures suggest that the growth in tomato exports and associated employment has led to upwards rural income mobility and poverty reduction in the research region.

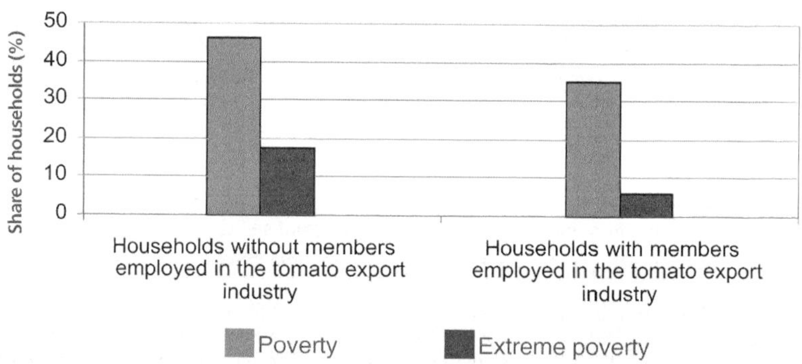

Note: Poverty and extreme poverty indicate the share of households living with per adult-equivalent incomes below a poverty line of 143 080 FCFA for poverty and 31 812 FCFA for extreme poverty.
These poverty lines are calculated from the ESAM I and II surveys in 1994 and 2000 (République du Sénégal, 2004), and are updated to the period of our survey (2005–2006) using consumer price indices (African Development Bank, 2006).

Figure 7.5: Comparison of poverty levels across households

6. CONCLUSIONS

During the past two decades, global supply chains have been restructured in response to the tightening of EU public standards and the increasing importance of private standards, especially for fresh food products such as fruits and vegetables. Large trading and retail companies have developed private standards that go further than public requirements with respect to food safety and quality, but also ethical aspects and the environment. The impact of developing countries' integration in such global high-standards markets on poverty and income inequality in these countries remains the subject of considerable controversy. Several authors argue that public and private standards in these supply chains create new barriers for developing countries' exports and lead to the exclusion of the small and poor farmers, while others state that they can create important benefits, including for the poor.

This chapter has analyzed the effects of increased foreign trade and investments in the tomato sector in Senegal on rural incomes and poverty, based on company and household survey data. Our study shows that, despite increasing standards, tomato exports have expanded rapidly and have importantly benefitted poor rural households through wage employment in the emerging agro-industry. Although these conclusions are obviously drawn from the specific sector that we studied, and caution should be taken in generalizing, we believe that these findings are particularly important.

First, our results challenge the general view in the literature that the gains from high-standards food trade are concentrated with foreign investors and large food companies while the poor in developing countries are increasingly marginalized. Our study shows that, even with extreme levels of supply base consolidation and complete vertical integration in the chains, there can be important benefits for the poor.

Second, the results show that important benefits may come through labour market effects rather than through product markets. Many empirical studies assume implicitly that there cannot be benefits for the rural poor when households are excluded as primary producers as a result of increasing standards. We show the importance of including the benefits through the labour market when assessing the overall impact for the rural poor. Related to this, we find that wage employment in the agro-industry is accessible for resource-poor and less educated households, indicating that such rural employment creation might be an important poverty-alleviation strategy.

Third, this case study on Senegalese tomato exports adds to the existing evidence of the possibilities of high-standards export development in Sub-

Saharan Africa and thereby contributes to the need for a balanced perspective on standards as barriers or catalysts to trade.

NOTES

1 See Jaffee and Henson (2004, 2005); Garcia Martinez and Poole (2004); Henson and Jaffee (2008); Maertens and Swinnen (2007) and Wilson and Abiola (2003) for a more detailed discussion.
2 See Gibbon (2003), Key and Runsten (1999), Maertens and Swinnen (2007); Swinnen (2007), and World Bank (2005) discuss the arguments on the exploitation and exclusion of small and resource-poor farmers.
3 For an overview of the evidence, see Maertens et al. (2009).
4 GLOBALG.A.P. (previously EUREPGAP) was established by a group of European retailers and specifies a series of protocols for the application of Good Agricultural Practices related to management, soil management, pesticide use, pollution management, harvesting, the handling of produce, personal hygiene, packing and storage, quality control, and so on. and provide guidelines for producers to comply with these standards (www.globalgap.org).
5 See Maertens et al., (2011) for details and regression analysis on the determinants of employment in the tomato export industry.
6 For details on the statistical methodology and the discussion of the results, refer to Maertens et al., (2011).
7 The poverty lines are calculated from the ESAM I and II surveys in 1994 and 2000 (République du Sénégal, 2004), and are updated to the period of our survey (2005–2006) using consumer price indices (African Development Bank, 2006).

REFERENCES

African Development Bank (2006), 'Selected statistics on African countries', XXV, Tunis: Statistics Division, Development Research Department, African Development Bank.

Aksoy, M.A. and Beghin, J.C. (2005), *Global Agricultural Trade and Developing Countries*, Washington DC: The World Bank.

Anderson, K. and Martin, W. (2005), 'Agricultural trade reform and the Doha Development Agenda', *The World Economy*, 28 (9), pp. 1301–1327.

Barrett, C.B., Reardon, T. and Webb, P. (2001), 'Nonfarm income diversification and household livelihood strategies in rural Africa: Concepts, dynamics and policy implications', *Food Policy*, 26 (4), pp. 315–331.

Barron, M.A. and Rello, F. (2000), 'The impact of the tomato agroindustry on the rural poor in Mexico', *Agricultural Economics*, 23 (3), pp. 289–297.

Carter, M.R., Barham, B.L. and Mesbah, D. (1996), 'Agricultural export booms and the rural poor in Chile, Guatemala and Paraguay', *Latin American Research Review*, 31 (1), pp. 33–65.

Danielou, M. and Ravry, C. (2005), 'The rise of Ghana's pineapple industry', *Africa Region Working Paper Series 93*, Washington DC: The World Bank, Africa Region.

Dercon, S. (1998), 'Wealth, risk and activity choice: cattle in western Tanzania', *Journal of Development Economics*, 55 (1), pp. 1–42.

Dolan, C. and Humphrey, J. (2004), 'Changing governance patterns in the trade in

fresh vegetables between Africa and the United Kingdom', *Environment and Planning*, 36 (3), pp. 491–509.
Dollar, D. and Kraay, A. (2004), 'Trade, growth and poverty', *Economic Journal*, 114 (493), pp. 22–49.
Dries, L. and Swinnen, J.F.M. (2004), 'Foreign direct investment, vertical integration and local suppliers: evidence from the Polish dairy sector', *World Development*, 32 (9), pp. 1525–1544.
Farina, E.M.M.Q. and Reardon, T. (2000), 'Agrifood grades and standards in the extended Mercosur: Their role in the changing agrifood system', *American Journal of Agricultural Economics*, 82 (5), pp. 1170–1176.
Fulponi, L. (2007), 'The globalization of private standards and the agri-food system', in J.F.M. Swinnen (ed.), *Global Supply Chains, Standards and the Poor*, Oxford: CABI Publishing.
Garcia Martinez, M. and Poole, P. (2004), 'The development of private fresh produce safety standards: Implications for developing and Mediterranean exporting countries', *Food Policy*, 29 (3), pp. 229–255.
Gibbon, P. (2003), 'Value-chain governance, public regulation and entry barriers in the global fresh fruit and vegetable chain into the EU', *Development Policy Review*, 21 (5–6), pp. 615–625.
GLOBALG.A.P., www.globalgap.org (accessed September 2010).
Gulati, A., Minot, N., Delgado, C. and Bora, S. (2007), 'Growth in high-value agriculture in Asia and the emergence of vertical links with farmers', in J.F.M. Swinnen (ed.), *Global Supply Chains, Standards and the Poor*, Oxford: CABI Publishing.
Henson, S. (2006), 'The role of public and private standards in regulating international food markets', Paper presented at the IATRC Symposium, May 2006, Bonn.
Henson, S. and Humphrey, J. (2008) 'Understanding the complexities of private standards in global agri-food chains'. Paper presented at the workshop: Globalization, Global Governance and Private Standards, University of Leuven, November 2008.
Henson, S. and Jaffee, S. (2008), 'Understanding developing country strategic responses to the enhancement of food safety standards', *World Economy*, 31 (4), pp. 548–568.
Humphrey, J., McCulloch, N. and Ota, M. (2004), 'The impact of European market changes on employment in the Kenyan horticulture sector', *Journal of International Development*, 16 (1), pp. 63–80.
Irwin, D.A. and Tervio, M. (2002), 'Does trade raise income? Evidence from the twentieth century', *Journal of International Economics*, 58 (1), pp. 1–18.
Jaffee, S. (2003), 'From challenge to opportunity: Transforming Kenya's fresh vegetable trade in the context of emerging food safety and other standards in Europe', *Agricultural and Rural Development Discussion Paper*, Washington DC: The World Bank.
Jaffee, S. and Henson, S. (2004), 'Standards and agro-food exports from developing countries: Rebalancing the debate', *World Bank Policy Research Working Paper No. 3348*, Washington DC: The World Bank.
Jaffee, S. and Henson, S. (2005), 'Agro-food exports from developing countries: the challenges posed by standards', in A.M. Aksoy and J.C. Beghin (eds), *Global Agricultural Trade and Developing Countries*, Washington DC: The World Bank.

Key, N. and Runsten, D. (1999), 'Contract farming, smallholders, and rural development in Latin America: the organization of agroprocessing firms and the scale of outgrower production', *World Development*, 27 (2), pp. 381–401.
Kherralah, M. (2000), 'Access of smallholder farmers to the fruits and vegetables market in Kenya', Unpublished document, Washington DC: International Food Policy Research Institute.
Klein, M., Aaron, C. and Hadjimichael, B. (2001), 'Foreign direct investment and poverty reduction', *World Bank Policy Research Working Paper No. 2613*, Washington DC: The World Bank.
Maertens, M. and Swinnen, J.F.M. (2007), 'Standards as barriers and catalysts for trade, growth and poverty reduction' *Journal of International Agricultural Trade and Development*, 4 (2), pp. 47–61.
Maertens, M. and Swinnen, J.F.M. (2009), 'Trade, standards and poverty: evidence from Senegal', *World Development*, 37 (1), pp. 161–178.
Maertens, M., Minten, B. and Swinnen, J.F.M. (2009), 'Growth in high-value export markets in Sub-Saharan Africa and its development implication', *LICOS Discussion Paper No. 245*, Leuven: LICOS.
Maertens, M., Colen, L. and Swinnen, J.F.M. (2011), 'Globalization and poverty in Senegal. A worst-case scenario?', *European Journal of Agricultural Economics*, 38 (1), pp. 31–54.
McCulloch, N. and Ota, M. (2002), 'Export horticulture and poverty in Kenya', *IDS Working Paper 174*, Sussex: Institute for Development Studies.
Minot, N. and Ngigi, M. (2004), 'Are horticultural exports a replicable success story? Evidence from Kenya and Côte d'Ivoire', *EPTD/MTID Discussion Paper*, Washington DC: IFPRI.
Minten, B., Randrianarison, L. and Swinnen, J.F.M. (2009), 'Global retail chains and poor farmers: Evidence from Madagascar', *World Development*, 37 (11), pp. 1728–1741.
Reardon, T., Codron, J.M., Busch, L., Bingen, J. and Harris, C. (1999), 'Global change in agrifood grades and standards: agribusiness strategic responses in developing countries', *International Food and Agribusiness Management Review*, 2 (3), pp. 421–435.
République du Sénégal (2004), 'La pauvreté au Sénégal: De la dévaluation de 1994 à 2001–2002', Dakar : Ministère de l'Economie et des Finances, Direction de la Prévision et de la Statistique.
Sautier, D., Vermeulen, H., Fok, M. and Bienabé , F. (2006), 'Case-studies of agro-processing and contract agriculture in Africa', Santiago: Rimisp-Latin American Center for Rural Development.
Swinnen, J.F.M. (2005), *When the Market Comes to You – or Not. The Dynamics of Vertical Co-ordination in Agro-food chains in Europe and Central Asia*, Report, Washington DC: World Bank.
Swinnen, J.F.M. (ed.) (2007), *Global Supply Chains, Standards and the Poor*, Oxford: CABI Publishing.
Swinnen J. and Maertens, M. (2007), 'Globalization, privatization, and vertical coordination in food value chains in developing and transition countries', *Agricultural Economics*, 37 (2), pp. 89–102.
Unnevehr, L.J. (2000), 'Food safety issues and fresh food product exports from LDCs', *Agricultural Economics*, 23 (3), pp. 231–240.
Warning, M. and Key, N. (2002), 'The social performance and distributional impact of contract farming: An equilibrium analysis of the Arachide de Bouche

Program in Senegal', *World Development*, 30 (2), pp. 255–263.
Weatherspoon, D.D. and Reardon, T. (2003), 'The rise of supermarkets in Africa: Implications for agrifood systems and the rural poor', *Development Policy Review*, 21 (3), pp. 333–356.
Wilson, J.S. and Abiola, V. (2003), *Standards and Global Trade: A Voice for Africa*, Washington DC: The World Bank.
World Bank (2005), 'Food safety and agricultural health standards: challenges and opportunities for developing country exports. Poverty Reduction and Economic Management Trade Unit and Agricultural and Rural Development Department', *Report No. 31207*, Washington D.C.: The World Bank.
World Bank (2008), 'World development report 2008: agriculture for development', Washington DC: World Bank.

PART III

Private food standards and global governance: legal perspectives

8. Transnational governance by contract: private regulation and contractual networks in food safety[1]

Fabrizio Cafaggi

1. TRANSNATIONAL PRIVATE REGULATION AND SUPPLY CHAIN

Transnational private regulation (TPR) in food safety is growing, adopting new models which influence both access to and exit from markets and the level of consumer safety. Private standards include rules not only concerning products and processes including traceability, but also extend to the use of chemicals and pesticides and their effects on the environment. TPR's impact differs across commodities – in some cases, competitiveness is primarily linked to price, while in others quality and safety are playing an ever more significant role. There seems to be a link between the development of TPR and the current structures of the supply chain in the agri-food industry.[2]

Different forms of global food safety regulation have recently emerged including public, private and hybrid forms (see Henson and Humphrey, 2009 and FAO/WHO, 2010). At the international level, standards have also been linked to the right to food. The Human Rights Council has recently devoted specific attention to the right to food and, in particular, issues relating to contract farming applying the Ruggie's 'protect, respect and remedy' framework to the food sector.[3] According to the reporter Olivier de Schutter, both state responsibility and corporate responsibility should lead to a different regulatory framework concerning contract farming[4] as the organizational choice of (agri)business models are not neutral with respect to the human right to food. Indeed, certain contractual arrangements are more 'right-to-food' compliant than others.[5]

There have also been several private regulatory initiatives involving supply chains and trade associations. The former preserve the strong nature of private initiatives as they are mainly designed through inner supply contracting. Those structures generally promoted by retailers, are often multi-national and involve the whole chain up to the farmers as due diligence requirements call for a supply chain approach. Trade association initiatives have largely been drafted by producers and retailers' associations. New private standard-setters are emerging, moving away from traditional coalitions of trade associations. Recent transformations illustrate the attempts to shift from a highly competitive regulatory landscape to forms of mutual recognition and transnational cooperation in private standard setting; however, the process is far from complete. The regulatory supply chain approach, adopted both in Europe and the US, has increased the importance of private regulation but at the same time has re-allocated the costs of regulatory compliance along the chain.

How does the new regulatory approach affect the relationships along the chain? The regulatory supply chain approach in industrial organization has important consequences for the definition of a risk-based approach to food safety regulation and hence to both public and private regulation.[6] It requires different risk assessment methodologies and different risk management instruments from the ones applied to control risks in individual, vertically-integrated firms. The emergence of hybrid regulatory arrangements, as a consequence of the increasing role of private standards, suggests that risk-sharing among the enterprises belonging to the chain may be designed to avoid shirking and to maximize collaboration between enterprises. This is especially so when emergencies arise, such as those which have characterized the recent food crises (including the spinach and sprouts, e-coli, mad cow/BSE, Chinese milk powder and beef hormone cases). The choice of the regulatory approach within the framework of the supply chain can further influence the allocation of regulatory power and the distribution of costs among the enterprises along the chain.

This chapter examines the role of regulation, and specifically TPR, in food safety and its relationship with the evolution of contractual practices within supply chains. It develops a coordinated approach, integrating the value chain perspective with regulatory theory, to show that co-evolutionary patterns contribute to explaining the changes in the supply chains and the increasing use of TPR. It examines the role of contractual governance in the implementation of transnational regulation, focusing on the role of transnational contracting, specifically that of network and collaborative contracts, for the regulation and monitoring of safety in food supply chains. It shows how TPR, for example, associated with traceability, affects the form and function of a supply chain and requires specific contractual arrangements among suppliers, and further, between suppliers and retailers to implement the safety standards and to monitor their compliance. Contractual networks in this framework can be used:

1. to design safety control systems along the supply chain

2. to detect risks and allow for prompt reaction before they spread, by conveying information to the relevant risk managers and by triggering remedial strategies.

For example, in the case of a product recall made by producers, in collaboration with retailers or with a public authority, well-designed network contracts may provide effective risk management tools. The analysis concludes by suggesting that policy design and implementation concerning food safety can be improved by implementing contractual governance at a global level, if supported by an adequate institutional framework and legislative reforms at the national level.

2. THE MUTUAL LINK BETWEEN REGULATION AND SUPPLY CHAIN GOVERNANCE: EXPLORING THE RELATIONSHIP BETWEEN INDUSTRIAL ORGANIZATION AND REGULATORY CHOICES

Regulation, in particular private regulation, influences the structure of the chain and its modes of coordination. However, the causal correlation is symmetric since the structure of the supply chain and its degree of integration affects the choice of regulatory instruments.[7] For instance, the choice between command-and-control, responsive, management-based or smart regulation influences the type of contract deployed to coordinate compliance by final producers, first- and second-tier suppliers. They range from standard contracts to relational contracts, from a sequence of bilateral linked contracts to the use of multilateral regulatory contracts. We will first examine transnational regulation and then analyse more specifically the administrative and liability rules concerning food safety, showing how they influence contractual governance.

Private regulation influences the structure of the market and the value created in the supply chain. More specifically, the increasing relevance of private standard-setting has had an effect on:

1. market concentration, reducing competition between big and small firms in developing countries
2. the shape and length of supply chains.[8]

In fact, regulatory coordination within the supply chain depends partly on the nature of the adopted standard.

The choice of standards may reflect different degrees of delegation between regulators (often the retailers) and regulatees (the producers/

suppliers). Performance and output standards presuppose a higher level of delegation by retailers to suppliers.[9] On the contrary, input standards reduce delegation and are used in a command-and-control framework, when retailers specify the standards in detail and monitor suppliers' implementation. There is some evidence that, unlike public regulation where regulators have moved from detailed input to broad output standards, in private regulation detailed prescriptions are often contractually required by retailer(s), which dictate the standards, leaving little or no discretion to suppliers.[10] The use of private standards is associated with technological control by the leading firm. Often downstream players, large food producers or retailers, provide the technology to meet the required standards thereby gaining full control over the manufacturing process. Two apparently conflicting patterns emerge: one leading towards increased hierarchy; the other promoting collaboration along the chain. Both, whether the identification of the 'technical' standards requires a stricter hierarchy, and whether quality management or performance standards call for more collaboration in the design or implementation stage, remain open questions.

Private regulation influences the structure of the market and the value created in the supply chain. More specifically, the increasing relevance of private standard setting has had an effect on market concentration, reducing competition between big and small firms in developing countries, and on the shape and length of supply chains (see Henson and Humphrey, 2009; Jaffe and Masakure, 2005). In fact, regulatory coordination within the supply chain depends partly on the nature of the adopted standard.

On the other hand, the form of the supply chain contributes to the definition of the regulatory strategy and the choice of regulatory instruments (see Lee et al., 2010).[11] Private standards, defined by actors within the supply chain, have pushed towards a market-based approach and the wider use of private certification to verify compliance with the rules. Therefore, not only the choices among different regulatory approaches but also the nature of the deployed standards are influenced by the structure of the supply chain.[12]

The degree of integration in the supply chain also affects the choice of the regulatory instrument, that is, the type of contract or company law device. Agri-food industry chains have experienced important changes in this respect (see UNCTAD, 2009). Both vertical integration and vertical disintegration are occurring, depending on the market and specific food commodity.[13] Investments in land by transnational corporations and sovereign funds are taking place after a period of disinvestment due primarily to the need to shift the risk of volatility in markets of agricultural commodities. Furthermore, depending on the degree of integration in the supply chain, diverse correlations between the instruments of private regulation and the degree of chain integration can be found.[14]

First, when vertical integration is in place, the main coordination tool is hierarchy, representing an example of private command-and-control regulation. In particular, when retailers integrate upstream buying suppliers, private standards become an internal affair of the retailer's company and their compliance is managed through internal committees, or other devices provided by company law. Second, when vertical disintegration occurs, private regulation is implemented primarily through integrated contracts, to a limited extent by tort law. There are at least two different examples of retailers' regulatory activity implemented through international contract law: private label safety regulations and branded product regulations.

Private label issues arise when retailers outsource production of food to be sold under their trademark. In relation to privately labelled products, the role of food safety standards goes well beyond a purely regulatory function, operating as one of the main devices to coordinate different nodes within the chain.[15] The retailer often organizes the production process to guarantee quality and safety standards. A second set of cases of 'de-verticalization' concerns big producers outsourcing part of the production process to smaller suppliers, often located in developing countries. (World Bank, 2005; Garcia Martinez and Banados, 2004). These activities are usually subject to strict private regulatory standards in order to preserve the reputation of the large final producers. In theory, private command-and-control regulation is available even in this scenario but unlike the approach taken in the vertically integrated chain example, contracts rather than company law are deployed. One option promotes the use of standard contracts, generally associated with input standards, while a second option provides for the use of incomplete contracts with unilateral completion, more likely to be associated with output standards, where the regulator/retailer defines the goals and the regulated/supplier selects the means.

3. PRIVATE REGULATION AND TRANSNATIONAL FOOD SAFETY

Regulatory changes concern both command-and-control and risk-based strategies, as well as private actors (the supply chain) and public actors (states and international government organizations (IGOs)). Three major changes have occurred:

1. the transfer of regulatory power from domestic to international actors
2. the increasing influence of private standard setting on food safety
3. the diversification of players within the private sphere which has brought about some degree of private regulatory competition.

The focus in private standard-setting has recently shifted from products to processes in order to detect hazards at the optimal point of the food chain. Hazard analysis and critical control points (HACCP) technique is now commonly adopted both in both public and private regulation. As a consequence the supply chain structure's duties to monitor and inform reflect the regulatory regime: the flow of information and the degree of its codification is deeply influenced by the type of regulation and the principle of traceability. Furthermore, the change is also meant to address environmental externalities in food processing. A second important changing pattern in supply chain governance is reflected in the link established by TPR between food safety and other policies, particularly environmental and social policies.[16] This interplay has powerful and important positive repercussions on the use of contractual governance for policy coordination (Cafaggi, 2011b). Commercial contracts along the supply chain include clauses on all of these aspects. In fact, while the commercial side concerning prices and quantities is relatively standardized, the regulatory part has become broader and more complex.

The competitive advantage of private regulation may contribute to more effective compliance. Importing states are weak enforcers of rules concerning transnational supply chains, hence, resorting to private regulation they delegate to industry players, in particular retailers in host states, the task of devising compliance mechanisms to be applied upstream in suppliers' countries (see Coglianese et al., 2009). Retailers have engaged in private regulatory competition, which partly increases market accountability mechanisms and partly augments regulatory fragmentation. Market accountability also operates within supply chains with contractual devices, for example, through self-enforcing contracts or by threatening contract termination or lack of renewal. Thus, suppliers might even have a stronger incentive to comply than they would have under their domestic legal regimes, enforced in courts (see Cafaggi, 2012a; Berdegué et al., 2005).

Private regulation also has its downsides. TPR often lacks legal accountability to consumers and other stakeholders where contractual governance shows its major weaknesses.[17] These stakeholders do not participate in the standard-setting process carried out primarily by industry 'experts'. The current design often implies a trade-off between higher effectiveness and lower accountability. However, this is not a necessary price as better institutional design can reconcile effectiveness and accountability, making private regulation a useful complement of transnational public regulation (Cafaggi, 2009a). Increasing accountability of TPR does not only meet democratic values but it also improves efficiency.[18]

As mentioned above, the transformation of private regulation, providing an increasing role for retailers and retail associations, emphasizes the potential conflict between regulatory competition and harmonization of rules. Retailers' private regulation has engendered an increasing number of standards, often competing at the regional level. Theoretically, the principal function of TPR is to reach a higher level of harmonization, often undermined by the differences existing in states' regulation. However, the proliferation of private standard-setters, often competing over standards of supply, modifies the regulatory landscape by substituting national public differentiation with private transnational fragmentation (Henson and Humphrey, 2009). Suppliers in developing economies must meet different standards to be able to access distribution systems in multiple regional areas, and often large retailers develop their own regimes to exercise competitive pressure over rivals. This fragmentation is particularly problematic in relation to food safety because it makes risk management extremely hard, especially when crises occur and common principles must be complied with in order to prevent outbreaks and pandemics. In such cases, it is necessary to opt for an institutional design that harmonizes rules, even within the private domain, that may increase costs of risk management, while a plurality of standards may constitute a useful competitive mechanism in other food safety areas. Two mutually non-exclusive options are available:

1. reducing the level of fragmentation through uniform standards
2. creating governance responses that can minimize the costs of regulatory fragmentation.

The following section of the chapter addresses the second response by focusing on a particular instrument across regulatory strategies: network contracts. It should be noted that a host of initiatives is trying to address fragmentation by way of promoting mutual recognition among private standards (the Global Food Safety Initiative (GFSI) and more broadly across fields by the ISEAL).

The link between private regulation, private standards and competition is relevant to further assess the strengths and limits of private regulation (see Maher, 2011). Private standards concerning food safety may constitute an instrument for product differentiation, thereby enhancing competition, or for product standardization, thereby hindering competition. But when adopted by coalitions of firms even those aiming at product differentiation may translate into anti-competitive devices to raise entry costs. They may constitute a barrier to trade by promoting processes of consolidation and aggregation, driving smaller producers out of the market.[19] Competition law, posing constraints on private regulation when it can create anti-competitive effects, ends up influencing the supply chain structure as well.

Agreements between trade associations in the agri-food industry, especially producers and distributors, have been promoted in different European countries to balance the contractual power of distributors. These agreements are mainly focused on price, but they also reflect concerns over the allocation of costs of the adoption of private standards. Competition law at the state level provides guidelines for standardization, including food products, in order to keep it compliant with general principles (see UK Competition Commission, 2008). Similarly, guidelines have been provided at the EU level. More difficult challenges concern competition law control over private standard-setting at the global level (see Firth et al., 2009).

4. FOOD SAFETY, TPR AND SUPPLY CHAIN GOVERNANCE BY CONTRACT

Having described some of the features of transnational private food safety regulation, we now turn to the contractual governance analysis of the supply chain as determined by the regulatory provisions.

Private regulation in food safety operates today through a set of complementary tools: codes of conduct enacted by trade associations at national and global levels, supply chain agreements and framework contracts. These regulatory standards are internalized into contracts with different techniques but, most importantly, they modify structure and governance of the contract. The supply chain approach in public regulation and the increased role of private standards call for stronger forms of contractual governance. The traditional, purely international commercial contracts are complemented by regulatory provisions that often integrate commercial and regulatory aspects. Governance by contract, however, requires specific models that enable more effective coordination among enterprises of the chain and which are capable of controlling the distributional consequences of the re-allocation of regulatory power along supply chains between farmers, producers and retailers. I will first address the general regulatory features of commercial contracts and then focus more specifically on the network form of contractual coordination among enterprises located along the chain.

The role of international contract law as an instrument of regulation is evolving and broadening. In the past, it has mainly been associated with *lex mercatoria* and the regulation of exchanges between merchants across different national legal systems. It was directed more at market design than market regulation. Today, contracts for exchanges within the food supply chain (and in particular, terms concerning quality and safety) are meant not only to complement state and international public regulation, but also to ensure the enforceability of regulation including international soft law, the Codex Alimentarius provisions and TPR.[20] Food safety provisions can be found in a number of contracts, from supply agreements, to mergers and acquisitions agreements, to credit and insurance agreements. Private standards, often defined in codes of conducts, are incorporated into these contracts. They concern products and processes and often cover food quality, food safety, and environmental concerns.[21] They prescribe rules controlling risks and risk management procedures specifying, for example, HACCP criteria.[22] These provisions are aimed at stabilising and even codifying arrangements for information transmission and risk management related to food quality and safety, which can potentially translate into illness outbreaks.

Contractual relationships may differ depending on the features of the supply chain, the nature of the product and the position occupied by each enterprise in the chain itself.[23] Different models of contractual governance may be used, according to the type of linkages between parties within the supply chain: *modular*, where parties can switch at low costs from one supply chain to the other; *relational*, where parties engage in strategic partnerships and exit costs increase; or *captive*, where suppliers are economically dependent on retailers and termination is often unilaterally defined.[24] In fact, several contractual models have been used to regulate food safety along the supply chain. Variations occur primarily in the first part of the chain, as in the case of contract farming (Da Silva, 2005). Farming contracts develop in various ways depending on the structure of the land, the size and ownership of the farm, the nature of the product and the technological requirements.[25] The contract choices depend on ownership of the land and the allocation of rights concerning farming choices.[26] For example, in tenancy or lease, the farmer pays a fee to the landowner and assumes the risks whereas in sharecropping, parties share the risks, profits and losses. The relationship between suppliers and retailers can also take various forms, translating into different models of risk-sharing and profit/loss allocation. In the traditional farming contract, the farmer supplies the commodity while the buyer supplies inputs like seeds, fertilizers, know-how and technological assistance. In joint ventures, a partnership between the farmer and the agribusiness is created with co-ownership and risk sharing. Furthermore, from a structural perspective, there may also be different variants.[27]

In some cases there exists a general framework contract, designed by the retailer and applied to all suppliers.[28] This scheme includes framework and executory contracts.[29] Another model deploys only bilateral contracts along the chain, reproducing in each contract principles and rules with common monitoring and enforcement mechanisms. This model is extremely weak and, despite the asymmetric contracting power along the supply chain, often only retailers are able to impose clauses on first-tier suppliers, while those on the second or third tier must delegate both contracting and compliance control to first-tier suppliers. These contracts are generally self-enforcing, with disputes solved through private dispute resolution mechanisms rather than through the courts (Cafaggi, 2012a).

An alternative model is the multi-party contract (see Cafaggi, 2008; 2011a). Typically this would constitute a consortium or a multiparty joint venture. These contracts often involve more than two parties, but even when they formally constitute a set of bilateral linked contracts, their assets' interdependence is relatively high and each contract along the supply chain replicates most of the regulatory clauses in order to regulate second- and third-tier suppliers consistently (Collins, 2009). Subscription to the same regulatory standards often implies a certain level of investment specificity, making it harder for suppliers to behave opportunistically. Retailers lock them in by defining their own standards above and beyond public regulation. They often include governance mechanisms directed at ensuring compliance, either by the contract participants or third-party certifiers, and non-judicial enforcement devices including, but not limited to, arbitration. The lock-in effect is particularly strong for private labels, and less so for trademarked products. Organizational models include cooperatives, both for production and service provision to farmers, and ordinary company models, often subject to specific agricultural legislation associated with special tax treatments.

As the abovementioned model shows, two important dimensions of using contracts as instruments of regulatory governance must be considered with regard to the accountability of transnational regulatory regimes:

1. the specificity of monitoring performances and sanctioning violations
2. the institutional framework within which these contracts operate.

5. CONTRACTUAL GOVERNANCE AND INSTITUTIONAL COMPLEMENTARITY BETWEEN DOMESTIC ADMINISTRATIVE REGULATION AND CONTRACT LAW

The institutional framework of contracting at the international level differs from that within nation states. These contracts and master agreements are concluded between suppliers located at different tiers and between suppliers and exporters, suppliers and importers, and suppliers and retailers located in different countries.[30] The retailer generally provides for the form of the contract but in some instances contracts may also be designed by producer groups.[31] State legislation strongly influences farming contracts, however, less so the contracts downstream at the end of the chain.

In order to have private standards in value chains, which often encompass enterprises located in different legal systems and with different contract laws, international agreements must define a framework to be implemented by single contracts among individual parties belonging to the chain. Especially in cases where bilateral contracting is used, the framework is imposed de facto by the chain leader. The multiplicity of contracts is often associated with multiple courts and often multiple jurisdictions which regulate the same supply chain in different, and sometimes conflicting, ways. As a result, transnational regulatory contracting is characterized by the presence of informal mechanisms and strong non-legal enforcement systems whose effectiveness is largely associated with the institutional and social framework, rather than the legal systems in which they operate.[32] Transnational governance by contract is then the result of various accountability mechanisms, all influencing effectiveness and compliance.

A key question for regulatory effectiveness via international contracting is monitoring compliance of food safety provisions. Since compliance is central to contractual governance we have to address who is responsible for compliance and through which instruments they must comply. Besides self-enforcing mechanisms, two additional factors have to be considered:

1. non-legal market and social accountability mechanisms
2. domestic public laws.

First, the supply chain regulatory approach outlined above partly promotes transfer of compliance control onto the chain. Thence, compliance mechanisms are contractually designed to meet due diligence requirements. Multinational liability often requires that due diligence extends beyond the corporate reach into contractual relationships with suppliers along the chain. Unlike the traditional domestic contracts, however, monitoring in international regulatory contracts is strongly complemented by third party intervention: on the one hand, through NGOs and the media, and on the other hand, through certifiers. Civil society and other market actors also play a significant role in ensuring proper monitoring, primarily via non-judicial enforcement.[33] Reputational mechanisms are set up; often, entire websites are dedicated to monitoring the conduct of either individual or groups of retailers and their compliance with contractual commitments or codes of conduct.[34] These mechanisms are reflected in the private monitoring system adopted within the chain, often including third-party monitoring, particularly by certifiers, and a sanctioning system, directed at deterring, blaming and shaming infringers rather than compensating losses suffered by consumers. In particular, monitoring compliance with food safety standards is often done by third-party certification, and rarely by first-party certification.[35] However, conventional consumer protection devices, in particular adjudication by national courts, still remain in place.

Second, international contracting including private regulatory standards is supplemented by domestic public laws, giving rise to vertical complementarity which affects both the design and enforcement of contracts. These include administrative regulation, criminal liability, product liability and sales law provisions for unsafe products. The vertical complementarity of regulatory systems, as we shall see, affects the form of contracts along the chain and eventually influences the shape of the chain itself. In addition, domestic contract laws are relevant because they fill gaps when regulatory contracts do not explicitly regulate matters. Not only this, but many other fragments of domestic legislation bear on the choice and content of international regulatory contracts. I proceed to give a brief illustration instrumental to examine the influence of domestic law(s) on transnational contractual networks.

Recent changes in the regulatory domain illustrate a preference for an *ex ante* preventative approach based on the precautionary principle over a regime of *ex post* detection of violations (see FAO, 2003). A good illustration is the influence of precautionary principle on the design of contractual governance. The precautionary principle characterizes food safety regulation in various domains.[36] The main objective of this change has been to minimize risks and to improve effectiveness and efficiency of control at the source of the hazard (see Vapnek, 2007, pp. 992–3). To promptly identify this source, traceability systems have developed under the pressure of both states and markets.[37] Traceability has increased the transparency of the regulatory process and the allocation of tasks along the chain. Transparency linked to traceability:

1. increases consumer confidence
2. ensures competition by differentiating products
3. decreases costs when product recalls are necessary
4. improves risk management when hazards emerge.[38]

Therefore traceability has become the foundation of risk-based regulation in food safety and beyond.[39] It is strongly correlated to the operation of the precautionary principle and the supply chain approach.

5.1. Comparing the Food Chain Approach in Europe and the USA and its Influence on Transnational Governance by Contract

Having illustrated the general transnational regulatory approach and its influence on contractual governance, we now add the domestic public regulatory regimes which endorse the supply chain approach. In Europe, administrative regulation concerning food safety has partially endorsed the food chain approach, placing responsibility concerning compliance with food safety standards on private enterprises along the chain (Vos and Wendler, 2006, p. 70; Alemanno, 2009, p. 171). Administrative regulation is often combined with criminal sanctions.[40] Private standards play a role in the enforcement of civil liability regimes but compliance with private standards alone is insufficient to immunize from liability, even when these standards are higher than those designed by national legislation.[41]

Food safety regulation is the outcome of administrative law and enforcement, civil liability and contract law in the US as well. Regulation is primarily carried out by the FDA and USDA with each adopting different strategies. While the former relies heavily on the cooperation of food companies, the USDA adopts a more traditional command-and-control approach. With the recent Food Safety Modernization Act (FSMA), the management-based approach has been strengthened.[42] The federal statute, in principle, does not pre-empt statutory and common law concerning liability.[43] The FSMA imposes the implementation of preventive controls on food facilities, and furthermore the adoption of corrective actions if prevention does not work properly.[44] These duties translate into the definition of procedures along the chain and a duty to monitor their compliance.[45] On the remedial side, FSMA introduces a mandatory recall authority defining a two-stage process where first voluntary recall is requested and in case of non-compliance, mandatory recall can be ordered.[46] However, neither the duties nor the remedies are explicitly associated with any organizational form that ensures proper implementation of the prevention measures. Contractual networks may constitute a viable measure to implement HACCP and to trigger corrective actions.[47] They are now part of the legislative framework but in relation to different issues. A specific FSMA provision on networks concerns the accredited laboratories that have to act when an emergency arises.[48]

In relation to civil liability, a flexible approach was taken in the Restatement (Second) of Torts § 402A, on the basis of which both sellers and retailers could generally be held liable for design defects. This rule had been applied to sellers of food for human consumption even before § 402A was approved.[49] The Restatement of Torts 3d § 7 defines the liability regime for defective food products, opting for a consumer expectation standard.[50] It dedicates a specific section to liability for product recalls. Liability for failure to recall can only arise when there is a breach of a statutory duty to recall.[51] Without such a duty, according to the Restatement, no liability could be found. It can be disputed, however, whether under a general negligence standard, failure to recall a product would constitute a violation of the duty of care. Clearly the new provisions of FSMA on product recalls open a new chapter in the litigation concerning liability for recall. American courts deploy a functional criterion to identify the party within the distribution chain that can most efficiently monitor the suppliers' compliance.[52] Depending on the structure of the distribution chain, this could be the distributor contractually closest to the supplier or the party with the greatest contractual power, often *also* the distributor, even if located further down the chain.

In Europe, the directive on product liability 85/274/EC has been applied to agricultural products since 1999, however no coordination of the relationship between the liability directive and the food safety regulation has been established, but for the provision that the regulation does not pre-empt the product liability regime. The supply chain approach in food safety regulation adopted with regulation 178/2002 is not followed in product liability, thus giving rise to a divergent regime, which increases the costs of defining organizational responses, including the shape of contractual networks.

The implications of the new regulatory regimes go to the core of product liability and affect also the potential shapes of the contractual networks, as will be illustrated below. If the retailers, either within their association or acting individually, are those who define private safety standards for suppliers, what causes of action are at the disposal of the final consumer? Would the consumer be able to hold retailers liable if the standards provided were defective? Can standards contribute to the existence of a 'design' defect? Is compliance by the suppliers with contractually-imposed standards sufficient to immunize them from liability? It is beyond the scope of this chapter to provide answers to these questions; however they should be kept in mind when considering the proposal concerning the use of a contractual network as a regulatory device to assess and control food safety-related risks.

6. GOVERNANCE BY CONTRACTUAL NETWORKS AND THE INFLUENCE OF GLOBAL 'PUBLIC' REGULATION ON DIFFERENT NETWORK MODELS

After describing how transnational private regulation and domestic public systems affect contractual governance, it is useful to move to the normative dimension and to contrast the two primary structural models of transnational governance by contract – bilateral and multi-party contracting.

Private regulation and the evolution of the supply chain, with increasing outsourcing and vertical disintegration, requires a contractual governance model that:

1. reduces transaction costs
2. increases cooperation to produce and transfer information concerning products' hazards along the chain and to the final (potential) consumer.[53]

The current practice is that of sequential bilateral contracting. I suggest that multi-party contracts can increase regulatory effectiveness and decrease transaction costs. This change would reflect the increasing importance of the supply chain as a unit of analysis of regulatory policies illustrated earlier.

Contractual networks can operate both as risk assessment and risk management devices in food safety. They have comparative advantages over both organizational and bilateral contracting models. To create an organization, a company for example, with the only purpose of organizing production and dissemination of information about food hazards along the supply chain would not be very cost effective. The real alternative is that of bilateral contracting. Bilateral contracts can certainly define duties to acquire and transfer information about safety hazards, but have serious shortcomings when it comes to coordination of multiple, numerous parties along the supply chain pursuing the same objective. Furthermore, they present drawbacks when corrective actions have to be undertaken simultaneously by multiple enterprises producing or selling hazardous foodstuffs. The analysis of the most recent food disease outbreaks clearly shows the difficulty of coordinating prompt market responses via bilateral contracting.[54]

Contractual networks, however, are not without costs. There are many components to these networks, which sometimes result in conflicting goals and interests within the network contract governing the supply chain. On the one hand, there is the private dimension represented by the food safety and quality supply management, mainly related to the governance of the chain. On the other hand, there are state and regional (for example, European) liability and regulatory systems requiring the formation of networks to provide organisational responses to 'public' regulatory needs. The two logics are often divergent. The first dimension has been illustrated in the previous section; the second dimension will be examined in the next section by looking at two examples of contractual networks influenced by liability and regulatory regimes in the area of information, and remedies for violations of food safety regulatory regimes. The analysis will show how the proposal, advocating the use of contractual networks as private regulatory instruments, must take into account public regulatory regimes and, in particular, liability regimes.

7. GLOBAL CONTRACTUAL NETWORKS AND PRIVATE REGULATION: IMPROVING GOVERNANCE DESIGN

Having described how regulation and liability may, in theory, affect different forms of private governance of risk regulation and having advanced the claim of contractual network superiority over other forms of contractual governance, I now turn to two illustrations. Two contractual networks associated to food safety regulation will be analysed:

1. food safety risk information for products on the market
2. product recalls, a voluntary measure that enterprises are 'invited' to adopt when the risks to human health are serious; in extreme cases, when there is inaction by private parties, product recalls are ordered by the public authority and implemented in a hierarchical mode, either directly by administrative authority or by way of judicial enforcement.

7.1. Information Contractual Networks

Coordination of information dissemination is extremely important in order to balance the right of consumers to be promptly informed about food hazards and the need to reduce the potentially devastating impact that alarm could cause to the industry when the risk does not materialize or is less serious than anticipated. Two main difficulties exist: multiple institutions and multiple standards. As to multiple institutions, often there is no entity predominantly responsible for information transmission of hazardous risks. The focus of the illustration is the private network, yet clearly its form is influenced by public regulation and by the media. In the EU, states form a network which manages the rapid alert system for food and feed where information has to be transmitted from the contact point to the state and from the latter to the network and the European Commission (Ref. 16/2011, 882/2005, 178/2002). Furthermore, the media plays a major role operating outside the institutional framework. Private chains have their own information channels organized differently from public ones. Information along the supply chain is defined by multiple standards determined by private regimes – ISO management standards like 22000 and public standards such as those enacted by EU regulations and by US FSMA. Standards concerning when, how and to whom information should be addressed may also diverge. These differences exist not only between the public and private spheres but also within the the public and within the private.

Private information regulation via contractual networks can help to harmonize standards and procedures to make foodstuffs traceable along supply chains, thereby favouring information flows concerning hazards. This, however, can only occur if there is a common framework which can either be provided by a standard-setting organization or by an agreement between the different private organizations which define safety standards. If multiple standards on product traceability are implemented, both consumer choices and risk control will be undermined; consequently, it might prove difficult to provide an effective contractual response.

Obligations concerning information about food safety hazards are often inserted into commercial bilateral contracts along the supply chain and linked with the implementation of HACCP. Information becomes crucial when a foodborne illness outbreak may occur. The accuracy and immediacy of information transfer is a mandatory condition for effectiveness of risk management. The use of bilateral contracts for communicating food hazards poses two problems: firstly, it increases the coordination costs, and secondly, reduces consumers' enforcement possibilities, since they cannot bring forward contractual claims against upstream third parties. The difficulties of incorporating extracontractual liability regimes have been illustrated above. To improve risk detection and risk management, it is crucial that all the links of the chain are involved in the regulatory process concerning production and dissemination of information about food safety hazards. Risk detection may become extremely difficult and costly if even a single node of the regulatory chain is excluded. Contracts must therefore include all the participants in the supply chain and distribute the responsibility to control safety of the production process and the final product, making information swiftly available throughout the chain.[55] Network contracts can contribute to codification of information requirements concerning safety, making individual transactions along the chain less specific, thereby reducing opportunism.

Once the regulatory procedure to trace the origins of a product and related risks is defined information can follow that track. There is, however, a need to identify the sources of hazards while monitoring compliance with regulatory standards. Contractual networks directed at information transmission should therefore govern the different sources of information concerning safety hazards: some are dependent on the fraudulent and negligent conduct of parties along the chain, whereas others arise out of risks unknown at the time of product safety design. Clearly, the negligent or fraudulent behaviour of any link of the chain can undermine the whole process of information dissemination. Network design should be instrumental, not only to ensure that the process of information gathering and dissemination is cost effective, but also to ensure that mistakes and frauds are quickly detected and corrected through effective peer monitoring.

There is a clear link between the supply chain, the regulatory model and the shape of the network. In a command-and-control model, the acquisition of information is instrumental to disseminate hierarchical instructions to the participants of the supply chain about how to minimize risks and liability. The leader, often a multinational retailer, dictates the model, generally associated with software programs. In a responsive regulation model, the shape of the network is functional to joint problem solving, often selecting on an *ad hoc* basis the party who is in the best position to detect the problem and disseminate information. Once information is acquired its dissemination is functional to the joint problem solving philosophy rather than the objective of minimizing liability. The shape of these contractual networks thus derives from the changes coming from the selected regulatory model, for example, the move from a public command-and-control system, based on (ineffective) on-site inspections, to a (primarily) private monitoring system, thus placing higher responsibility on the supply chain and on the process of information gathering and dissemination. An important yet often neglected role in regulating information about foodstuff hazards is played by certification schemes.[56] Certifiers are generally third parties, paid by suppliers but chosen by retailers, who certify compliance with food safety requirements.[57] Given their strategic monitoring function, they should ideally be part of the information network to constitute an additional and more effective source of consumer information.[58] Their importance is also related to requirements that certification schemes impose, increasingly influencing the organization of the supply chain as the GLOBALG.A.P. example shows.[59] The contractual network form therefore plays at least two important roles: first, it increases the available information and knowledge about food hazards; second, it enhances the effectiveness of monitoring compliance and solves the problems associated with the knowledge of the hazards. As mentioned above, the network often replicates the form generated by the technology of traceability[60] but may vary in relation to the components of the chain where it is easier to solve the problem.

Once information has become available, the decision-making process, aiming to minimize risks of harm, may require the use of a contractual network different from that deployed to gather information. While information concerning the cause of the hazard (for instance, adulteration) may primarily concern the production level, the management of risk is better performed at the distribution or retail level, where consumers become exposed to risks. Therefore, decision-making power may be allocated differently within the network, depending on the specific function to be performed in relation to the same hazard: risk assessment or risk management. The creation of two different flows of information may also be compatible with a single contractual network with different architecture of information circulation. The design of the network may reflect different obligations among parties depending on the specific function: a modular network may satisfy these needs.

So far we have assumed that parties can freely design the network. However, the multi-level regulatory regime as described in section 5 poses constraints in relation to the shape of the network given the liability regimes that allocate burdens in respect of acquiring and disseminating information along the chain. Liability rules do not directly limit contractual freedoms but pose de facto constraints by allocating the burdens of informing the final consumers about the hazard.[61] In theory, parties could design a different and even opposite allocation of information duties from that consistent with liability rules. Deviation in network design from that mirroring liability towards third parties may be justified when the goals of problem-solving and of deterring unlawful behaviour follow different logics. However, the costs of *ex post* litigation, if the enterprises along the chain comply with contractual obligations rather than liability rules, might be rather high. It is thence reasonable to believe that the parties would internalize liability regimes into network design and try to avoid serious conflicts.

In Figure 8.1, the information network is centred on the final producer because the liability and the regulatory regime are organised around that

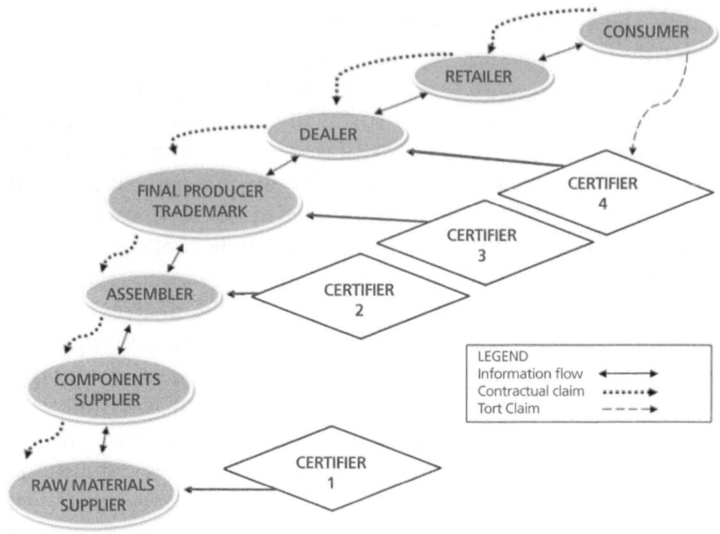

Figure 8.1: Information contractual network with vertical information

knot. The two lines indicate the potential liability regimes (contractual and extra-contractual) if information is not (adequately) provided. The information about the risk comes from harmed consumers, reaching the final producer through retailers and distributors. The producer of the final good has the responsibility to design the architecture of the information channels so that information will be efficiently produced and disseminated to the other members along the supply chain, both up to the producers of raw materials and down to the other distributors and retailers. In this particular form, the flow of information is vertical and goes from the harmed consumer up to the final producer and is then redistributed both horizontally and vertically. The final producer should design the network in such a way as to ensure that information concerning hazardous sources can be quickly generated and disseminated in compliance with HACCP principles.[62] In this context, traceability plays a strategic role as it codifies information and permits fast identification of product hazards.[63] In theory, this network design should match the information duties imposed by a liability regime centred on producers when they also internalize problem solving. In addition, the contractual network will presumably reflect the notification regime designed by EU regulation 1788/2002 specified and amended by regulation 16/2011 on the rapid alert system.

In the contractual network model shown in Figure 8.2, the leading organizing role shifts to retailers. The flow of information is, unlike the previous model, both vertical and horizontal. A contractual network for information transmission regarding food-related hazards, centred on the retailer, entails that information rules must be implemented at both the distribution and production level.[64] The retailer organizes the information flows both downstream to consumers and upstream to the producers. This model operates when the product is a private label and sold only by one chain of retailers with their trademark. Clearly, if the product is sold by multiple retailers, it would also be necessary to have inter-retailer communication. This model corresponds to a supply chain in which the retailer has greater market power and consequently has control over the channels of communication throughout the chain.[65]

7.2. Contractual Network for Risk Management: Handling Product Recalls

Information dissemination may not be sufficient to tackle food safety hazards. When hazards become known it might be necessary to react and reduce the risk for consumer health and the environment. The recall of the product is often the necessary path in order to reduce the risk of pandemic outbreaks. Therefore, a second area in which regulation has been playing an increased role is that of product recalls and withdrawals.[66] Currently, legislation does not indicate how recalls should be organized; it simply indicates who bears responsibility. The practice reflects partly the administrative regulation, which is also based on network, and partly the commercial aspects, organized via bilateral contracting. In this context,

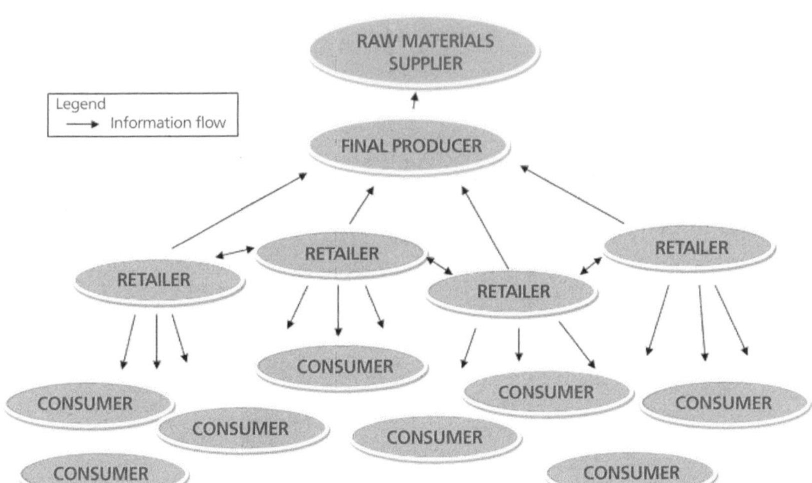

Figure 8.2: Information network centred on retailers

contractual networks may prove to be useful to organize product recalls (see Figure 8.3). They constitute a regulatory insrument that can increase effectiveness and minimize harm.[67] Before deciding about recalls the public has to be informed about the risks posed by hazardous foodstuff. Often recalls are only the final step in a procedure that requires firstly that consumers are informed of the risks and then, when the source is identified and the risk cannot be handled by the consumer, that the product has to be recalled. Recalls require that information is transmitted to retailers, professional customers engaged in the restaurant and catering business and final consumers. They call for the direct involvement of producers in collaboration with downstream distributors to ensure that the product is promptly taken out of the market and that proper information is disseminated in respect of the relevant risks. Often retailers contractually transfer the costs of recalls onto producers.[68]

The creation of a contractual network is one possible organizational response to the emergence of hazards that require recalls. The operation of a network would reduce coordination costs and reflect the supply chain approach. The particular shape of the contractual network is mainly influenced by the regulatory regime, which places the main burden on the producer, within a framework of coordination with the other parties.[69] Recalls were regulated in Europe, and now with FSMA there is also cross-sectorial regulation in the US. For the purposes of this chapter, recalls are conceived as risk management devices consistent with the precautionary

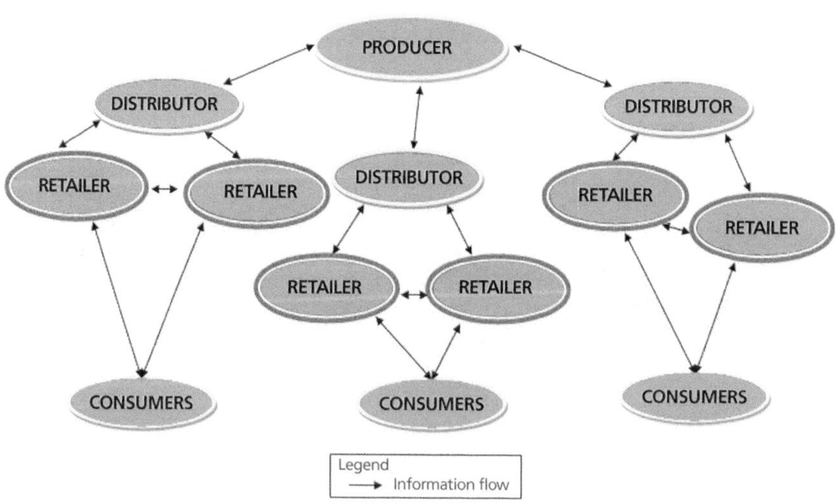

Figure 8.3: Risk management and product recalls

principle.[70] Risk management implies responding to the emergence of hazards concerning the product and its consumption.

Recalls are generally voluntary, and only as a last resort are they ordered by agencies or courts when serious health-related risks arise.[71] The European Regulation 178/2002 enables all food operators along the supply chain to initiate a recall procedure.[72] Product recalls in the US were also used before the FSMA.[73] The FSMA has now adopted an approach similar to the European one, where recalls are first 'invited' and then ordered in case of inaction.[74] The reputational harm that may be linked to any refusal to recall a product from the market usually induces producers and distributors to 'voluntarily' recall the product, often in agreement with public authorities.

As it was the case for the information approach, contractual network parties are not entirely free to design the contractual network that would manage the product recall. Both regulatory and liability constraints affect the potential shape of the contractual network. In respect of the design of the network, attempts should therefore be made to internalize the allocation of burdens to recall hazardous products, imposed by both public and private regulation. The liability regime under which voluntary recalls operate also affects the structure of the network.[75] Product liability regimes still place the highest burden on the producer for a product whose defects existed at the time the product was put in the market.[76] This implies that the producer tends to be the key player in product recall networks, ensuring coordination among retailers and along the supply chain.

To place strict liability on the retailer if the product is defectively designed because the private standards contractually imposed on the suppliers are inadequate might provide the corrective incentives for product recall. In these cases, retailers' liability not only requires identifying the best monitor but also the 'real' manufacturer: it calls for the identification of the party who designed the product or, at least, the party who defined the technical standards to be satisfied by the product.[77] Private standard-setting implies that the standard-setter should be held liable for failure to meet the standards, which they themselves defined and those which the certifiers have designed. When, as is usually the case for transnational standards, they are stricter than the domestic public standards, the liability regime should reflect the private standards and the commitments made by the sellers.

8. THE ACCOUNTABILITY OF PRIVATE CONTRACTUAL REGULATORY REGIMES AND THE CHALLENGES AHEAD

The above analysis has shown that private regulatory regimes in food safety are growing for two main reasons:

1. the adoption of the food chain approach both in public and private regulation
2. the particular features of agricultural commodities which require strong adaptation to each supply chain, increasing the number of commodity specific regulations.

These changes are likely to broaden the use of regulatory contracts as an instrument to coordinate supply chain participants in their implementation of public and private safety regulation. In turn, regulation calls for closer coordination, which makes sequential bilateral contracting extremely expensive and not very effective. Traditional bilateral contract models should be replaced by multi-party network models, which can involve all the main players along the supply chain, favouring joint problem-solving procedures. The structure of the network contracts reflects the changes in regulatory units of analysis, from the single firm to the supply chain.

Both the design and enforceability of these multi-party contracts must be the outcome of privately devised mechanisms since domestic contract law and international business transactions do not yet provide adequate support to regulatory functions. Hence, in order to implement effective processes of information production and transfer regarding food safety hazards, enterprises located along the supply chain must create international contractual networks to provide incentives for risk detection and the transfer of information about food-related risks. As demonstrated in section 7, freedom of contract is constrained by both regulatory requirements and by liability regimes. The adopted form of the network and the number of participants to the regulatory contract will be dependent upon the specific feature of the supply chain and its safety requirements, which change from commodity to commodity (from milk to poultry, from coffee to tomatoes).

Important drawbacks linked to this proposal remain in respect of their accountability to the final consumers, which are the potential beneficiaries of these new regulatory schemes.[78] Often safety codes are unilaterally drafted without the involvement of suppliers, consumer or environmental associations, or other NGOs (however, see the case of the coffee sector in

Giovannucci and Ponte, 2005). Participatory rights are not well defined. Notice and comment is rare and not well enforced, while judicial review is almost non-existent. For this reason, consumer public law often complements private regulation affecting the distribution of liabilities and costs along the chain.

9. FOOD SAFETY AND CONSUMER PROTECTION: ADDRESSING THE ACCOUNTABILITY DEFICIT AND ITS INFLUENCE ON REGULATORY CONTRACTUAL NETWORKS

Food safety is primarily designed to protect consumers' health, while food safety standards, incorporated in international contracts, are aimed at governing the food chain. Thus, consumer enforceability plays a strategic role in defining compliance incentives. Emphasis on the governance of the supply chain or on consumer protection varies, so consumers may be defined as direct or indirect beneficiaries of these agreements, depending on the relevant technical instruments: for example, a code of conduct, a protocol, guidelines or soft law.[79] Neither individual consumers nor consumer associations are technically part of the bilateral contracts, which makes it difficult to enforce them if violations occur causing harm to the final consumers. Legal systems define the different ways in which these contracts can be directly enforced by consumers and/or their associations:

1. by virtue of the '*action directe*' by the consumer against the supplier
2. by requiring unequivocal statements that their contracts are for the benefit of third parties
3. by allowing enforcement using implied terms of consumer contracts
4. by granting individual or class remedies under civil liability
5. by qualifying violations as unfair commercial practices.[80]

Contracts within the supply chain between retailers and suppliers, including food safety provisions, may qualify as contracts for the benefit of third parties (individual consumers and/or collective organisations) and can be enforced by them.[81] It would be easier to consider the contractual network as a contract for the benefit of consumer safety emphasizing the collective interest. Consumers may bring a claim for breach of warranty against the immediate seller when the warranty concerns compliance with food safety requirements. Clauses concerning food safety may constitute implied terms or may otherwise be 'integrated' within the contract by reference to general clauses such as good faith.[82] Consumers can enforce the provisions against the retailer even if such a clause is not explicitly included in the sale contract.

If retailers give firm commitments to comply with codes of conduct or protocols concerning food safety, violations have occurred, for example, according to European law against unfair trade practices, the retailer can be enjoined or forced to pay damages to individual consumers or consumer organisations.[83] The most common avenues are civil liability, in particular product liability and unfair competition law. The development of aggregate litigation in Europe and its consolidated function in the US may provide strong accountability devices to *ex post* control the regulatory activities of retailers and producers. Aspects of the difficulties, just described, can be minimized by shifting from bilateral to multi-party network contracts among the participants to the supply chain. What this chapter makes clear is that consumer law, including regulation and liability affects the shape of the supply chain and the allocation of liabilities therein.

10. GOVERNANCE BY CONTRACTS AND ACCOUNTABILITY: CHALLENGES TO TRANSNATIONAL PRIVATE REGULATION

Governance by contract is part of the menu of the so-called 'new modes of governance', although it is not often included in the list.[84] As we have seen, the emergence of contractually-based private regulatory regimes poses important challenges with respect to legitimacy and accountability towards consumers, but also in relation to smallholders in developing countries, which can be penalised by asymmetric contractual powers. Not only do consumers have a low level of participation in contractual design and standard-setting within the food supply chain approach, they also have very weak enforceability powers before courts. The accountability of these regimes is based mainly on the enforcement strength of NGOs and, to a limited extent, on competitors who may vary across industries and countries.

The illustrations above show the potential tensions between different contractual networks along the same supply chain; that is, networks created mainly by retailers to govern food safety along the chain by means of private technical standards and networks established to respond to regulatory needs concerning hazard information and product recalls. The identification of the key link in the network and the distribution of compliance and monitoring costs may vary if the network is retail or producer driven. Clearly the shape of the regulatory network should be responsive to the role and positions of the final consumers together with effective internal organization among the chain's participants. While they have little voice regarding contracting along the chain due to the insufficiencies of current contract law described in the section above, civil liability can provide a 'voice' in the regulation driven network. The different shapes of the contractual networks can thus be responsive to the role of liability regimes towards consumers. This tension may be solved in different ways: by imposing the primacy of a liability-driven network, or by improving coordination of the contractual network with the liability regime. In the latter case, enterprises along the chain will be able to arrange their own internal organisational structure, which will be affected by the liability regime but not necessarily entirely shaped by it. Liability regimes can amount to a limited response but do not provide satisfactory answers to accountability demands by the beneficiaries of the regulatory process, primarily consumers. International contractual governance requires a serious legal reform of network contracts in terms of design and monitoring, in order to ensure that consumer and environmental voices are heard, both in relation to contractual design and the enforcement of private safety standards. Multi-party regulatory contracts can be regulated to ensure enforceability by third parties when contractual provisions define new rights. Such reforms must, for the time being, be implemented at the state or regional level (European, North American, Latin American) by enacting appropriate legislation. However, it would be desirable for institutions like UNIDROIT, WHO and FAO to take the opportunity soon to make a proposal going beyond contract farming to encompass the entire supply chain.

11. CONCLUDING REMARKS

Food safety has long become a global regulatory issue. Today, the food safety regime is governed by a multi-level system where different co-regulatory modes operate (see FAO, 2003). Its private dimension has always been quite strong. However, in the past, it was sector-specific and predominantly producer driven. Today, it is increasingly retail driven, with a stronger transnational dimension, cutting across different commodities. Rule-making is taking place at the transnational level, based on the combination of international soft law, private codes and guidelines. More specifically, a shift from product to process standards, related to traceability requirements and new quality management standards, has taken place both in public and private regulation.[85] This change has increased the need for a supply chain approach since the production process regulation almost by definition includes all the nodes in the chain. However, it has also had an important side effect: the integration of environmentally-friendly techniques into supply chain production standards as, for example, the integrated pesticide management programmes (IPM) shows.

Compliance is ever more in the hands of the supply chain management, and of importing countries' firms, often ensuring the effectiveness of private control, exercised either within the supply chain or by third-party certifiers (see Meidinger, 2009, p. 233). Private transnational food safety regulation provides staggering illustrations of regulatory power changes: shifts from states to transnational and from the public to the private are taking place. The final result is not replacement but rather the existence of new forms of institutional complementarity between private and public regulation.[86] Transnational private standards are thence emerging both as the result of a change in regulatory regimes and as a response to the need for stronger global supply chain governance. The move from at-the-border public control to direct suppliers' responsibility associated to retailers' on-site inspections and third-party certifiers is both the cause and result of a changed regulatory strategy (see Blair et al., 2008). Important changes have occurred in the private domain, where retail-driven regulation has burdened producers, mainly located in exporting countries, with higher costs for safety monitoring procedures.[87] These transformations have not, however, deeply involved the civil liability regimes, which remain centred around the supplier or the importer.[88]

The consolidation of transnational private regulation and the increasing role of retailers call for a new conceptual framework and new regulatory instruments. The unit of regulatory analysis should become the supply chain rather than the single multi-national firm, and, as a consequence, the primary regulatory instrument should be the multi-party contractual network rather than sequential bilateral contracting. Network contracts can be horizontal among the farmers, vertical between farmers, processing food firms and retailers, or may be a combination of both.

The role of contractual networks as regulatory instruments to produce and disseminate information and to manage risks has to be more strongly promoted. Private regulation, even more than administrative regulation, highlights the weaknesses of sequential bilateral contracting, thus posing strong coordination problems, and emphasizes the need for a network approach to contractual governance of food safety regulation. The use of networks can reduce monitoring costs in allocating tasks among different participants to the supply chain and allow for the utilisation of information technology as a 'bonding' device among enterprises along the chain. Furthermore, common technology platforms, linked with HACCP, may reinforce cooperative links along the chain. Unlike the bilateral contract model, where coordination is not contractually designed but operates *de facto*, the network model would ensure greater and more effective coordination among all the sources of hazard information and contribute to codifying information through pre-defined procedures. The source of information may be any part along the chain or the final consumer. The coordinator of the contractual network does not have to coincide with the source of information but has to be able to exercise control over the flow.

The use of contractual networks is certainly not a panacea, though it can warrant incremental advantages over other organizational models in ensuring compliance with safety standards along the supply chain. Its comparative advantages over other models of regulatory coordination are dependent upon several factors including the market concentrations, both up and downstream.[89] For the time being it is both states' and corporate responsibility to ensure an adequate legal framework for effective regulation of food safety. It would be desirable that, given the transnational structure of food supply chains, a more tailored regulation of contractual governance will be the outcome of international public-private partnerships (see Garcia Martinez et al., 2007).

The multiplicity of regulatory instruments gives rise to several questions relevant to further research. First, they increase costs of compliance for producers, who are often subject to multiple, and not necessarily converging, sets of rules. Second, they do not send a clear signal to consumers who may suffer more than they benefit from private overregulation. Thirdly, regarding their rule-making procedures, they give rise to general concerns relating to the legitimacy and accountability of the relevant processes and products. Finally, enforcement is still quite diverse. For a supply chain it is mainly performed through self-enforcing contracts. Judicial control is understood to constitute a last resort. For codes enacted by private, retail or producer associations, internal compliance procedures are not very effective. The emergence of co-regulation at the national level improves enforcement mechanisms by bringing about a mixed system of rules made by private actors and enforced by administrative agencies with or without the contribution of courts, but the supply chain approach calls for a selective monitoring and enforcement activity by administrative agencies.

NOTES

1 An earlier version of this chapter was presented at Tsing-Hua University in May 2009 at a

conference jointly organised by NYU Law School and Tsing-hua University. The paper was then presented at Fordham Law School faculty workshop in September 2011. It is part of a research project on transational governance by contract supported by Scuola Superiore Della Pubblica Amministrazione (SSPA). Thanks to K. Davis, M. Patterson, C. Scott, R. Stewart, M. Trebilcock and B. Zipursky, for useful comments on earlier drafts. Thanks to Gary Gereffi for stimulating conversations on the topics and to Federica Casarosa and Stephanie Law for research assistance.

2 See FAO Technical Papers on Fisheries and Aquaculture (2011) where the analysis distinguishes different models of supply chains associated with different regulatory strategies and contracting practices (p. 90 ff). For a more detailed analysis, see Cafaggi, on file with the author.

3 See De Schutter, 2010, 2011.

4 In his recommendations, the Rapporteur clearly refers to forms of cooperative partnerships along the chain (point 47): 'Governments should support the organization of farmers into cooperatives or other types of producers' organization that can improve farmers' bargaining position and help then to move up the value chain into the produce packaging, processing and marketing operations and help them to acquire the inputs and sell their products under better circumstances' (De Schutter, 2010, p. 19).

5 De Schutter, 2010, p.15. 'In the view of the Special Rapporteur, farmer-controlled enterprises, joint ventures and community supported agriculture schemes provide interesting and complementary ways to rethink the political economy of food chains for the benefit of small-scale farmers.'

6 For the purposes of this chapter, the term 'supply chain approach' will also include the management-based approach to private regulation. Both refer to changes in public regulation, first in Europe and then in the US, which have transferred the power and costs of regulatory compliance to operators along the supply chain.

7 See FAO, Technical Papers on Fishers and Aquaculture, 2011, p. 111 ff. referring to a 2007 OECD/FAO study where three types of supply chains have been found: vertically integrated, collaborative and importer driven. The report states that the influence of private standards varies according to the type of supply chain. On the role of the global value chain in inter-firm relationships, see Humphrey and Schmitz, 2008, p. 258 ff.

8 See Henson and Humphrey, 2009, and FAO/WHO, 2010.

9 In performance standards, the regulator, the retailer in this case, defines the target or the outcome while the regulatee, the supplier, chooses the means to achieve the target.

10 See FAO/WHO, 2010 p. 17: 'The big industry players who have been known to insist with authorities on the importance of regulations that allow them flexibility in designing and implementing their food safety systems are now less willing to accord flexibility to their suppliers.'

11 This paper focuses on the relationship between market concentration on either the supply or demand side and supply chain forms.

12 According to Lee et al., 2010, p. 3, while retailer-driven supply chain focus on safety standards, producer-driven supply chains emphasize product differentiation, which includes quality, environmental and social concerns.

13 For example, in fisheries there is evidence that supply chains are highly differentiated as to the use of intermediaries: in Europe retailers have direct contracts, in the US brokers are used, and in Asia a combination of the two techniques is deployed.

14 See FAO/WHO, 2010, p. 109. This report suggests a direct correlation between private standards and supply chain integration: 'the more direct the supply relationship and the more integrated the supply chain, the more private standards are likely to enter the equation. Where retailers contract directly producers or processors, they are able to impose more controls, including products and process standards.'

15 See, in relation to the wine industry, Cafaggi and Iamiceli, 2010b.

16 See Henson and Humphrey, 2009. This occurs with carbon footprint labelling; see Stewart et al., 2009.

17 FAO/WHO, 2010, emphasizes the lack of stakeholder inputs in private standard-setting.

18 On the relationship between accountability and efficiency in transnational private

regulation, see Cafaggi, 2011.
19 See Henson and Humphrey, 2009, p. 3; Smith, 2009. For an overview of the existing standards see FAO, 2007.
20 On the use of contract law as a device to 'harden' international soft law, see Cafaggi, 2011b.
21 See the case of Barilla, an Italian pasta producer and final producer of wheat products, who in order to achieve a high quality level of raw products, negotiated a wide number of supply contracts (contratti di coltivazione) with individual or organised farmers which strictly defined not only the final product to be provided but also its qualitative and technological characteristics. In this case, the contract included both food quality and safety provisions, which are tightly intertwined in the production phase; in particular, technological requirements focused on the protein content of wheat, its colour and the gluten quality. The latter two were mainly related to the genetics of the wheat cultivated, while the former descended from the agricultural practices adopted. Thus, the contracts were negotiated with suppliers of specific types of wheat and imposed strict control over the use of phytosanitary.
22 See the Guidelines of Federalimentare, the Italian national food association, on the recall system: Federalimentare, 2004.
23 The importance of distinguishing the different supply chains according to the nature of the product has been emphasized in empirical work; see Gereffi et al., 2005, p. 78 ff.
24 See Gereffi et al., 2005. For a more detailed analysis of the correlation between regulatory choices and contractual practices, see Cafaggi, 2012b.
25 For a wide survey, see Vermeulen and Coluta, 2010. They identify six business models including contract farming, management contracts, tenant farming and sharecropping, joint ventures, and farmer-owned business and upstream/downstream business links.
26 According to Vermeulen and Coluta, 2010, p. 31–32, the correlation between land ownership and control over production choices may lead to different contractual models depending on the combination of smallholders and agribusiness.
27 For a survey in the wine industry, see Cafaggi and Iamiceli, 2010a.
28 See the Italian case of supply chain coordination between the UNAPROA (National Association of Fruit and Vegetable Producers) and Auchan and SMA (constituting a large distribution chain), which signed a framework contract in 2003 concerning their mutual obligations in the distribution of apples. The contracting parties also drafted a template for supply contract to be used in the following negotiations among the local distributors and the individual supplier. In particular, it included the provision of specific safety requirements to be evaluated in the product supply. See art. 3.4. of the template contract: 'The supplier guarantees that the Product will provide the feaures provided by Reg. 85/2004 and complies with, concerning the private label products, to the purchase technical specifications issued on . . . by the quality service of the Auchan/SMA group, while for the Products "1^{c} price" and "conventional" complies with the technical specifications determined by mutual agreement by the parties.'
29 See again the case of Barilla (note 21), where each contract includes the 'Disciplinare Barilla di coltivazione e conservazione del grano duro' in which the safety requirements are clearly defined for each phase. In the field of wine, the increasing phenomenon of private label wines distributed by final big retailers is producing similar effects.
30 Food safety provisions may be found in framework or master agreements and/or in an SLA (Service level agreement) that details standards of performance with which suppliers have to comply.
31 See note 28 above, concerning the framework contract between the UNAPROA (National Association of Fruit and Vegetable Producers) and Auchan and SMA.
32 See in relation to the US, Gilson et al., 2009, p. 431; and McLeod, 2007.
33 See the case of the Ethical Trading Initiative (ETI), which was developed in 1998 after campaigns by trade unions and NGOs, and is mainly targeted at big supermarket chains and large textile companies. The ETI turned the spotlight on bad working conditions in corporate supply chains. The participation of trade unions and NGOs is then included in the monitoring and verification group in order to push and enhance the application of the

code of conduct. For a deeper analysis, see Schaller, 2007.

34 See again, the ETI in which the code of conduct, drafted by the all members of the association, provides that, in case of breaches, retailers and suppliers should agree on a realistic timeframe in which measures for improvement have to be implemented. Only if a supplier refuses to cooperate and all other measures have failed should commercial relationships be terminated. See the ETI code Annex on Violations guidelines, available at www.ethicaltrade.org/sites/default/files/resources/Alleged%20Code%20Violations%20-Guidelines%202009_0.pdf

35 See the EU Commission communication, *EU best practice guidelines for voluntary certification schemes for agricultural products and foodstuff*, 2010. References to certification are made also in the FDA, Food Safety Modernisation Act, 2010 (hereafter FSMA) in reference to imported food, Sect. 303. See also FAO, 2006; Hatanka et al., 2005.

36 See Gray et al., 2011, p. 65 ff. suggesting that the differences between Europe and the US do not necessarily focus on the precautionary principle.

37 See EU regulation 178/2002, art. 18.

38 The correlation between traceability and information is clear in the European system. See art. 18 of EC Regulation 178/2002.

39 See again art. 18 of EC Regulation 178/2002. Nonetheless, traceability and, in general, food safety is not to be interpreted as a way to limit freedom of establishment and to provide services, see Commission v. France, [2008] ECJ C-389/05 (17 July 2008), where at para. 98 and 99 it states that: 'As regards food safety and the traceability of semen, in contrast to what the French Republic submits, Article 18 of Regulation No 178/2002 cannot be interpreted to justify the restrictions stemming from the system at issue. That article concerns the field of food safety, the requirements of which relating to traceability can be met by a system providing that the semen insemination service is carried out by qualified and properly identified persons, without the application of restrictions such as those resulting from the system at issue. Furthermore, that Member State has not in any way proved that granting exclusive rights over defined geographical areas to authorised centres and making the issue of an inseminator's licence subject to concluding an agreement with the managing director of such a centre are proportionate and necessary measures for the purposes of guaranteeing food safety and traceability. No evidence has been submitted to prove that the obligations imposed on inseminators as regards the quality and use of the semen and the checking of whether those obligations have been observed require the granting of those exclusive rights or the condition imposed for the issue of the licence.'

40 See, for example, Scott, 1990, p. 785 ff part. p.792 ff. For a broader examination concerning European law, see Hodges, 2005, p. 241. For a comparative perspective concerning England and France, see Whittaker, 2005.

41 The approach taken by product liability law in Europe (i.e. Directive 374/85/EC), which is still primarily centred around the manufacturer, seems at odds with the development of the regulatory regime which is moving towards a brand-oriented regulatory regime that places responsibility on the most influential actors along the supply chain. This approach is complemented by sales law, placing primary responsibility on the retailer through warranty in the sales contract; see Cafaggi, 2009b, p. 215.

42 See, FSMA.

43 There are several provisions that explicitly exclude prevention in FSMA; see, for example, sect. 103.

44 See FSMA; section 103 introduces hazard analysis and preventive controls: 'The owner, operator or agent in charge of a facility shall, in accordance with this section evaluate the hazards that could affect food manufactured, processed, packed or held by such facility, identify and implement preventive controls to significantly minimize or prevent the occurrence of such hazards and provided assurances that such food is not adulterated under section 402 or misbranded under section 403(w) monitor the performance of those controls, and maintain records of this monitoring as a matter of common practice.'

45 See FSMA, section 103 e) on corrective actions: 'The owner, operator or agent in charge

of a facility shall establish procedures to ensure that, if the preventive controls implemented under subsection c) are nor properly implemented or are found to be ineffective

(1) Appropriate action is taken to reduce the likelihood or recurrence of the implementation failure
(2) All affected food is evaluated for safety; and
(3) All affected food is prevented from entering into commerce if the owner, operator or agent of such facility cannot ensure that affected food is not adulterated under section 402 or misbranded under section 403(w)'.

Then the FSMA defines the duty to monitor compliance in subsections (d) and (f).

'(d)Monitoring and effectiveness. The owner, operator or agent in charge of facility shall monitor the effectiveness of the preventive controls implemented under subsection c to provide assurances that the outcomes described in subsection c are achieved...
(f) Verification. The owner, operator, agent in charge of a facility shall verify that
(1) Preventive controls implemented under subsection (e) are adequate to control the hazards identified under subsection (b)

The owner, operator or agent is conducting monitoring in accordance to subsection (d).'

46 See FSMA, section 206 on mandatory recall authority:
'(a)Voluntary procedures..."the secretary shall provide the responsible party with an opportunity to cease distribution and recall such article..."
(b) Prehearing order to cease distribution and give notice
(1) If the responsible party refuses to or does not voluntarily cease distribution or recall such article within the time and in the manner prescribed by the secretary, the secretary may by order require to
(a) immediately cease distribution of that article.'

47 See below at text accompanying notes 74 *et seq.*

48 The statute imposes the creation of 'a national food emergency response laboratory network that provides ongoing surveillance, rapid detection and surge capacity for large-scale food related emergencies, including national adulteration of the food supply.'

49 See the US Kratz v. American Stores Co. 59 A.2d 138.

50 In particular, it applies the consumer expectation test: 'Under § 2 (a) a harm causing ingredient of the food product constitutes a defect if a reasonable consumer would not expect the food product to contain that ingredient.'

51 See § 11 Restatement (Third) Torts, Products liability: 'One engaged in the business of selling or otherwise distributing products is subject to liability for harm to persons or property caused by the seller's failure to recall a product after the time of sale or distribution if:
(1) a governmental directive issued pursuant to a statute or administrative regulation specifically requires the seller or distributor to recall the product.'

52 For examples of non-food product cases stating the policy that liability should be placed on the most efficient accident avoider along the distribution chain, see Daly v. General Motors corp. 572 P.2d 1162; Leary ex rel Debold v. Syracuse Model Neighborhood corp 799 N.Y.SS. 2d 867; Promaulayko, 562 A.2d at 206: 'the effect of requiring the party closest to the original producer to indemnify parties farther down the chain is to shift the risk of loss to the most efficient accident avoider.' See also Peterson v. Lou Bachrodt Chevrolet Co. 329 N.E.2d 785: 'Imposition of liability upon wholesalers and retailers for defective product is justified on ground that their position in marketing process enables them to exert pressure on manufacturer to enhance safety of product.' In addition, see Godoy v. Abamaster 302 A.D.2d 754 defining policy rationales to distribute liability along the distribution chain in relation to a defective meat grinder.

53 It has been claimed that modularity and technical standardisation can be understood as devices to achieve modularity and reduce the danger of opportunism created by asset specificity. Thus, it can expand the range of choices and allow for or facilitate a move away from vertical integration; see Blair and O'Hara, 2009.

54 Consider, for example, the concerns raised relating to issues of coordination in the recall of turkey contaminated with salmonella in August 2011. See www.theatlantic.com/life/

archive/2011/08/the-turkey-recall-another-sign-our-food-system-is-broken/243455/

55 See art. 18.1 of EC Regulation 178/2002 on traceability. See also art.13 of EC Regulation 1169/2011 stating: 'This regulation shall apply to food business operators at all stages of the food chain, where their activities concern the provision of food information to consumers.' Moreover, to facilitate the recall process, Unilever includes specific information duties in its purchase agreements with suppliers; see www.unilever.com/images/USCCAGGeneralTermsConditionsofPurchasecm13272811.pdf

56 See in the UK, Hazlewood Grocery Ltd v. Lion Foods Ltd [2007] EWHC B5 (QB), [2007] EWHC B5 (QB) where the judge acknowledged the breach of contract between a supplier and a final producer, also taking into account the absence of the most updated certification system.

57 See for example in Italy Cass. pen., 8 marzo 2001, n. 16065, Foro it. 2001, II, 506.

58 *Supra* note 35. for an analysis of the benefits and drawbacks of certification, see FAO, 2009.

59 GLOBALG.A.P. requires the creation of producers groups without specifying the exact legal form; see section 5.1 of the General Regulations, available at www.globalgap.org/cms/front_content.php?idart = 1440 See the cases presented in Deutsche Gesellschaft für Technische Zusammenarbeit (GTZ) mbH, 2010.

60 Traceability plays a crucial role in implementing effective strategies when outbreaks and pandemics develop. This is a key factor for risk assessment and management and can only function if an agreed procedure is designed along the chain. For the European system, see Regulation 178/2002 on general food law, art. 18.1: 'The traceability of food, feed, food-producing animals, and any other substance intended to be, or expected to be incorporated into a food or feed shall be established at all stages of production, processing and distribution.'

61 See in the US Restatement (Third) Torts, Products Liability: § 10 Liability of commercial product seller or distributor for harm caused by *ex post* sale failure to warn.

62 Information concerning safety is generally codified and related to specific risks in order to select the most appropriate risk management procedure.

63 Traceability performs many other functions which are connected to the use of the network form: 'Traceability can serve a number of objectives: facilitating tracking for food safety reasons, differentiating products for marketing purposes, reducing information costs for consumers desiring to know more about food products, regaining consumer confidence and product reputation after an outbreak, decreasing costs to companies faced with product recalls and generally improving the management of food supplies.' See Vapnek, 2007, p.1003.

64 The European system includes the retailer but does not reflect the more recent evolution of private safety regulation. See art. 19.2. of the Regulation 178/2002: 'A food business operator responsible for retail or distribution activities which do not affect the packaging, labeling, safety or integrity of the food shall, within the limits of its respective activities, initiate procedures to withdraw from the market products not in compliance with the food-safety requirements and **shall participate in contributing to the safety of the food by passing on relevant information necessary to trace a food, cooperating in the action taken by producers, processors, manufacturers and/or the competent authorities**.' (bold by the author).

65 The liability regimes are often conceived with regard to the first vertical models, and then design duties to inform accordingly. In a proposal made elsewhere, I tried to sketch a more complex approach where parties could design contractual obligations independently of the system of liability. See Cafaggi, 2009b, p.215.

66 See Cafaggi, 2009b, p. 215.

67 See the Carrefour statement concerning their product recall system: 'Within two hours, a product can be recalled in each banner. In France, like in other countries where the Group operates, an on-call system gives suppliers and stores 24/7 contact with the Quality Department, which works in close association with the supply chain. Withdrawal messages are sent to all stores within less than 2 hours. A crisis team is set up immediately for all significant withdrawals/recalls.' Available at www.carrefour.com/cdc/responsible-

commerce/product-safety-and-quality/.

68 See, for example, Walmart Suppliers' Agreement available at www.sec.gov/Archives/edgar/data/828064/000095015304000722/p68961exv10w57.txt where under recalls, it is stated that: 'If Merchandise is the subject of a Recall, whether initiated by Supplier, Company or a government entity (including the issuance of safety notices), Supplier shall be responsible for all matters and costs associated with the Recall, including but not limited to:

(a) Consumer notification and contact;
(b) All expenses and losses incurred by Company in connection with such Recall (and where applicable, any products with which the Recalled Merchandise has been packaged, consolidated or commingled), including but not limited to refunds to customers, lost profits, transportation costs and all other costs associated therewith; and
(c) Initial contact and reporting of the Recall to any government agency having jurisdiction over the affected Merchandise.

If a government agency initiates any inquiry or investigation relating to the Merchandise or similar goods manufactured or supplied by Supplier, Supplier shall notify Company immediately thereof **and take reasonable steps to resolve the matter without exposing Company to any liability or risk**.' (bold by the author)

69 Under EC Regulation 178/2002, art. 17 provides that: 'Food and feed business operators at all stages of production, processing and distribution within the businesses under their control shall ensure that foods or feeds satisfy the requirements of food law which are relevant to their activities and shall verify that such requirements are met', and art. 19, footnote 113. See in the Italian caselaw, Cass. Pen., n. 7692/2007, CED Cass. pen. 2008, 2, 713, and previously Cass. Pen., 14 maggio 1998, Cattaneo, Dir. e giur. agr., 2000, p. 498; in tema v. anche Cass. Pen., 13 novembre 1997, Perini, Dir. e giur. agr., 1998, p. 3081; Cass. Pen., 1 febbraio 1995, n. 2350, Profeta, Dir. e giur. agr., 1996, p. 2348.

70 See for the European system, Recital 20 and art. 7 of EC Regulation 178/2002. On the comparative analysis of the precautionary principle in food safety, see Gray et al., 2011, p. 65 ff.

71 The FSMA regulates product recall in section 206. Further implementing regulations are expected. The creation of a network of laboratories is specifically indicated in the Statute in section 202. See also FDA, 2011. See also the recent case of Peanuts Corporation of America which received a request by the Food and Drug Authority in order to recall its product due to salmonella contamination, which, after the refusal to recall by the firm, was followed by an inspection warrant in an attempt to gain access to the company's distribution records. See the information available at www.fda.gov/Safety/Recalls/MajorProductRecalls/Peanut/FDA%E2%80%99sInvestigation/default.htm.

72 See EC Regulation 178/2002 on general food law, art. 19.1: 'If a food operator considers or has reason to believe that a food which it has imported, produced, processed, manufactured or distributed is not in compliance with the food safety requirements, it shall immediately initiate procedures to withdraw the food in question from the market where the food has left immediate control of that initial food business operator and inform the competent authorities thereof. Where the product may have reached the consumer, the operator shall effectively and accurately inform the consumers of the reasons for its withdrawal, and if necessary, recall from consumers products already supplied to them when other measures are not sufficient to achieve a high level of health protection.' See Alemanno, 2006, p. 35 ff.; Mac Maolain, Hart 2007; Barack, 2009, p. 173.

73 In the US, the Food and Drug Authority includes within the industry guidelines that the main goal to pursue is information of the customer, then each part of the chain is responsible to the notification of the recall to customers, while the decision about the recall depends on the point of the chain where the problem has been raised. See the product recall strategy clarified in the US Food Safety Authority at www.fda.gov/Safety/Recalls/IndustryGuidance/ucm129259.htm.

74 See FSMA, Section 206.

75 See in Italy Cass. Pen., 20 dicembre 2004, n. 3712, in *Dir. e giur. agr.*, 2005, p. 662.

76 See in Italy Cass. Pen., 19 marzo 2008, n. 18767.
77 See M.A. Geistfeld, 2005. See also Smith v. Alza Corp 948 A.2d 686 N.J. Super App. 2008: 'The purpose of the product seller immunity provisions in the Products liability Act is to reduce litigation costs borne by innocent retailers and wholesalers in product liability actions'; West v. KKL, LLC 2008 WL 4664232: '"The middleman" provisions of the Kentucky Product Liability Act (KPLA) were designed to protect only those distributors, wholesalers, or retailers, who have no independent responsibility for the design or manufacture of a product'; Yrak v. Dan's Supermarket Inc 188 P.3d 487: 'When one party in an action under the Product Liability Act is merely a passive retailer, the strict liability fault, lies, if any with the manufacturer not with the passive retailer.'
78 On these questions see Black, 2008, p. 137 ff.
79 On the distinction between regulatees and beneficiaries and the notion of regulatory relationship, see Cafaggi, 2011b, p.38. For a similar perspective on the relation between regulators, regulatees and beneficiaries see Buthe, 2010.
80 For a comparative analysis, see the essays by Grundmann, Aubert de Vincelles and Whittaker in Cafaggi (ed.) 2011a.
81 Legal systems differ significantly in relation to the extent that third parties are permitted to enforce contracts. Thus, consumer protection may vary across the supply chain depending on the choice of applicable law.
82 See Hazlewood Grocery Ltd v. Lion Foods Ltd [2007] EWHC B5 (QB), [2007] EWHC (Q B), where the compliance to the most updated safety controls were included in the contract as implied terms.
83 See Dir. 2005/29 art. 10: This Directive does not exclude the control, which Member States may encourage, of unfair commercial practices by code owners and recourse to such bodies by the persons or organizations referred to in Article 11 if proceedings before such bodies are in addition to the court or administrative proceedings referred to in that Article.'
84 See Scott and Trubek, in: de Búrca and Scott (eds), 2006; Sabel and Zeitlin, 2008.
85 See FAO, 2003, and Henson and Humphrey, 2009, underlining the similar evolution in public regulation with the consolidation of HACCP.
86 On different perspectives concerning institutional complementarities, compare Buthe and Mattli, 2011, and Cafaggi, 2011b.
87 For the materials of the conference, 'Private agri-food standards and a sustainable future for African agriculture', 27–28 March 2008, London, available at www.agrifood-standards.net/en/global/agrifood_standards_workshop_2008.html.
88 The FAO proposal of introducing shared liability as part of the food chain approach has not been followed by national systems, where liability is still distinguished according to the position in the chain and joint and several liability is more the exception than the rule. The network approach I have proposed distinguishes between liability towards consumers and means to allocate liability along the chain so as to maximize consumer protection and efficient allocation.
89 On the relationship between market concentration and competition and standards, see Lee et al., 2010.

REFERENCES

Alemanno, A. (2006) 'Food safety and the single European market', in C. Ansell and D. Vogel (2006) *What's the Beef*? Cambridge: MIT Press, pp. 237–258.

Alemanno, A. (2009) 'Solving the problem of scale: the European approach to important safety and security concerns', in G. Coglianese, A.M. Finkel and D. Zaring (eds) (2009) *Import Safety: Regulatory Governance in the Global Economy*, Philadelphia: University of Pennsylvania Press, 171–189.

Barack, A. (2009) 'A disadvantageous dichotomy in product safety law', *European*

Business Law Review, 20 (1), 173–198.
Berdegué, J. A., Balsevich, F., Flores, L. and Reardon, T. (2005) 'Central American supermarkets' private standards of quality and safety in procurement of fresh fruits and vegetables', *Food Policy*, 30, 254–269.
Black, J. (2008) 'Constructing and contesting legitimacy and accountability in polycentric regulatory regimes', *Regulation and Governance*, 2 (2), 137–164.
Blair, M. and O'Hara, E. (2009) 'Outsourcing, modularity and the theory of the firm', Industry Studies Association, Annual Association Conference, May 2009, available at http://papers.ssrn.com/sol3/papers.cfm?abstract_id= 1443357
Blair, M., Williams, C. and Lin, L. –W. (2008) 'The roles of standardization, certification and assurance services in global commerce', *Comparative Research in Law and Political Economy*, w.p. 12/2008, available at http:// www.comparativeresearch.net/papers.jsp?pubyear = 2008
Buthe, T. (2010) 'Private regulation in the global economy: A (P)Review', *Business and Politics*, 12 (3), 1–38, available at http://0-www.bepress.com.biblio.eui.eu/ cgi/viewcontent.cgi?article = 1328&context = bap
Buthe, T. and W. Mattli, (2011) *The New Global Rules. The Privatization of Regulation in the World Economy*, Princeton: Princeton University Press.
Cafaggi, F. (2008) 'Contractual networks and the small business act: towards European principles?', *European Review of Contract Law*, 4, 493–539.
Cafaggi, F. (2009a) 'Legitimacy of private regulators: recombining voice, exit and loyalty', Paper presented at The Hague Conference, 8–9 October 2009.
Cafaggi, F. (2009b) 'Product safety, private standard-setting and information networks', in Muir Watt, H. and F. Cafaggi (eds) (2009), *The Regulatory Function of European Private Law*, Cheltenham: Edward Elgar, pp. 207–242.
Cafaggi, F. (ed.) (2011a) *Contractual Networks, Inter-firm Cooperation and Economic Growth*, Cheltenham: Edward Elgar.
Cafaggi, F. (2011b) 'New foundations of transnational private regulation', *Journal of Law and Society*, 38 (1), 20–49.
Cafaggi, F. (2012a) 'Enforcing transnational private regulation – models and patterns', in F. Cafaggi (ed.) (2012) *Enforcement of Transnational Private Regulation*, forthcoming, Cheltenham: Edward Elgar.
Cafaggi, F. (2012b) 'Private regulation and contractual practices in global supply chains', on file with the author.
Cafaggi, F. (2012c) 'Regulatory strategies and contracting practices in food safety transnational regulation', on file with author.
Cafaggi, F. and Iamiceli, P. (2010a) (eds) *Inter-Firm Networks in European Wine Industry*, EUI WP 2010/19, available at http://cadmus.eui.eu/bitstream/handle/ 1814/15654/LAW_2010_19_rev.pdf?sequence = 5
Cafaggi, F. and Iamiceli, P. (2010b) 'Inter-firm networks in European wine industry – a comparative analysis' in F. Cafaggi and P. Iamiceli (eds) *Inter-Firm Networks in European Wine Industry*, EUI WP 2010/19, 107-146, available at http://cadmus.eui.eu/bitstream/handle/1814/15654/LAW_2010_19_rev.pdf? sequence = 5
Coglianese, G., Finkel, A. and Zaring, D. (eds) (2009) *Import Safety: Regulatory Governance in the Global Economy*, Philadelphia: University of Pennsylvania Press.
Collins, H. (2009) 'The weakest link: Legal implication of the network architecture of supply chains', in T. Amstutz and G. Teubner (eds) (2009) *Networks – Legal*

Issues of Multilateral Co-operation, Oxford and Portland, OR: Hart.
Da Silva, C.A.B. (2005) *The Growing Role of Contract Farming in Agri-food Systems Development: Drivers, Theory and Practice*, Rome: FAO, available at http://www.fao.org/fileadmin/user_upload/ags/publications/AGSF_WD_9.pdf
De Búrca, G. and Scott, J. (eds) (2006) *Law and New Governance in the EU and the US*, Oxford and Portland, OR: Hart.
De Schutter, O. (2010) *Agribusiness and the Right to Food*, Report of the special rapporteur on the right to food, A/HRC/13/33.
De Schutter, O. (August 2011) Note produced by the special rapporteur, *The Right to Food*, A 66/262.
Deutsche Gesellschaft für Technische Zusammenarbeit (GTZ) mbH (2010) *Integrating Smallholders into Global Supply Chains – GLOBALG.A.P. Option 2 Smallholder Group Certi?cation Generic Manual: Lessons learnt in pilot projects in Kenya, Ghana, Thailand and Macedonia*, GIZ: Eschborn, available at www.gtz.de/en/dokumente/gtz2010-en-globalgap-group-certification.pdf
ETI (2001) *Code: Annex on Violations Guidelines*, available at www.ethicaltrade.org/sites/default/files/resources/Alleged%20Code%20Violations%20Guidelines%202009_0.pdf
EU Commission (2010) *EU Best Practice Guidelines for Voluntary Certification Schemes for Agricultural Products and Foodstuff*, 2010/C 341/04, OJ C 341/5 16.12.2010.
FAO (2003) *Strategy for a Food Chain Approach to Food Safety and Quality: A Framework Document for the Development of a Future Strategy Direction*, available at www.fao.org/DOCREP/MEETING/006/Y8350e.HTM
FAO (2006) *Food Safety Certification*, FAO: Rome.
FAO (2007) *Private Standards in the United States and European Union Markets for Fruits and Vegetables – Implications for Developing Countries*, FAO: Rome.
FAO (2009) *Certification in the Value Chain for Fresh Fruits – The Example of the Banana Industry*, p. 9 ff, FAO: Rome.
FAO Technical Papers on Fisheries and Aquaculture (2011) *Private Standards and Certification in Fisheries and Aquaculture: Current Practice and Emerging Issues*, 55.
FAO/WHO Standards Programme (2010) *Consideration of the Impact of Private Standards*, CX/Cac/10/33/13.
FDA (2011) *Biennial Report to Congress on the Food Emergency Response Network Submitted Pursuant to 202(b) of the FDA Food Safety Modernization Act*, available at www.fda.gov/Food/FoodSafety/FSMA/ucm271966.htm
Federalimentare (2004) *Linee Guida di Federalimentare per la Gestione delle Non-Conformità*, 26 Ottobre 2004, available at www.federalimentare.it/Documenti/LineeGuida/Gestione_non_conformita_26ott04.pdf
Firth, A., Raybould, D.M. and Singleton, E.S. (2009) 'Commission notice 2001/C3/02 on guidelines on the applicability of Article 81 of the EC Treaty to Horizontal Cooperation Agreements', pp. B94/33–B94/56, *Comparative Law of Monopolies*.
Garcia Martinez, M. and F. Banados (2004) 'Impact of EU organic product certi?cation legislation on Chile organic exports', *Food Policy*, 29, 1–14.
Garcia Martinez, M., Fearne, A., Caswell, J.A. and Henson, S. (2007) 'Co-regulation as a possible model for food safety governance: opportunities for public–private partnerships', *Food Policy*, 32, 299–314.

Geistfeld, M.A. (2005) *Principles of Products Liability*, New York: Foundation Press.
Gereffi G., Humphrey, J. and Sturgeon, T. (2005) 'The governance of global value chains: an analytic framework', *Review of International Political Economy*, 12 (1), 78–104.
Giovannucci, D. and S. Ponte (2005) 'Standards as a new form of social contract? Sustainability initiatives in the coffee industry', *Food Policy*, 30, 284–301.
Gilson, R.J., Sabel, C.F. and Scott, R.E. (2009) 'Contracting for innovation: vertical disintegration and inter-firm collaboration', *Columbia Law Review*, 109, 431–502.
Gilson, R.J., Sabel, C.F. and Scott, R.E. (2010) *Braiding: The Interaction of Formal and Informal Contracting in Theory, Practice and Doctrine*, available at http://ssrn.com/abstract = 1535575
Gray, G., Rogers, M. and Wiener, J. (2011) 'Beef, hormones and mad cows', in J.B. Wiener, M.D. Rogers, J.K. Hammitt and P.H Sand (eds) (2011), *The Reality of Precaution. Comparing Risk Regulation in the United States and Europe*, Resources For the Future Press/Earthscan.
Hatanaka, M., Bain. C. and Busch, L. (2005) 'Third-Party Certification in the Global Agrifood System', *Food Policy*, 30, 354–369.
Henson, S. and J. Humphrey (2009) 'The impact of private food safety standards on the food chain and on public standard setting processes', Paper prepared for FAO/WHO, May 2009, available at ftp://ftp.fao.org/codex/cac/CAC32/al329Dbe.pdf (accessed March 2012).
Hodges, C. (2005) *European Regulation of Consumer Product Safety*, New York: Cambridge University Press.
Humphrey, J. and Schmitz, H. (2008) 'Inter-firm relationships in global value chains: trends in chain governance and their policy implications', *International Journal of Technological Learning, Innovation and Development*, 1 (3), 258–281.
Jaffe, S. and Masakure, O (2005) 'Strategic use of private standards to enhance international competitiveness: vegetable exports from Kenya and elsewhere', *Food Policy*, 30, 316–333.
Lee, J., Gereffi, G, and Beauvais, J. (2010) *Global Value Chains and Agri-Food Standards. Challenges and Possibilities for Smallholders in Developing Countries*, available at www.pnas.org/cgi/doi/10.1073/pnas.0913714108 (accessed February 2012).
Mac Maolain, C. (2007) *EU Food Law*, Oxford; Portland, OR: Hart.
Maher, I. (2011) 'Competition law and transnational private regulatory regimes: marking the cartel boundary', *Journal of Law and Society*, 38 (1), 119–137.
McLeod, W.B. (2007) 'Reputations, relationships and the enforcement of incomplete contracts', *Journal of Economic Literature*, 45 (3), 595–628.
Meidinger, E. (2009) 'Private import safety regulation and transnational new governance', in G. Coglianese, A.M. Finkel and D. Zaring (eds) (2009) *Import safety: Regulatory Governance in the Global Economy*, Philadelphia: University of Pennsylvania Press, 233–253.
Sabel C.F. and Zeitlin, J. (2008) 'Learning from difference: the new architecture of experimentalist governance in the EU', *European Law Journal*, 14 (3), 271–327.
Schaller, S. (2007) *The Democratic Legitimacy of Private Governance – An Analysis of the Ethical Trading Initiative*, INEF Report 91/2007, available at http://inef.uni-due.de/page/documents/Report91.pdf

Scott, C. (1990) 'Continuity and change in British food law', *Modern Law Review*, 53, 785–801.

Scott, J. and D.M. Trubek (2002) 'Mind the gap: law and new approaches to governance in the European Union', *European Law Journal*, 8, 1–18.

Smith, G. (2009) *Interaction of Public and Private Standards in the Food Chain*, OECD Food, Agriculture and Fisheries Working Papers, No. 15, OECD Publishing.

Stewart R.B., B. Kingsbury and B. Rudyk (2009) *Climate Finance – Regulatory and Funding Strategies for Climate Change and Global Development*, New York: New York University Press.

UK Competition Commission (2008) *The Supply of Grocery in the UK Market Investigation*, 30 April 2008, available at www.competition-commission.gov.uk/rep_pub/reports/2008/fulltext/538.pdf

UNCTAD (2009) *World Investment Report: Transnational Corporations, Agricultural Production and Developments*, UNCTAD: Geneva.

Vapnek, J. (2007) 'Legislative implementation of the food chain approach', *Vanderbilt Journal of Transnational Law*, 40 (4), 987–1014.

Vermeulen, S. and L. Coluta (2010) *Making the Most of Agricultural Investment: A Survey of Business Models That Can Provide Opportunities for Smallholders*, London/Rome/Bern, IIED/FAO/IFAD/SCD, available at http://www.ifad.org/pub/land/agri_investment.pdf

Vos, E. and F. Wendler (2006) 'Food safety regulation at EU level', in E. Vos and F. Wendler (eds) *Food Safety Regulation in Europe – A Comparative Institutional Analysis*, Antwerp and Oxford: Intersentia, pp. 65–138.

Whittaker, S. (2005) *Liability for Products: English Law, French Law and European Harmonisation*, Oxford: Oxford University Press.

World Bank (2005) *Food Safety and Agricultural Health Standards: Challenges and Opportunities for Developing Country Exports*, Agriculture and Rural Development Discussion Paper, Washington DC: World Bank, available at http://siteresources.worldbank.org/INTRANETTRADE/Resources/Topics/Standards/standards_challenges_synthesisreport.pdf

9. Food safety-related private standards: the WTO perspective

Gretchen H. Stanton[1]

INTRODUCTION

The international trade agreements of the World Trade Organization (WTO) have been negotiated by the governments of the 155 countries/territories that are members of the WTO. These are normally seen as the rules that are to be respected by governments when establishing national requirements that affect international trade. The discussions at the various WTO committees are therefore among government representatives and normally about government policies. However, in June 2005, a representative of the small Caribbean island nation of St. Vincent and the Grenadines complained about restrictions that affected the ability of the country to sell bananas to the European Union (EU). This complaint, raised in the context of a meeting of the WTO Committee on Sanitary and Phytosanitary Measures (SPS committee) in Geneva, was not about the official pesticide residue requirements of the EU or of its member states, but rather about requirements established by a private, non-profit organization, GLOBALG.A.P. (known at that time as EUREPGAP). By raising this specific trade concern, the small island triggered discussions at the WTO that have involved and divided more countries with respect to international food safety and health concerns than any other issue to date.

THE WTO AGREEMENTS

To understand why this issue has become so hotly debated, it is necessary to go back in time to the creation of the WTO. The WTO is an organization of member governments[2] who have developed a set of rules to govern international trade. The first set of rules, the General Agreement on Tariffs and Trade (GATT), was adopted in 1948, and was subsequently modified and expanded. In 1994, the member governments agreed to replace the interim organization which oversaw the implementation of the GATT with a permanent organization, the WTO. At the same time, they adopted a new set of trade agreements which entered into force on 1 January 1995.

One of the WTO agreements is the Agreement on the Application of Sanitary and Phytosanitary Measures, more commonly referred to as the SPS agreement. The SPS agreement consists of 14 articles and three annexes, establishing legal rights and obligations on the governments of WTO member countries. Article 2 sets out the basic rights and obligations, which are further elaborated upon in subsequent articles. As part of these basic rights and obligations, Article 2.1 recognizes the right of governments to impose restrictions on international trade when the restrictions are necessary to protect human, animal and plant life from certain risks, or to protect the territory of the country from damage caused by pests. More specifically, SPS measures are described, in Annex A.1, as any measure taken with one of the following objectives shown in Table 9.1:

Table 9.1: Definition of SPS Measures

Any measures taken to Protect	**From**
Human and animal health	Additives, toxins, disease-causing organisms in foods, beverages or feedstuffs
Human health	Animal- or plant-carried diseases
Animal and plant health	Pests, diseases, disease-causing or disease-carrying organisms
The territory of a country	Other damage from the entry or spread of pests

Source: Legal texts of the World Trade Organization, Agreement on the Application of Sanitary and Phytosanitary Measures, the 'SPS Agreement'.

WTO member governments have committed themselves to impose food safety or quarantine requirements on imported products only in a manner that complies with the SPS agreement. This has not been an easy undertaking for any country. Governments have had to distinguish the requirements for health protection from those proposed to ensure quality, composition, environmental protection or other purposes. Although these different requirements may be contained in a single piece of national legislation, different WTO rules apply depending on the purpose of the requirement. For the health protection measures, according to Article 2.2 of the SPS agreement, governments must ensure that the requirement is justified on the basis of scientific evidence of potential health risks, unless it is a temporary measure imposed to deal with an emergency situation in accordance with Article 5.7.

To ensure such scientific justification, Article 3.1 encourages governments to base their nation's SPS requirements on the standards adopted by three international, intergovernmental organizations as identified in Annex A.3. For food safety, these are the standards adopted by the joint Codex Alimentarius Commission of the Food and Agriculture Organization (FAO) and World Health Organization (WHO) of the United Nations (Codex). For animal health and animal diseases that are transmissible to humans (zoonoses), the SPS agreement recognizes the standards of the World Organization for Animal Health, known as the OIE because it was previously called (in French) the Organisation Internationale des Epizooties. For plant protection, the relevant international standard-setting body is the Commission on Phytosanitary Measures, operating under the International Plant Protection Convention (IPPC) of the FAO.

If a government uses these international standards as the requirement for products entering its territory, it is considered not only to have a scientific justification, but also to meet the other obligations of the SPS agreement. This 'presumption of conformity' contained in Article 3.2 also presumes conformity with any SPS-related obligations under the GATT agreement as well. When a government decides not to use these international standards as the basis for its national requirement, Article 3.3 requires that the government must be able to justify its SPS requirement on the basis of a scientific assessment of potential risks to human (animal or plant) health. A similar requirement applies when there is no relevant international standard, and is spelled out in Article 5.1, which requires that SPS measures be based on risk assessments appropriate to the circumstances. While each country may decide what level of health protection it wants to provide to its consumers, it must, according to Article 5.6, select the requirements with the least negative impact on international trade that provide the desired level of health protection. In addition, the impact of these requirements on the trade of developing countries, many of whom may have difficulties meeting sophisticated hygiene requirements but are highly reliant on agricultural export income, must be considered (Article 5.4). According to Article 4, governments must also accept other SPS measures that provide an equivalent level of health protection, if this can be demonstrated by a foreign supplying country.

The SPS agreement also sets rules regarding how governments can control, test and inspect traded goods to ensure that these comply with the food safety, plant and animal health requirements. These rules, in Article 8 and detailed in Annex C, indicate, *inter alia*, that the information requested of foreign suppliers can be no more than what is necessary to ensure compliance with the SPS requirement, and that any charges for the testing, inspection or certification of these imported goods can be no more than the actual costs for such services.

One of the aims of the WTO agreements is to provide more information and transparency regarding international trade. Article 7 and Annex B of the SPS agreement establish transparency obligations with respect to SPS measures. WTO governments are obliged to give advance notice of their intention to impose new SPS requirements that may affect international trade and differ from the relevant international standards. A notification about proposed new requirements must be sent to the WTO secretariat, for distribution to all WTO members (and the public at large). This is to be done while the proposed new requirements are still in draft form, and comments from trading partners must be solicited and considered. A reasonable period of time, normally six months, should be provided between the final adoption of a new requirement and its entry into force, to allow other countries to adapt without losing the ability to sell their products. This advance notice and delay is not required when SPS measures are taken to address emergency health situations, although notification is still required and comments must subsequently be considered. The SPS committee has elaborated formats and recommendations regarding the implementation of the transparency provisions (WTO, 20 June 2008, article 7).

SPS-RELATED PRIVATE STANDARDS

General public awareness of the BSE (bovine spongiform encephalopathy, or mad cow disease) problem in the United Kingdom largely coincided with the entry into force of the SPS agreement. The BSE problem caused a serious deterioration of public confidence in governmental food safety authorities in the United Kingdom, and to a lesser extent in other European countries. Governments struggled to make the public understand relative risks, and the limited possibility for government officials to regulate and inspect all aspects of food production and processing. In the United Kingdom, the 1990 Food Safety Act required all firms along the supply chain to prove they had undertaken all possible steps to ensure their product was safe and would not cause harm.

This liability clause had far-reaching repercussions, first in the United Kingdom, and later throughout Europe and other parts of the world. It also helped give rise to the increased use of private standards that address food safety. Private standards are any common requirements that have been established by non-governmental entities, including wholesale or retail stores, national producer associations or civil society groups. These can include, for example, the requirement of a fast-food chain that only a certain variety and grade of potato may be used for production of the French fries it sells, or the requirement of a home furnishings store chain that only products certified as coming from sustainable forests will be sold, or the system for certification of sustainable forestry managed by a civil society group. Sometimes agreement is reached by various business associations within a country or region to follow a common private standard, such as to not purchase products produced by child labour.

Private standards for food products have a relatively long history. They have been used to differentiate the quality of products or to address particular (real or manufactured) consumer preferences. Examples are private standards for organically produced foods, 'fair trade' practices, sustainable fisheries, and so on. They have proliferated in recent years and accompanied other important trends in the food sector, including the concentration of retail grocery chains in many developed countries and the resultant direct contracting of production by larger retailers.

DISCUSSIONS AT THE WTO

In contrast to the WTO's globally negotiated disciplines on government actions, private standards are seen by many developing countries as going in exactly the opposite direction. The private standards address a mix of SPS and other objectives, including social and environmental concerns that may not be related to food safety or plant/animal health protection. These private requirements may address consumer perceptions of what is safe or unsafe without reliance on scientific evidence. Private standards may require the use of production practices that are common in developed countries, but unknown and perhaps unsuitably costly for developing country producers.

In January 2007, the WTO secretariat prepared a background paper on private standards for the SPS committee (WTO, 24 January 2007). At the time, the United Nations Conference on Trade and Development (UNCTAD) estimated the number of private schemes at 400 and increasing. The private standards schemes range from those developed by individual firms to collective industry-wide international schemes. Private standard schemes are not exclusive to a particular country, geographical region or level of development. The same factors and companies driving the use of private standards are at work in developed, developing and least developed countries.

Table 9.2 gives examples of private standards. The list of standards given in the table is an illustrative one; it is far from exhaustive. The 13 schemes identified serve to demonstrate some of the diversity of the 400 plus schemes in operation.

Table 9.2: Examples of private standards

Individual firm schemes	Collective national schemes	Collective international schemes
Tesco Nature's Choice	Assured Food Standards	GLOBALG.A.P.
Carrefour Filière Qualité	British Retail Consortium Global Standard – Food	International Food Standard
	QS Qualität Sicherheit	Global Food Safety Initiative
	Label Rouge	ISO 22000: Food safety management systems
	Food and Drink Federation/British Retail Consortium Technical Standard for the Supply of Identity Preserved Non-Genetically Modified Food Ingredients and Products	Safe Quality Food (SQF) 1000 and 2000 ISO 22005: Traceability in the feed and food chain

Source: WTO, 'Private Standards and the SPS Agreement', 24 January 2007, document symbol G/SPS/GEN/746. See also 'Typology of Global Standards – Communication from the United Nations Conference on Trade and Development (UNCTAD)', 26 February 2007, WTO document symbol G/SPS/GEN/760.

The categorization used in Table 9.2 between individual firm schemes, collective national and collective international schemes is one of several possible categorizations. Further distinctions can be drawn between pre- and post-farm gate standards, or between business-to-business standards and collective schemes, or between 'hidden' requirements and standards tied to a particular labelling or logo scheme visible to consumers. Collective schemes may also tackle a particular supply chain issue or objective, at a national or international level. The schemes listed in Table 9.2 cover all these categories. For example, while GLOBALG.A.P. is primarily a pre-farm gate standard, the British Retail Consortium (BRC) Global Standard and the International Food Standard are aimed at packing and processing facilities. Similarly, while the Assured Food and Label Rouge schemes are linked to logos displayed on food packaging, the GLOBALG.A.P. scheme is not. Likewise, the joint Food and Drink Federation/British Retail Consortium Technical Standard and the ISO

22005 scheme tackle specific supply chain issues at both a national and international level.

Table 9.2 demonstrates the diversity of private standards. It highlights the rise of private standard-setting coalitions which are seeking to harmonize industry-wide efforts to control particular risks. The proliferation of standards schemes nationally and internationally is stimulating a trend towards 'benchmarking', which provides a means to compare requirements. For example, GLOBALG.A.P. has a process through which other schemes may be 'benchmarked' against its own standards, such as the ChileGAP scheme for fresh fruit. Another example of this process is the Global Food Safety Initiative (GFSI). The GFSI was founded with the idea of 'benchmarking' national schemes internationally against a set of key elements, so that a product certified as complying with one scheme will be accepted by buyers normally requiring certification against another scheme. It is important to note, however, that benchmarking does not necessarily imply equivalence in the sense of the SPS agreement. The SPS agreement requires that governments accept other ways of producing or treating a product if the end result is equally safe. This can make it possible for farmers in poorer countries to use less costly methods of production without compromising the health of consumers elsewhere in the world. Benchmarking, on the other hand, compares the processes that are used, not the end result.

Private standards are not mandatory; suppliers are not required by law to meet them. Compliance with private standards is a choice on the part of the supplier. When private standards become the industry norm, however, the choice is limited. Consolidation in food retailing is a key factor. If a small number of food retailers account for a high proportion of food sales, the options for suppliers who do not participate in either an individual or collective retailer standard scheme can be reduced considerably. The retailer scheme may be applied de facto as the industry norm by all actors in the supply chain. Thus the choice of whether or not to comply with a voluntary standard becomes a choice between compliance or exit from the market. In this way, the distinction between private voluntary standards and mandatory 'official' or 'public' requirements becomes blurred.

In the SPS committee, the discussions so far have focused on three themes:

1. Do private food safety standards present barriers or opportunities for access to foreign markets?
2. Do private standards have a positive or deleterious impact on economic development in poorer countries?
3. Is there a legal basis for disciplining private food safety standards in the WTO?

Do Private Food Safety Standards Present Barriers or Opportunities for Access to Foreign Markets?

Some trade officials and the private standard-setting bodies maintain that the standards set by the private sector help suppliers improve the quality of their products and gain access to higher-quality markets. Most of the private standards require compliance with very specific processes at every step of the production chain. The private standards make producers aware of what the buyer wants, and detail what the producer must do in order to have a final product that meets this standard. Those producers who are able to comply with these private requirements can sell their products to buyers in high-quality markets.

Others argue that private standards can be both more restrictive and more prescriptive than official import requirements. Many private standards, for example, require that the level of pesticide residues in a food be substantially less than the level the government has said is acceptable. While the official requirement may be described in terms of the characteristics of the final product, private standard schemes impose the process to be used to achieve the desired food safety outcome.

Some trade officials, especially from developing countries, also argue that the proliferation of private standards, in contrast to the use of harmonized international standards as foreseen in the SPS agreement, increases transaction costs. Instead of producing to meet a single, internationally known standard, farmers have to meet different requirements for each buyer. Another concern is the cost of certification of compliance with the private standards. Many governments provide inspection and certification services at no cost, or charge only to cover actual expenses. Certification of compliance with private standards is done by private companies, at a direct cost to producers or exporters. For these reasons, many developing country trade officials argue that private food safety standards act as additional barriers to market access.

Do Private Standards have a Positive or Deleterious Impact on Economic Development in Poorer Countries?

In the discussions at the WTO, trade officials have argued that private standards can be more effective than government programmes in improving hygiene and safety for farmers and processors in developing countries. These standards provide detailed requirements for every step of the production and processing chain, and a direct incentive to meet these requirements. They reach down to the level of each individual producer or processing plant, avoiding some of the delays and problems of more general national or regional programmes.

Yet officials from both developed and developing countries have indicated that it is primarily small producers that are most concerned about private standards. The costs of complying with private standards, and the additional cost of certification, can make the development of export-oriented schemes virtually impossible for small-scale producers. It is particularly difficult for small and medium-scale producers who do not have the necessary capital and cannot afford the initial investment costs. Once certified, the small producers often cannot maintain the costs of continual re-certification, which are high in proportion to the value of their production. At the same time, there is often no price premium for products that meet the private standards, but those that do not are excluded from certain markets.

While these negative repercussions affect small producers in all countries, there are proportionally many more small producers in developing countries. In addition, small producers in developing countries often lack basic infrastructure and support services. It is not surprising that this issue was first raised in the WTO by a small developing country, and it has primarily been developing countries that have pressed for action on this issue at WTO.

Is there a Legal Basis for Disciplining Private Food Safety Standards in the WTO?

The third focus of discussions in the SPS committee has been with regard to the status of these private standards under WTO agreements. This has been the most controversial area of discussion. Some trade officials, and particularly those of European and North American countries, express the view that setting standards for products purchased is a legitimate private sector activity with which governments should not interfere. They argue that exceeding official food safety requirements does not result in any violation of national laws, and that there could be benefits for those producers who can meet higher requirements.

Other trade officials express a contrary view, arguing that the SPS agreement makes governments in importing countries responsible for the standards set by their private sectors. They maintain that the private standards do not always meet the WTO requirements for transparency and scientific justification of food safety measures and may be more trade-restrictive than necessary to protect health. These trade officials, primarily representing developing countries, want to see governments take action to limit the ability of the private sector to set safety requirements that go beyond what has officially been determined as safe.

The very first article of the SPS agreement states that the agreement applies to 'all sanitary and phytosanitary measures which may, directly or indirectly, affect international trade'.[3] Its definition of a 'sanitary or phytosanitary measure' (Annex A, paragraph 1) refers to 'any measure applied' to achieve certain types of health protection. This does not seem to exclude the types of measures imposed by the private standards. On the other hand, the obligations under the SPS agreement are addressed to WTO members, that is, the governments representing member countries. This raises the question of whether the agreement covers actions taken by the private sector, or only those taken by governments (at national or sub-national levels).

Article 13 of the SPS agreement indicates that:

> Members are fully responsible under this Agreement for the observance of all obligations set forth herein. Members shall formulate and implement positive measures and mechanisms in support of the observance of the provisions of this Agreement by other than central government bodies. Members shall take such reasonable measures as may be available to them to ensure that non-governmental entities within their territories, as well as regional bodies in which relevant entities within their territories are members, comply with the relevant provisions of this Agreement. In addition, Members shall not take measures which have the effect of, directly or indirectly, requiring or encouraging such regional or non-governmental entities, or local governmental bodies, to act in a manner inconsistent with the provisions of this Agreement. Members shall ensure that they rely on the services of non-governmental entities for implementing sanitary or phytosanitary measures only if these entities comply with the provisions of this Agreement.

The last three sentences of Article 13 deal with 'non-governmental entities', and the role of members in ensuring that such entities comply with the SPS agreement. The term 'non-governmental entities' is not defined in the SPS agreement. While some have argued that it would cover private standards bodies, others believe that only private entities that have been contracted by a government to carry out regulatory tasks would be included.[4] Even if this article applies to private standards bodies, it is likely that the 'reasonable measures' to be taken by a particular government to ensure that a specific non-governmental entity complies with the SPS agreement would have to be considered on a case-by-case basis.

Some countries have suggested that the SPS committee should develop, or request, a legal ruling on whether the SPS agreement applies to private food safety standards. But in the WTO such interpretations can come only from a consensus agreement among all members, or through formal legal dispute cases. Given the divergence of views on this issue, a consensus on the interpretation of this provision is highly unlikely. To date, there has been no WTO jurisprudence that would help in determining what are the 'reasonable measures' available to ensure that non-governmental entities comply with the SPS agreement. Many delegates to the SPS committee, and in particular those from developing countries, wanted the SPS committee to address the issue of SPS-related private standards. Several information meetings were organized for delegates to the committee with representatives of various private standard-setting bodies.

In July 2008 the chairman of the SPS committee circulated a questionnaire soliciting specific suggestions from members regarding what the SPS committee could do to:

1. reduce the negative effects that SPS-related private standards have on international trade, especially for developing countries
2. enhance the potential benefits arising from private SPS standards for developing countries.

The questions sought views as to whether the committee should limit the focus of its work to certain categories of private SPS standards (for example, collective international schemes, collective national schemes, or also individual firm schemes). Members were also asked whether a study which compared private standards with corresponding Codex, IPPC and OIE standards would be useful, and if so, how such a study could be done practically – and what the committee could do with the results of any study. Views were sought on the value of organizing periodic information sessions with private standard-setting bodies or joint meetings with the WTO Committee on Technical Barriers to Trade, and also on how the SPS committee might coordinate on this issue with the Codex, IPPC and OIE, or with other organizations such as UNCTAD and the World Bank. Specific examples of where private standards facilitated compliance with official SPS requirements were solicited, along with views on whether the SPS committee should eventually pursue a legal analysis of the relationship between the SPS agreement and private standards. The countries that replied to this questionnaire were invited to participate in an ad hoc working group to assist the chairperson.

A summary of the responses to these questions was circulated as a WTO document, which also proposed a plan of action for the SPS committee (WTO, 25 September 2008). One action agreed by the SPS committee was to encourage all WTO members and observers to provide any relevant information regarding studies or analysis which they have undertaken or of which they are aware for consideration by the ad hoc working group. Of particular interest are the studies that have been undertaken by UN Food and Agriculture Organization (FAO) with respect to food safety standards, and by the World Organization for

Animal Health (OIE) regarding animal health and welfare standards, discussed below. No trade problems have been identified with regard to private standards in the plant protection area. The SPS committee also agreed in October 2008 to undertake a study identifying trade problems or benefits from specifically identified private standards, and subsequently the identification of possible actions that could be taken by the SPS committee or WTO member governments.

The first step was the circulation of a second questionnaire to all WTO members soliciting specific examples of products, markets and private standards that were considered to be creating problems for trade, or providing benefits. Members were asked to provide as much detail as possible regarding these standards and their effects on producers and exporters of the product, including how the private standards differed from official and Codex or OIE standards, whether the producers most affected were small, medium or large enterprises, costs of compliance and of certification, and information on positive effects of the standards (WTO, 8 December 2008).

The responses to the questionnaire were compiled and circulated in a document for further consideration by the SPS committee at its meetings in June and October 2009 (WTO, 10 December 2009). There was a lot of controversy regarding some of the responses. Very few responses identified positive benefits from private standards. Some trade officials had solicited information directly from producers and exporters in their countries. However, the trade officials noticed that many producers and exporters did not know which requirements were established by governments and which by the private sector. The producers and traders knew only that to be able to sell their product in a market, they had to comply with certain requirements. Some of the replies to the questionnaire concerned official requirements set by governments, not private standards. Another problem with some of the responses to the questionnaire was that they covered issues not within the scope of the SPS agreement, such as requirements for organic foods or labour standards. Information on the costs of complying with the private standards, and the costs of certification, was often missing, or not very precise.

A commonly cited problem in the responses was the requirement of certain private standards that the level of pesticide residues permissible in food products could not exceed one-half, or in some cases one-third, of the acceptable level established by the government of the importing country. Other examples were retailers that required the processing of poultry and beef products allegedly for disease control reasons, in ways that exceeded the government requirements. High costs of certification of compliance with the private standards was a common complaint.

As the next step, WTO members were requested to suggest concrete and appropriate actions that the SPS committee, or member governments themselves, might take to minimize any negative effects of SPS-related private standards and to enhance any potential benefits from these standards. These proposals for actions were first discussed by the ad hoc working group in October 2009, and discussions continued in 2010. The working group identified 'Possible Actions for the SPS Committee Regarding SPS-related Private Standards' in early 2011. At its March 2011 meeting, the committee agreed to pursue five actions recommended by the working group (WTO, 6 April 2011). While WTO members remain highly divided as to whether private standards legally fall within the scope of the SPS agreement, the committee agreed to develop a working definition of private standards related to SPS, and limit any discussions to private standards identified in the definition. In addition, the committee agreed that information regarding the work of Codex, IPPC and OIE as well as relevant developments in other WTO councils and committees should be regularly shared in the committee. Members agreed to educate relevant private sector bodies in their countries so that they understand the issues raised in the SPS committee and the importance of the international standards of Codex, IPPC and OIE. The committee also agreed to explore co-operation with these three bodies in developing information material underlining the importance of international SPS standards.

As noted previously, this issue is also under active consideration by the Codex and the OIE.

CODEX DISCUSSIONS

At its 32nd session in June–July 2009, the FAO/WHO Codex Alimentarius Commission (CAC32) considered a report prepared by FAO consultants regarding the impact of private standards on the food chain and on the public standard-setting process (Henson et al., n.d). The report focused specifically on standards related to food safety, and why there was a need for private standards. Four drivers of increased control along food chains were identified:

1. real and/or perceived risks along the food chain
2. heightened interest among consumers and businesses for food safety matters
3. the globalization of the food supply
4. the responsibility taken by the private sector in ensuring food safety.

The study compared different types of private standards with the standard-setting process in Codex and analysed potential challenges for Codex in terms of the speed and complexity of its standard-setting processes. Actions proposed for consideration by the Codex Alimentarius Commission included the admission of collective private standards organisations as observers to the Codex, and changes in the Codex operating procedures to better respond to the challenges and opportunities presented by private food standards.

The discussions in the Codex Alimentarius Commission in many ways paralleled those in the WTO SPS committee (Joint FAO/WHO Food Standards Programme, 29 June–4 July 2009). Many developing country delegates did not support the recommendations of the study, and emphasized the negative effects that private food safety standards had on small producers and exporters in their countries. They maintained that Codex should be the sole international reference organisation for food safety. Others noted that private standards were a market reality and important for the diversification of some markets.

The Codex Alimentarius Commission was of the opinion that Codex standards should be benchmarks for private food safety standards and agreed to monitor developments in the WTO and work in cooperation with the OIE and the IPPC to consult on a common position on this matter. The Commission also agreed that a study be conducted to analyse the role, cost and benefits of private standards for consideration by the Codex Executive Committee and the Commission. In addition, the Codex secretariat was asked to prepare an analysis of the speed of the Codex standard-setting process, as this had been identified as one of the possible reasons for the emergence of private standards.

A new study (CX/CAC 10/33/13) was prepared by the FAO and WHO and considered during the 33rd Session of the Codex Alimentarius Commission (5–9 July 2010, paras. 218–243). The main conclusions of the paper were that there was a tendency for individual firm standards to be more stringent than relevant Codex standards without scientific basis, whereas collective food safety standards were largely consistent with Codex. A general exception to this related to traceability requirements. Private food safety standards were, however, more prescriptive than Codex standards in stating how food hygiene requirements should be met. Since the standards in most cases were prepared with extremely limited opportunity for developing country input, the prescriptions contained within the standards were often inappropriate in developing country contexts and difficult or impossible to apply in small-scale food businesses in developing countries. The cost of certification disproportionately penalized small-scale producers and multiple certification requirements were a major problem that should be avoidable given that there are minimal differences among many of the existing standards.

Some delegations welcomed the paper as more balanced than the report discussed at CAC32 while others were of the opinion that the paper seemed to favour private standards and put the onus on developing countries to meet these standards. The chairperson concluded that legal trade implications of private standards were best dealt with in the WTO while Codex, FAO and WHO should engage with global private standard-setting bodies and encourage their participation in Codex as observers. The chairperson noted the willingness of FAO to make closer contact with private standards organizations. The Commission agreed to refer the matter to regional coordinating committees to conduct further analysis of the problems encountered with private standards and to make recommendations for follow-up by the next session of the Commission. The analysis should include the financial burden, especially on small- and medium-sized enterprises (SMEs), due to the proliferation of private standards. Private standard-setting bodies should be encouraged to limit the number of audits and to work more cooperatively among themselves. A side event on private standards was organized by the FAO and WHO on the session-free day of the Commission on 8 July 2010.

The Codex Secretariat had prepared an analysis of the speed of the Codex standard-setting process, which had been mentioned as one reason for the proliferation of private standards. This analysis was discussed at the 63rd Session of the Executive Committee in December 2009 (CX/EXEC 09/63/8; see Joint FAO/WHO, December 2000) and a further study taking into account the setting of numerical standards and work management approaches of different committees was discussed at the 64th Session of the CCEXEC in June/July 2010 (CX/EXEC 10/64/4). The Executive Committee concluded that the analysis contained in the working document had been positive, showing that Codex work in general was progressing much better than was the prevailing impression and that this message should be actively communicated to all relevant parties. The Executive Committee concluded further that the analysis had helped to identify the work-management approaches of Codex Committees that facilitate advancement of texts in the Codex step process. The Executive Committee recommended that Codex Committees consider adopting the good practices identified.

OIE DISCUSSIONS

The OIE also questioned its members regarding the role of private standards in the animal health and welfare area. OIE member governments adopted a resolution regarding the implication of private standards in international trade of animals and animal products in May 2008 (OIE International Committee, 25–30 May 2008). This resolution requested the Director General of the OIE 'to work with relevant public and private international organizations with the objective that concerns of Members are taken into consideration and that private standards, where used, are consistent with and do not conflict those of the OIE'. The OIE secretariat has provided regular updates to the SPS committee and submitted a document entitled 'Considerations Relevant to Private Standards in the Field of Animal Health, Food Safety, and Animal Welfare' (WTO, 25 February 2008). An OIE ad hoc working group was established to consider private standards in the areas of animal health and welfare. This group met in October 2009 to review the results of a questionnaire sent to OIE members and relevant organizations and to prepare recommendations for future action by the OIE. The group's report[5] was reviewed by the Code Commission in February 2010 and was published as an annex to the Code Commission report in March 2010, including the complete version of the report of the OIE questionnaire (Report of the Meeting of the OIE Terrestrial Animal Health Standards Commission, 8–12 February 2010, p. 701).

Most of the 68 OIE members responding to the questionnaire recommended that the OIE work more closely with private standard-setting organizations in an effort to avoid negative effects of private standards. The OIE convened a meeting with private organizations, with the participation of the WTO secretariat, in February 2010 to exchange information and consider possible next steps.

At the OIE 78th General Session (23–28 May 2010) the private sector's views on private standards were presented by a representative of the not-for-profit global alliance for a Safe Supply of Affordable Food Everywhere (SSAFE). In the related General Session Resolution No. 26,[6] members recommended that the OIE maintain and strengthen appropriate links and dialogue with relevant global private standard-setting bodies and global private industry organizations, with the aim of encouraging the compatibility of private standards with OIE standards and fostering communication with national governments and consumers on the safeguards offered by official standards. The Final Report of the 78th General Session is available on the OIE website.

Following the recommendations of Resolution 26, the OIE convened a meeting in September 2010 with some global standard-setting bodies and other stakeholders to discuss future collaboration. The report of this meeting was released in October 2010 as an annex to the report of the

Terrestrial Code Commission's September meeting. Information on OIE activities relating to private standards for sanitary safety and animal welfare may be found at: www.oie.int/eng/normes/en_Implications%20of%20private%20standards.htm

CONCLUSIONS

The discussions on SPS-related private standards at the WTO, as well as in the Codex and OIE venues, are characterized by such widely differing views among countries that it is difficult to foresee their outcome. Many countries, and particularly developing countries, see the proliferation of SPS-related private standards as potentially serious and unjustified barriers to international trade. They are concerned, in particular, about the additional costs and difficulties these standards present to small producers and exporters already challenged by the official requirements of their potential buyers. However, the concerns of many developing country governments go beyond the commercial effects. Many officials see the proliferation of private standards as a phenomenon that, if allowed to continue unchecked, will undermine the value and credibility of the international standards developed by Codex and OIE, and even of the official SPS requirements of governments. What confidence will consumers have in a determination by the European Food Safety Agency, or the US Food and Drug Administration, or any other government regulatory body that a certain level of pesticide residues presents no risk to human health, if major supermarket chains refuse to sell products unless they contain less than half of the officially 'safe' level? Why should government experts invest their time and resources in developing international Codex and OIE standards regarding safe products, if a growing number of commercial buyers impose their own 'safety' requirements?

However, other governments vehemently defend the right of the private sector to set voluntary standards that allow companies to differentiate their products and respond to the perceived demands of their consumers. Official requirements normally focus on maximum residue levels, or permitted additives, and nothing prevents companies from preferring lower levels or fewer additives. These countries argue that the WTO SPS agreement does not apply to the normal commercial practices of the private sector, and hence any actions in this regard should be limited.

At this point in time, the most likely compromises are those that allow governments to continue to discuss this issue at the WTO and in other international venues while they find ways to ensure the private standard-setting bodies are made aware of the concerns raised by developing countries. Enhancing the knowledge and understanding of all stakeholders, governmental and private, of the real and perceived effects of SPS-related private standards may open the way to ensuring that such requirements result in safer foods and facilitate trade, particularly for developing countries.

NOTES

1 The author is a Senior Counsellor in the Agriculture and Commodities Division of the World Trade Organization, and Secretary of the WTO Committee on Sanitary and Phytosanitary Measures. The views expressed are those of the author only and do not necessarily represent the views of the World Trade Organization or of its members.
2 WTO members do not have to be recognized sovereign states; customs territories with control of imports and exports can become members of the WTO (for example, the Separate Customs Territory of Taiwan, Penghu, Kinmen and Matsu). For ease of reading, however, the term 'countries' will be used in this chapter when referring to WTO members.
3 The full text of Article. 1.1 of the Agreement on the Application of Sanitary and Phytosanitary Measures reads as follows: 'This Agreement applies to all sanitary and phytosanitary measures which may, directly or indirectly, affect international trade. Such measures shall be developed and applied in accordance with the provisions of this Agreement'.
4 For a more detailed analysis of Article 13 and of other articles of the SPS and TBT agreement, see WTO, 9 October 2007. This document contains legal analysis carried out by O'Connor and Company, a law firm based in Brussels (MB8).
5 Final Report – OIE Questionnaire On Private Standards, Executive Summary available at www.oie.int/eng/normes/en_executive%20summary.pdf (accessed 30 April 2010).
6 Resolution No. 26. 'Roles of public and private standards in animal health and animal welfare'.

REFERENCES

Henson, S. and Humphrey, J. 'The impacts of private food safety standards on the food chain and on the public standards-setting process', Paper prepared for FAO/WHO and published as ALINORM 09/32/9D-Part II, available at ftp://ftp.fao.org/codex/CAC/CAC32/al329Dbe.pdf (accessed 30 April 2010).

Joint FAO/WHO Food Standards Programme (29 June–4 July 2009), 'Report of the thirty-second session of the Codex Alimentarius Commission', Rome, Italy, available at www.codexalimentarius.net/web/archives.jsp?year = 09 (accessed 24 April 2010).

Joint FAO/WHO Food Standards Programme (5–9 July 2010), 'Report of the thirty-third session of the Codex Alimentarius Commission', Geneva, Switzerland, available at www.codexalimentarius.net/download/report/744/al33REPe.pdf (accessed 24 April 2010).

Joint FAO/WHO Food Standards Programme (8-11 December 2009) 'Report of the sixty-third session of the Executive Committee, Geneva, Switzerland, available at www.codexalimentarius.net/download/report/735/al33_03e.pdf (accessed 18 February 2011).

Legal texts of the World Trade Organization, Agreement on the Application of Sanitary and Phytosanitary Measures, the 'SPS Agreement'. available at www.wto.org/english/docs_e/legal_e/15-sps.pdf (accessed 18 February 2011).

OIE (23–28 May 2010), 'Final Report of the 78th General Session', available at www.oie.int/eng/OIE/actes/en_rfinal.htm.

OIE, 'Implications of private standards in international trade of animals and animal products', available at www.oie.int/eng/normes/en_Implications %20of%20private%20standards.htm.

OIE International Committee (25–30 May 2008), 'Resolution No. XXXII', 76th General Session, available at www.oie.int/fileadmin/Home/eng/About_us/docs/pdf/A_RESO_2008_webpubpdf (accessed 12 March 2012).

OIE, 'Questionnaire on Private Standards Final Report', Executive Summary, available at www.oie.int/eng/normes/en_executive%20summary.pdf (accessed 30 April 2010).

Report of the Meeting of the OIE Terrestrial Animal Health Standards Commission (8–12 February 2010), Paris, available at www.Oie.Int/Tahsc/Eng/En_Reports.Htm (accessed 30 April 2010).

WTO Agreement on the Application of Sanitary and Phytosanitary Measures, available at www.wto.org/english/docs_e/legal_e/15-sps.pdf (accessed 18 February 2011).

WTO (24 January 2007), 'Private Standards and the SPS Agreement', document symbol G/SPS/GEN/746, available at http://docsonline.wto.org/gen_search.asp?searchmode = simple (accessed 30 April 2010).

WTO (26 February 2007), 'Typology of Global Standards – Communication from the United Nations Conference on Trade and Development (UNCTAD)', document symbol G/SPS/GEN/760, available at http://docsonline.wto.org/DDFDocuments/t/G/SPS/GEN760.doc, (accessed 18 February 2011).

WTO (9 October 2007), 'Private Voluntary Standards within the WTO Multilateral Framework', document symbol G/SPS/GEN/802, submitted by the United Kingdom, available at http://docsonline.wto.org/gen_search.asp?searchmode = simple (accessed 30 April 2010).

WTO (25 February 2008), 'Considerations Relevant to Private Standards in the Field of Animal Health, Food Safety and Animal Welfare', Submission by the World Organisation of Animal Health to the WTO Committee on Sanitary and Phytosanitary Measures, document symbol G/SPS/GEN/822, available at http://docsonline.wto.org/gen_search.asp?searchmode = simple (accessed 30 April 2010).

WTO (20 June 2008), 'Recommended Procedures for Implementing the Transparency Obligations of the SPS Agreement', document symbol G/SPS/7/Rev.3, available at http://docsonline.wto.org/gen_search.asp?searchmode = simple (accessed 24 November 2010).

WTO (25 September 2008), 'Private Standards – Identifying Practical Actions for the SPS Committee – Summary of Responses', document symbol G/SPS/W/230, available at http://docsonline.wto.org/gen_search.asp?searchmode = simple (accessed 24 November 2010).

WTO (8 December 2008), 'Questionnaire on SPS-related Private Standards', document symbol G/SPS/W/232, available at http://docsonline.wto.org/gen_search.asp?searchmode = simple (accessed 30 April 2010).

WTO (10 December 2009), 'Effects of SPS-Related Private Standards – Compilation of Replies', document symbol G/SPS/GEN/932/Rev.1, available at http://

docsonline.wto.org/gen_search.asp?searchmode = simple (accessed 30 April 2010).
WTO (6 April 2011), 'Actions Regarding SPS-related Private Standard', document symbol G/SPS/55, available at http://docsonline.wto.org/DDFDocuments/t/G/SPS/55.doc (accessed 25 April 2012).

10. Private standards, global governance and international trade: the case of global food safety governance

Jan Wouters, Axel Marx and Nicolas Hachez[1]

1. INTRODUCTION

Foodstuffs are increasingly produced and traded globally. Developing and newly industrialized countries, often with weaker environmental, health and safety regulatory frameworks, are becoming major producers of agricultural and other food products. This rise in their production capacity is affecting the way foodstuffs are produced and handled. As a result, regulatory gaps have been forming in global food governance. Many critics have argued that existing multilateral and governmental initiatives are currently incapable of effectively addressing the numerous global regulatory challenges associated with food, such as food safety or food quality, which result from trade liberalization and increased globalization.

As a result of this state of play, the global food trade has been witnessing for some years the emergence of new 'non-state' initiatives aiming to fill these regulatory gaps. These initiatives seek to govern supply chains across the globe according to a set of 'standards' addressing the issues of the safety and the quality of food, but also the sustainability of its production methods.[2] This movement partakes of a wider evolution which is intensively followed by the academic world, using a multiplicity of denominations to describe it, such as the important rise of private standards in supply chain management (Swinnen, 2007; Henson and Humphrey, 2008), the uptake of civil regulation (Vogel, 2008), the certification solution (Gereffi et al., 2001), the certification revolution (Conroy, 2007) and the proliferation of the voluntary standards movement (ISEAL Alliance, 2009). These new regulatory initiatives are developing very quickly and are not limited to food products.[3] Internationally traded goods and services and internationally operating economic actors are indeed increasingly being subjected to privately developed standards and to certification schemes focusing on issues as diverse as technical product specifications (see, for example, the thousands of ISO standards defining technical requirements for as many products), social standards (for example, the SA8000 scheme developed by Social Accountability International and generally the fair trade movement), environmental and natural resources management standards (for example, the sustainability labels granted by the Forest Stewardship Council or the Marine Stewardship Council) and consumer health and safety standards (for example, GLOBALG.A.P. and other food safety standards).

These private standards, mainly developed in Europe and the United States, are consequently becoming important regulatory instruments in the context of global food governance. Many large retailers are using these private standards and certification schemes worldwide to govern their supply chains (Vandenbergh, 2007). In this regard, Cafaggi (this volume) insists on the decisive position gradually gained by a small number of western retailers for the purpose of setting food safety and quality standards. This gradual emergence of private standards is generating a heated debate on their relation to international trade law. It is alleged that private standards may represent barriers to the trading of a number of products and may therefore run counter to the objectives pursued by international trade rules. Combating barriers to the trade in food products is indeed the reason why, in the context of the World Trade Organization (WTO) principles and rules have been adopted to control and reduce the trade-restrictive effects of, for example, food safety measures. These rules are laid down in the Agreement on the Application of Sanitary and Phytosanitary Measures (SPS Agreement). However, at the time the SPS Agreement was negotiated and adopted (1994), private standards had not yet invaded the food chain, and this evolution had admittedly not been envisioned by the drafters of the Agreement. However, times have changed, and some authors now even claim that private standards are challenging the legitimacy and effectiveness of established multilateral trade institutions such as the WTO (Henson and Humphrey, 2008). As the WTO itself recognizes: 'a stable and mutually supportive relationship between standards regimes and international trade rules is central to the effective functioning of the trading system. [. . .] Standards are essential for addressing market failures. [. . .] But the design and operation of standards must [. . .] avoid [. . .] unwarranted obstacles to competition and trade' (World Trade Organization, 2005a, p. iii).

This chapter focuses on the nexus between private standards as an important global governance tool and on the multilateral trading system. The governance of food is taken as a case-study to explore this issue further as the operation of the SPS Agreement directly links private food safety standards to the multilateral trading system. The chapter argues that private standards are institutionalized market governance instruments which can be used in innovative policy arrangements to address global governance challenges. In order to fulfil their potential as an integral part of such policy arrangements the relationship of private standards with, and their place in, the multilateral trade regime needs to be clarified. This chapter seeks to add to this clarification effort. The next section, Section 2, is devoted to a description of the emergence of private standards as a governance tool and argues that private standards are becoming an integral part of new policy arrangements regulating the globalized food trade. Sections 3 to 5 address the issue of the interactions of private food safety standards with the multilateral trading system. After a short presentation of the supposed underlying assumptions of the SPS Agreement in section 3, the chapter presents the issues posed by private food safety standards in relation to the trade-liberalization agenda pursued by the SPS Agreement (section 4). It then examines the extent to which private standards may or may not be said to fall into the scope of the SPS Agreement, and whether the latter may have any traction on their potential trade-restrictive effects (section 5). The final section attempts to present a regulatory model under which private food safety standards could find their place within the multilateral trade regime and to formulate recommendations to the relevant actors on ways to put that model into practice (section 6).

2. THE EMERGENCE OF PRIVATE STANDARDS AND THEIR INSTITUTIONALIZATION AS NEW POLICY ARRANGEMENTS

As indicated above and explained at length elsewhere in this volume, the global food sector is increasingly being subjected to standards developed and enforced by a variety of private actors (industry, NGOs, multistakeholder coalitions, and so on[4]). Private standards may have diverse substantive scopes, as some focus exclusively on food safety and quality (for example, the BRC Global Standards), while others also address environmental and social issues (for example, the GLOBAL G.A.P. Standard). They may also espouse very different design and governing schemes, for example in respect of the process of 'certification', which guarantees to a buyer of food products that the producer complies with the standard considered. Some of those standards materialize for the consumer as a label visible on products (for example, Label Rouge in France), while others are strictly business to business and are not directed at consumers (for example, GLOBALG.A.P.). This complexity is making it difficult to present a rationalized picture of private food safety governance today.[5] The somewhat erratic emergence of private standard initiatives in the food sector may be said to be sparked by many interrelated factors which are progressively 'institutionalizing' private standards in current food governance regimes. In this section, we try to uncover those factors and explain why private food standards have become policy instruments which can hardly be dispensed with today (see also Cafaggi, this volume).

First of all, following many different food crises,[6] consumers have grown more conscious of food safety risks and may be thought to adjust their purchasing behaviour in relation to the perceived reliability of food. Moreover, general knowledge of foodborne diseases or illnesses[7] is expanding, causing food safety to become an increasingly important health issue, and to receive more media attention. In the United States, the Center for Disease Control and Prevention (2007) estimates that 76 million people suffer yearly from foodborne illnesses, accounting for 325 000 hospitalizations and more than 5000 deaths. As a consequence, supermarket chains and large producer groups have made food safety a key concern and a differentiating factor in the marketing of food products.[8] The competition in food products has therefore arguably to some degree shifted from prices to quality and safety (Henson and Reardon, 2005).

Secondly, and related to the first point, brand protection is becoming a key issue for many leading companies in the food sector. The proliferation, diversification and internationalization of NGOs establishing themselves as genuine counter-powers through the use of media strategies, have forced companies to take civil society concerns into account (Bartley, 2003; Cashore, 2003; O'Rourke, 2003; Fung, 2003; Gereffi et al., 2001; Marx, 2008). Gereffi et al. (2001) note, for example, that protests and direct actions against brand-name retailers are only 15 years old, but are regarded as extremely powerful tools to force retailers to take environmental, social and safety issues into consideration (see also Bartley, 2003). Joining a private standards initiative can thus be an effective strategy to protect a firm's reputation, especially when independent external parties certify products and production processes and hence provide assurance on the efforts made by firms to manage food-related issues (Marx, 2008).

Thirdly, in line with a general trend, food markets have become increasingly globalized, and food products now circulate much more extensively from one geographic zone to another. This leads to an increased diversity in food products on local markets, and to more difficulties in tracing the origins of such products. It has become much more difficult for single governments to keep track of the range of products present on their domestic markets, and to keep up with the assessment of all the risks associated therewith. In the recent past, public food safety regulations have not been able to prevent some major food crises, such as mad cow disease to name only one (see Stanton, this volume, pp. 235–253). States therefore tend to limit command-and-control regulation of food, and to place a kind of default responsibility on the food chain actors in case of food safety problems. An early example of such regulatory design is the due diligence requirement contained in the UK Food Safety Act (UKFSA) of 1990, which provides that food retailers can escape liability for non-compliance with food safety laws if they can demonstrate that they have taken all precautions in this regard.[9] It is often said that the possibility of being held liable for food safety issues did prompt a response from the food industry, resulting in the development of private standards (Henson, 2008; Food and Agriculture Organization, 2007). Mirroring the UKFSA, the EU Food Law Regulation of 2002 also currently provides for a quite stringent responsibility threshold for commercial actors involved with food products.[10] In this connection, Cafaggi (this volume, pp. 195–234) discusses interesting developments on the articulation of public (national, regional and international) regulations and private standards. Private standards may thus be said to be used by the private sector as a tool to pre-empt food safety problems and reassure consumers, but also as a signal to governments that corporations are exercising due diligence to prevent incidents from happening, which would permit them to escape liability if the cases arise.

Fourthly, the structure of food markets has changed along with globalization and nowadays hands a premium to large global actors. The number of key actors in the food chain has reduced as their size grew. Major retailer groups have particular influence as they are the 'gatekeepers' of the food markets: they decide which products they will offer to their customers, and therefore which products will access a defined market. Such concentration and increase of bargaining power allow these retailer groups to impose practically any condition they want on their suppliers and contractors, from payment deadlines to the safety features of the food products they sell (Organisation for Economic Co-operation and Development, 2006a). The rapid spread of private standards owes very much to this new market configuration. To be sure, many private standards are developed by large retailer groups and are imposed contractually on their suppliers. As to the legal mechanisms through which private standards are spreading throughout the supply chain, Cafaggi (this volume) offers a very thorough analysis of global food safety governance by way of contractual mechanisms.

Finally, the institutionalization of private standards is taking place in a context of profound changes in the role of states in market regulation.

Many observers have argued that a partial and progressive shift is occurring since the 1980s from public to private, or public-private governance, on certain issues. Van Tatenhove et al. (2000, p. 48) identified the following major evolutions:

a. the traditional divides between state, market and civil society are disappearing
b. the interrelations between these spheres increasingly exceed the nation-state
c. this results in new coalitions between state agencies, market actors and civic parties both at local and global levels (see also Haufler, 2003; Cashore et al., 2004; Visseren-Hamakers and Glasbergen, 2007; Abbott and Snidal, 2009a; Marx, 2011).

Given that this reconfiguration of governance is an attempt to adapt to the globalizing evolution of economy and politics, these new regulatory forms are often considered as more promising than purely public policy-making strategies, at least for certain issues, among which food governance is one (Beierle, 1998; Karkkainen et al., 2000; Coglianese and Nash, 2001). As a result of all the above, governance schemes dominated by private standards are therefore in the process of decisively shaping global food governance (Henson, 2008).

Understanding the context in which private standards operate is important in order to assess their potential impact on and interrelatedness with public policy-making. Private standards are increasingly becoming part of larger policy arrangements and may in some instances be said to contribute to achieving aims traditionally entrusted exclusively to purely public regulation. The interconnection and interaction between private standards and public policy-making is becoming increasingly complex since many public policy arrangements are starting to make use of private standards. This trend fits within the redefinition of policy-making outlined above and the role of the state therein, and opens up opportunities for innovative policies (Liefferink et al., 2000; Jänicke, 1990). As Osborne and Gaebler famously claimed in *Reinventing Government*, the state should no longer row but steer (Osborne and Gaebler, 1992). Private standards are an interesting mechanism by which governments can achieve certain policy goals and promote change (steer) without excessive regulatory burdens (row). The ways in which governmental regulation interacts with private standards are diverse (Smith, 2009).

First of all, governments can delegate to private standard entities or refer to private standard schemes in public regulations. Several governments require exporters to meet the privately developed HACCP procedure (Hazard Analysis and Critical Control Points), traceability and quality standards, using either public or private auditors and laboratories. Secondly, governments are increasingly using private standards in their day-to-day activities. Meidinger (2003) provides the example of how forest certification is used by US government agencies to certify publicly owned forests. Henson and Humphrey (2008) report that the UK Food Standards Agency has instructed enforcement authorities to take into account membership in private standard schemes for determining the frequency of inspection of production facilities. In this way, private initiatives play a large role in the public oversight of numerous products and services. Thirdly, governments are increasingly using private standards in public procurement. Given the budgets of many governments for public procurement, this adds to the overall effectiveness of private standards and generates a significant impact on their further development. Several European countries have developed and are implementing extensive national sustainable procurement policies (see Steurer et al., 2007; Mechel et al., 2006). Thirdly, as we already emphasized, governments can leave the substance of regulation to private actors in certain fields, and encourage the development of private standards in diverse ways, by setting responsibility rules (see the UK Food Safety Act responsibility mechanism above), or by creating or supporting labelling schemes for product differentiation.

All of these elements have favoured the emergence of private food safety standards, which major food actors impose on their suppliers, and which often go beyond the requirements of public regulation (see Fulponi, 2007). Such private standards reassure consumers as to the safety of the food they purchase, position food products into the competition for safety and quality, and shield the major food actors from liability in case of a sanitary crisis. These driving forces, which represent structural changes in the global food market, institutionalize private standards in global food governance. As a result, their interaction with the multilateral trading regime is becoming increasingly relevant. This is discussed in the next section.

3. GLOBAL FOOD SAFETY AND TRADE LIBERALIZATION: THE ASSUMPTIONS UNDERLYING THE SPS AGREEMENT AND THEIR SUITABILITY FOR GLOBAL FOOD GOVERNANCE

With a number of far-reaching international agreements, an effective adjudicatory body and an active dispute settlement practice, international trade law is one of the most vibrant international legal regimes, embodied in a fully-fledged international organization, the World Trade Organization (WTO). As made explicit in the preamble of the Agreement Establishing the World Trade Organization (signed in Marrakech on 15 April, 1994), the main purpose of the rules of international trade is to facilitate trade among countries and to reduce as much as possible the barriers that inhibit the circulation of goods and services between 'national' markets. A particular type of product that is strongly connected to the international trade agenda is food. Such products are among the most widely traded goods worldwide, and their export accounts for a very large share of many countries' gross domestic product. It is therefore important that food products can be traded widely and easily throughout the world, taking into account existing or required safety measures. In order to minimize the impact of the food safety agenda on free trade, the WTO has laid down principles and rules which attempt to control and reduce the trade-restrictive effects of food safety measures.

The main rules are laid down in the Agreement on the Application of Sanitary and Phytosanitary Measures (SPS Agreement, see generally Scott 2007 and Stanton, this volume, for a detailed overview). The SPS Agreement supplements the Agreement on Technical Barriers to Trade (TBT Agreement), which sets general disciplines for all standards except those which qualify as 'SPS measures'.[11] The SPS Agreement recognizes the legitimate right of states to regulate the safety of the food which is present in their territories (Preamble and Art. 2.1.), but the exercise of that right is constrained by a number of disciplines and the general obligation to base SPS measures on scientific evidence (Art. 2.2). The SPS Agreement also adds a presumption of conformity for SPS measures which are based on the 'international standards, guidelines and recommendations' adopted for food safety by the Codex Alimentarius Commission (Art. 3 and Annex A).[12] Such reference to 'international standards' is aimed at encouraging the global harmonization of SPS measures, and therefore minimizing the barriers to trade created by the food safety agenda. Certain authors have analyzed this provision as a delegation, by the WTO, of the power to internationally legislate appropriate food safety standards (Büthe, 2008). This 'positive integration' of food safety rules by way of 'quasi-legislation' (Marceau and Trachtman, 2002, p. 838) or 'legislation by proxy' raises a number of concerns, for example, that the WTO, whose mandate is to facilitate trade, is encroaching on other regulatory fields (see Charnovitz, 1999–2000 and Reich, 2004). In light of the above, it is now interesting to take a look at the spirit of the SPS Agreement and at the assumptions which underlie it in order to be able to assess whether it is fit to play its role as a centrepiece of today's global food safety regulatory regime, notably given the recent emergence of private food safety standards.

3.1. The International Law Nature of the SPS Agreement

The SPS Agreement is a treaty and therefore has international legal status. In that sense, it only binds the states which have agreed to it. As is clear from the wording of the Agreement itself, it is first and foremost addressed to members and, insofar as it applies to 'all SPS measures', the SPS Agreement was essentially designed to deal with public regulation. A likely reason for this is that, at the time of the inception of the SPS Agreement, private food safety standards did not have the prevalence they now enjoy. Article 1.1 and Annex A of the Agreement, which define SPS measures, do not however explicitly exclude private standards from the scope of the Agreement (Stanton, this volume), and it is therefore not inconceivable that the disciplines of the SPS Agreement – as well as those of the TBT Agreement – could also be applied to private standards.

However, such application would have to take place through the mediation of WTO Members.[13] Article 13 of the SPS Agreement indeed states that:

> Members are fully responsible under this Agreement for the observance of all obligations set forth herein. Members shall formulate and implement positive measures and mechanisms in support of the observance of the provisions of this Agreement by other than central government bodies. Members shall take such reasonable measures as may be available to them to ensure that non-governmental entities within their territories, as well as regional bodies in which relevant entities within their territories are members, comply with the relevant provisions of this Agreement. In addition, Members shall not take measures which have the effect of, directly or indirectly, requiring or encouraging such regional or non-governmental entities, or local governmental bodies, to act in a manner inconsistent with the provisions of this Agreement. Members shall ensure that they rely on the services of non-governmental entities for implementing sanitary or phytosanitary measures only if these entities comply with the provisions of this Agreement.

As will be discussed below (section 5.), no authoritative interpretation of Article 13, notably by the WTO Dispute Settlement Body, is yet available, and therefore it is quite difficult to determine what it entails for governments and private standard-setters.

3.2. The Trade Focus of the SPS Agreement

The SPS Agreement is, in conformity with the mission statement of the WTO, a trade agreement, and not a food safety agreement. It seeks to apply the WTO trade rules to the trade in food products, and to harmonize food safety regulations in order to lower trade barriers on food products resulting from those regulations. As such, it seeks to apply the safeguard clause of article XX (b) of GATT 1994 (Lowenfeld, 2008).

As a result, the WTO does not decide on any substantive food safety issues. It is only concerned with the scientific justification and 'harmonization' of food safety measures in order to reduce barriers to trade. In order to pursue those goals, the SPS Agreement designates the Codex Alimentarius Commission as the relevant standard-setter in the field of food safety, without intervening in its work. Therefore, any food safety regulation complying with an applicable Codex Alimentarius Standard is deemed compliant with the SPS Agreement. Only when a food safety regulation sets a more stringent level of protection is the SPS Agreement liable of being breached (except when scientifically justified). Any food safety regulation which is more lenient than a Codex Alimentarius Standard does not violate the SPS Agreement (see Kalderimis, 2004). In short, the SPS Agreement is not concerned about setting a high standard of food safety, but leaves, by delegation, that task to the Codex Alimentarius Commission, the standards of which it imposes as upper limits on the level of protection that members can choose to apply (save, again, scientific justification).[14] It can therefore be feared that the manner in which the SPS Agreement is configured risks making it more concerned about the international trade agenda than about the food safety agenda. Some authors even argue that the SPS Agreement was designed to establish a 'practical hierarchy' putting WTO trade rules above non-trade rules (Kalderimis, 2004). However, as discussed in section 2, the dynamics of food markets and food governance have significantly evolved since the inception of the SPS Agreement.

4. ISSUES RELATING TO PRIVATE FOOD SAFETY STANDARDS AND FREE TRADE

If private standards are increasingly regarded as strong tools to increase safety levels in food products, they also create problems of their own, notably as they have exclusionary effects on certain products, mainly on those originating from developing countries. These exclusionary effects can be divided into three categories: market access, developmental aspects, and legal/procedural concerns (Stanton, this volume; World Trade Organization, 2007a). Another major concern is the legitimacy of such standards. In the next sub-sections we briefly analyze the main terms of discussion on these issues. Stanton (this volume) addresses more specifically the debates going on in the SPS Committee concerning those questions.

4.1. Market Access Problems

Since the large retailer groups setting private food safety standards act as 'gatekeepers' to (western) food markets, complying with their standards has in many cases become a de facto mandatory requirement for accessing such markets (World Trade Organization, 2009a, para. 27). The problem is made worse when the private standards overtake public food safety regulation, as it is often the case. Moreover, as per the SPS Agreement, public regulation may not be used for protectionist purposes and must normally be based on science and/or scientific principles, which critics allege may not always be the case for private standards (World Trade Organization, 2007a, p. 3). Other market access problems triggered by private standards emerge from the fact that several standardization schemes may coexist, compete and contradict each other. Stanton (this volume) for example identifies more than 400 private standard schemes. This would result in situations where, on one local market, the same product would have to comply with (and possibly be certified under) several different and potentially conflicting standards in order to be sold to different supermarket chains, involving a multiplication of compliance costs (World Trade Organization, 2009a, para. 33). What is more, such lack of harmonization can result in discrimination between products, either inside or outside of a defined standardization scheme, as private actors do not have to be consistent in the stringency of their food safety measures, contrary to national SPS measures under the SPS Agreement (see Arts. 2.3 and 5.5).

4.2. Development Impact

Developing countries have pointed out that complying with private standards is very burdensome as such standards often require significant upgrades in production facilities and costly certification procedures, involving several inspections by independent reviewers. These cost implications often mean that small and medium food producers in export markets (especially in developing countries) who are not able to pay the price of compliance, are de facto excluded from the potential supply pool of most wholesaling and retailing actors in numerous major markets (Maertens and Swinnen, 2009; Organisation for Economic Cooperation and Development, 2006b, pp. 16, 20 ; World Trade Organization, 2009a, paras. 27, pp. 29–31, 36; UN Conference on Trade and Development, 2009; see also Stanton, this volume). This can have a major developmental impact, since the GDPs of many developing countries depend heavily on the exportation of food products and the bulk of their economic fabric is often composed of small farming enterprises.[15]

4.3. Legal/Procedural Issues

The growing pervasiveness of private standards also raises questions of a more legal/procedural nature (see Stanton, this volume). For example, a complaint may be that private standard-setters, when they adopt or modify a standard which will apply on a large scale and have substantial market access and development implications, do not have to notify those standards in advance, to publish them or to observe a transition period to allow time for all relevant parties to comply with or switch to the new standard, contrary to the provisions of the SPS Agreement (see Art. 7). In other words, the criticism is that these standard-setters do not use a transparent procedure which contains several criteria with which private standards should comply and which is open to independent review as is the case with, for example, the SPS Agreement (2009, paras 31 and 37). Also, in case of conflict between several standards, or in case of dispute concerning the application or interpretation of a standard, adjudicatory mechanisms may often be lacking to resolve the conflict or dispute, and the complaining party then has to surrender to the views of the private standard-setters.

4.4. Legitimacy Debate

No one denies that private standards in fields like food safety have come to play a governing role in global affairs and have an impact, positive or negative, on a number of constituencies, as well as on a number of other policy fields. The fact that they are developed by private (business) actors outside of any legal mandate, following unilateral procedures, and the fact that they may run counter to international or domestic legal rules, raises doubts as to the legitimacy of such private standardization schemes (see, for example, Greenpeace, 2010). In this respect, many authors wish to explore how to ensure that complex private regulatory processes (notably contract-based) which do not stem from democratic political entities, show public accountability, taking the public interest and not only self-interested private designs into consideration (Freeman, 2000; Cafaggi, this volume).

Even in multi-stakeholder governance systems the issue of which preferences dominate is crucial. Simple confrontation of interests and points of view does not necessarily produce socially optimal regulation. As Lobel (2004, p. 458) argues:

> [i]n order to be effective, the governance model must not accept a naïve account of the win-win theme. Situations in which multiple interests are mutually enforcing are context-specific. [...] The governance school must therefore develop a richer basis for approaching collaboration in situations of pervasive competition, power imbalances, and limited resources.

In order to be legitimate, governance systems need to be regarded as 'appropriate' by the public they seek to govern, and as such be congruent with that public's normative references (Zürn, 2004). Legitimacy can derive from many factors, but most importantly the sense of 'appropriateness' conveyed by legitimacy stems in large part from the belief that a regulation, be it public or private, actually reflects the preferences of society at large and consequently pursues the public interest (see, for example, Bernstein, 2005). In order to achieve this, questions of institutional design are of importance, notably in that legitimacy in modern time's rule-making is strongly associated with the necessity for it to be 'democratic' (Keohane, 2003). The question of democratic legitimacy in private global governance is a hotly debated one, and discussions are unsettled as to what democratic legitimacy requires regarding private regulation. A few basic principles, such as participation, transparency, and accountability, however dominate the academic discourse on those issues (Hachez and Wouters, 2011; Fuchs et al., 2009). Indeed, it is argued that wide participation of the affected actors is crucial (De Búrca, 2008), and that the rule-making process may not be captured by powerful interests. As Black (2008) argues, institutions in 'polycentric regulatory regimes', characterized by the meeting of a plurality of actors seeking to play a governance role, may have a crucial role to play in guaranteeing participation and limiting the possibilities of capture. The actions of private actors may lack transparency towards the public (see Hale, 2008) and are not usually controlled by systems of checks and balances as are those of public authorities (World Trade Organization, 2009a, paras. 31 and 37).

In this context the issue of accountability mechanisms is equally of importance, as the public must be able to control the outcomes of the rule-making process (Freeman, 2000). An accountability relationship may be defined, in a general fashion, as a relationship 'in which an individual, group or other entity makes demands on an agent to report on his or her activities, and has the power to impose costs on the agent' (Keohane, 2006, p. 77). Such accountability relationships are well-determined in the traditional administrative hierarchy, but they are much less clear in private governance arrangements. First of all, private actors often exercise regulatory activities in the absence of a clear legal mandate (Scott, 2002), which raises questions about the real responsibilities and possible liability of private actors in the exercise of their regulatory roles (Cafaggi, 2005). Most importantly, whereas public authorities have to justify their actions before their citizens according to a legal framework setting limits to their competences, it is rather unclear who is entitled to hold private regulators into account for their regulatory activities, what interests they really represent and defend, and where they are allowed to go (see Cohen and Sabel, 2005). In that respect, Black (1996) notes, for example, that courts have been puzzled when it came to judicially reviewing private regulations as the distinction between private and public law, and hence the scope of action of the court, sits uneasily between the private status of the actor and the public repercussions of its regulatory activities.

In general, the fact that regulatory functions are progressively being transferred from the state to a mix of functionally differentiated public and private arrangements also transforms the nature of the relationship between the regulator and the regulatees. Whereas the accountability of public actors in a traditional democracy can be regressed to electoral, judicial or administrative mechanisms available to a limited body of citizens, accountability channels in private governance arrangements may be much more diffuse and erratic, for example, as they use the levers of the consumer or financial markets (see Donahue and Nye, 2002). While electoral, judicial or disciplinary mechanisms may give rise to well-defined sanctions at the end of a reasoned assessment process, accountability mechanisms in private (and especially market-based) regulatory settings, such as product boycotts or naming and shaming campaigns orchestrated by watchdog NGOs, are also much more difficult to assess and do not always respond to the democratic exigencies of due process.[16] Likewise, participation in private regulatory settings tends to become more complex given the size and elusiveness of the public concerned, no longer composed of 'citizens', but of 'stakeholders', that is, the ensemble of people affected by or holding a stake in a (regulatory) activity. In matters of food safety, the pool of persons which could hypothetically claim participation rights could soon become limitless, since it would include economic actors such as producers and retailers, those economically and environmentally affected by those economic activities, such as the people working in the food industry or living near its factories, and also consumers of food products, that is, the entire world population. All these elements contribute to a lot of uncertainty over the legitimacy of global governance, and of private standards in particular.

5. A LEGAL ANALYSIS OF PRIVATE STANDARDS IN LIGHT OF WTO RULES

In light of the above, certain countries have for some time raised the issue of private standards before the SPS Committee (World Trade Organization, 2005b, pp. 6 ff.) and requested that measures be taken in order to reduce the exclusionary and other trade-restrictive effects of private standards (World Trade Organization, 2009b, para. 6; Stanton, this volume). Such submissions notably argued that:

> The SPS Agreement recognizes the role of the International Standard Setting Bodies (OIE, Codex Alimentarius and the IPPC) as the only authorities for establishing SPS standards. However, the proliferation of standards developed by private interest groups without any reference to the SPS Agreement or consultation with national authorities is a matter of concern and presents numerous challenges to small vulnerable economies. These standards are perceived as being in conflict with the letter and spirit of the SPS Agreement, veritable barriers to trade (which the very SPS Agreement discourages) and having the potential to cause confusion, inequity and lack of transparency. (World Trade Organization, 2007b, p. 1)

As many of the private standards in question are more demanding than public regulations abiding by the disciplines of the SPS Agreement, the conflict would supposedly have to be solved by granting primacy to public regulation over private standards. Article 13 of the SPS Agreement (see above) is cited as particularly relevant to that effect, although it needs to be clarified (World Trade Organization, 2005b). The latter provision's scope is indeed unclear since the SPS Agreement was drafted in a time when private standards had not yet invaded the market. Arguably, the disconnect between the underlying assumptions of the SPS Agreement and today's global food market reality, and the anguish that the issue of private standards causes to countries eager to export their products to the wealthy west, is reflected in this account of a statement by the Argentine representative to the SPS Committee:

> The representative of Argentina recalled that the international community had generated international agreements to ensure that trade standards were not unnecessarily stringent so as to act as barriers to international trade and countries had devoted time and financial and human resources to attend all the international meetings where standards were discussed, developed and implemented. If the private sector was going to have unnecessarily restrictive standards affecting trade and countries had no forum where to advocate some rationalization of these standards, twenty years of discussions in international fora would have been wasted. The representative of Argentina was convinced that the rational and legal aspects of these kinds of regulations had to be addressed.' (World Trade Organization, 2005b, p. 7)

However, the question of the applicability of the SPS Agreement to private standardization schemes is a thorny issue which has not yet been settled authoritatively, notably by the Dispute Settlement Body. Article 1.1 of the SPS Agreement does not explicitly exclude private standards adopted for health and safety issues from its scope, even though no definite determination has yet been made in this respect. Also, the actual obligations of WTO members under Article 13 are still unclear, notably as to what the phrase 'reasonable measures [. . .] to ensure that non-governmental entities within their territories [. . .] comply with the relevant provisions of this Agreement' might concretely encompass, and as to what kind of organizations the phrase 'non-governmental entities' refers (Wouters and Geraets 2012).

The vagueness of Articles 1.1 and 13 of the SPS Agreement and their public international law nature has led some authors to consider that the SPS Agreement is not applicable to private standards and, as such, cannot be used as a lever to discipline them (Henson, 2008; Chia-Hui Lee, 2006). The EU, for instance, has relied on the purely private character of such standards to argue before the SPS Committee that:

> Even if these standards, in certain cases, exceeded the requirements of EC SPS standards, the EC could not object to them as they did not conflict with EC legislation. [. . .] The representative of the European Communities encouraged developing countries, particularly LDCs, to discuss this issue with non-governmental organizations since, in many respects, the [private standards'] requirements reflected their concerns. The current accumulation of such standards constituted an opportunity to emphasize the value of official standards, since private standards were often much more demanding. (World Trade Organization, 2005b)

A report on those issues commissioned by the UK for presentation to the SPS Committee concluded on the other hand that 'private standard-setting bodies are non-governmental entities under Article 13 of the SPS Agreement', and that 'WTO Members appear to have positive obligations in relation to making sure that non-governmental actors do not act inconsistently with the SPS Agreement' (World Trade Organization, 2007c, pp. 54–55). Other authors have also noted that the effectiveness of the SPS Agreement and an analogous interpretation of Article 4 and the Code of Good Practice of the TBT Agreement could command that Article 1.1 and Article 13 of the SPS Agreement be interpreted as applying to the trade effects of private standards when they related to health and safety issues in food products (Casey, 2007).

The Secretariat of the SPS Committee accordingly pointed out that an avenue for disciplining private standards outside of the SPS Agreement framework would be the TBT Agreement, which covers food standards that relate to issues other than human, animal and plant health and which enjoins members to take reasonable measures so that non-governmental bodies would comply with its annexed Code of Good Practice for the Preparation, Adoption and Application of Standards. The Secretariat indeed notes that private food safety standards often contain elements, such as social and environmental requirements, which fall outside the scope of the SPS Agreement, but well within the scope of the TBT Agreement (World Trade Organization, 2007a, p. 5).

Until recently, the SPS Committee seemed to have taken account of the limits of a legalistic analysis of the impact of private standards on international trade, but it is now poised to take on the matter from a more practical standpoint (World Trade Organization, 2008a, p. 10). In 2008 the Secretariat of the SPS Committee proposed a multi-track approach to solving the private standards issue. It suggested putting a 'group of interested Members' in charge of monitoring private standards developments, reporting to the SPS Committee, requesting the organization of information sessions about private standards, and so forth. In 2011, the SPS Committee decided on a number of soft private standards-related 'actions', and notably resolved to develop a working definition of private standards relevant to the discussions in the framework of the SPS Agreement, and to increase information, communication and sensitization about such private standards (see World Trade Organization, 2011 and Stanton, this volume).

To date, no WTO member has decided to use the 'hard way', by way of WTO dispute settlement or otherwise, of trying to enforce the SPS Agreement against private standards directly, or against another member harbouring private standard-setters. Interested countries are, however, increasingly vocal about their perceived need for something to be done about it so as to preserve the balance of interests and obligations contained in the SPS Agreement (World Trade Organization, 2009b; Stanton, this volume).

6. THE WAY FORWARD: HOW TO RECONCILE PRIVATE FOOD SAFETY STANDARDS AND INTERNATIONAL TRADE LAW?

The discussions concerning the applicability of WTO disciplines to private standards have so far resulted in an empty shell. There is uncertainty as to whether the scope of the SPS Agreement encompasses private standards, and there is uncertainty as to what leverage the SPS disciplines could have in order to reduce the trade-restrictive effects of private standards. The growing pervasiveness of private standards in the face of the repeated assertions that they run counter to the liberalization and harmonization objectives of the SPS Agreement arguably challenges the suitability and relevance of the latter in addressing the trade-offs that now exist between food safety issues and free trade objectives. The fact that the enforcement of the SPS Agreement against private standards is almost never advocated, and the fact that the SPS Committee seems to address the issue by trying to reduce trade barriers caused by private standards by soft methods also tend to confirm this diagnosis (World Trade Organization, 2008a, p. 4).[17]

6.1. Towards a New Configuration for the Global Regulation of Free Trade and Food Safety: the Role of Private Standards in Global Governance and New Policy Arrangements

At this juncture the question can be raised as to what strategy should be put in place in order to facilitate trade in food products while acknowledging the new realities in private food safety standard-setting. The starting point of our reflection is that the most vocal WTO members in the current debate on private standards tend to have an overtly negative view of private standards, considering them redundant and restrictive of trade (World Trade Organization, 2009a, para. 29). Responses to a questionnaire that the Secretariat of the SPS Committee circulated among its members showed that 'some respondents were categorical that private standards could not facilitate compliance with international standards', and that '[a] number of members [were of the opinion] that there was no evidence that private standards contributed to the compliance of official SPS requirements, and it was noted that most private standards did not correctly address SPS issues' (World Trade Organization, 2008a, pp. 8 and 9). Even though it may appear that the scope of the survey was perhaps not entirely clear to all respondents (Stanton, this volume), the views expressed therein clearly reflect a strictly public approach to food safety, on the basis of the international standards identified in the SPS Agreement. This would imply that any conflict or overlap between applicable public and private standards should result in the former trumping the latter. We hold that this view might be misguided for a number of reasons.

First of all, even in the absence of private standards, the SPS Agreement would in any case probably not be an appropriate instrument for balancing the objectives of free trade and food safety. Next to the fact that the current international system has so far proven rather weak in harmonizing and disciplining domestic measures (Cafaggi, this volume), it could be argued that the focus on scientific justification, and the quasi-legislative status given to Codex Alimentarius standards, potentially allow the free trade agenda to pre-empt food safety and other objectives and may, in the long run, hamper the democratic development of global food safety rules (see Kalderimis, 2004; Charnovitz, 1999–2000; Reich, 2004; Ewers, 2000). The proliferation of private food standards that go beyond the requirements of WTO-vetted Codex Alimentarius standards sharpens this tension and challenges even more the suitability of the SPS model for delivering high/required levels of food safety.

Secondly, as the SPS Committee itself recognizes, private standards also have trade-enhancing effects (World Trade Organization, 2009a, paras 38 ff.; Stanton, this volume). It could, for example, be argued that through their de facto binding effects and pro-active compliance mechanisms private standards generate several advantages. These include a contribution to the modernization of industry in developing countries, fostering foreign direct investment, helping to solve food safety issues in industrialized countries, helping compliant products receive access to higher priced markets and, where price-based competition is reduced, allowing producers to enter into more stable business relationships (Stanton, this volume; Organisation for Economic Co-operation and Development, 2006b, pp. 13 ff.). The fact that private standards hand a premium to safe and qualitative products should not be overlooked in this connection.

Thirdly, as argued above, private standards schemes offer a response to the growing awareness and demands of consumers for extra precautions in matters of food safety. The fact that such extra precautions had to be taken by the private sector may correspond to a decreasing reliance of consumers (at least in the EU – see Food and Agriculture Organization, 2007, p. 143) on public authorities in the field of food safety after the latter were not able to prevent the various food crises of the late 20th and early 21st centuries. In this regard, as indicated above, private standardization schemes seem to espouse a new generation of food laws emphasizing the duty of the food chain actors to cater for the safety of food products rather than focusing on the requirements that such products have to meet (Fulponi, 2007).

For all these reasons, private food standards can be said to potentially serve a useful purpose and, in any case, they are viewed as fairly effective in delivering high levels of food safety to consumers (Organisation for Economic Co-operation and Development, 2006a). It is now incontestable that private standards are decisively shaping the global regulatory environment for food products (Henson, 2008), to the point that certain 'producers [. . .] are simply not aware of international standards [identified in the SPS Agreement] and focus on meeting the private standards in their export markets' (World Trade Organization, 2009a, para. 20). In other words, 'private standards are here to stay' (Organisation for Economic Co-operation and Development, 2006a, p. 7) and, even more, 'food safety is expected to remain the most important private standard in the future' (Fulponi, 2006, p. 10).

If one accepts this preliminary conclusion, a sound strategy in addressing private standards would be to try to make them part of the solution by embedding them in new policy arrangements acceptable to all. Of course, the exclusionary effects of private standards, the proliferation of different types of private standards, and their legitimacy deficits are worrisome and need to be taken up. Those issues should be squarely addressed, but not at the expense of the level of food safety demanded by consumers, which could be the case if the SPS Agreement were to be applied too strictly (see above).

Does all of this imply that the SPS Agreement should be modified in order to take account of the private standards phenomenon? This option is sometimes brought up, but the practical possibility of doing so seems to be very weak at present (World Trade Organization, 2007c, p. 95). The diverging views of different groups of countries make it quite unlikely that a consensual solution will be found. What stance should WTO members then take to try to reconcile the different views and issues under consideration?

One could recommend that all actors acknowledge the potential of private standards as governance tools, while working to address their problematic sides, namely their exclusionary socio-economic effects in specific countries and between producers, the lack of transparency due to the proliferation of different systems and their legitimacy deficits. In other words, major national players and the WTO should not make a case against private standards as a matter of principle, but should design, in partnership with the other relevant actors, strategies to bring private standards in line with the free trade objective, without jeopardizing the search for optimal levels of food safety. In a way, the Secretariat of the SPS Committee seems to be exploring this path in a recent note (World Trade Organization, 2008a), but certain factions of member states seem resolute that the logics of the SPS Agreement must be preserved and continue to govern the global food safety regime (World Trade Organization, 2009b). The same debates are also taking place in other relevant international organizations, such as the OIE and Codex Alimentarius, further evidencing the resistance of certain states to any compromise regarding private standards (Stanton, this volume).

The approach sketched in this chapter draws from the 'new' and 'reflexive' governance schools (see Teubner, 1983; Van Tatenhove et al., 2000; Karkkainen et al., 2000; Sabel et al., 2000), according to which, put briefly, states should not attempt to shape all aspects of life in society through prescriptive legislation, but should rather place themselves in a position of 'catalyst', 'facilitator' or 'orchestrator' of regulations which are set by the (public or private) actors which are most effective, representative, competent and knowledgeable in the relevant field (Abbott and Snidal, 2009b). This includes schemes like self-regulation, third-party standardization and certification and delegated regulation. This would allegedly provide for more dynamic regulation. In doing so, public authorities should 'steer' and 'channel' the effects of those decentralized regulatory initiatives toward the public interest, the defence of which is their very mission (see Abbot and Snidal, 2009b; Aman, 2000–2001; Stewart, 2003; Lobel, 2004). This implies capitalizing on the positive effects of private standards while taking measures to correct their shortcomings.

This new governance model can apply to the case of private standards in the food safety and free trade regulatory contexts. Private standards are effective in setting high degrees of food safety, which responds to consumer demands and is arguably in the public interest, while at the same time they create trade and development problems and raise doubts as to their legitimacy. The relevant public and private actors should thus reflect on:

a. how the positive contribution of private standards to the food safety agenda can be enhanced, while
b. tackling the negative effects of private standards on trade and development
c. rationalizing the erratic proliferation of private standards schemes
d. bringing more legitimacy into private standards schemes.

These four issues should constitute the axes of the private standards strategy of all relevant actors, be they the WTO and the other relevant international organizations, the national authorities or private actors in the food chain.

6.2. Acknowledging and Fostering the Positive Contribution of Private Standards

With regard to point (a) above, Bernstein and Hannah (2008, p. 604) argue that 'WTO rules should not be developed that militate against the adoption of [private food safety standards]. Neither should the WTO let itself be pulled into the political game of overtly deciding which standards are authoritative'. The implications of such a recommendation for the WTO are multiple.

First, it entails that one ought to revisit the strategy which designates the Codex Alimentarius Commission and other international organizations for setting standards as global reference points for public food safety regulations across the world. The composition and standard-setting processes of the Codex Alimentarius Commission seem to indicate that the organization is de facto skewed toward business interests (see for example, Victor, 1999–2000, pp. 887 ff.; Braithwaite and Drahos, 2000, pp. 401 and 408). In the same vein, the focus on science, which is at the heart of the SPS Agreement and of the operation of the Codex Alimentarius Commission (which is an expert-based agency of the FAO and WHO), may have to be complemented by other guiding principles. Quite a number of SPS measures, on top of having scientific (or precautionary) foundations, may also be taken for moral or cultural reasons, which should not be disputable per se (Echols, 2001), especially if such measures are adopted following a democratic debate.

In this connection, it would seem appropriate that a more fundamental debate be introduced in the SPS Committee on what kinds of standards are really appropriate, and notably what role private standards could play in the food safety/free trade conundrum. Notably, these actors should consider launching a debate on the role and added value of Codex Alimentarius standards in relation to the private standards phenomenon, as well as on the well-founded character of the option to base harmonization strategies on scientific justifications. Indeed, science, despite its aura of objectivity, has been argued to be a poor guide for judging the appropriateness of food safety measures, which rely on many more factors (Winickoff et al., 2005). In this regard, it comes as no surprise that the case-law of the WTO Dispute Settlement Body has been quite hesitant on the question of the value of scientific evidence for deciding on SPS Agreement disputes (Gruszczynski, 2010). Such a strategy would, however, imply entirely revisiting the foundations of the SPS Agreement, and the debate might therefore be stillborn given the entrenched positions of the members of the SPS Committee on these issues, and the insistence of some that the SPS Agreement be applied and enforced as such.

Secondly, it can be argued that the success and level of trust enjoyed by private standards among consumers and retailers come from the fact that such standard-setting schemes are dynamic and seek to stick to consumer demands as quickly and closely as possible (see Henson and Humphrey, 2009). This is notably due to the fact that food safety standards or environmental standards may be one of the elements which differentiate products in the eyes of consumers. A constant emulation between private food safety standards can therefore be deemed to exist, and a 'ratcheting up' of the general level of food safety may be thought to ensue. In this regard, various authors have underlined the potentially positive effects of the 'competition for a regulatory share' which may take place among various regulatory actors, notably in terms of effectiveness and legitimacy (see, for example, Black, 2009). In addition, the liability rules encouraging actors in the food chain to take all possible precautions in matters of food safety oblige the latter to constantly follow evolutions in the field of food safety in order to make sure that their standardization schemes are as up to date and protective as possible.

In sum, this chapter argues, along with other authors, that states should, in terms of the substance of global food governance, leave a 'transnational regulatory space' (Bernstein and Hannah, 2008) to the actors of the food chain and buttress the substantive quality of private standards, for example, by means of responsibility rules. The setting of minimal food safety requirements to prevent possible 'races to the bottom' is also recommended. It could be argued that this 'reflexive' model may have better chances of delivering high levels of food safety than the current public model. It should be reckoned that such extended leeway conceded to private actors could at times lead to abuses or ill-suited standards. This is why certain safeguards should be put in place in order to monitor the substance of private standards. Such safeguards should allow concerned actors to challenge the relevance of a standard before an independent body. This independent adjudicatory body could be the WTO Dispute Settlement Body, though the latter might be suspected to have a trade bias in its decision-making (Reich, 2004). On the other hand, setting up new multilateral organizations can be costly and ineffective.

6.3. Mitigating the Negative Effects of Private Standards

Private standards generate exclusionary effects on the producers of certain countries (cf. point (b) above). The evidence on this is still piecemeal but is nonetheless growing. The exclusionary effects of private standards normally only apply to producers that are not able to comply, but on the other hand, private standards may have positive effects for compliant producers. Studies have shown that exclusionary effects are more likely to hit smallholders in developing countries, which do not have the resources necessary to bear the cost of compliance, such as the upgrade of their facilities or product certification fees. A major contributing effort should thus be made by public and private actors to mitigate those exclusionary effects, for example, by providing information, financial aid and technical support to those excluded stakeholders (Organisation for Economic Co-operation and Development, 2006b; Henson and Humphrey, 2009). This solution has already often been brought forward, and it is beginning to be applied by private standardization schemes themselves. GLOBALG.A.P. has, for example, developed a 'Smallholder Involvement' programme, which notably allows for small producers to obtain 'group certification' of their product in order to spread the costs of the procedure.[18] One could also imagine that private and public actors would provide funding or grant discounts to help small producers in developing countries meet certain compliance requirements.

More generally it can be recommended that a global fund be created which provides financial and technical assistance to producers to comply with different standards. Such an initiative could be initiated by a joint effort from national authorities in co-operation with the major private actors in the global food market. From the last survey conducted by the SPS Committee, it appears that a number of financial, technical and informational[19] initiatives aimed at helping weaker actors comply with private standards are emerging (World Trade Organization, 2009a, paras. 48–49).

Besides providing financial and technical assistance to comply with private standards, initiatives should be developed in order to provide up-to-date information on different private standards and what they aim to achieve, on how to apply for certification, on the procedure for certification, the costs of certification, and so on. The SPS Committee has also emphasized the importance of good information for producers to be able to comply with private standardization schemes. This is why it has proposed in a recent note that the group of interested members request, when necessary, that information sessions be organized with private standard-setters. This suggestion was equally encouraged by exporting states (World Trade Organization, 2008a, pp. 5 and 11). GlobalG.A.P. and other standard-setters have, in this connection, already attended SPS Committee meetings (SPS Committee, 2007). This information provision and diffusion strategy should be developed further. In a joint effort, GTZ and the World Bank have launched the Trade Standards Practitioners Network (TSPN network) which centralizes information about standards with the aim of 'integrating developing country producers into the value chain'.[20] This initiative could be expanded into the development of a genuine independent private standards observatory controlled by a board of independent experts, including academics.

6.4. The Proliferation of Private Standard-setting Schemes and the need for Harmonization and Cooperation

A specific concern expressed in relation to private standards is that several different schemes may exist on the same market, and producers might have to comply with all of them individually in order to sell their products to all retailers on the market, thereby multiplying compliance costs. Moreover, this multiplication of private standards may be puzzling in the cases where such standards contradict either each other or the legislation in force on a market (UN Conference on Trade and Development, 2009). This proliferation of different schemes is precisely what the SPS Agreement seeks to combat through its harmonization strategy.

It makes sense that private standards would have to comply with the applicable laws. The fact that in some cases such standards go beyond the exigencies of local (or international) law (World Trade Organization, 2009a, para. 24) should not be disfavoured per se as this feature is part of the improvement dynamics of the private regulation model. A more difficult issue arises when private standards contradict each other, as there often is no conflict mechanism to determine which standard must prevail over the other. To address the issue of the discrepancies between various standards, private standard-setters have already taken action. Some standard-setters are involved in processes of 'benchmarking' standards against one another, allowing producers which comply with one standard to be deemed compliant with all the other standards against which that standard is benchmarked. Examples include GLOBALG.A.P.[21] and the Global Food Safety Initiative (GFSI).[22] Although they are showing certain limits, and standard owners may at times be reluctant to use the flexibility required by the benchmarking exercise (UN Conference on Trade and Development, 2009), these initiatives are an important step forward in mitigating the negative trade effects of private standards. They should, however, not be pushed to the point where all standards would be considered as equivalent. Conversely, the Codex Alimentarius Commission supports the view that its own standards should be the benchmark of all other standardization initiatives (Heilandt, 2009). We believe, in turn, that this could result in eliminating the incentive that private standardization schemes have to compete with each other for higher levels of food safety. In the cases of conflict not solved by benchmarking processes, some sort of adjudicatory body could intervene and apply conflict rules defined in advance.

6.5. Guaranteeing the Legitimacy of Private Standards

As to issue (c) above, one must note that the legitimacy of a regulatory measure is, next to its effectiveness, an important component of the 'validity' of such a norm, understood as the recognition, in a certain regulatory regime, that the norm in question may have the regulatory effects that its authors intended to give it (Ost and Van De Kerchove, 2002). If public authorities are going to co-operate with global private actors in the field of food safety, it is quite natural that they would require these actors to be legitimate and to act in a legitimate way. Assessing the legitimacy of domestic public regulation does not normally pose insoluble problems for lawyers. In this regard, the constitutional rules of the concerned legal order are of particular relevance. Pushing the search for legitimacy one step further, the democratic character of a regulatory order is a particularly important factor as it reflects the responsiveness and accountability of such order toward the 'public' (see section 4.4 above) (Hachez and Wouters, 2011). There are reasons to believe that the democratic ideal should also apply – *mutatis mutandis* – to global governance initiatives involving private actors (see, for example, De Búrca, 2008; Meidinger, 2008; Scholte, 2008; Cohen and Sabel, 2005).

In global governance settings, where no democratic constitution allocates power and authority (Brunkhorst, 2002), and where regulatory functions are the shared responsibility of national, international, public and private actors alike, the legitimizing framework becomes blurred and the prospect of a global democratic order is far off (see Held, 1995). It would therefore be useful if all actors concerned with food products reach a consensus on what they understand by 'legitimacy' in that context. This chapter does not intend to add to the debate as to what the notion of (democratic) legitimacy should encompass in global governance settings. The literature on the subject is rich (see, for example, Buchanan and Keohane, 2006; De Búrca, 2008; Bernstein and Cashore, 2007; Bernstein, 2008; Wallner, 2008; Black, 2008; Zürn, 2004; Risse, 2006; Dingwerth, 2007; Hachez and Wouters, 2011) and in various ways seeks to make the concept revolve around certain principles such as the inclusive and egalitarian participation of all interested parties, the transparency of the decision-making process, the accountability of the decision-makers toward the relevant public, and more generally the search for the public interest (see, for example, Fuchs et al., 2009; Henson and Humphrey, 2009). The application of the legitimizing principles agreed upon by the relevant actors of food safety regulation could then be promoted among, or imposed upon, private standard-setters, for example, through the use of a 'Code of Practice' for the development and application of standards, on the model of the Code annexed to the TBT Agreement.

An interesting initiative in this regard is the ISEAL Alliance,[23] which is an independent membership association which includes several leading multi-stakeholder and independent private standardization initiatives committed to strengthening and promoting 'credible standards and conformity assessment by developing capacity building tools to strengthen members' activities and by promoting credible voluntary social and environmental certification as a legitimate policy instrument in global trade and development' (ISEAL Alliance, 2010). Although the ISEAL Alliance focuses on social and environmental standards, this example is very relevant to this chapter, as food safety standards also often contain social and environmental components, and social and environmental private standards can also be analyzed as potential barriers to trade. The main instrument in ISEAL's policy is its Code of Good Practice for Setting Social and Environmental Standards (ISEAL Alliance, 2010). Application of the Code of Good Practice by private standard-setters is thus supposed to result in credible and legitimate standards.[24] The Code of Good Practice is based on the internationally recognized ISO rules for developing standards, on the TBT code of good practice, and on the TBT and SPS agreements. Harmonization of differing standards and the development of international standards to mitigate the trade-restrictive effects of standards is also an important component of the code.

The initiative of the ISEAL Alliance constitutes a reference for private standards initiatives in terms of standard design. The Marine Stewardship Council is 'certified' by the ISEAL Alliance while other initiatives such as GLOBALG.A.P. are trying to follow some of its tenets (Greenpeace, 2010). Although the idea of a 'one-size-fits-all' solution should be treated with caution, the idea of 'benchmarking' private standardization schemes for legitimacy is, in our view, quite promising. This could be driven by national or international public authorities, and enable them to help private standards become a more legitimate policy instrument to tackle global challenges. Public oversight of private standards initiatives could thus enhance the legitimacy of private standards.

7. CONCLUSION: THE NEED FOR A PLURALISTIC FOOD SAFETY GOVERNANCE

Increasingly, private standards are becoming important policy instruments for addressing global challenges. This chapter focused on private standards in the context of global food safety governance and linked that issue to international trade law. It argued in favour of a pluralistic view of global regulation in which all leading actors, such as developed and developing countries, the World Trade Organization and the other relevant international organizations, public and private standard-setters and major actors in the food chain, have to bring part of the solution. In this regard, Smith (2009) convincingly argues that public and private standards, often viewed as working at cross-purposes, may in fact prove quite complementary. In addition, none of the regulatory actors possesses all the capacities and competences to take on single-handedly the challenges posed by the regulation of global issues such as food safety or international trade. At the same time, in a global governance context characterized by the absence of institutionalized checks and balances, a conjunction of all regulatory forces allows for a reduction of the risk that a global issue involving the public good be captured by the particular interests encapsulated in intergovernmental horse-trading, business profit-seeking or NGO activism (Abbott and Snidal, 2009a).

We further argued that private standard-setters (most importantly large western retailer groups) have now come to dominate the food safety regulatory environment. As a result, private standards have become the prime determinants of access to most western food markets. In light of these evolutions, the logic behind the SPS Agreement appears somewhat flawed, and the latter is increasingly regarded as having lost its grip on the global food safety regulatory environment, which now largely develops independently from the rules of world trade. This disconnect has many negative consequences, most notably the erratic proliferation of different public and private regulatory schemes and the potential exclusion of the weaker actors of the food chain from the lucrative western markets. In addition, the legitimacy of private standards in regulating issues as important as food safety is questioned. In order to re-equilibrate the relationship between the objective of free trade and the food safety regulatory environment, several recommendations addressed to public and private regulators alike were put forward. These recommendations derive from the 'new' or 'reflexive' governance scholarship, and involve the public authorities (WTO and members) relying on the assets of private food safety standards and focusing on correcting their downsides.

Firstly, public actors need to acknowledge the effectiveness of private standard-setters in delivering high levels of food safety and generally leave more space for private actors to define the substance of food safety regulation while buttressing the quality of those regulatory initiatives with 'framework' rules such as liability regimes or minimal protection thresholds. Secondly, public and private actors should focus on reducing the exclusionary effects that private food safety standards may have on the weaker actors in the food chain, and reduce the discrepancies and contradictions between private standards. Practically, this may induce the creation of a global fund for technical and financial assistance in order to comply with private standards, information and capacity building programs via a private standards observatory, the design of mechanisms to harmonize and benchmark private standards, and the adoption of rules to solve conflicts between contradictory standards. Finally, public and private actors should ensure the legitimacy of private food standards by identifying the minimal features of legitimate standards and applying them to private standardization schemes, for example, through the promotion and implementation of a code of good practice.

A number of private standard-setters have demonstrated their willingness to address these concerns in a pro-active and constructive way, by providing information, by setting up smallholder involvement programs, or by issuing codes of good practice for the development of standards. A more elaborate and systematic public policy towards private standards might address these issues further and enable private standards to play an important role in new policy arrangements to address global challenges.

NOTES

1 This chapter draws on a paper prepared for the project 'Managing Biosafety and Biodiversity in a Global World' funded by the European Commission (DG External Relations) within the framework of the pilot-program on Transatlantic Methods for Handling Global Challenges. The authors thank the participants of the Workshop on 'Managing Biosafety and Biodiversity in a Global World' organized by the University of California, Berkeley (11–12 December 2008) for their comments and insights. A subsequent version of this paper was presented at the Postgraduate Legal Research Workshop on 'Transnational Regulation of Food Safety and Quality – Issues of Harmonisation, Diversity and Legitimacy', UCD Dublin, 4–5 December 2009. The useful comments of the participants to the workshop are acknowledged, with special thanks to Colin Scott and Donal Casey.

2 In this volume Cafaggi offers a description of the way networks of contracts pervading the supply chain are now partially regulating the issue of food safety.

3 Several international initiatives are being developed in order to make private standards more professional and efficient. The growth figures of many private standards initiatives have been consistently high during the last decade. The global market for Marine Stewardship Council-labelled products, for example, grew in 2008 by nearly 100 per cent to reach a retail value of close to 1 billion USD. The number of companies who were awarded MSC Chain of Custody certification and hence we are able to supply MSC material within an audited and traceable supply chain grew to nearly 600 in total and includes major retailers in the United States and Europe (Marine Stewardship Council Annual Report 2007/2008, available at www.msc.org/). Major national (GTZ) and multilateral (World Bank) organizations are supporting the development and professionalization of private standards, and in this regard have, for example, established the Trade Standards Practitioners Network (TSPN) (see generally http://tradestandards.org/en/).

4 Stanton (this volume) offers an interesting descriptive table (Table 9.2) of the different types of standards.

5 See however Henson and Humphrey (2009, pp. 3 ff.), who offer a very detailed analysis of the various types, forms and processes of private standards.

6 Food products have indeed been the source of numerous high profile health and safety crises in the last decades, which have made durable impressions on consumers: mad cow disease, foot and mouth disease, dioxin in poultry meat, lethal bacteria in US spinach and most recently the presence of melamine in Chinese powdered milk. See, for example, Ansell and Vogel, 2006.

7 Foodborne illnesses are defined as diseases, usually either infectious or toxic in nature, caused by agents that enter the body through the ingestion of food. According to the

World Health Organization (2007), every person is potentially at risk of catching a foodborne illness.

8 This is, however, only true to some extent, as supermarkets are of course not willing to suggest that food products sold in their stores are 'more' or 'less' safe than other products that they sell. The official discourse from supermarkets is therefore that all their products are safe (see Havinga, 2006, p. 528). This may be why private food safety standards tend to be business to business (B2B) standards. See, for further elaboration, the distinction made by Henson and Humphrey (2008) between 'risk management standards' (among which food safety standards) and 'product differentiation standards'.

9 UK Food Safety Act 1999. Section 21 (available at www.legislation.gov.uk/ukpga/1990/lb/section/21), which reads as follows: 'it shall be a defence for the person charged to prove that he took all reasonable precautions and exercised all due diligence to avoid the commission of the offence by himself or by a person under his control'.

10 Regulation (EC) No. 178/2002 of the European Parliament and of the Council of 28 January 2002 laying down the general principles and requirements of food law, establishing the European Food Safety Authority and laying down procedures in matters of food safety, *O.J.* 1 Feb. 2002, L31/1. See Article 17(1): 'Food and feed business operators at all stages of production, processing and distribution within the businesses under their control shall ensure that foods or feeds satisfy the requirements of food law which are relevant to their activities and shall verify that such requirements are met.'

11 The full definition, contained under No. 1 of Annex A of the SPS Agreement, is:
'Sanitary or phytosanitary measure – Any measure applied:
(a) to protect animal or plant life or health within the territory of the Member from risks arising from the entry, establishment or spread of pests, diseases, disease-carrying organisms or disease-causing organisms;
(b) to protect human or animal life or health within the territory of the Member from risks arising from additives, contaminants, toxins or disease-causing organisms in foods, beverages or feedstuffs;
(c) to protect human life or health within the territory of the Member from risks arising from diseases carried by animals, plants or products thereof, or from the entry, establishment or spread of pests; or
(d) to prevent or limit other damage within the territory of the Member from the entry, establishment or spread of pests.
Sanitary or phytosanitary measures include all relevant laws, decrees, regulations, requirements and procedures including, *inter alia*, end product criteria; processes and production methods; testing, inspection, certification and approval procedures; quarantine treatments including relevant requirements associated with the transport of animals or plants, or with the materials necessary for their survival during transport; provisions on relevant statistical methods, sampling procedures and methods of risk assessment; and packaging and labelling requirements directly related to food safety.'
In the wide range of SPS measures, this chapter focuses particularly on measures which concern food safety.

12 SPS measures concerning animal health and zoonoses should be based on the standards developed by the International Office of Epizootics, and SPS measures concerning plant health should be based on the standards developed in the framework of the International Plant Protection Convention. International standards under the SPS Agreement may also encompass other standards developed by any other relevant international organization which is open for membership to all WTO Members 'as identified by the SPS Committee', that is, the body in charge of overseeing the functioning of the SPS Agreement. The SPS Committee has to date identified no other relevant organization.

13 This is unless the SPS Agreement were to be recognized as having direct effect. The WTO is neutral as to the direct effect of its rules, leaving it to its members to decide on the effects of the WTO agreements in their national legal orders. In the EU, WTO legal rules are in principle not considered as having direct effect (at least for the purpose of reviewing European Community law measures against WTO rules – see Hachez, 2008–2009; and World Trade Organization, 2007c, p. 10).

14 Certain authors, however, argue in favour of a more reasoned relationship between domestic regulations and international standards (see, although more in the context of the TBT Agreement, Howse, 2006, p. 383).

15 With regard to the situation in South America, see America, World Trade Organization, 2009b, para. 17. See also generally Chia-Hui Lee, 2006, pp. 25–27. It should be noted that some studies show that producers who are able to participate in the private standards schemes do reap socio-economic benefits from their participation (see Maertens and Swinnen, 4–5 November 2008).

16 In this respect, see the distinction between 'internal' and 'external' modes of accountability developed notably by Keohane (2003, pp. 141 ff.).

17 Members of the SPS Committee were asked the question, 'If the results of [a] study showed that in some specific cases private standards requirements exceed the international standards, what actions could the SPS Committee take?' The responses were summarized as follows: 'Several specific actions were proposed in response to this question. It was suggested that such results should be immediately published to ensure that not only the private standard-setting bodies but the public at large was made aware of the conclusions. Other suggestions included: analyzing the rationale and justification for such discrepancies and whether there was any discriminatory element (for example, if the private standards apply only on the basis of country of origin); determining whether there was any corresponding price compensation or whether the higher standards created an additional market opportunity; developing guidelines to governments regarding vigilance and control over private standards; meetings with the private standard-setting bodies; workshops with competent government authorities, consumer organizations and other relevant stakeholders; assistance to developing countries to comply with private standards; and requesting scientific justification of the private standard-setting bodies.' Most members, however, considered that a legal analysis of the relationship between the SPS Agreement and private standards would be "useful" or "essential"' (World Trade Organization, 2008a, p. 9).

18 See www.globalgap.org/cms/front_content.php?idcat = 70.

19 See, for example, the compendium of studies about private standards compiled by the Secretariat of the Standards and Trade Development Facility (World Trade Organization, 2008b). 'The Standards and Trade Development Facility (STDF) is a global program in capacity building and technical co-operation established by the Food and Agriculture Organization of the United Nations (FAO), the World Organization for Animal Health (OIE), the World Bank, the World Health Organization (WHO) and the World Trade Organization (WTO). The strategic aims of the STDF are: (i) to assist developing countries enhance their expertise and capacity to analyze and to implement international sanitary and phytosanitary (SPS) standards, improving their human, animal and plant health situation, and thus ability to gain and maintain market access; and (ii) to act as a vehicle for awareness raising on the importance of SPS issues, coordination among technical cooperation providers, the mobilization of funds, the exchange of experience and the dissemination of good practice in relation to the provision and receipt of SPS-related technical co-operation.' See www.standardsfacility.org/Overview.htm.

20 See http://tradestandards.org/en/index.aspx.

21 See, for GLOBALG.A.P.: www.globalgap.org/cms/front_content.php?idart = 44&idcat = 29&lang = 1&client = 1.

22 See http://www.mygfsi.com/.

23 In full, the International Social and Environmental Accreditation and Labelling Alliance. See www.isealalliance.org/. For an interesting study of ISEAL in relation to the debate about public accountability, see Courville, 2006, pp. 271–300.

24 Still, according to the preamble of the code, 'ISEAL does not consider its members to be the only bodies that can legitimately develop environmental and social standards and conformity assessment procedures. Legitimacy in this area of work is determined by the suitability of the processes through which these standards are developed, adopted and implemented. The ISEAL Code of Good Practice for Setting Social and Environmental Standards provides a benchmark to assist standard-setting organisations to improve how they develop social and environmental standards.'

REFERENCES

Abbott, K. and Snidal, D. (2009a), 'The governance triangle: regulatory standards institutions and the shadow of the state', in W. Mattli and N. Woods (eds), *The Politics of Global Regulation*, Princeton: Princeton University Press, pp. 44–88.

Abbott, K. and Snidal, D. (2009b), 'Strengthening international regulation through transnational new governance: overcoming the orchestration deficit', *Vanderbilt Journal of Transnational Law*, 42, 501–578.

Aman, A. C. (2000–2001), 'The limits of globalization and the future of administrative law: from government to governance', *Indiana Journal of Global Legal Studies*, 8, 379–400.

Ansell, C. and Vogel, D. (2006), *What's the Beef?*, Cambridge, US: M.I.T. Press.

Bartley, T. (2003), 'Certifying forests and factories: states, social movements, and the rise of private regulation in the apparel and forest products fields', *Politics and Society*, 31, 43–464.

Bernstein, S. (2005), 'Legitimacy in global environmental governance', *Journal of International Law and International Relations*, 1, 139–166.

Bernstein, S, (2008), 'Do intergovernmental and non-state governance institutions rest on different bases of legitimacy?', 1 June 2008, available at www.allacademic.com/meta/p254253_index.html (accessed 1 March 2011).

Bernstein, S. and Cashore, B. (2007), 'Can non-state global governance be legitimate? An analytical framework', *Regulation and Governance*, 1, 347–371.

Bernstein, S. and Hannah, E. (2008), 'Non-state global standard setting and the WTO: legitimacy and the need for regulatory space', *Journal of International Economic Law*, 11, 575–608.

Beierle, T. (1998), 'Public participation in environmental decisions: An evaluation framework using social goals', *Resources for the Future, Discussion Paper No. 99-06*, available at www.rff.org/Documents/RFF-DP-99-06.pdf (accessed 1 March 2011).

Black, J. (1996), 'Constitutionalising self-regulation', *Modern Law Review*, 59, 24–55.

Black, J. (2008), 'Constructing and contesting legitimacy and accountability in polycentric regulatory regimes', *Regulation and Governance*, 2, 137–164.

Black, J. (2009), 'Legitimacy and the competition for a regulatory share', *LSE Law Society and Economy Working Paper No. 14/2009*, available at http://eprints.lse.ac.uk/24559/1/WPS2009-14_Black.pdf. (accessed 1 March 2011).

Braithwaite, J. and Drahos, P. (2000), *Global Business Regulation*, Cambridge, UK: Cambridge University Press.

Brunkhorst, H. (2002), 'Globalising democracy without a state: strong public, weak public, global constitutionalism', *Millenium: Journal of International Studies*, 32, 675–690.

Buchanan, A. and Keohane, R.O. (2006), 'The legitimacy of global governance institutions', *Ethics and International Affairs*, 20, 405–437.

Büthe, T. (2008), 'The globalization of health and safety standards: delegation of regulatory authority in the SPS agreement of the 1994 agreement establishing the World Trade Organization', *Law and Contemporary Problems*, 71, 219–255.

Cafaggi, F. (2005), 'Gouvernance et responsabilité des régulateurs privés', *Revue Internationale de Droit Economique*, 19, 111–163.

Casey, D. (2007), 'Private food safety and quality standards and the WTO', *University College Dublin Law Review*, 7, 65–89.

Cashore, B. (2003), 'Legitimacy and the privatization of environmental governance: How non-state market-driven (NSMD) governance systems gain rule-making authority', *Governance – An International Journal of Policy and Administration*, 15, 503–529.

Cashore, B., Auld, G. and Newsom, D. (2004), *Governing Through Markets – Forest Certification and the Emergence of Non-state Authority*, New Haven and London: Yale University Press.

Center for Disease Control and Prevention (2007), 'Infectious Disease Information', 1 October 2007, available at www.cdc.gov/ncidod/diseases/food/index.htm (accessed 1 March 2011).

Charnovitz, S. (1999–2000), 'The supervision of health and biosafety regulation by World Trade Rules', *Tulane Environmental Law Journal*, 13, 271–302.

Chia-Hui Lee, G. (2006), 'Private food standards and their impacts on developing countries', *European Commission – DG Trade Unit G2 Paper*, available at http://trade.ec.europa.eu/doclib/docs/2006/november/tradoc_127969.pdf (accessed 1 March 2011).

Coglianese, C. and Jennifer N. (2001), 'Environmental management systems and the new policy agenda', in C. Coglianese and J. Nash (eds), *Regulating from the Inside: Can Environmental Management Systems Achieve Policy Goals?*, Washington D.C.: Resources for the Future, pp. 1–26.

Cohen, J. and Sabel, C. (2005), 'Global democracy?', *N.Y.U. Journal of International Law and Politics*, 37, 763–797.

Conroy, M. (2007), *Branded! How the Certification Revolution is Transforming Global Corporations*, Gabriola Island, BC: New Society Publishers.

Courville, S.(2006), 'Understanding NGO-based social and environmental regulatory systems: why we need new models of accountability', in M. Dowdle (ed.), *Public Accountability – Designs, Dilemmas and Experiences*, Cambridge, UK: Cambridge University Press, pp. 271–300.

De Búrca, G. (2008), 'Developing democracy beyond the state', *Columbia Journal of Transnational Law*, 46, 101–158.

Dingwerth, K. (2007), *The New Transnationalism: Private Transnational Governance and its Democratic Legitimacy*, Basingstoke: Palgrave Macmillan.

Donahue, J. and Nye, J. (eds) (2002) *Market-Based Governance – Supply Side, Demand Side, Upside, and Downside*, Washington D.C.: Brookings Institution Press.

Echols, M. A. (2001), *Food safety and the WTO – The interplay of Culture, Science and Technology*, London/The Hague/New York: Kluwer Law International.

Ewers, J. (2000), 'Dueling risk assessments: why the WTO and codex threaten U.S. food standards', *Environmental Law*, 30, 387–412.

Food and Agriculture Organization (2007), 'Private standards in the United States and European Union markets for fruit and vegetables – implications for developing countries', *FAO Commodity Studies No. 3*, available at ftp://ftp.fao.org/docrep/fao/010/a1245e/a1245e00.pdf (accessed 1 March 2011).

Freeman, J. (2000), 'The private role in public governance', *N.Y.U. Law Review*, 75, 543–675.

Fuchs, D., Kalfagianni, A. and Havinga, T. (2009), 'Actors in private food safety governance: the legitimacy of retail standards and multistakeholder initiatives with civil society participation', *Agriculture and Human Values*, 11 (online version).

Fulponi, L. (2006), 'Private voluntary standards in the food system: The perspective of major food retailers in OECD countries', *Food Policy*, 31, 1–13.

Fulponi, L. (2007), 'The globalization of private standards and the agri-food system', in J.F.M. Swinnen (ed.), *Global Supply Chains, Standards and the Poor: How the Globalization of Food System and Standards Affects Rural Development and Poverty*, Oxford and Cambridge: CAB International, pp. 5–18.

Fung, A. (2003), 'Making social markets: dispersed governance and corporate accountability', in J. Donahue and J. Nye, (eds), *Market-Based Governance – Supply Side, Demand Side, Upwards, and Downwards*, Washington, D.C.: Brookings Institution Press, pp. 145–172.

Gereffi, G., Garcia-Johnson, R. and Sasser, E. (July–August 2001), 'The NGO-industrial complex', *Foreign Policy*, 125, 56–65.

Greenpeace (January 2010), 'Assessment of the GLOBALG.A.P. aquaculture certification programme', available at www.greenpeace.de/fileadmin/gpd/user_upload/themen/meere/GlobalGapAssessmentBriefing20.05.10.pdf (accessed 1 March 2011).

Gruszczynski, L. (2010), 'The standard of review in international SPS trade disputes – Some new developments', Paper presented at the Third Biennial Conference of the ECPR Standing Group on Regulatory Governance on the theme 'Regulation in the Age of Crisis', UC Dublin (17–19 June 2010), available at http://regulation.upf.edu/dublin-10-papers/7F4.pdf (accessed 1 March 2011).

Hachez, N. (2008–2009), 'Case C-308/06, International Association of Independent Tanker Owners and Others: the requirement of direct effect in the judicial review of EU Law against international law', *Columbia Journal of European Law*, 15, 143–164.

Hachez, N. and Wouters, J. (2011), 'A glimpse at the democratic legitimacy of private standards – Assessing the public accountability of GLOBALG.A.P.', *Journal of International Economic Law*, 14, 677–710.

Hale, T. (2008), 'Transparency, accountability and global governance', *Global Governance*, 18, 73–94.

Haufler, V. (2003), 'New forms of governance: certification regimes as social regulations of the global market', in E. Meidinger, C. Elliott and G. Oesten (eds), *Social and Political Dimensions of Forest Certification*, Remagen-Oberwinter: Forstbuch, pp. 237–248.

Havinga, T. (2006), 'Private regulation of food safety by supermarkets', *Law and Policy*, 28, 515–533.

Heilandt, T. (2009), 'The relationship between the SPS committee and the international standard-setting organizations', Workshop organized by the Secretariat of the WTO, Geneva, 26 October 2009, presentation available at www.wto.org/english/tratop_e/sps_e/wkshop_oct09_e/codex_e.ppt (accessed 1 March 2011).

Held, D. (1995), *Democracy and the Global Order – From the Modern State to Cosmopolitan Governance*, Cambridge: Polity Press.

Henson, S. (2008), 'The role of public and private standards in regulating international food markets', *Journal of International Agricultural Trade and Development*, 4, 63–81.

Henson, S. and Humphrey, J. (2008), 'Understanding the complexities of private standards in global agri-food chains', 18 November 2008, available at www.ids.ac.uk/index.cfm?objectid=7AE181C1-F99E-834D-33B7CF2AEE885CB3 (accessed 1 March 2011).

Henson, S. and Humphrey, J. (2009), 'The impacts of private food safety standards on the food chain and on public standard-setting processes', Study prepared for the FAO/WHO, May 2009, available at www.fao.org/docrep/012/i1132e/i1132e00.pdf (accessed 1 March 2011).
Henson, S. and Reardon, T. (2005), 'Private agri-food standards: implications for food policy and the agri-food system', *Food Policy*, 30, 241–253.
Howse, R. (2006), 'A new device for creating international legal normativity: The WTO technical barriers to trade agreement and "international standards", in C. Joerges and E.-U. Petersmann (eds), *Constitutionalism, Multilevel Trade Governance and Social Regulation,* Oxford, Hart Publishing, pp. 383–396.
ISEAL Alliance (2007), 'Governmental recognition of international standards under the TBT and government procurement agreements', ISEAL – DFID Private Standards and Public Policies Conference, London, October 2007, available at www.isealalliance.org/sites/default/files/P005_ISEAL_Std-Setting _Code_v5.01.pdf (accessed 1 March 2011).
ISEAL Alliance (2009), 'Strategic plan 2009–2013', February 2009, available at www.isealalliance.org/ (accessed 1 March 2011).
ISEAL Alliance (2010), 'ISEAL code of good practice for setting social and environmental standards', June 2010, available at www.isealalliance.org/sites/default/files/P005_ISEAL_Std-Setting_Code_v5.01.pdf (accessed 1 March 2011).
Jänicke, M. (1990), *State Failure – The Impotence of Politics in Industrial Society,* Cambridge, Polity Press.
Kalderimis, D. (2004), 'Problems of WTO harmonization and the virtues of shields over swords', *Minnesota Journal of Global Trade*, 13, 305–352.
Karkkainen, B., Fung, A. and Sabel. C. (2000), 'After backyard environmentalism. Towards a performance-based regime of environmental regulation', *American Behavioral Scientist*, 44, 692–709.
Keohane, R.O. (2003), 'Global governance and democratic accountability', in David Held and Mathias Koenig-Archibugi (eds), *Taming Globalization – Frontiers of Governance*, Cambridge: Polity Press, pp. 130–159.
Keohane, R.O. (2006), 'Accountability in world politics', *Scandinavian Political Studies*, 29, 75–87.
Liefferink, D., Andersen, M.S. and Enevoldsen, M. (2000), 'Interpreting joint environmental policy-making: between deregulation and political modernization', in A. Mol, V. Lauber and D. Liefferink (eds), *The Voluntary Approach to Environmental Policy*, Oxford, Oxford University Press, 2000, pp. 10–31.
Lobel, O. (2004), 'The renew deal: the fall of regulation and the rise of governance in contemporary legal thought', *Minnesota Law Review*, 89, 342–470.
Lowenfeld, A. (2008), *International Economic Law*, 2nd ed, Oxford and New York: Oxford University Press.
Maertens, M. and Swinnen, J. (2008), 'Private standards, the organization of global supply chains, and their impact on developing countries', paper presented at the workshop 'Globalization, global governance and private standards', Leuven, 4–5 November 2008, on file with authors.
Maertens, M. and Swinnen, J. (2009), 'Food standards, trade and development', *Review of Business and Economics*, 54, 313–326.
Marceau, G. and Trachtman, J.P. (2002), 'The technical barriers to trade agreement, the sanitary and phytosanitary measures agreement, and the general agreement on tariffs and trade – A map of the World Trade

Organization law of domestic regulation of goods', *Journal of World Trade*, 36, 811–881.
Marx, A. (2008), 'Limits to non-state market regulation', *Regulation and Governance*, 2, 253–273.
Marx, A. (2011) 'Global governance and the certification revolution', in D. Levi-Faur (ed.) *Handbook of the Politics of Regulation*, Cheltenham: Edward Elgar.
Mechel, F., Meyer-Ohlendorf, N., Sprang, P. and Tarasofsky, R. (2006) *Public Procurement and Forest Certification: Assessing for Policy, Law, and International Trade*, 29 May 2006, Berlin: Eco-Logic in association with Chatham House, available at http://ecologic.eu/download/projekte/900-949/933/933_final_report.pdf (accessed 1 March 2011).
Meidinger, E. (2003), 'Forest certification as environmental law making by global civil society', in E. Meidinger, C. Elliott and G. Oesten (eds), *Social and Political Dimensions of Forest Certification,* Remagen-Oberwinter: Forstbuch, pp. 293–330.
Meidinger, E. (2008), 'Competitive supragovernmental regulation: how could it be democratic?', *Chicago Journal of International Law*, 8, 513–534.
Organisation for Economic Co-operation and Development (2006a), Directorate for Food, Agriculture and Fisheries, Committee on Agriculture, Working Party on Agricultural Policies and Markets, 'Final report on private standards and the shaping of the agro-food system', 31 July 2006, OECD Doc. No. AGR/CA/APM(2006)9/FINAL.
Organisation for Economic Co-operation and Development (2006b), Directorate for Food, Agriculture and Fisheries, Committee on Agriculture, Working Party on Agricultural Policies and Markets, 'Private standards schemes and developing country access to global value chains: challenges and opportunities emerging from four case studies', 3 August 2007, OECD Doc. No. AGR/CA/APM(2006)20/FINAL.
O'Rourke, D. (2003), 'Outsourcing regulation: analyzing nongovernmental systems of labor standards and monitoring', *Policy Studies Journal*, 31, 1–29.
Osborne, D. and Gaebler, T. (1992), *Reinventing Government*, New York: Basic Books.
Ost, F. and Van De Kerchove, M. (2002), *De la Pyramide au Réseau – Pour une Théorie Dialectique du Droit*, Brussels: Publications des Facultés Universitaires Saint-Louis.
Reich, A. (2004), 'The WTO as a law-harmonizing institution', *University of Pennsylvania Journal of International Economic Law*, 25, 321–382.
Risse, T. (2006) Transnational governance and legitimacy', in A. Benz and Y. Papadopoulos (eds), *Governance and Democracy: Comparing National, European and International Experiences*, London: Routledge.
Sabel, C., Fung, A. and O'Rourke, D. (2000), 'Ratcheting labor standards. Regulation for continuous improvement in the global workplace', *KSG Working Paper No. 00-010; Columbia Law and Economic Working Paper No. 185*, Columbia Law School, Pub. Law Research Paper No. 01-21, available at http://papers.ssrn.com/sol3/papers.cfm?abstract_id=262178 (accessed 1 March 2011).
Scholte, J.-A. (2008), 'Reconstructing contemporary democracy', *Indiana Journal of Global Legal Studies*, 15, 305–350.
Scott, C. (2002), 'Private regulation of the public sector: a neglected facet of contemporary governance', *Journal of Law and Society*, 29, 56–76.

Scott, J. (2007), *The WTO Agreement on Sanitary and Phytosanitary Measures – A Commentary*, Oxford: Oxford University Press.

Smith, G. (2009), 'Interaction of public and private standards in the food chain', *OECD Food, Agriculture and Fisheries Working Papers, No. 15*, OECD Publishing, OECD Doc. No. AGR/CA/APM(2006)21/ FINAL.

SPS Committee (2007), news release on 'Private standards are a mixed blessing, committee hears', 28 February 2007 and 1 March 2007, available at www.wto.org/english/news_e/news07_e/sps_28feb_1march07_e.htm (accessed 1 March 2011).

Steurer, R., Berger, G., Konrad, A. and Martinuzzi, A. (2007) *Sustainable Public Procurement in EU Member States: Overview of Government Initiatives and Selected Cases*. Brussels: European Commission DG Employment, Social Affairs and Equal Opportunities, available at www.sustainability.eu/pdf/csr/policies/Sustainable%20Public%20Procure ment%20in%20EU%20Member%20States_Final%20Report.pdf (accessed 1 March 2011).

Stewart, R. (2003), 'Administrative law in the twenty-first century', *N.Y.U. Law Review*, 78, 437–460.

Swinnen, J. (ed.) (2007), *Global Supply Chains, Standards and the Poor: How the Globalization of Food Systems and Standards Affects Rural Development and Poverty*, Oxford and Cambridge: CAB International.

Teubner, G. (1983), 'Substantive and reflexive elements in modern law', *Law and Society Review*, 17, 239–286.

Uk Food Safety Act (1990), 29 June 1990, avaliable at www.legislation.gov.uk/ukpga/1990/16(UKFSA) (accessed 1 March 2011).

UN Conference on Trade and Development (2009), 'Comparative study on the GLOBALG.A.P. fruit and vegetables standard and the EU organic agriculture regulation', Discussion paper for the Ad Hoc Meeting of 10–11 December 2009 on Facilitating Access of Small Organic Farmers in Developing Countries to Supermarket Shelves, 2 November 2009, available at www.unctad.org/sections/wcmu/docs/ditc_tedb_ted0019_en.pdf (accessed 1 March 2011).

Vandenbergh, M. (2007), 'The new Wal-Mart effect: the role of private contracting in global governance', *UCLA Law Review*, 54, 913–970.

Van Tatenhove, J., Arts, B. and Leroy, P. (2000), 'Political modernization', in J. Van Tatenhove, B. Arts and P. Leroy (eds), *Political Modernization and the Environment – The Renewal of Environmental Policy Arrangements*, Dordrecht: Kluwer Academic Publishers, pp. 35–52.

Victor, D.G. (1999–2000), 'The sanitary and phytosanitary agreement of the World Trade Organization: an assessment after five years', *N.Y.U. Journal of International Law and Politics*, 32, 865–937.

Visseren-Hamakers, I. and Glasbergen, P. (2007), 'Partnerships in forest governance', *Global Environmental Change – Human and Policy Dimensions*, 17, 408–419.

Vogel, D. (2008), 'Private global business regulation', *Annual Review of Political Science*, 11, 261–282.

Wallner, Jennifer (2008), 'Legitimacy and public policy: seeing beyond effectiveness, efficiency, and performance', *The Policy Studies Journal*, 36, 421–446.

Winickoff, D., Jasanoff, S., Busch, L., Grove-White, R. and Wynne, B. (2005), 'Adjudicating the GM food wars: science, risk, and democracy in world trade law', *Yale Journal of International Law*, 30, 81–123.

World Health Organisation (2007), 'Food safety and foodborne illness', March 2007, available at www.who.int/mediacentre/factsheets/fs237/en/ (accessed 1 March 2011).

World Trade Organization (1994), 'Agrement on the Application of Sanitary and Phytosanitary Measures', opened for signatures 15 April 1994, 1867 UNTS 493 (entered into force 1 January 1995), available at www.wto.org (accessed 1 March 2011).

World Trade Organization (2005a), 'Exploring the links between trade, standards and the WTO', *World Trade Report*, available at www.wto.org/english/res_e/booksp_e/anrep_e/world_trade_report05_e.pdf (accessed 1 March 2011).

World Trade Organization, Committee on Sanitary and Phytosanitary Measures (2005b), 'Summary of the meeting held on 29–30 June 2005', Note by the Secretariat, 11 August 2005, WTO Doc. No. G/SPS/R/37.

World Trade Organization, Committee on Sanitary and Phytosanitary Measures (2007a), 'Private Standards and the SPS Agreement', Note by the Secretariat, 24 January 2007, WTO Doc. No. G/SPS/GEN/746.

World Trade Organization, Committee on Sanitary and Phytosanitary Measures (2007b), 'Private Industry Standards', Communication from Saint Vincent and the Grenadines, 28 February 2007, WTO Doc. No. G/SPS/GEN/766.

World Trade Organization, Committee on Sanitary and Phytosanitary Measures (2007c), 'Private voluntary standards within the WTO multilateral framework', Submission by the United Kingdom, 9 October 2007, WTO Doc. No. G/SPS/GEN/802.

World Trade Organization, Committee on Sanitary and Phytosanitary Measures (2008a), 'Private standards – identifying practical actions for the SPS committee – summary of responses', Note by the Secretariat, 25 September 2008, WTO Doc. No. G/SPS/W/230.

World Trade Organization, Committee on Sanitary and Phytosanitary Measures (2008b), 'Research and researchers on private standards', Note by the Secretariat, 8 December 2008, WTO Doc. No. G/SPS/GEN/891.

World Trade Organization, Committee on Sanitary and Phytosanitary Measures (2009a), 'Effects of SPS-related private standards – descriptive report', Note by the Secretariat, 15 June 2009, WTO Doc. No. G/SPS/GEN/932.

World Trade Organization, Committee on Sanitary and Phytosanitary Measures (2009b), 'Legal framework for private standards in the WTO', Communication from Mercosur (Argentina, Brazil, Paraguay and Uruguay), 30 September 2009, WTO Doc. No. G/SPS/W/246.

World Trade Organization, Committee on Sanitary and Phytosanitary Measures (2011), 'Action regarding SPS-related private standards', 6 April 2011, WTO Doc. No. G/SPS/55.

Wouters, J. and Geraets, D. (2012) 'Private Food Standards and the World Trade Organization: Some Legal Considerations', *World Trade Review*, 11, 1–11.

Zürn, M. (2004), 'Global governance and legitimacy problems', *Government and Opposition*, 39, 260–287.

11. Conclusion: private standards – a global governance tool?

Axel Marx, Miet Maertens, Johan Swinnen and Jan Wouters

INTRODUCTION

During the last three decades, many scientists have discussed the impact of globalization. Some critics have argued that existing multilateral and governmentally driven initiatives are incapable of addressing the global challenges that result from trade liberalization and increased economic globalization. At the same time, one can observe the emergence of new non-state market regulatory initiatives. These private regulatory initiatives aim to govern supply chains across the globe according to a set of 'private' standards. The literature refers in this context to the rise of private standards in supply chain management (Swinnen, 2007), the rise of civil regulation (Vogel, 2008), the certification solution (Gereffi et al., 2001), the certification revolution (Conroy, 2007) and the proliferation of the voluntary standards movement (ISEAL Alliance, 2009). Many new private regulatory initiatives are developing very quickly and are gaining ground. Ecolabel Index, a global directory of ecolabels, counted 429 ecolabels, based on private standards, in 246 countries in 25 industrial sectors in the second half of 2011 (Ecolabel Index, 2011). In addition, the United Nations Conference on Trade and Development (UNCTAD) estimated the total number of private food safety standard schemes to be 400 in January 2007 (Wolff and Scannell, 2008). These private systems are becoming important instruments in the context of global governance and regulation. Dingwerth (2007) identifies private standards as one of three distinct forms of global governance besides intergovernmental governance (such as the United Nations and the World Trade Organization) and transgovernmental governance (such as the International Organisation of Securities Commissioners).

The use of private standards by firms in their international operations is currently studied in economics, law and political science. Political scientists and governance researchers have mainly concentrated on social and environmental standards, especially in the sectors of forestry and apparel, and have focused on questions of emergence, legitimacy and classification. Economists have largely paid attention to the diversity of private food standards and how they change supply chain relations. Legal scholars have approached private standards as a new form of international normsetting through contracts and assessed the degree to which this constitutes an accountable and legitimate way of rule-making.

The different chapters in this book illustrate the importance and diversity of private standards schemes, advance the state-of-the art and bring together insights from different disciplinary angles. Throughout the contributions two key issues are addressed from different perspectives, which are linked to the overall question of whether private standards are a global governance tool. First, several contributions focus on private standards in relation to public standards and policy-making. Henson and Humphrey (Chapter 4) aim to provide clarity regarding the nature of private food standards and how they relate to and differ from public regulations and international guidelines on food safety. They focus on the diversity of private standards, analyse the reasons why they have become important and assess the degree to which they go beyond public regulations. Van Waarden (Chapter 2) analyses the interaction between private and public regulation in an historical perspective and with a focus on private initiatives in managing natural resources. Marx, Bécault and Wouters (Chapter 3), in their discussion of the legitimacy and effectiveness of the Forest Stewardship Council, highlight the many ways public and private policies interact in the context of forest governance. Cuyvers and De Meyer (Chapter 5) assess the degree to which private standards complement or replace public standards with regard to labour standards on a global scale. Wouters, Marx and Hachez (Chapter 10) focus on food safety standards and analyse the relation with international trade law and public food safety standards developed by the Codex Alimentarius. Finally, Cafaggi (Chapter 8) provides a general regulatory framework for the analysis of transnational private regulation of food standards. His key focus is on the use of contractual network governance for regulating and monitoring safety in food supply chains.

Second, other contributions assess the degree to which private standards have potential distributional implications and create inequalities across and within countries and regions due to different patterns of adoption. Maertens and Swinnen (Chapter 6) and Colen, Maertens and Swinnen (Chapter 7) assess the development implications of private food standards by analysing structural changes in food supply chains that are induced by increasing standards and the implications for rural households in developing countries. Stanton (Chaper 9) assesses the degree to which these private standards constitute potential barriers to trade and provides an insight into current internal debates in the World Trade Organization (SPS Committee) on this issue.

In this concluding chapter, we focus on the interconnections between different chapters and findings with the aim of assessing private standards as a tool for global governance. Global governance is here defined as the transnational regulation of transnational public policy problems, by either governmental, intergovernmental or non-governmental actors (Rosenau, 1999; Weiss and Thakur, 2010). In the next section, we assess the degree to which private standards are truly global. We first consider the emergence of private standards and who is involved in the private standard-setting systems. We argue that private standards have emerged mainly in high-income countries and that there is actually little evidence available to make an assessment of whether private standards are set by a global group of stakeholders or not. We then consider the distribution of the adoption of private standards across the globe and the implications this has for low-income countries. The available evidence is inconclusive and some trends might support an argument that the adoption of private standards will differ as a function of the nature of private standards, for example, food safety standards versus environmental standards. In the subsequent section, we focus on the interaction between private standards and public policy with the aim of assessing whether private standards complement public policy-making and hence could be considered as an important governance tool. The chapter ends with a conclusion.

GLOBALIZATION AND PRIVATIZATION OF STANDARDS

Private standards initiatives started to emerge in different economic sectors (food production, textiles, forestry) with regard to the management of different aspects of the production and marketing process, ranging from quality control issues to social and environmental issues. These initiatives have been developed by individual firms and multinational corporations, corporate associations, non-governmental organizations (NGOs) or coalitions of NGOs. Several types of private standards initiatives exist and they differ on many different parameters, *inter alia*, with regard to how standards are developed, how they are governed and how they are implemented (Abbott and Snidal, 2009b; Marx, 2011; van Waarden, 2011; Henson and Humphrey, this volume). The rise and proliferation of private standards initiatives can clearly be situated in Europe and North America. Some of these standards were developed to address certain policy gaps and failures, such as a lack of social and environmental protection or food safety in the South, but most of them were established by Northern NGOs and firms. In the food safety area, most initiatives started off as retailer-driven initiatives which then consolidated in network types of organizations such as EUREPGAP and GLOBALG.A.P. The Forest Stewardship Council was established by a coalition of many different NGOs, such as European-based nature conservation NGOs and World Wildlife Fund (WWF) and Northern firms such as Home Depot. The Marine Stewardship Council, now an independent organization, emerged out of a coalition between Unilever and WWF.

The further demand for private standard initiatives, mainly social and environmental ones, was subsequently sparked by many interrelated factors which institutionalized private standards in current governance regimes. Again, the interaction of factors was most prominent in Europe and North America. From a theoretical perspective, Bartley (2011, pp. 444–446) has elaborated possible explanations for the demand of private standards systems and identified two main, partially complementary, theoretical approaches. A first theoretical approach, mainly rooted in political institutionalism, approaches private regulation from the perspective of social actors (NGOs) and sees private standards as a NGO-driven institutional capacity-building project in order to achieve their aims. Rather than being confrontational towards firms or trying to influence firm behaviour via lobbying governments to implement regulatory standards, NGOs are increasingly using a co-operative strategy towards firms, of which certification based on private standards is the most prominent example. As Bartley (2011, p. 445) notes, 'private efforts have also been perceived by many NGOs as a way to bypass political roadblocks'. The institutionalisation of private standards systems in governance regimes occurs in a wider political context of profound changes regarding the role of states and the general shift from government to governance and from the nation State to the globe (Wouters et al., this volume).

A second theoretical approach, rooted in institutional economics, starts from the perspective of firms and highlights the importance of information asymmetries which arise via NGO actions such as 'naming and shaming' and consumer demand for ethical products. In this perspective, firms have an incentive to solve information problems by creating or joining private standard-setting initiatives (Bartley, 2011). In addition, firms may have incentives to engage in private standard-setting and adoption because it increases consumer confidence in product safety and quality, and hence increases consumer demand; or because private standards can be used as a strategic tool to differentiate products, thereby creating market segmentation and softening competition (Swinnen and Vandemoortele,

2011). An important insight from the economics literature is that private food standards may also serve to pre-empt government regulation (Swinnen and Vandemoortele, 2011; McCluskey, 2007). Private firms may choose a level of standards that minimize their own costs before governments or international organizations set standards. McCluskey and Winfree (2009) argue that an important advantage of private over public standards is that the former are more flexible in response to changes in consumer tastes and preferences, and to changes in technology. These different explanations for the emergence and development of private standards, pre-empting government regulation, addressing information asymmetries and direct targeting of firms by NGOs, are mostly based on an analysis of what has happened in the United States and Europe, indicating the prominence of private standards in those regions. This is not to argue that private standards do not affect developing countries, but that they originated in developed countries. The question of whether there are significant private standards in developing countries and how they might differ from the established ones in Europe and the United States is hardly researched. Most research so far has focused on a handful of leading European and American examples.

One can observe that there is significant variation across private standard-setting schemes with regard to who is involved in the standard-setting and implementation processes (Abbott and Snidal, 2009a; SOMO 2003a; 2003b). Several initiatives include transnational firms, associations of firms across international borders and international NGOs in the standard-setting process and have a global scope (for example, GLOBALG.A.P., FSC and MSC). It is however often not entirely clear how their representative function works, and neither is there a clear strategy with regard to stakeholder mapping and stakeholder representation. Schemes such as the Forest Stewardship Council (FSC) have an elaborate system of balancing interests. The FSC is a multi-stakeholder membership-based organization with a governance structure consisting of a general assembly in which the members are represented, a board of directors and an executive director. The General Assembly of FSC members is the highest decision-making body in the FSC and is made up of the three membership chambers (tripartite structure): environmental, social and economic, which are further split into sub-chambers North and South. The purpose of the chamber structure is to maintain the balance of voting power between different interests without having to limit the number of members (FSC_US, 2010). But even in case of the Forest Stewardship Council, the distribution of representatives from the North and South is uneven (Marx et al. Chapter 4, this volume). Other private standards initiatives do not involve international representation in standard-setting and are rather national or regional, mainly European and American, initiatives (for example, standards set by the British Retail Consortium). Such standards can nevertheless spread globally as many different firms across the world adopt and implement the standards.

Concerning global adoption, little solid empirical evidence is available. In the case of forest private standards there are indications that the adoption of private standards is mainly limited to the global North (Auld, et al., 2008; Marx and Cuypers, 2010a; Pattberg, 2006; Rayner et al., 2011). For other private standards less empirical studies are available that analyse global adoption and distribution. Hence, at this stage it is impossible to draw any definite conclusions with regard to the global adoption of private standards.

Depending on the underlying trends one might conclude on the one hand that the geographical scope of private standards is limited or on the other hand that it is already quite extensive and growing. In the coming years it will become clearer whether private standards are truly globalizing or whether the adoption of these standards remains limited to a subset of countries and how we might explain this. In addition, the trends may very well develop differently for food safety schemes vis-à-vis schemes for the improvement of environmental or labour management. With regard to food safety standards it should be stressed that these schemes govern the core business of the agri-food sector, namely food quality, which is a prerequisite for access to markets. The incentives for firms to engage with these regulatory standard-setting systems are very high, as emphasized in several chapters in this book. In addition, EUREPGAP only transformed itself into GLOBALG.A.P. in September 2007. Hence, one could expect that private food standards will spread more globally in the future and that the adoption of private food standards will continue to increase in the coming years.

A different trend might develop in the context of private environmental and labour governance standards. They are not related to the core business (or bottom line) of many firms and the incentives are different. Some studies conclude that several hypothesized incentives, such as willingness to pay premium prices for certified products, are in some cases absent (Carrera et al., 2006) or only appear under conditions when all other decision factors are identical (Hiscox and Smyth, 2005). Other incentives, such as reputation control in the context of labour standards, are present but only hold for a limited number of firms within specific market-niches, which in turn limits the adoption rate and geographical scope (Marx, 2008; O'Rourke, 2005). In addition, other studies have observed the limited adoption of forest management standards on a global scale and relate this to the costs involved in gaining certification. The high financial barriers exclude many forest owners or forest concession holders from the private standards process. This exclusion is prominent in developing countries. (Auld et al., 2008; Gullison, 2003; Marx and Cuypers, 2010a). These observations might indicate that there are limits to the geographical diffusion and adoption of environmental and labour standards.

The potential exclusion of developing countries has raised a number of concerns especially with regard to private food standards. These are:

1. that standards act as new non-tariff barriers diminishing the export opportunities of the poorest countries who face multiple constraints in complying with stringent standards and upgrading their supply chains
2. that poor farmers and smallholder suppliers are excluded from high-standards food supply chains because of their inability to comply with high food safety standards
3. that these farmers are exploited in the chains because stringent standards decrease the bargaining power of small farmers vis-à-vis large food exporters and multinational food firms, and increase the possibilities for rent extracting in the chain.

These fears are substantiated by recent debates within the World Trade Organization (see Stanton, this volume) and have also been formulated with regard to other private standards (Marx and Cuypers, 2010a). Standards are therefore often seen as barriers to trade and barriers to development for poor countries. However, the arguments are subject to debate and empirical studies have come to diverse conclusions about the effects of increasing and tightening food standards on trade and development.

The chapters in this book show that increasing and tightening private food standards is not necessarily a barrier to the participation of poor countries in international agricultural trade or to development in these countries. The chapters by Maertens and Swinnen (Chapter 6) and Colen, Maertens and Swinnen (Chapter 7) in particular, demonstrate that private standards can bring about positive development effects for rural development and poverty reduction.

The potential of private standards as catalysts for international trade will partially depend on the geographical distribution of these standards across the globe, that is, significant adoption in developing countries. At this moment, it is difficult to assess what the geographical scope and underlying dynamics (speed of adoption) of these systems are. For some schemes, mainly business-driven private food standards, little information is available. For other systems we can observe that they operate internationally but also that many countries remain outside the standard-setting process.

PRIVATE, PUBLIC AND PRIVATE-PUBLIC STANDARDS

The most prominent private standards initiatives, which receive the bulk of attention in the academic literature and which are discussed in this book, such as Social Accountability (Cuyvers and De Meyer, Chapter 5), Forest Stewardship Council and Marine Stewardship Council (van Waarden, Chapter 2) and GLOBALG.A.P (Wouters et al., Chapter 10; Swinnen, Maertens, Henson and Humphrey, Chapter 4) are entirely private in the sense that the different functions, including standard-setting, adoption, implementation, conformity assessment and enforcement (as described by Henson and Humphrey, Chapter 4) are performed by private entities. However, not all private standards are purely private, as different entities may be involved in one or more of the aforementioned functions.

Abbott and Snidal (2009a) have recently developed a classification system of private standards based on the actors involved in setting the standards. They distinguish between three major actors – the state, firms and non-governmental organizations – which develop rules and standards, either separately or together. These three actors form the 'governance triangle' (see page 63). Within this triangle, Abbott and Snidal distinguish seven zones, depending on how many actors are involved in defining standards. They place new, regulatory initiatives in each of these zones. Three zones contain initiatives whereby one of the aforementioned actors develops the standards, three zones contain initiatives whereby two actors develop standards and one zone contains standard-setting initiatives which are developed by the three actors jointly. A typical example of state-driven initiative is the OECD Guidelines for Multinational Enterprises. These are recommendations, accepted by governments, made to multinational firms regarding socially responsible business operations. The Responsible Care Program in the chemical sector or GLOBALG.A.P. in the agri-food sector are leading examples of business-driven initiatives, whereas the Clean Clothes Campaign exemplifies a NGO-driven initiative. The UN Principles for Responsible Investment are a result of NGO and state co-operation and the UN Global Compact of state and business co-operation. An initiative in which all actors are involved is the Kimberley Process relating to the governance of conflict diamonds. Finally, there are many leading initiatives in which businesses and NGOs collaborate, such as several forest certification initiatives. Abbott and Snidal's classification clearly suggests that the standard-setting process is not entirely private since there are many examples of systems in which the state or international organizations are involved.

As pointed out by Henson and Humphrey (Chapter 4), private food safety standards are closely related to public food safety legislation and are, in fact, a response to public regulation. Many private standards appear to be closely related to public policy. Private standard-setting includes the composition of a set of principles, norms and criteria. Often these principles and criteria refer to some extent to public (international) law and norms – as do, for example, the principles on which the standards of the FSC are based. Principle 1 refers to all applicable laws and international treaties. In practice, this principle brings together a whole range of laws and acts from multiple levels of governance. If one takes the example of the Forest Stewardship Council in the US (FSC_US, 2010), principle 1 covers more than 50 laws and acts ranging from the international level,[1] treaties with tribes,[2] federal laws and policies,[3] state law and policies[4] and local rules and policies.[5] Principle 4 refers to the conventions of the ILO and includes conventions on *inter alia* the minimum wage (C131), migrant workers (C143), occupational safety and health (C155), indigenous and tribal people (C169), forced labour (C29), freedom of association (C87), the right to organize and collective bargaining (C98), equal remuneration (C100), abolition of forced labour (C105), discrimination (C111), minimum age (C138) and worst forms of child labour (C182) (Cuypers and De Meyer, Chapter 5). Consequently, with regard to principles and norms private standards are not solely or even mainly private but rooted in a multi-level system of public (international) norms and laws. In a way, private standards act as a catalyst to enforce via one system a whole range of public rules which are developed on multiple levels.

Finally, the privateness of the implementation of private standards falls apart in two aspects: the supply side of implementation (enforcement) and the demand side (drivers for adoption). The supply side concerns the implementation process *sensu stricto*, namely the enforcement of standards. In order to enforce standards many private standard-setting schemes have developed an elaborate system of monitoring. Monitoring is a control mechanism which allows for the assessment of the implementation of standards and mainly consists of auditing systems. Monitoring refers to the assessment of conformity with standards by independent third parties. The conformity of products and processes to standards must be assessed and demonstrated in order to be certified. In order to provide assurance that parties which carry out conformity assessments are fitted for the task, accreditation systems are put in place. Accreditation aims to guarantee that a conformity assessment body is competent to carry out tasks such as auditing and inspection, and to come to the right conclusion as to whether a product complies with a defined standard. Often the private standard-setting body accredits independent organizations to perform the conformity assessment. Hence monitoring involves an independent certification body which performs the conformity assessment and often takes the form of auditing sites. This is solely done by private actors, either international consultancy firms, NGOs or local organizations (Blair et al., 2008).

The demand side concerns the use of private standards schemes and focuses on the drivers for adoption of private standards of both a private as well as public nature. First of all, from a purely private perspective one can identify incentives for firms to adopt private standards. There is a rising demand from customers (consumers and firms) and stakeholders (NGOs) that products comply with minimum requirements with regard to safety, environmental and/or social issues. Hence, there is a growing need for business management instruments that enable firms to comply with the demands of customers and stakeholders. Consequently, private standards systems are increasingly becoming a regular management instrument for firms. This is especially true in the context of risk and reputation management. Concerning risk management, more and more firms are making use of private standards to monitor suppliers and the quality (measured by different parameters) of the products they are offering. In the food processing industry, in particular, with the increasing liability borne by firms, private standards are used as a risk management tool (Henson and Humphrey, Chapter 4). In this context, private standards are mainly business-to-business tools and are used relatively little for the purpose of external communication. Private standards as a means of reputation management are used mainly by firms that supply directly to consumers and are (very) sensitive to negative publicity as this can impact on both sales and share value. For instance, a number of prominent clothing brands (for example, Adidas, Nike) that wish to avoid 'sweatshop' claims work with private standards organizations to monitor employment conditions in their supply facilities (Marx, 2008).

Secondly, from a public policy perspective one can identify several ways in which private standards schemes interact with public policy-making. One can identify at least five ways in which public policy-making is influencing the adoption of private standards. First, an increasing number of governmental bodies are complying with private standards. The most prominent example concerns forest management which is based on private standards. Many governments are applying for forest management certificates for forests which are under their ownership (Marx and Cuypers, 2010a). Secondly, in certain cases, new laws with regard to the management of natural resources require that owners or concession-owners apply for private standards. Bolivia's New Forest Law 1700, for example, requires that private forest owners and concession holders apply for third-party forest management certificates based on private standards (Carey and Guttenstein, 2008).

Thirdly, private standards are increasingly used in public procurement policies in European countries. Many countries and local governments are increasingly using sustainability criteria when purchasing goods. Certificates, such as FSC or Max Havelaar, provide in one label the information with regard to these sustainability criteria/standards and hence are often used when governments have to decide on buying specific goods (Meidinger, 2007; Mechel et al., 2006)

Fourthly, especially in the food sector, liability and due diligence clauses in legislation can provide incentives for the adoption of private standards. In this book, Wouters et al. (Chapter 10) and Henson and Humphrey (Chapter 4) argue that the boost in private food regulation was driven by changes in legislation which were implemented after the food crises. The UK Food Safety Act (section 21) of 1990 provides that food retailers can escape liability for non-compliance with food safety laws only if they can demonstrate that they have taken all precautions in this regard. A related dynamic might unfold with regard to forest standards. In the European Union, private forest standards are increasingly considered as a legality verification/due diligence tool in the context of FLEG (Forest Law Enforcement and Governance) initiatives. For example, article 6 of EU Regulation 995/2010 on the prevention of sales of illegal timber and timber products within the EU recognizes forest certification, based on private standards, as an assurance of compliance with applicable legislation.

Fifth, many multilateral organizations use private standards as a tool to stimulate the sustainable management of natural resources in developing countries. These organizations include the World Bank (WB) and WB Global Environmental Facility (GEF), International Tropical Timber Organisation (ITTO), Food and Agriculture Organization (FAO) and other UN and multilateral organizations involved in development co-operation (Marx and Cuypers, 2010b). In addition, many individual country initiatives aim to support private standards for the governance of natural resources. Publicly funded technical assistance agencies are increasingly promoting the uptake of private standards schemes. The United States Agency for International Development (USAID), for example, supports efforts to improve the management of forests as a means to promote sustainable social and economic development. USAID achieves this by providing assistance to foreign governments at the national, state and local levels, as well as non-governmental organizations and local communities. Through this assistance, they support on-the-ground efforts to reduce illegal logging, improve the management of protected forest areas, promote agroforestry, empower communities to responsibly manage local forest areas, and promote the adoption of reduced impact logging techniques. Forest private standards initiatives are an important tool in this context (Marx and Cuypers, 2010b). Another example is provided by Germany's Gesellschaft für Internationale Zusammenarbeit (GIZ) GmbH. The forest certification section of the Programme Office for Social and Ecological Standards of GIZ supports the process of forest certification internationally in selected developing countries.

CONCLUSION

Do private standards constitute a global governance tool? At the end of this volume, we can only provide an inconclusive and partially contradictory answer. The assessment of private standards as a complement to public policy clearly shows the many ways in which private standards and public policy-making are interrelated. In some cases, private standards enforce public international and national law and in other cases they are explicitly mentioned in public legislation, as is the case in EU Regulation 995/2010 for the implementation of public legislation. In other cases, governments recognize the importance of private standards in their procurement policies, which constitutes a significant influence on the markets of products which are privately regulated. Assessing it from this perspective, one could argue that private standards are increasingly institutionalized as an instrumental governance tool. Alternatively, the assessment of the global nature of private standards provides on the other hand indications that private standards are possibly a governance tool mainly in developed countries, having emerged in Europe and the United States. In addition, government support in terms of public procurement is mainly a European phenomenon. The global adoption of these systems is yet to be empirically assessed. For some private standards, such as forest standards, there are indications that adoption is limited so far to developed countries. For many others, more empirical research is required to make an assessment. Taken together, a picture might emerge of a governance tool which is mainly active in only a selected number of countries.

This is not to argue that this is a definite conclusion. Many private standards are of a recent date. In addition, the diffusion of adoption might vary depending on the nature of private standards. Hence, it could very well be the case that private food standards will diffuse more globally than other private standards. With regard to food standards, it is also difficult to make a more general assessment of global diffusion because many private standards are administered by retailers and firms who do not provide full information on where they operate. As a result, their global distribution might de facto be already more pronounced than in comparison with other private standards.

One of the interesting aspects of the private food standards case is that one can observe a very significant rise in their importance after new legislation with regard to food safety was enacted (for example, the liability clause in the UK Food Act). This legislation allocated the default responsibility for food safety to retailers, which provided important incentives to develop control systems. A similar default responsibility is currently included in EU Regulation 995/2010 on the prevention of sales of illegal timber and timber products within the EU. Importers of timber products must provide for legality verification, that is, attestation that the forest products originate from legally harvested forest. Article 6 explicitly mentions that this legality verification can take the form of third-party certification based on private standards. This legislation will become operational from 2013 and constitutes an interesting natural experiment to analyse the effect of anchoring private standards in public legislation on the dynamics of private forest standards. An analysis of the effects of the legislation on private standards adoption, forest owners and patterns of trade will constitute an interesting case for future research. Comparisons with the dynamics of food standards and their potential on influencing trade patterns (barriers/catalysts to trade) is another interesting area for future research. In addition, as is the case in the area of food standards (see Henson and Humphrey, Chapter 4), one can expect a proliferation of standard-setting schemes in the forest sector, some of which will be purely firm-based but with strong independent monitoring and certification systems. First, it will be interesting to see whether this hypothesis will be confirmed since it will shed light on the question of how the field of private standards develops in light of changes in regulation. Secondly, if private standards will proliferate in the forest sector, issues of competition and coordination will emerge. The analysis of how competition and coordination evolves constitutes another area for future research.

As a result, the question of whether private standards are a global governance tool cannot be answered definitely at the current time. Private standards are becoming an important governance tool, but their global impact might be limited. In addition, as many chapters in this volume highlighted, several other questions with regard to private standards, such as their legitimacy, are still outstanding. The aim of this volume was to bring together scholars from different disciplines, working on different private standards, to address some of these questions and share insights which are fruitful for cross-fertilization. As indicated above, a more thorough comparison between private food standards and private forest standards might constitute an especially fruitful area for further multi-disciplinary research. This might consolidate knowledge which can then be applied to other private standards and sectors.

NOTES

1 These include Convention on Nature Protection and Wild Life Preservation in the Western Hemisphere (Washington, DC, 1940), Convention on Wetlands of International Importance Especially as Waterfowl Habitat (Ramsar, Iran, 2 February 1971), United Nations Conference on the Human Environment (UNCHE) (Stockholm, Sweden, June 1972), Convention Concerning the Protection of the World Cultural and Natural Heritage (Paris, France, 16 November 1972), Convention on International Trade in Endangered Species of Wild Fauna and Flora (CITES) (Washington DC, 1973), International Plant Protection Convention (IPPC) (1979 Revised Text) (Rome, Italy, 1979), Convention on the Conservation of Migratory Species of Wild Animals (Bonn, Germany, 23 Jun 1979), Amendment to the Convention on International Trade in Endangered Species of Wild Fauna and Flora (Art. XI) (Bonn, Germany, 23 June 1979), Convention on Environmental Impact Assessment in a Transboundary Context (Espoo, Finland, 1991), Convention for the Conservation of Anadromous Stocks in the North Pacific Ocean (Moscow, Russia, 11 February 1992), Agenda 21, United Nations Convention on Environment & Development UNCED, (Rio de Janeiro, Brazil, June 1992), Forest Principles (UNCED) (Rio de Janeiro, Brazil, June 1992), Convention on Biological Diversity (UNCED) (Rio de Janeiro, Brazil, 5 June 1992), Framework Convention on Climate Change, (UNCED) (Rio de Janeiro, Brazil, 1992), Rio Declaration on Environment and Development (UNCED) (Rio de Janeiro, Brazil, 1992) and International Tropical Timber Agreement (Geneva, Switzerland, 1994).

2 These include varied treaties with American Indian nations, tribes, and bands in the United States. Particular note should be made of treaties which established off-reservation treaty rights.

3 These include the Lacey Act (concerning trade in illegally taken fish, wildlife or plants) (1900, 1969, 1981, 1989, 2008), Federal Insecticide Act (1910), Plant Quarantine Act (1912), Migratory Bird Treaty Act (1918, 2006), Federal Insecticide, Fungicide and Rodenticide Act (FIFRA)/Federal Environmental Pesticide Control Act (FEPCA) (1947, 1972), Federal Plant Pest Act (1957), Wilderness Act (1964), National Historic Preservation Act, including in relation to American Indian sites (1966), National Environmental Policy Act (1969, 1975, 1982), Occupational Safety and Health Act (OSHA) (1970), Federal Water Pollution Control Act/Clean Water Act (1972, 1977), Endangered Species Act (1973, 1978, 1979, 1982), Resource Conservation and Recovery Act (RCRA) (1976, 1984)., Comprehensive Environmental Response, Compensation and Liability Act (CERCLA, commonly known as 'Superfund') (1980, 1986), Coordinated Framework for the Regulation of Biotechnology, Office of Science and Technology (1986), Pollution Prevention Act (1990), Executive Order (EO) 12898 – Federal Actions to Address Environmental Justice in Minority Populations and Low-Income Populations (1994), Federal Food, Drug, and Cosmetic Act (2002), Energy Policy Act (2005), federal policy on income taxes, capital gains taxes, inheritance taxes, reforestation tax credits, and other relevant taxes and federal business practices law and

US Farm Bill.

4 These include forest practices acts, endangered species acts, environmental quality acts, wildlife laws, water quality protection laws, water resources laws, land use laws, cultural protection acts, business practices laws, fire practices laws, river compacts and wild and scenic rivers acts, natural communities conservation acts and tax policies.

5 These include county rules or guidelines regarding particular habitat types, county land use policies, including, general plans (or their functional equivalents) and zoning ordinances (or their functional equivalents), regional (multi-county) land use policies, county building codes, county tax policies, including policies for income taxes, property taxes, and special assessment districts.

REFERENCES

Abbott, K. and Snidal, D. (2009a) 'Strengthening international regulation through transnational new governance: overcoming the orchestration deficit', *Vanderbilt Journal of Transnational Law*, 42 (2) pp. 501–578.

Abbott, K. and Snidal, D. (2009b) 'The governance triangle: regulatory standards institutions and the shadow of the state', in W. Mattli and N. Woods (eds), *The Politics of Global Regulation*, Princeton: Princeton University Press.

Auld, G., Gulbrandsen, L. and McDermott, C. (2008) 'Certification schemes and the impacts on forests and forestry', *Annual Review of Environment and Resources*, 33, 187–211.

Bartley, T. (2011) 'Certification as a mode of social regulation', in D. Levi-Faur (ed.) *Handbook on the Politics of Regulation*, Cheltenham: Edward Elgar, pp. 441–452.

Blair, M., Williams, C. and Lin, L. (2008) 'The new role for assurance services in global commerce', *Journal of Corporation Law*, 33 (2) pp. 325–360.

Carey, C. and Guttensetein. E. (2008) *Governmental Use of Voluntary Standards: Innovation in Sustainability Governance*, London: ISEAL Alliance.

Carrera, F., Stoian, D., Campos, J.J., Morales, J. and Gustavo, P. (2006) 'Forest certification in Guatemala', in B. Cashore, F. Gale, E. Meidinger and D. Newsom (eds), *Confronting Sustainability: Forest Certification in Developing and Transitioning Countries*, New Haven, Connecticut, USA: Yale School of Forestry and Environmental Studies, pp. 363–406.

Conroy, M.E. (2007) *Branded! How the Certification Revolution is Transforming Global Corporations*, Gabriola Island BC, Canada: New Society Publishers.

Dingwerth, K. (2007) *The New Transnationalism: Private Transnational Governance and its Democratic Legitimacy*, Basingstoke: Palgrave Macmillan.

Ecolabel Index (2011) *Global Directory*, available at: www.ecolabelindex.com/ (accessed 14 October 2011).

Gereffi, G., Garcia-Johnson, R. and Sasser, E. (2001) 'The NGO-industrial complex', *Foreign Policy*, 56–5.

Gullison, R. (2003) 'Does forest certification conserve biodiversity?' *Oryx*, 37 (2) pp. 153–165.

FSC_US (Forest Stewardship Council US) (2010) Appendix A: Relevant laws, treaties and agreements. Available at: www.fscus.org/images/documents/standards/Laws%20and%20Policies%20noted%20for%20relevance%20to%20forest%20management%20in%20the%20US.pdf

Hiscox, M. and Smyth, N. (2005) 'Is there a demand for labor standards: Evidence from field experiments in social labelling.' Working Paper 2008-0058,

Weatherhead Centre for International Affairs, Harvard University.
ISEAL Alliance (2009), *Strategic plan 2009–2013*, available at www.isealalliance.org/
Marx, A. (2008) 'Limits to non-state market regulation: A qualitative comparative analysis of the international sport footwear industry and the Fair Labor Association', *Regulation and Governance*, 2 (2) pp. 253–273.
Marx, A. and Cuypers, D. (2010a) 'Forest Certification as a global environmental governance tool. What is the macro-impact of the Forest Stewardship Council?', *Regulation and Governance*, 4 (4) pp. 408–434.
Marx, A. and Cuypers, D. (2010b) 'Halting deforestation and forest certification. What is the impact of the Forest Stewardship Council?', *Leuven Centre for Global Governance Studies Working Paper.*
Marx, A. (2011) 'Global governance and the certification revolution: types, trends and challenges', in D. Levi-Faur (ed.) *Handbook on the Politics of Regulation*, Cheltenham: Edward Elgar, pp. 590–603.
McCluskey, J. (2007) 'Public and private food quality standards: recent trends and strategic incentives', in J.F.M. Swinnen (ed.) *Global Supply Chains, Standards and the Poor*, Oxford: CABI Publishing.
McCluskey, J.J. and Winfree, J.A. (2009) 'Pre-empting public regulation with private food quality standards', *European Review of Agricultural Economics*, 36 (4) pp. 525–39.
Mechel, F., Meyer-Ohlendorf, N., Sprang, P. and Tarasofsky, R. (2006) *Public Procurement and Forest Certiciation: Assessing the Implications for Policy, Law and International Trade*, Berlin: Eco-Logic in association with Chatham House.
Meidinger, E. (2007) 'Beyond Westphalia: competitive legalization in emerging transnational regulatory systems', in C. Brütsch and D. Lehmkuhl (eds) *Law and Legalization in Transnational Relations*, London and New York: Routledge, pp. 121–143.
O'Rourke, D. (2005) 'Market movements: nongovernmental strategies to influence global production and consumption', *Journal of Industrial Ecology*, 9 (1–2) pp. 115–128.
Pattberg, P. (2006), 'Private governance and the South: lessons from global forest politics', *Third World Quarterly*, 27 (4) pp. 579–793.
Rayner, J., Buck, A. and Katila, P. (2011) *Embracing Complexity: Meeting the Challenges of International Forest Governance. A Global Assessment Report by the Global Forest Expert Panel on the International Forest Regime*, World Series Volume 28, Vienna: International Union of Forest Research Organizations.
Rosenau, J. (1999) 'Toward an ontology for global governance', in M. Hewson and T. J. Sinclair (eds), *Approaches to Global Governance Theory*, Albany, NY: State University of New York.
SOMO (2003a) *Report of SOMO Workshop on Complaints Mechanisms in the context of monitoring and verification of codes of conduct*. Amsterdam: SOMO.
SOMO (2003b) *Monitoring and Verification Terminology Guide. For the garment and sportswear industries*. Amsterdam: SOMO.
Swinnen J. (ed.) (2007) *Global Supply Chains, Standards and the Poor: How the Globalization of Food Systems and the Standards Affects Rural Development and Poverty*, Oxford and Cambridge: CAB International Publishing.
Swinnen, J. and Vandemoortele, T. (2011) 'Trade and the political economy of food standards', *Journal of Agricultural Economics*, 62 (2) pp. 259–280.
van Waarden, F. (2011) 'Varieties of private market regulation: problems and

prospects', in D. Levi-Faur (2011) *Handbook on the Politics of Regulation*, Cheltenham: Edward Elgar.

Vogel, D. (2008) 'Private global business regulation', *Annual Review of Political Science* 11, pp. 261–282.

Weiss, T. and Thakur, R. (2010) *Global Governance and the UN: An Unfinished Journey,* Bloomington: Indiana University Press.

Wollf, C. and Scannell, M. (2008) 'Implications of private standards in international trade of animals animal products', 76th General Session of the World Organisation for Animal Health, Paris, 25–30 May 2008.

Index